'BANDIT COUNTRY'

'BANDIT COUNTRY'

Toby Harnden

Hodder & Stoughton

First published in 1999 by Hodder and Stoughton
A division of Hodder Headline
A Hodder and Stoughton/Lir book

ISBN 0 340 71736 X

Typeset by Hewer Text Ltd, Edinburgh
Printed and bound in Great Britain by
Clays Ltd, St Ives plc

Hodder and Stoughton
A division of Hodder Headline
338 Euston Road
London NW1 3BH

For my parents,
Keith and Valerie Harnden

Contents

'BANDIT COUNTRY'

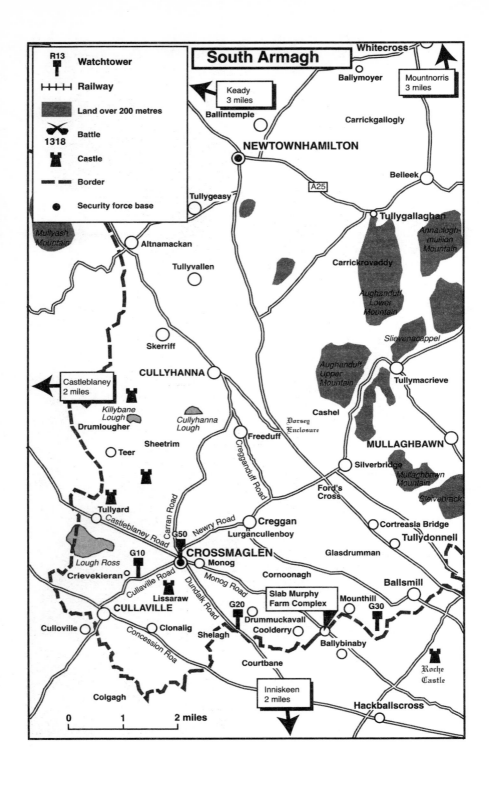

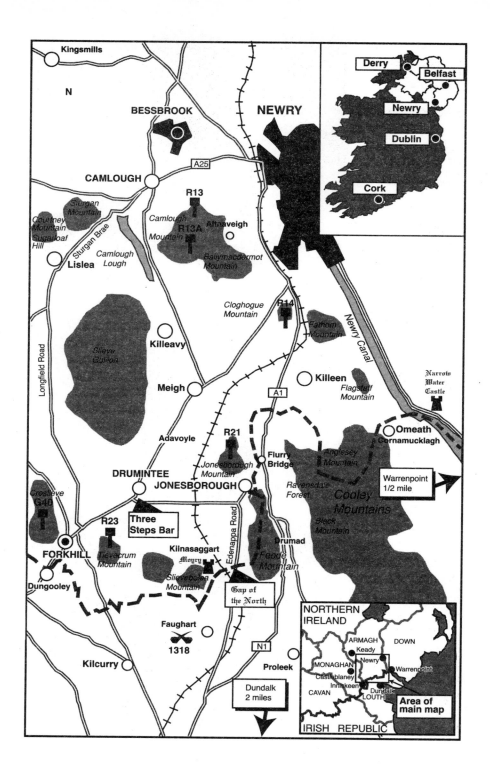

Preface

For the past three decades, South Armagh has exerted a powerful hold on the British and Irish imagination and my journey from teenage recollections of the death of Robert Nairac and the Narrow Water massacre to the completion of this book has been a long one. Many people have assisted me along the way and to all those who helped lay the foundations for this project and believed in it despite all the obstacles, I wish to express my profound gratitude.

My aim has been to go some way towards providing answers to a series of questions. Why is South Armagh such a place apart? What sort of people have joined the IRA and how do they live their lives? What has driven these men to the point where the end will justify any means? What has it been like for the outsider to be pitted against such men? Why has the South Armagh Brigade been consistently more effective than the IRA in any other area? What has been the human cost of this fight for Irish freedom? I have tried throughout to approach these issues by focussing on the thoughts, actions and experiences of the participants themselves, using their own words in preference to my own as often as possible.

This is a contemporary history with all the freedoms and limitations which that entails. Detachment from a subject such as South Armagh is impossible and any belief that objectivity can be attained is flawed. But this is not intended to be a work for one side or the other. I have attempted to use language free from value judgements and I do not spare the reader the sometimes gruesome details of the events I deal with. If relatives of victims find some passages distressing, I hope they will understand that the goal of presenting as full a truth as possible would not have been served by attempting to airbrush distasteful realities. The main omissions are those necessary for legal reasons; most notably, the pseudonyms 'the Surgeon' and 'the Undertaker' have had to be given to two of the most senior figures within the South Armagh Brigade.

The following institutions have all been invaluable sources of information and their staffs unfailingly helpful. In Belfast: the Linen Hall Library; Queen's University Library; Central Library; Lisburn Road Library; and the Public Record Office of Northern Ireland. In Dublin: the *Irish Times* library. In London: the *Daily Telegraph* library. In Dundalk: the Louth County Library. In Newry: the Newry Divisional Library. Yvonne Murphy and Ciaran Crossey, of the incomparable Political Collection at the Linen Hall, were not only extremely industrious, interested and proactive during my researches but also read and criticised the early manuscript. I acknowledge with thanks the assistance of Mr J. Daniel Thompson CBE, Her Majesty's Coroner for South Down, in making inquest files available for my inspection and the Deputy Keeper of Records, Public Record Office of Northern Ireland for granting me permission to quote from material deposited there.

People who have helped me in different ways include: Eddie Bell, Paul Bew, Carolyn Boyes, Kelvin Boyes, Suzanne Breen, Liam Clarke, Renee Coady, Karen Davies, Jim and Patricia Flynn, Roger Goodwin, Michael Hanlon, Conor Hanna, David Hanna, Elaine Keogh, Peter Levaggi, Alan Lewis, Mark Long, Phelim McAleer, Jason McCue, Martin McCullough, Diarmuid McDermott, Tony McGleenan, Alistair McQueen, Ed Moloney, John Mullin, Séamus Murphy, Jeanette Oldham, Susan Phoenix, Shawn Pogatchnik, Sarah Ramsey, Darwin Templeton, Chris Thornton, Kevin Toolis, Ben Webster, Jeremy Weller and Beanie Wilgaus. I thank them all.

Nick Lewis unknowingly started the whole thing off. Mark Devenport gave me access to his carrier bags full of material on arms buying in America, which I have drawn on extensively in Chapter 10. Articles in *Creggan*, the Journal of the Creggan Local History Society, and *Seanchas Ard Mhacha*, the Journal of the Armagh Diocesan Historical Society, were immensely useful in researching

Chapters 3 and 4. Michelle McDowell and Gina Inglis of the Law faculty at Queen's University transcribed countless hours of taped interviews with good humour and efficiency. The Reverend Mervyn Kingston of Creggan parish church generously made the text of his exhibition available to me. At the *Daily Telegraph*, I owe a debt of gratitude to Charles Moore and Susan Ryan for giving me the opportunity to be sent to Northern Ireland and to Neil Darbyshire and his colleagues on the news desk who have been consistently supportive and often pretended not to notice when I was preoccupied with book writing. Sheila Fullerton kindly allowed me to use her house overlooking the beach at Cranfield in County Down, a beautiful setting and the place where most of the writing was done.

Given the nature of my subject, it is inevitable that the majority of those who helped me most will wish to remain anonymous. Many serving and retired members of the security forces spoke to me with great frankness and without official authorisation. Some trusted me with information which, if treated carelessly, could jeopardise their lives. Despite warnings that no one would speak to me in South Armagh, many people there received me with warmth and friendliness. I found republicans courteous and prepared to take a chance with me and tell a story they believed had been ignored for too long; whatever my personal feelings about their actions, I could not help but be impressed by their dedication to their cause and the genuineness of their commitment. All those who gave formal interviews are listed at the end of the book; without their assistance, publication would not have been possible. Any comments or communication about the book can be addressed to me at: tobyharnden@hotmail.com.

Finally, I would like to thank my ever-faithful companion Finn for reminding me so often that a walk at Shaw's Bridge would be more productive than another hour at my desk, and Claire Flynn for her love, support and encouragement.

Belfast
September 1999

Prologue

Codeword Kerrygold

'There's a massive bomb beside South Quay station, Marsh Wall, Isle of Dogs, London,' said the caller in a slow South Armagh brogue. His voice was calm and deliberate; it was not the first time he had delivered such a message. 'Evacuate immediately. Codeword Kerrygold.' Anne Brown, a switchboard operator at the *Irish News* in Belfast, felt her heartbeat quicken as she wrote down the words on the pad in front of her. Aware that a mistake on her part could lead to the deaths of scores of people, she requested that the caller repeat the details. 'Was the codeword Kerrygold?' she asked. 'Same as the butter,' he answered and hung up.

In the decade she had worked at the newspaper, Mrs Brown had dealt with dozens of coded warnings but this was one she had never expected to hear. It was 5.54 p.m. on Friday 9 February 1996 and just over 17 months earlier the IRA had declared a ceasefire; like many in Northern Ireland, she had believed that the Troubles were over.

At 5.28 p.m., another man had dictated a statement from the IRA's Army Council to John Murray, a reporter with RTÉ, the Irish Republic's state broadcasting corporation. 'It is with great reluctance that the leadership announces that the complete cessation of military operations will end at six o'clock on February 9th,' the statement said. 'The cessation presented a historic challenge for everyone and Óglaigh na hÉireann [the IRA] commends the leadership of nationalist Ireland at home and abroad. They rose to the challenge. The British Prime Minister did not. Instead of embracing the peace process, the British government acted in bad faith, with Mr Major and the Unionist leaders squandering this unprecedented opportunity to resolve the conflict.' The statement was signed 'P. O'Neill', the *nom de guerre* under which the Provisionals had issued warnings and claimed responsibility for attacks over the previous 25 years.

On both sides of the Irish Sea, few could bring themselves to believe that the statement or the warnings were genuine. When RTÉ's main evening news began at 6.01 p.m., there was no mention of the IRA announcement. Fifteen minutes later, an officer from Scotland Yard telephoned the *Irish News* to ask Anne Brown to go through once more what the South Armagh caller had told her. John Bruton, the Irish premier, went ahead with a 6.30 p.m. engagement at a Dublin art gallery while his aides made desperate attempts to reach Sinn Féin officials. Commander John Grieve, head of the Metropolitan Police's anti-terrorist branch, later admitted that when he was paged by detectives with a message to call Sir Paul Condon, the Met's Commissioner, he thought it must be a practical joke.

Four officers had initially been despatched from Limehouse station shortly after 6 p.m. to close the Docklands Light Railway station at South Quay. But there was confusion about exactly where the IRA had said the bomb was and over the next hour another 16 officers were sent out to set up cordons and clear the streets. Some buildings were evacuated only for their occupants to be sent back ten minutes later; others very close to South Quay station knew nothing about the bomb warnings. At 6.48 p.m., PC Roger Degraff and another officer spotted a blue car transporter parked outside South Quay Plaza between two office blocks and next to a row of shops.

Inside the transporter was more than 3,000 lbs of explosives made up of ammonium nitrate fertiliser mixed with icing sugar in plastic sacks. The sacks were in two compartments in the back of the transporter and packed around 'booster tubes'. Designed to increase the power of the blast, the tubes had been made from parts of scaffolding poles drilled with holes and stuffed with 10 lbs of Semtex high explosive. Attached to the booster tubes were lengths of improvised detonating cord made from plastic tubing filled with PETN and RDX, the two constituent elements of Semtex. The bomb was to be set off by a nail attached to a kitchen timer which would complete an electrical circuit, sending power through to two detonators which would activate the detonating cord and, in turn, set off the booster tubes and trigger the main explosive charge. Shortly after the bomb lorry was parked, a 'memo park' timer, invented for absent-minded motorists who needed prompting that their meters were about to run out, had been used to 'arm' a mercury tilt switch anti-handling devices. The kitchen timer had been set for two hours so that it would run out at 7 p.m.

The two policemen walked around the lorry and quickly concluded that if the IRA warnings were genuine, the bomb was probably inside the vehicle. Degraff went to the cab and was about to look inside when he stopped himself. Had he opened the door, he would have set off the anti-handling device and activated the bomb. Realising he needed to clear the row of shops next to the transporter, Degraff rushed into a newsagent's store at 6.56 p.m. and told Inam Bashir and his assistant, John Jefferies, to leave immediately. Bashir, who had been at work at the family business since 5 a.m., said he would first shut up the shop while a sceptical Jefferies observed: 'We are in a ceasefire.'

A minute before 7 p.m., a blue flash could be seen several miles away as the bomb exploded; Bashir and Jefferies were blown through two walls and their bodies buried by tons of rubble. Degraff, 30 yards from the device, felt a deep rumble and a rush of wind as he was blown off his feet. For a fraction of a second, the hundreds of people still working in Canary Wharf, one of Europe's tallest tower blocks, felt that the building was about to collapse. 'I was lying curled up in a ball listening to glass and debris falling from all the buildings,' Degraff said afterwards. 'I lay there for a while, waiting for something big to fall on me.' Barbara Osei, 23, who had been cleaning offices with her brother Isaac, was sprayed with hundreds of tiny slivers of glass; she was blinded in one eye and her face, arms and hands were so badly cut she needed 300 stitches. Members of the Berrezag family, Moroccans who worked as cleaners at the Midland Bank branch in South Quay, were even closer to the blast. Their car was virtually destroyed as they sat in it; Zaoui Berrezag, 51, suffered severe head injuries and never fully recovered his memory. Graeme Brown, an advertising designer, was knocked out; he woke a few minutes later surrounded by the water from a burst main. 'It was bizarre,' he said the next day. 'I knew it wasn't a bomb, because we don't get them in London any more, do we?'

Soon, Docklands was echoing to the sound of police and ambulance sirens, wailing alarms and breaking glass as the residents of council flats knocked their shattered windows out into the streets below. Debris had been spread over a radius of 300 yards; where the transporter had been, there was a crater 32 ft wide and 10 ft deep. The blast had caused an estimated £150 million of damage to property. Its impact was felt world-wide, with television bulletins across the globe leading with the news. The IRA had struck another blow at the heart of the British establishment less than three years after devastating the City of London for the second time in 12 months. As the home of merchant banks, television and advertising companies and, in Canary Wharf, the *Mirror* and *Telegraph* newspaper groups, Docklands was an ideal prestige target.

While political argument raged during the next few days, two funerals went almost unnoticed. The traditional Islamic colours of gold and green were draped over Inam Bashir's coffin as it was driven from his home in Streatham to Croydon mosque for a private service. His elderly father Shere, who had to be supported by his second son as he went into the mosque, was to die within a year. John Jefferies' father, a widower, was nearly beside himself with grief at the loss of his only son who had still lived with him. White chrysanthemums had been arranged into guitar-shaped bouquets as a tribute to the amateur musician who had often busked at Underground stations. As the mourners gathered at Lewisham crematorium in south London, they listened in silence to a tape of Jefferies' own rendition of a song he had written and recorded for a new girlfriend just a few days before the bomb. He had called it *Glad to be Alive*.

Chapter One

The Boss

'From Carrickmacross to Crossmaglen, the polisman he did vow
There are more rogues than honest men and anyone will allow'
(The Dealin' Men of Crossmaglen, traditional ballad, c1900)

'If there is ever a big meeting and they are all there and a target is
given, then the Crossmaglen boys are on their way to do the job as
soon as they get out of the door.'
(South Armagh informer, Military Intelligence Report, 1975)

Inside a cattle shed five miles west of the Ring of Gullion and 200
yards beyond the border into the Irish Republic, nine men
worked silently and methodically as the light faded into the
late afternoon gloom of a cold January day in 1996. Some were
farmhands; others made a living doing odd jobs or driving lorries and
tractors around the South Armagh borderlands. Most had been
involved in smuggling for many years, profiting from the hated
line that had divided Ireland for three quarters of a century by
moving contraband to and fro across the United Kingdom's only land
boundary. Led by 'the Surgeon', the notorious commander of the
South Armagh Brigade, they were among the most trusted volunteers in the IRA's heartland; between them, they had been involved
in several hundred attacks on the security forces. But this job
was different, and each man knew the significance of what he was
there to do.

Micheál Caraher, an IRA sniper responsible for the deaths of up to eight soldiers and policemen, was there. So too were Séamus McArdle and Bernard McGinn, key members of the back-up team used to get Caraher in place and protect him as he fired a single .50 (half-inch) calibre bullet from a high-powered American sniper rifle. Frank 'One Shot' McCabe, one of the senior figures behind the sniper attacks, was also in the shed; an eight-year sentence for possession of explosives and a firearm had not dulled his desire to see Ireland united. A man who had earned his reputation as an IRA volunteer in a unit which shot soldiers and bombed Army bases on the Continent worked alongside his elder brother. Each man had been told by either the Surgeon, a thick-set man with piercing blue eyes, or Michael 'Micksey' Martin to rendezvous that morning at the galvanised iron shed, situated at the end of a long lane near Donagh's crossroads and close to the Drumlougher border crossing between South Armagh and County Monaghan. Once gathered, they had been given the word from 'the Boss' that South Armagh had been entrusted with the task of making, transporting and detonating a huge bomb. A bomb for England.

At one end of the cattle shed was a stack of sacks, each containing a hundredweight of ammonium nitrate agricultural fertiliser. As one man split the sacks, the others shovelled the contents into an electric barley crusher plugged into the power shaft of a tractor. The barley crusher, designed to break down animal feed, was used to grind the granules of fertiliser into tiny particles. Once each lot of fertiliser was of the requisite consistency, several bags of icing sugar were added and the two ingredients were stirred together to make a light brown substance. The side panels had been removed from the back of a lorry converted into a car transporter, revealing a hidden compartment. The compartment, lined with plastic sheeting, was then packed with three tons of explosives. After the job had been completed, the barley crusher was washed and then towed away behind the tractor by Caraher. The Surgeon took charge of the car transporter with the explosives inside; a red Peugeot 205 'scout car' drove ahead to check the roads were clear. The next day, the shed would revert to being a cattle byre; all that had been required to transform it into a temporary bomb factory had been a friendly farmer and a watertight roof.

According to Detective Inspector Alan Mains, the RUC officer who led the Docklands inquiry in Northern Ireland, the plan to blow up South Quay had been drawn up at least six weeks before the bomb was mixed. On 30 November 1995, President Clinton had told a cheering crowd gathered outside the City Hall in Belfast: 'You must say to those who still would use violence for political objectives: you are the past; your day is over.' It was a neat rejection of the IRA's slogan 'Tiocfaidh ár Lá', Irish for 'Our Day will Come', which had often been accompanied by a clenched fist salute as it was shouted from the dock. But even as Clinton was speaking, work was already in progress in South Armagh and across the border in North Louth to construct the car transporter that would be loaded with the Docklands bomb. Nowhere else in Ireland was the commitment to the IRA's armed struggle so strong. From the day the IRA ceasefire had been declared in August 1994, there had been extreme scepticism in South Armagh about the 'peace strategy' of Gerry Adams and Martin McGuinness, the Sinn Féin leaders; sometimes this bordered on open contempt. South Armagh volunteers had heard the clever words of British prime ministers and American presidents before and set little store by them.

The very mention of South Armagh can send a shiver down the spine of any one of the tens of thousands of soldiers who have served there since the Troubles began. Branded 'Bandit Country' in 1975 by Merlyn Rees, then Northern Ireland Secretary, no other part of the world has been as dangerous for someone wearing the uniform of the British Army. Some 123 soldiers have been killed in the South Armagh area since August 1971, around a fifth of all military casualties in Northern Ireland, along with 42 Royal Ulster Constabulary officers and 75 civilians. According to RUC statistics, the area within a 10-mile radius of the heart of South Armagh has seen 1,255 bomb attacks and 1,158 shooting incidents since the Troubles began.

Situated in one of the six counties of Ulster which make up Northern Ireland, South Armagh is around 192 square miles in area and home to approximately 23,000 people. As defined by both the British Army and the IRA, it is enclosed to the east by the A1, the main Belfast-to-Dublin road, to the south and west by the border with the Irish Republic and to the north by an imaginary east-west line running through Mountnorris and Keady. The population of

South Armagh is overwhelmingly Roman Catholic, almost exclusively so in the land south of the A25 road. It has been in this 120-square-mile southern portion of South Armagh, including the town of Crossmaglen and the villages of Cullyhanna, Forkhill, Drumintee and Jonesborough, that the overwhelming number of Army and RUC casualties has occurred.

History and landscape are rooted deep in the psyche of the people of South Armagh. At the centre of both sits Slieve Gullion, whose bulk looms through the mist high above the watchtowers, fields and blackthorn hedges like a slumbering giant keeping guard over South Armagh and Ulster's ancient frontier. At the base of the mountain, the granite peaks of the ring dyke stand sentinel as if protecting their master through the ages. On six of the peaks stand the modern watchtowers, the latest in a long line of military fortifications built by the invader in the vain hope of subjugating the natives of a countryside in which the outsider has never been welcomed. When the mist clears, eight counties can be seen from Slieve Gullion's summit, 1,840 ft above sea level.

For the British soldier, Crossmaglen – known as XMG to the military, and Cross to locals – is a place of hostility, isolation and the constant threat of death. Before going out on patrol, troops are briefed that every gorse bush, stone wall or ditch, every cowshed, milk churn or bale of hay could hide a bomb; if a sniper decided to strike, the victim would probably never even hear the crack of the bullet being fired. In the Square in Crossmaglen, site of a thriving market each month and the place where eight soldiers have met their deaths in the past quarter century, an IRA memorial has been erected. The inscription reads: 'Glory to you all praised and humble heroes who have willingly suffered for your unselfish and passionate love of Irish freedom.' Just eight miles north of Crossmaglen is Newtownhamilton, where a substantial number of Protestants live; soldiers consider it the 'softest' posting in South Armagh and some joke that the acronym NTH stands for 'No Terrorists Here'.

Captain Nick Lewis said of his time in South Armagh with the Coldstream Guards in 1996:

> Conditions at Crossmaglen and Forkhill had to be experienced
> to be believed. In terms of space and light, the mortar proofing

made it a bit like being in a submarine. In Crossmaglen there were more men than beds and no windows. You were banned from being outside or sitting in the sun because of the mortar and sniper threat. Outside in the baronial fiefdom of South Armagh, IRA members operated, intimidated and plotted and went about their daily business of farming, smuggling and drinking. It made us wonder just whose freedom was being constrained.

The sense of helplessness, frustration and incomprehension felt by the ordinary soldier had changed little in the 20 years since Captain Tony Clarke, of the Parachute Regiment, had recalled the experience of serving in Crossmaglen in his memoir *Contact*. He wrote:

> I get the feeling of being one of those shooting-gallery targets that go round on a conveyor-belt, endlessly waiting for some-one to knock it down. South Armagh, still light-years away from civilisation, still living in the dark ages, where barbarity and cruelty are the prime factors of a successful life. Where stealing and killing are as natural a part of living as breathing is to most of us.

For republicans, Crossmaglen is their stronghold, the capital of the *de facto* independent republic of South Armagh.

Proximity to the border, the absence of a Protestant community, the undulating terrain and the powerful sense of rebellion throughout history have all combined to make South Armagh the ideal operating ground for the IRA. Hostility towards authority stretches back to the Middle Ages and smuggling became widespread as soon as the border was drawn up. Moving goods across the border under cover of night and concealing illicit merchandise in vehicles while keeping one step ahead of the law became skills as useful to the IRA man as to the smuggler. Modern-day republicanism in South Armagh is simply the latest manifestation of its independence and refusal to submit to the Queen's Writ or any other rule from beyond its hinterland.

Constables Sam Donaldson and Roy Millar, who were blown up in August 1970 by a car bomb left outside Crossmaglen, were the first RUC men to be killed by the IRA during the modern Troubles. But for centuries enforcers of the law had been meeting their end in South Armagh. The security forces were soon to find that IRA members were often interchangeable with those for whom defiance of authority was already a way of life. Before the Troubles began, a small-time South Armagh smuggler was fined and ordered to pay compensation at Forkhill Petty Sessions Court after admitting stealing farm animals in Northern Ireland and selling them at Dundalk market. By the 1990s, the same man was a major criminal with an annual turnover of hundreds of thousands of pounds; he was also an IRA volunteer playing a central role in mounting bomb attacks in the City of London. In the intervening years, Sergeant Albert White, who had investigated the theft of the farm animals, had been shot dead by the Provisionals in Newry and the courthouse in Forkhill had been destroyed by a bomb.

Since the early 1970s, South Armagh has effectively been under the control of the IRA. Road signs warn not of children crossing but of a Sniper at Work, the red triangle framing the silhouette of a masked gunman waving an Armalite. A few miles from the barn where the South Quay bomb was mixed, a mock advertisement declares: 'Richardson's Fertiliser. Tried and tested at home and abroad by P.I.R.A.'

The Army presence in South Armagh is centred around its headquarters at Bessbrook Mill, a 19th century linen factory situated in a Quaker model village whose founder, John Grubb Richardson, laid down that there be no pawnshop or pub within its boundaries. Bessbrook was named by John Pollock, an 18th century linen manufacturer, after his wife Elizabeth or 'Bess' and Camlough river or 'brook'. In the grounds of the converted mill is one of the busiest helipads in Europe and a garden of remembrance peppered with Mourne granite memorials to the soldiers who have been killed in South Armagh. The commanding officer there controls the three joint RUC-Army bases at Crossmaglen, Forkhill and Newtownhamilton; village police stations in 1971, they are now mini-fortresses strengthened at a cost of millions of pounds to withstand mortar and bomb attack.

Since the mid-1970s virtually all military movement has been by helicopter to avoid casualties from landmines planted under the roads; even the rubbish from the security force bases is taken away by air. As the threat of surface-to-air missiles and heavy machine-guns has increased, helicopters have flown in twos and later threes for mutual protection. Even in the early 1990s, the IRA would set up illegal roadblocks to demonstrate its invulnerability. The border between South Armagh and North Louth has become the traditional dumping ground for the bodies of men executed by the IRA after confessing to the capital offence of being an informer. In August 1998, the Omagh bomb, which killed 29 people, was put together in South Armagh by Provisionals who had defected to the so-called 'Real IRA'.

South Armagh's strategic position on the border and the formidable strength of armed republicanism there have meant that it has long been the place where new weapons and prototype bombs have been tested after being produced by the IRA's Dublin-based engineering department. The South Armagh Brigade has pioneered the use of mortars with eight of the 11 new types manufactured since 1974 being first fired by the Crossmaglen IRA unit. Semtex was first used by the IRA in South Armagh and radio-controlled bombs were developed there. Bicycles, torches, Irish tricolours and the bodies of informers have all been elaborately booby-trapped with bombs. In August 1993, a tractor was loaded with explosives and a dummy placed in the driver's seat before it was guided by radio control into the village of Belleek. Five years later, a Real IRA member from South Armagh perfected a bomb that could be detonated by calling a mobile phone.

Within the IRA, the South Armagh Brigade has always enjoyed a degree of autonomy. During the organisation's ceasefire of 1975, the South Armagh Brigade carried on killing; after the 1994 ceasefire, Frank Kerr, a Post Office worker, was shot dead by South Armagh volunteers during an IRA robbery in Newry.

IRA leaders in South Armagh have gone to extraordinary lengths to ensure their men would escape capture and imprisonment. On 9 May 1992, Mark Flynn, a young volunteer from Silverbridge, was preparing a 180 lb bomb in a derelict house on the Tullymacrieve Road in Mullaghbawn. The device was to be activated by the light from a flash bulb; designed to be placed in a wheelie bin and to kill soldiers on foot patrol, it represented a significant advance in IRA bomb technology and had therefore been fitted with a self-destruct charge that would destroy forensic evidence. As Flynn moved the bomb, this charge exploded, blowing off his right thumb and two fingers, burning his upper body and face and blinding him. He was rushed across the border to hospital by his companions, Joe McCreesh and Paddy Murphy, both IRA men in their early twenties. The following morning, McCreesh and Murphy were arrested in a hijacked car that contained a balaclava and fragments of bloodstained wood. After the security forces sealed off the area, a forensic scientist was flown in by helicopter to examine the derelict house. She was able to reconstruct a wooden A-frame in the house and take samples that matched exactly the fragments of wood found in the hijacked car, thereby establishing an evidential link between the three young IRA men and the bomb.

On 23 September 1992, four months after Flynn had been blinded, the South Armagh Brigade hijacked a van near Newry, packed it with 3,500 lbs of explosives, drove it to Belfast and abandoned it outside the Forensic Science Laboratory in Newtownbreda. At 8.45 p.m., 40 minutes after a coded warning had been issued, the device exploded, almost demolishing the laboratory and damaging 1,002 homes in the area, most of them on the loyalist Belvoir estate. The blast was felt up to 12 miles away and the bomb was later assessed as probably the biggest ever to be detonated in Northern Ireland. In the event, the wood samples which incriminated Flynn, McCreesh and Murphy had been safely locked away in a vault and were not damaged in the blast. Flynn was so badly injured that charges were not proceeded with while McCreesh and Murphy were both convicted of attempting to remove evidence linked to the premature explosion in Mullaghbawn.

The South Armagh Brigade's efficiency, militancy and independence made it the obvious choice to be entrusted with bringing about the end of the ceasefire in February 1996. Having been given the job, the South Armagh men set about their task with skill and some relish. Starting with a Ford Cargo lorry once owned by British Gas and parts cannibalised from two other lorries, a new vehicle was constructed by a team of IRA associates skilled at cutting and welding. The end result was a blue vehicle that looked like an ordinary car transporter. In fact, it was the outer casing of a mobile bomb, the platform at the back concealing a void into which the explosives would be crammed. At the McKinley farm in Mullaghbawn, ramps were made so that a trailer could be loaded onto the back of the transporter to make it look as if it was carrying an ordinary load. Bits of aluminium used in making one of the ramps were later found on a Mitsubishi flatbed lorry owned by 32-year-old Patrick McKinley. Commander John Grieve, head of SO13, the Met's anti-terrorist unit, later speculated that the inspiration for the design of the bomb lorry might have come from a film. 'It's always been one of my thoughts,' he said, 'after seeing Gene Hackman in *The French Connection* during my childhood, that that's where they got the idea of burying the bomb right down deep in the bodywork.'

The IRA was as meticulous about planning the movement of the bomb from South Armagh to South Quay as it had been in constructing the car transporter. Never before had an IRA vehicle bomb been fully assembled in Ireland and driven to its destination in England without using any of the 'sleeper' units or the logistical support network in place. Once the vehicle had been built, a 'dummy run' to London was carried out to help the IRA volunteer selected to drive the bomb familiarise himself with the motorway system and the routine at the ferry ports. The dummy run was also a way of testing out anti-terrorist procedures; the IRA was well aware that during the ceasefire the authorities had let their guard drop in a number of areas. A reconnaissance of the Docklands area had already been carried out by two South Armagh volunteers who had confirmed that vehicles were not being checked on the way in or out of Docklands.

Even before the ceasefire, South Quay had been identified by the South Armagh Brigade as a suitable target. Since 1991, the IRA leaders in the area had been the driving force behind the 'England campaign' and had proved spectacularly successful. In April 1992, a massive bomb at the Baltic Exchange in the City of London had killed three, injured 91 and delivered a devastating blow to the financial heart of the United Kingdom. A year later, the City had again been the target when two men drove 2,200 lbs of homemade explosives into Bishopsgate. The blast killed a newspaper photographer and caused damage estimated at more than £500 million.

Séamus McArdle, from Silverbridge, was chosen by the Boss to drive the transporter to South Quay. Aged 27, he had more than 10 years as an IRA volunteer behind him but had never been arrested in Northern Ireland; he was viewed as a 'clean skin' whose fingerprints had not been taken by the RUC and whose absence from South Armagh would not attract suspicion.

On Monday 15 January 1996, McArdle picked up final instructions from the Boss and collected the transporter, which had a trailer loaded on the back, from a farm in North Louth. He then drove it 50 miles to Belfast ferry terminal and onto the 7 p.m. Stena Sealink ferry to Stranraer on the west coast of Scotland. As he did so, McArdle noted that there was no weighbridge in use to check for abnormally heavy loads. This time, the secret compartments within the transporter were empty; on his next journey they would be filled with explosives. After arriving at Stranraer at 9.30 p.m., McArdle drove the transporter to the BP truck stop at Carlisle where he met another South Armagh volunteer. They booked into rooms 14 and 16 under the name Murphy and stayed the night there.

The next day, the pair went to Carlisle Car Auctions and bought a Renault 25 and a Peugeot 205. They drew attention to themselves by paying £600 for the Renault, which was well over the odds, and the difficulties they had loading it onto the transporter without using ramps. After the auction, the two parted company. McArdle drove the transporter back to South Armagh via Stranraer and Belfast while the other volunteer returned in the Peugeot via Holyhead and Dun Laoghaire. That night, the transporter, with the Renault on the back, was parked outside Caesar's night-club near Jonesborough, just a few yards south of the border on the A1.

Once the bomb had been mixed and packed into the transporter, everything was in place for the Docklands attack. On Wednesday 7 February, McArdle picked up the transporter and trailer from the border farm and travelled the same route as he had on the dummy run, catching the 7 p.m. ferry from Belfast and staying at the Carlisle truck stop. He also linked up with a scout car which was to accompany him to London. McArdle booked in as 'Mr Hoey', the name of a prominent South Armagh volunteer. For both the dummy and the bomb runs, the transporter had been fitted with false numberplates bearing the registration 575 7IB, which had been taken from a car transporter broken up for scrap in Cullaville, two miles from Crossmaglen. As a precaution against the vehicle being traced later, McArdle booked the transporter in at the truck stop using the registration 575 7BI.

On the Thursday morning, McArdle continued his journey south down the M6, stopping at the Hollies service station in Staffordshire and then at a truck stop on the M25 at South Mimms in Hertfordshire. At this stage, McArdle was joined by another South Armagh volunteer and they spent the night nearby. They rose early on Friday 9 February, the day of the blast, and drove through the Dartford Tunnel to a piece of waste ground on an industrial estate at River Road in Barking, arriving in the early afternoon. The pair were then taken in the scout car to eat at a nearby café and prepare themselves for the final and most hazardous part of the IRA operation – the 11-mile journey to South Quay.

While at Barking, the 575 7IB numberplates, which identified it as an Irish vehicle, were substituted with English plates bearing the registration C292 GWG; the plates were later found to have been made at a repair garage in Crossmaglen. The transporter was now what was known in the anti-terrorism world as a 'ringer vehicle'. A similar transporter owned by a man in Tandragee in North Armagh had the genuine registration C292 GWG; an IRA supporter had stolen its licence disc during the first two weeks of January. This meant that if the bomb transporter's registration was run through a police computer it would appear to be the Tandragee vehicle. McArdle and his colleague then unloaded the trailer from the back of the transporter and primed the device by linking the timing and power unit (TPU) in the cab to the bomb compartment at the back. At about 4.15 p.m., the transporter, driven by McArdle, and scout car left River Road and travelled down the A13. Security camera footage at South Quay showed the lorry arriving at 5.04 p.m. and the two IRA men getting out of the cab. Before they did so, McArdle checked that the TPU, a wooden box containing timers and wires, was set correctly; a red warning light would have come on had there been a problem. He then removed a wooden dowel pin from the side of the TPU and flicked a switch; the bomb was now 'armed' and the two-hour kitchen timer ticking away.

Although in most respects the Docklands bomb had been a classically successful South Armagh operation, a few tiny clues were to lead to Séamus McArdle's eventual conviction. After appeals for information, more than 850 people telephoned the Met's anti-terrorist hotline. The 199th caller to be logged was Arthur Ward, a lorry driver who reported having seen seeing an unfamiliar car transporter and trailer parked at River Road on the day of the explosion. He had stopped, he later told Woolwich Crown Court, because 'I am nosy'. Officers picked up every scrap of urban detritus they could find on the River Road site. The search provided the key to the inquiry, named Operation Heron by the Met. Inside an old tyre were found a copy of *Truck and Driver* magazine, receipts for a parking ticket at South Mimms and a packet of Screenies windscreen wipes, and a lorry tachograph sheet. There were broken pieces of a 575 7IB numberplate nearby. The trailer was also there; particles of PETN explosives and paint scrapings eventually led to it being linked to the transporter and traced back to South Armagh. Police believed that the presence of a British Telecom engineer working up a nearby telegraph pole had panicked the IRA men into thinking they could be under surveillance and deciding not to burn the tyre and its contents.

For 14 months, police did not know who had driven the bomb to South Quay, although three thumbprints from the same person had been found on the *Truck and Driver* magazine, an ashtray at the Carlisle truck stop and a ferry ticket stub handed in at Stranraer on the return leg of the dummy run. In April 1997, the RUC took the fingerprints of Micheál Caraher, McArdle and two other members of an IRA sniper team captured in South Armagh by the SAS. A match was made between McArdle's thumbprints and those sent over by the Met; 'triple thumbprint man' had been identified.

The Renault and Peugeot cars had been located at the McKinley farm, and on 7 June 1996 Patrick McKinley had been arrested during a massive security swoop codenamed Operation Fisherton. Both McKinley and McArdle faced trial on charges of conspiring to cause an explosion while McArdle was also charged with murdering Inam Bashir and John Jefferies. At their joint trial, which began at the Old Bailey in January 1998, it was established that the two cars bought in Carlisle had ended up at the McKinley farm within 48 hours. Ramps on the trailer found at River Road were almost identical to those on the Mitsubishi lorry he had rebuilt. McKinley's defence was that the cars had been sold to him by Patrick Goodfellow, a Bessbrook man with IRA links who had hanged himself from a beam in his roof space two weeks before Operation Fisherton. The judge directed that he be acquitted.

Also arrested during the Docklands investigation was Kevin 'Fred' Loye, a barman from Mullaghbawn. Loye was known to be a republican and a friend of Micksey Martin, one of the four most senior IRA men in the South Armagh Brigade. In April 1994, Martin, at that time wanted for gunrunning offences in America, and Loye were arrested after a high speed car chase that ended in Ballsmill in South Armagh. When the security forces opened fire, Martin crashed his car and was wounded in the right thigh; Loye remained silent during five days of questioning and claimed through his solicitor that he had been thumbing a lift. Loye was arrested again in June 1996 after one of the six coded warnings about the Docklands bomb was traced to a telephone box in Drogheda in County Louth. The box was removed and several of Loye's fingerprints found on it; he again refused to answer any questions and was released without charge.

McArdle's defence at the Old Bailey was ingenious. He told the jury he spent 10 or 15 days a year working for a powerful South Armagh farmer known as 'the Boss'. Some of the work would be legal, feeding cattle or transporting hay, but some of it would involve smuggling diesel or kegs of beer across the border. He knew that the Boss was a senior IRA man and admitted running messages for him that probably had something to do with the IRA. Faced with fingerprint evidence that linked him to both the dummy and the bomb runs, McArdle said that he had been asked by the Boss in January to do a job for him that involved bringing back cars from England. This he had done and when he arrived in Carlisle for a second job in February the Boss had told him that the job 'was going to be different this time' and asked him to drive the transporter further south. McArdle said he had handed the transporter over to another driver at South Mimms and hitched a lift home. He knew nothing about the bomb and assumed the Boss had used him because 'he trusted me in the past and his own customers through smuggling and that, so he probably would have knew I'd keep it to myself'.

McArdle told the Old Bailey that he could not identify the Boss because of possible reprisals. 'I can't scream because I would be putting myself in danger and my family in danger,' he said. But questioning by the judge elicited that the Boss owned a farm and dealt in cars, lived six or seven miles from Dundalk, was aged between 45 and 50 and was balding. At least one member of the Old Bailey jury believed McArdle's story and, with the jury unable to reach a unanimous verdict, a retrial was ordered. Following a second trial at Woolwich Crown Court in May 1998, McArdle was convicted of conspiring to cause an explosion and sentenced to 25 years' imprisonment. As he left the dock, his supporters from South Armagh cheered and waved two fingers to signify that he would serve less than two years in jail before being released under the Good Friday Agreement which Sinn Féin had endorsed the previous month.

Although he had lied about the extent of his role in the Docklands bomb, it seems McArdle had largely stuck to the truth about the man who was behind the IRA operation as a guard against being caught out in cross-examination. During the two trials, he gave enough details about the Boss to leave few doubts among the initiated about the man he was referring to.

The Boss had been the central IRA figure in South Armagh for more than 25 years and, by the time of McArdle's trial, was also the IRA's Chief of Staff, the leader of the world's most feared paramilitary organisation. His importance had only begun to be revealed publicly 13 years earlier when an armour-plated Ford Cortina carrying four RUC officers was blown apart at Killeen as it escorted a lorry carrying a Brinks Mat gold bullion consignment across the border in May 1985. All four were killed when a 900 lb radio-controlled bomb packed into an articulated trailer on the hard shoulder was detonated. Afterwards, Sir John Hermon, then RUC Chief Constable, joined a line of his officers who had spread out across a field next to the main Belfast-to-Dublin road for the grim task of gathering the remains of their colleagues. As the line advanced slowly, one officer knelt down and picked up a severed hand. 'Fingerprint bag, please,' he called. Another RUC man said: 'I know that hand, it belongs to Tracy Doak.' It was a left hand and, although the little and ring fingers were missing, he had recognised a gold band on the middle finger. The ring finger, on which a diamond engagement ring had been worn, was never found. Constable Tracy Doak, 21, the driver of the Cortina, had been due to marry a fellow police officer that year.

At her funeral at Ballywatt Presbyterian Church near Coleraine in County Derry, the Reverend Ian Hunter told the congregation that Constable Doak had been murdered, like so many others, 'by an unseen enemy and faceless men who do their deeds in secret and in hiding'. But Hermon, who was becoming increasingly depressed about the number of RUC losses in South Armagh and Newry, knew exactly who the unseen enemy was. Shaken by what he had seen at Killeen, Hermon decided to let the IRA know that its hierarchy in South Armagh was being watched and revealed during a radio interview that a 'wealthy pig smuggler' living in the Irish Republic had been responsible for the Killeen attack.

The pig smuggler's name was Thomas 'Slab' Murphy. He owned and controlled the Slab Murphy farm complex straddling the border some two miles south-east of Crossmaglen. A bachelor, he lived at the farm with his elderly widowed mother Elizabeth. Murphy was the Boss McArdle had referred to and the use of the surname at the Carlisle truck stop during the Docklands dummy run was possibly an in-joke about the provenance of the bomb plot. While Murphy is still relatively unknown to the public and has never been convicted of a criminal offence, since 1970 his name has been familiar to every senior Army and RUC officer who has served in South Armagh. Exercising power in the same way as a feudal lord controlling his vassals, Murphy rules his domain through courtiers and henchmen authorised to act on his behalf. The few who cross him are dealt with mercilessly. 'If you meet Tom Murphy driving along the road he just heads straight for you and you have to go into the ditch,' said a neighbour. 'You'd never ask him a question about what goes on for fear you might end up in a bag on the side of the road.'

The Slab Murphy farm complex, partly in Ballybinaby in County Louth in the Irish Republic and partly in Cornoonagh in County Armagh in Northern Ireland, has been at the epicentre of IRA activity in South Armagh since the birth of the Provisionals. For nearly three decades, grid reference 957128 at 71 Larkins Road, where the farm is situated, has been observed by scores of successive Army surveillance teams dug in close to Border Crossing Point (BCP) 28. In 1986, several million pounds was spent building watchtowers at Drummuckavall and Glasdrumman – known to the Army as Golf Two Zero and Golf Three Zero respectively – to dominate the area to the north of the Slab Murphy farm complex. By the 1990s, Murphy was judged by MI5 to be the single biggest domestic threat to the United Kingdom. The resources devoted to curtailing his activities are probably greater than those deployed against any other individual this century.

Docklands had been Tom Murphy's operation from start to finish. When the IRA Army Council met in October 1995 to decide in principle that the ceasefire should be brought to an end, it seemed natural that Murphy and his South Armagh Brigade should be left to take care of the practicalities. In the years before the IRA ceasefire of August 1994, South Armagh had played an increasingly important role within the 'England Department'.

Despite rumours in 1996 of an IRA split or a coup by three members of the Army Council, both MI5 and RUC officers now agree that all seven men were party to the collective decision. According to intelligence sources, the seven were: the Sinn Féin leadership triumvirate of Adams, McGuinness and Pat Doherty; Kevin McKenna, the Chief of Staff, from County Monaghan; Brian Keenan, the Belfast Marxist who had masterminded the IRA's bombing campaign in England in the 1970s; Martin Ferris, a former head of the IRA's Southern Command who had been convicted of smuggling a huge consignment of weapons from America; and Tom Murphy. McKenna and Murphy had been unhappy about the ceasefire from the outset. The others had become more and more exasperated by what they saw as the British government's unwillingness to convene all-party talks with Sinn Féin at the table.

As political stasis had set in, the balance of opinion on the Army Council had shifted towards a resumption of violence and in South Armagh a 'return to war' was considered overdue by 1996. Jim McAllister, a former Sinn Féin councillor from Crossmaglen who has been the authentic voice of republicanism in the area since the early 1980s, said:

> Within active republicans the feeling became as those months passed by that there was definitely nothing going to come out of it. And the feeling then became: 'Give it another month, give it another two months, then we'll see.' When Canary Wharf [Docklands] did come there was no great sadness; it was what they expected. And there was also a very, very strong attitude amongst the people here that that's the place for the bombs: 'London, keep them over there. I don't want one, I've had

enough of them, bang it out to hell over there.' Genuinely there
was no great sorrow for London. None.

McAllister was chosen by the republican leadership to travel to
England to observe McArdle's second trial.

TOM Murphy left Glasdrumman school at the age of 14 and
began to take charge of the family farm when his father,
Joseph, died five years later. Today, he presides over a
smuggling empire with an annual turnover of millions of pounds.
Since October 1996, when Kevin McKenna stepped down after
nearly a decade in post, he has been the IRA's Chief of Staff. Balding
and heavily built, Murphy has a lolloping gait and an imposing
presence. Apart from the IRA and smuggling, his only passion is
Gaelic football and he often watches matches around the Louth area.
Although he drinks little, he can sometimes be found on Saturday
nights in the bar at the Ballymascanlon Hotel outside Dundalk, where
darts matches are held. Still unmarried, Murphy has lived alone at the
farm since his mother died in 1992 at the age of 72.

A Garda Síochána (Irish police) Special Branch profile of Murphy
dated March 1998 describes him as 'Smuggler, PIRA Army Council.
Strongly built, 5 ft 11 in tall. Balding' and states that oil smuggling
within his farm complex is his principal source of income and a major
money-spinner for the IRA. Oil and petrol tanks are situated on both
sides of his hedge, which marks the border, and a gravity feed system
takes the fuel underground from one state to the other. At the
moment, fuel is bought in the Irish Republic and transferred to the
tank in Northern Ireland because of the low value of the Irish pound;
in the past, when sterling was weaker, the system worked vice versa.
Once the fuel is in the northern tank, it is piped into a shed used as a
loading bay and a portable electric pump used to fill up tankers to
take it away to be sold.

Murphy first became involved in the oil business in the early
1980s having already made a fortune in the previous decade from
smuggling grain, pigs and cattle. A succession of oil companies have
traded from the family farm; the latest, Ace Oils, was set up in 1992.
The situation of the Slab Murphy farm complex, with the dwelling
house in the Irish Republic and most of the land in Northern Ireland,

made it ideal for these activities and the layout of the farm has been used to maximum advantage. The border runs directly along the rear wall of the farmhouse and through several sheds built by Tom Murphy; linked to the house are two offices which are in Northern Ireland and oil tanks on both sides of the border. Much of Murphy's smuggling has been funded by European subsidies. At one stage he was driving lorryloads of pigs from the Republic, filing a claim for a subsidy of £8 per pig at the UK Customs Post in Newry and then driving the pigs back across the border ready for another round trip. Monty Alexander, a former RUC sergeant with long experience in South Armagh, said:

> Smuggling has always been rife down there. In the 1970s, there was a guy in Dundalk who was hiring pigs out to people who would drive them across the border and back again. It got to the stage where the pigs were collapsing with fatigue they'd been on the road for so long. When the subsidies shifted to grain, there was a smuggler with a lorry full of sand with a thin layer of grain on top of it. The joke was that he nearly got caught on because the grain had been so long on top of the sand that it started to sprout.

Tom Murphy is still one of the most prolific smugglers in Ireland and also charges other smugglers, many of whom have no connection to the IRA, a toll for those using Larkins Road. Oil tankers thunder up and down Larkins Road by day and night, the drivers often turning off their lights after dark to avoid easy detection. Murphy keeps deer worth about £50,000 on land at Cornoonagh and a herd of cattle near Kells in County Meath on land he rents for £45,000 a year. Neither police nor customs officials on either side of the border are able to estimate with any confidence exactly how much Tom Murphy is worth; he has become master of the South Armagh practice of exploiting the border by, in the words of one local, 'working each side to the middle and paying no one'. He evades VAT and income tax in both jurisdictions and pays all bills in cash. Although he has no bank account in his own name, Murphy is believed to have hundreds of thousand of pounds in various bank and offshore accounts held by relatives or under aliases. He changes vehicles frequently but in 1998 was driving a blue Isuzu Trooper jeep and a black BMW diesel 325; the Irish police had a list of another 13 cars, vans and lorries at his disposal. An RUC Special Branch collator's index of suspects compiled in 1988 listed Murphy thus: 'MURPHY, Thomas (Slab). Dob 27/1/44. On the run. Lives B'binaby HBX [Hackballscross]. Wanted re attempted murder XMG 72, possession of explosives and firearms.' Murphy was in fact born on 26 August 1949 and the date listed is one of several false dates of birth he has used over the years. Aware that he is still technically wanted for terrorist offences in Northern Ireland, he ventures north of the border only to attend the occasional IRA gathering.

Murphy and his brothers, Patrick, five years older, and Francis, seven years his junior, inherited the nickname 'Slab' from their father. It was, however, with Tom Murphy that the nickname became primarily associated. Family nicknames are often used in South Armagh and other rural areas to differentiate between those with a common surname. In the locality of Ballybinaby — which derives its name from the Irish *Bealach Ben Bhuí* or 'way by the yellow hill' — there are 'Miller', 'Mason' and 'Paramour' Murphys while a little further afield 'Nelly' and 'Corney' Murphys can be found. 'Tom's father was a big slab of a man and the name just stuck,' said Paddy Short, the loquacious publican who has been an unofficial spokesman for the people of Crossmaglen throughout the Troubles. 'It could be an occupation, a character trait or some sort of physical characteristic that gives a nickname. I've known all three boys since they were this high and would come to the market in Cross and they were always known as the Slabs.' Tom Murphy is thought to have joined the IRA in the mid 1960s and by 1968 was listed as being a member of the unit in Inniskeen in County Monaghan. Some time in the late 1960s or early 1970s, he spent six months in England. Francis Murphy, then 18, was charged in May 1973 with the attempted murder of British soldiers during a cross-border gun battle at Coolderry; he was acquitted.

In their younger days, the two older Murphy brothers were well-known local sportsmen and both played Gaelic football for Roche Emmets; Patrick has been club treasurer for the past 25 years. A team photograph taken after a victory over Inniskeen in a Crossmaglen tournament on 8 August 1970 shows a youthful Tom Murphy grinning at the cameraman. Three days later, Constables Donaldson and Millar were blown up by men from the Inniskeen IRA unit, of which Tom Murphy was at that time a member. In 1979, Tom Murphy joined Naomh Malachi Football Club along with his friend Tom Conlon and the team won the County Louth junior championship during their first season, beating the Naomh Martin side in the final on 14 October. The match report in the *Dundalk Democrat* noted: 'The former Roche pair Conlon and Murphy gave the full-back line a very solid look. Murphy fielded well and Conlon earned marks for his "dead" ball kicking.' Patrick Murphy had been Mid-Ulster junior heavyweight boxing champion from 1966 to 1968, once losing on points to Danny McAlinden, later to become British professional heavyweight champion.

Brigadier Peter Morton, who served in South Armagh as the Crossmaglen company commander in 1973 and commanding officer of the Parachute Regiment's 2nd Battalion in 1976, said that 'Murphy's gang' was already notorious when he first arrived in Northern Ireland. 'The officer who handed over to me pointed to the Slab Murphy farm complex on a map and said: "This is where everything stems from." And he was absolutely spot on. During my time in South Armagh and subsequently in headquarters at Lisburn or the Ministry of Defence, I never had any reason to change my views on that.'

The Slab Murphy farm complex, Brigadier Morton believed, was linked to the deaths of Corporal Terence Williams and Trooper John Gibbons in May 1973. He recalled:

> I had just lost my best company sergeant major to an IRA bomb and the two lancers were winding up the command wire, which led across the border to an area not terribly far from Murphy's. All these things seemed to have that common thread. They never ended at Murphy's but they were never far away. The troopers were just finishing off the incident when they pulled the wire where it went through a wall and the whole wall disintegrated. It was one of the first occasions when they put a secondary device in. My commanding officer and I had taken off in a helicopter and we were just about over the top of this thing and the helicopter rocked like hell. We were just bloody lucky

that we weren't a few yards one way or the other or the whole thing would have come down. But sadly those two guys were killed in that because they were very close to the wall.

Murphy was later to perfect the use of secondary devices at Narrow Water near Warrenpoint in August 1979 when 11 soldiers were killed in a radio-controlled explosion 32 minutes after seven of their colleagues had perished in the initial blast.

Brigadier Morton was one of the first Army officers to draw attention to Tom Murphy's smuggling activities. He explained:

> I watched him from a little Sioux helicopter. Big pig lorries would drive up to a pig pen close to the farm, but just north of the border. The driver would unload the pigs into the pig pen and then the lorry would depart. There would be no one at the pig pen at all. Then a truck driven by a farmhand would come from the Slab Murphy farm complex, go to the pig pen, pick up the pigs and go back to the farm. The pigs had crossed an international land boundary but really they'd just moved within Tom Murphy's farm.

Tom Murphy featured prominently in military intelligence reports of the early 1970s and he and Francis inspired fear because of their readiness to settle an argument with their fists. 'They were awful ignorant fellows,' said a Ballybinaby woman who went to dances in Dundalk and Monaghan with them. 'As kids we would call them the Slob Murphys and were told to steer clear of them because they were always fighting. My mother said they were a bad lot.' In January 1977, an informer being 'run' by an Army staff sergeant working for military intelligence at Bessbrook Mill reported:

> On 31 Dec 76 the MURPHY brothers, accompanied by about seven other men, went to the Newmore Hotel, CARRICKMA-CROSS, to 'sort out' the bouncer, John Howard, a former professional wrestler against whom 'Slab' MURPHY held a grievance. HOWARD received advanced warning and fled. The gang left when they failed to find HOWARD, but not before

'Slab' pulled the speakers off the stage and bent the microphone stand.

The staff sergeant noted that his source was referring to: 'The MURPHY brothers of BALLYBINABY (GR 957128), Thomas "Slab" and Francis Joseph.'

The same informer, identified in documents by the number 3/0020, implicated Tom Murphy in the shooting of Lance Corporal David Hind two days after the incident in the Newmore Hotel. 'Slab Murphy had a hand in the killing,' he told the staff sergeant. Hind was on patrol on the Dundalk Road outside Crossmaglen when he was hit twice during a burst of automatic gunfire from close to St Joseph's Secondary School. One of the bullets passed through his back, rupturing his liver and heart and killing him instantly; two fusiliers were wounded. The informer reported that the shots had come from a 'pill-box' mounted on the back of a flatbed lorry; large enough to contain two or three men, it had been constructed from sandbags and hidden by bales of hay. The night before the attack, eight men had loaded the lorry at Coolderry Bridge, less than a mile from the Slab Murphy farm complex. Shortly after Hind had been killed, an Army patrol commander spoke to a man in Crossmaglen who had seen the gunmen. 'No names, no names,' he said. 'I shouldn't be talking to you now.' The patrol commander concluded that the man had recognised the volunteers and was genuinely afraid of reprisals should he identify them.

Tom Murphy was believed by the RUC and Army to have been involved with the development of IRA mortars in the early 1970s. In March 1979, the IRA claimed its first victim in a mortar attack when Private Peter Woolmore was killed by a direct hit as he relieved himself in the 'ablutions block' inside Newtownhamilton security force base. It was the first use of the Mark 10 mortar, made up of 45 lbs of fertiliser explosives packed into a gas cylinder and set off by a propellant ignited by a photo flash bulb. Mark 10 mortars later killed nine police officers at Corry Square RUC station in Newry in 1985 and were used in attacks on Downing Street in 1991 and Heathrow airport in 1992. Nine mortars were fired at Newtownhamilton base at one-second intervals using an electronic sequential timer unit which gave the volunteers involved just 90 seconds to get away from the lorry before the first was launched. A tenth mortar was set on a timer to explode 30 minutes later and had the dual aim of catching soldiers engaged in the follow-up operation and destroying evidence. Fired from the back of a tipper truck and with a total weight of 120 lbs, the Mark 10s were by far the largest mortars used by the IRA in the 1970s; prototypes had been tested extensively in North Louth.

An RUC investigation into the Newtownhamilton attack concluded that it had been a textbook IRA operation involving between 15 and 20 volunteers. 'The scouting and execution was carried out successfully in that at no time did any member of the security forces suspect or identify any of the participants,' the investigator concluded. 'The lorry was very precisely placed and the line of fire was extremely accurate. The position also afforded the greatest protection from view from the camp.' Another investigator wrote that 'the style, expertise and resources evident in the attack' were characteristic of 'the Crossmaglen Group'. A few days later, an informer told his handler that he had heard a man, identified here as K, boasting in a Dundalk pub about having driven the tipper truck. According to his handler, the informer said: 'The man that drove the lorry that mortared Newtownhamilton base was K from Kilcurry . . . K was bragging about this in the Lisdoo Arms . . . K goes around with Thomas Slab Murphy.' The handler commented: 'Murphy refers to Thomas "Slab" Murphy, RC, DOB 1950, Ballybinaby, Hackballscross. Traced PIRA.'

A unique aspect of the IRA in South Armagh, and one that accounts for much of its success, is the remarkable continuity of personnel over nearly three decades of conflict. Most of the men who fought alongside Tom Murphy in the early 1970s remain senior IRA figures today. Murphy's deputy, a man known as 'the Undertaker', is now the IRA's director of finance; he has long been a member of Northern Command, the body which controls the IRA in what it describes as the 'occupied six counties'. Micksey Martin has organised scores of IRA operations and is still one of Tom Murphy's most trusted lieutenants. Pat Thompson, a Murphy protege before his arrest in 1975, is considered to be 'adjutant' to the IRA's Chief of Staff, effectively the eyes and ears of the Boss in South Armagh. The RUC believes Thompson has represented

South Armagh at recent meetings of the IRA's General Army Convention, its supreme decision-making body. While British Army units have come and gone and the captains and majors of the early days have long since retired as colonels, brigadiers or even generals, the same volunteers still form the backbone of the IRA. Some of the South Armagh Brigade's gunmen and bombers are in their forties or fifties; few in Belfast would be still active beyond their twenties.

Family ties within the republican movement in South Armagh are stronger than in any other part of Ireland. Many volunteers can trace their ancestors back to the Defenders and Ribbonmen of the 18th and 19th centuries; their more recent forebears fought in the IRA's 4th Northern Division in the 1920s and its border campaign of 1956 to 1962. In RUC and Army files during the modern Troubles, the same names crop up again and again with several large clans, all interlinked by marriage, forming the nucleus of the movement. But the job of the security forces has been made all the more difficult because many members of these clans are not linked to the IRA and some of the staunchest republicans have been concerned mainly with the politics of a united Ireland. The almost obsessive secrecy of some of those who are deeply involved means that even close relatives might not know they are IRA volunteers.

The Murphy, Martin, O'Callaghan, Caraher and Moley clans are all staunchly republican. Both Micksey Martin and his brother Jim are leading IRA men. Micksey Martin has served sentences in the Republic for possessing explosives in 1975 and in America for attempting to procure arms in 1989. Jim Martin was convicted of assaulting a Garda officer in 1975 and the attempted murder of one soldier and the murder of two others in 1973. He was also charged in connection with the arms procurement case in America but charges were dropped. A nephew, Eugene Martin, was an IRA volunteer who died in a car crash in April 1996.

Eugene O'Callaghan was sentenced to ten years in prison in 1980; he had been captured the previous year on board a boat loaded with bomb-making equipment at Lough Ross near Cross-maglen. He and his brother Patsy, a senior republican, grew up at Monog, a townland on the road from Crossmaglen to Ballybinaby which Captain Clarke described as 'a seedy collection of unkempt dwellings, rusty cars and hate-filled people'. Peter John Caraher, a veteran of the Border Campaign, still presides over republican rallies in South Armagh. One of his sons, Micheál, helped to mix the Docklands bomb and was the IRA's principal sniper in the 1990s. Another son, Fergal, was shot dead by the Royal Marines in 1990 and a daughter, Maria, was elected as a Sinn Féin representative in 1996. Brendan Moley, blown up by his own bomb in 1988, left his brothers Séamus and Aidan to keep the republican flame burning. Both were implicated along with Micksey Martin in the 1989 arms-buying conspiracy.

Eamon Larkin, a Sinn Féin councillor who broke with the Provisionals in 1986 and joined Republican Sinn Féin, said that family links stretching back more than a hundred years would be a factor when assessing whether a young man should be recruited to the republican movement. 'In a rural environment like South Armagh everyone knows everyone else's strengths and weaknesses. Not only do they know them for one generation but they know them for maybe three generations of families and you would be able to give judgement on them.' John Grieve found that examining family networks was one of the keys to unlocking the puzzle of who was involved in the Docklands bomb. He said:

> You can narrow it down. I've always been very interested in family trees, the nephews, the nieces, the classic robber stuff: 'Who's the brother-in-law and then who's the brother-in-law's sister?' Those networks, which become very incestuous, sometimes seem to jump a generation and then it's just some youngster and his dad hasn't actually figured very much at all; you just know him to be the son and then you get the grandfather. You could map it into these families and say that it's amongst them.

Eamon Collins, a customs officer who joined the IRA's Newry unit in 1979 and spent six years working with the South Armagh Brigade, made essentially the same point when he said: 'Whatever republicans do in South Armagh, they like to keep it in the family.' Collins was an IRA 'intelligence officer' who would gather information on potential targets and set them up to be shot. In 1985, he gave the RUC a full account of his IRA activities and briefly agreed to give evidence against his comrades before retracting the statement and being acquitted on several charges of murder on a legal technicality. In January 1999, after speaking out against the IRA and Tom Murphy, Collins was abducted, bludgeoned and stabbed to death.

Collins said that he had once asked Brendan Burns, who was blown up with Brendan Moley, how the IRA in South Armagh had been so successful:

> Brendan said it was quite simple. They had taken a number of people and they had worked with them over a period of years, gradually acclimatising them to the type of warfare they were going to be involved in, rather than putting them in at the deep end quickly, which is what happens in the urban areas. South Armagh developed a slow process of training the volunteer. They would have taken raw recruits and put them in with skilled people and took them on. They didn't push them too hard. And they got them used to what they were going to be faced with. And over a period of years, as Brendan said, people working together in close proximity with each other, experiencing operations, came to trust and depend on each other. In fact they would have been loath to meet up with other people or to operate with volunteers outside their own immediate circle.

This system meant that there were fewer mistakes and therefore fewer arrests in South Armagh than in any other IRA brigade area. Only a handful of South Armagh IRA men have been convicted of serious offences and nine killed on 'active service' in 27 years of conflict. Operations are planned meticulously and on a 'need to know' basis with only the unit commander knowing all the details of how an attack would be carried out. Junior volunteers would be ordered to hijack a vehicle or keep lookout for Army patrols but they would not find out the target of the attack until it was over. Only those who had performed these relatively straightforward tasks satisfactorily and proved they could be depended on were then given more important tasks. Murphy also taught the value of caution and to this day South Armagh IRA men will call off an operation if there is the slightest hint it could have been compromised or conditions are not right. Trust has to be earned but it is also based on how a person's family is regarded. Betrayal has been rare because such an act is regarded as unnatural, cutting across blood ties as well as those of fealty. As Collins was to find out, the penalty for betrayal was death.

Chapter Two

'Fighting Men'

'In Crossmaglen the fire burns true
The patriotic flame will never die
And when you hear the battle cry
It will be the fighting men of Crossmaglen'
(*The Fighting Men of Crossmaglen,*
IRA ballad, 1970s)

'The only bandits I ever saw in South Armagh were wearing British uniforms.'

(Peter John Caraher, Cullyhanna, 1998)

A van backfiring as it drove through west Belfast signalled the start of the Troubles in South Armagh. It was 7.30 a.m. on Saturday 7 August 1971 and a jittery sentry, hearing two loud bangs, shouted out that the Springfield Road base was under attack. An NCO from the Parachute Regiment who was on desk duty inside grabbed his rifle, ran into the street and, dropping down on one knee, fired two shots into the back of the van. Arthur Murphy, a Silverbridge man who was in the passenger seat, looked across at his friend Harry Thornton, a 29-year-old father of six from nearby Tullydonnell, and saw him slump forward as half his head was blown off.

The two men had been staying in digs in the lower Falls area and had just set off for Carryduff in County Down, where they were working on a sewerage contract. A search of the van yielded only a bag of tools and two lunch boxes. That afternoon, leaflets headed 'Murder, Murder, Murder' were being handed out in west Belfast and there were angry scenes as Murphy, his face swollen and bandaged, was driven from the police station to hospital; two RUC officers, Sergeant John Magowan and Constable Raymond Proctor, were later cleared of assaulting him. A few hours before Thornton was buried on the Monday morning, internment was introduced and 342 IRA suspects arrested in Army swoops across Northern Ireland. Kevin McMahon, a schoolteacher from Cullyhanna, was the only person from South Armagh to be interned but the shooting of Thornton had already raised local feelings to fever pitch.

Nationalists view Thornton's death as South Armagh's Bloody Sunday, the spark that started the conflagration that was to rage for more than 25 years. On the night of his funeral, there was a riot in the Square in Crossmaglen and a bus and the car of the town's RUC sergeant, Willie Murtagh, were torched. An Irish tricolour was hoisted to the top of the Markethouse in defiance of the Union flag – soon to become known to locals as 'the Butcher's Apron' – flying from the RUC station. One of those who addressed the angry crowd outside the station was Peter John Caraher, then aged 43 and listed by the RUC as a veteran of the IRA's Border Campaign of 1956 to 1962. During the Troubles, he was to lose one son, Fergal, to a Royal Marine's bullet, while another, Micheál, helped mix the Docklands bomb in 1996 and became the South Armagh Brigade's principal sniper. Among the young rioters were Volunteer M, an 18-year-old from Crossmaglen, and 15-year-old Pat Thompson who lived in Tullydonnell. Volunteer M, who came from one of the area's staunchest republican families, had already acted as a lookout during a failed IRA attack on the Crossmaglen RUC station in August 1969. During his career as an IRA volunteer he was to be captured and imprisoned twice, shot three times, extradited from Northern Ireland to the Republic and served with an exclusion order from Great Britain. Pat Thompson also joined the IRA and was to be convicted of murdering four soldiers at Tullydonnell in 1975 and serve 16 years of a life sentence in the Maze jail.

Peter John Caraher, who was arrested during the riot and spent the night in a cell, recalled the presence of another soon-to-be IRA man that night: Michael McVerry, 21, the first Provisional IRA 'officer commanding' (OC) in Crossmaglen. 'That night, Micky McVerry and a group of other fellows almost took Crossmaglen barracks over with their bare hands and a couple of nail bombs,' he said. 'They got through the window and were inside and if they'd had a couple more men they'd have done it.' McVerry was to fight another day; he had his right hand blown off the following year when he was preparing a mortar bomb and by the time he was shot dead during an attack on the Keady security force base in November 1973 he was believed by the RUC to have been involved in the killing of 26 people.

The death of Thornton, a near neighbour, prompted Thompson to join the IRA. While this was essentially a 'gut reaction' to events, he said 27 years later, he was under no illusions about what lay ahead. 'It was a decision which I didn't take lightly because there's only one of three things that could happen: you get killed, you go to jail or you survive.' Volunteer M said: 'Harry Thornton's death and internment was the trigger here. Units were organised and by the spring of '72 the number of shootings was unbelievable. Every time the Brits walked out of the barracks there was an IRA unit waiting for them. We took on a lot of foot patrols in rural areas and almost every day there was two or three attacks.'

From August 1971, scores of young men in South Armagh applied to join the IRA. A discreet approach would be made to one of the older republicans and the potential recruit would soon find himself being interviewed by the local OC. 'They couldn't be vetted quick enough there was that many,' said Volunteer G, from Forkhill. 'In our 3rd Battalion area from Drumintee to Keady we had maybe 60 or more people involved. That's how many volunteers we had. We had to turn people away.' Fired up by the scenes on television of rioting in Belfast and Derry in 1970, Volunteer G had bought a gun even before he joined the IRA. 'Me and a friend decided we wanted to do something about what was happening,' he said. 'We went camping in County Kerry with a tent and we got talking to this fellow and told him what we were looking for. He was able to get us a Steyr rifle. It cost us seven quid, which was all we had with us for the holiday.' After taking part in rioting and throwing petrol bombs at RUC jeeps, he joined the IRA. He recalled:

I was 17 years old when I was accepted. There was a ceremony in which I held the tricolour, came to attention and swore the oath of allegiance to uphold the honour of the Republic. Afterwards we were taught military drill and a bit of weapons training. We were taken south of the border to this rich man's house with a swimming pool and everything and taught how to handle a Thompson and a .303. We weren't allowed to fire them because there wasn't enough ammunition at that stage.

As the IRA became more organised, volunteers began to specialise in areas such as sniping, explosives, logistics or intelligence. Volunteer Raymond McCreesh, who was to become the third of ten IRA hunger strikers to die in 1981, used his job as a milkman in Jonesborough and Drumintee to gather information for the IRA; he was designated an intelligence officer. Others would be known as operations officers and were responsible for planning attacks. Volunteer G said:

I took the job of quartermaster. I looked after the arms dumps. If there was an operation on I would be told to get such and such to a particular area and I would make sure it was there. It was very easy to move weapons around. To prevent leaks, only one or two of us would know where things were kept. There was a link man between me and GHQ Staff in Dublin. I would ask for gear and he would give me about a quarter of what I asked for. There was never enough.

Constable Sam Malcomson volunteered to be stationed at Crossmaglen a few weeks after Thornton had been shot. The posting was already considered exceptionally dangerous. He and Constable Albert McCleary took over from Constables Russell McConnell and Jimmy Poole, who had been shot and seriously wounded. McConnell and Poole had replaced Constables Sam Donaldson and Roy Millar when they were blown up in August 1970. Malcomson, then aged 22, saw the attitude towards the RUC change dramatically during the year he spent in Crossmaglen. 'At first you saw the decent and respectable side of people,' he said. 'You did come across smuggling but to me there were greater crimes than old timers smuggling a few hundredweight of potatoes or a few sheep or cattle across the border. Smuggling was part of their life; they lived on the border and any community living on a border took advantage of the situation.'

But before long, the police were being shunned. Malcomson recalled:

> There was a shop in Crossmaglen where we would go into to buy our newspapers and milk. Then we noticed the shopkeeper being very hesitant. I remember saying to her: 'Look, I think we are causing a problem by coming in here.' And this woman's attitude suggested to me she wanted to say: 'Yes, I mean, we've been threatened, we've been told not to serve you.' We then made a decision that we wouldn't put her life at risk by coming into her shop any more. We didn't want maybe some morning to be called to a scene where the IRA had shot the shopkeeper because of us. There had been this shift. I put that down to the hardcore republican people coming in, imposing their will on the people and saying: 'You will do this, you will do that, you won't talk to the security forces.' At that stage, we lost contact with the ordinary people.

For a time, soldiers stationed in Crossmaglen were allowed out when they were off duty. Volunteer M remembered them drinking in Paddy Short's bar 'like typical squaddies with bright, flowery shirts from Cyprus or wherever they had been last . . . they would get a bit of banter but it was good natured. But gradually people began to get more hostile towards them.' Jim McAllister explained how on one occasion he expressed his dissatisfaction that local publicans were serving the soldiers:

> The Irish national anthem was played at the end of the night. Everybody stood up except me. I refused to stand and I got a few dodgy looks for it. I was asked why I didn't stand and I said I wouldn't stand with them soldiers there. The soldiers were standing quite respectfully; that's actually what annoyed me. If they hadn't stood I would have stood. They were here basically occupying the town and they were standing. It didn't make sense to me.

But the honeymoon period for the Army was short-lived. 'The area closed down against them, refused to serve them in shops, pubs, cafés, anywhere,' McAllister said. 'They couldn't get a box of matches.' It was, he claimed, the result of a realisation that the Army, far from protecting the people of South Armagh, was oppressing them. He said:

> It wasn't a thing enforced upon the people; the people done that themselves. It's a type of boycott which, of course, is an Irish word; we are quite good at that kind of thing. Paddy Short puts it the best way that anybody could ever put it. Somebody once asked Paddy: 'How do you treat the British army around Crossmaglen?' He replied: 'The Brits? You wouldn't even ignore them.' We live here as if they are not here. People just walk past, act as if they weren't there, step across them, walk around them, carry on their own conversation.

Paddy Short is the uncle of Clare Short, who became Minister for Overseas Development when Tony Blair's Labour government was elected in 1998. During a visit to Crossmaglen in 1983, Miss Short said: 'It is ridiculous that British troops are here in Crossmaglen. The claim is that they're in Ireland keeping the peace between two communities. But there is only one community in South Armagh so what the heck are they doing here?' She added that she accepted 'the legitimacy of the nationalist community to resist through force' but in recent years has refrained from commenting on Irish matters.

The IRA unit that killed Constables Donaldson and Millar by booby-trapping a Ford Cortina had been made up of volunteers from Navan in County Meath and Inniskeen in County Monaghan commanded by Seán Mac Stiofáin, the first Chief of Staff of the Provisional IRA. Mac Stiofáin had led the attack on Crossmaglen barracks in 1969 in which Volunteer M had acted as a lookout. The Cortina had been stolen from outside the Ardmore Hotel in Newry on 7 August 1970 and abandoned on the Lisseraw Road outside Crossmaglen two days later. Its doors were locked and the IRA had attached one end of a wire to the driver's light and the other to a 15 lb gelignite bomb. The car remained there until the following evening when Donaldson and Millar drove down from Crossmaglen RUC station to set about forcing the lock on the driver's door with a length of curtain rail.

When the door opened, the driver's light went on, sending an electrical current to the bomb, which exploded. The policemen were caught by the full force of the blast and flung over a hedge into a field. Up to a dozen locals rushed to the scene and an ambulance was called. Donaldson's face had been damaged beyond recognition by broken glass; he was moaning and trying to stand up. Millar lay on his back, still conscious and able to speak even though one of his legs had been blown off. Millar had been going out with a local girl called Ann Donaldson – who was no relation to Sam – and her brother Joe was one of those who had run to the field. Earlier that day, the two men had been sitting in Joe Donaldson's house just off the Dundalk Road while the policeman talked about taking sandwiches to Derry for the Apprentice Boys parade at the weekend. As Joe Donaldson leant over him, Millar asked: 'Is Ann alright?' When Sergeant McCrum, the station sergeant, arrived, Millar said to him: 'God save me, I'm going to die. You're a good sergeant, I like you. You're a good man and I'll meet you in heaven.' Constable Millar died in Daisy Hill Hospital in Newry at 10.33 a.m. the next day, a few hours after Constable Donaldson.

The killings were openly condemned by many in Crossmaglen and among the wreaths at Donaldson's full police funeral in Kilkeel in County Down were a number from South Armagh, including one from the Oliver Plunkett Youth Club in Crossmaglen. A month later, a Mass and memorial service for the two constables, both Protestants, were held in St Patrick's Church in Crossmaglen; relatives of the dead men and detectives taking part in the murder inquiry were among the congregation. Willie Murtagh, the policeman whose car was set alight on the night of Harry Thornton's funeral, read the lesson. Volunteer M said:

> I knew Constable Donaldson very well and Constable Millar boarded here in a local house. I was genuinely sorry for them when they were killed. There was no pleasure in that. They were victims of the British presence here. They were genuine victims of what had been wrong and continues to be wrong in the Six

Counties. But in the atmosphere of the time down here killing
them was an unpopular act.

A little over two weeks after Thornton's funeral, Corporal Ian
Armstrong was shot dead from across the border at Courtbane. Two
Ferret armoured vehicles had crossed the border into the Republic
and were cut off and prevented from returning back to Northern
Ireland by a group of about 150 locals. An IRA unit was duly
summoned and opened fire with a GO2 rifle and Thompson machine-
gun, killing Armstrong and wounding another soldier. The incident,
which ended with one of the Ferrets being set alight before it was
towed away to Dundalk by gardaí, was the one of the first indications
that the level of support for the IRA in South Armagh and North
Louth was something out of the ordinary.

Sam Malcomson said the extent of the change in atmosphere was
brought home to him in August 1972 when a Ferret was blown up by
a 600 lb landmine outside Crossmaglen. Trooper Ian Caie was
thrown out of the vehicle and trapped underneath the turret. 'A
crowd had gathered by the time we reached the scene and they were
jeering the Army,' said Malcomson. 'He was lying under this vehicle
dying and those people were willing him to die and taunting the rest
of the patrol. I can remember seeing the muscles in his hand moving;
there was still life in him. If it had happened in war conditions it
would have been kinder to have shot that lad to finish him off.' But
Malcomson was able to put the dangers of serving in South Armagh
to the back of his mind. 'To me it was a great adventure, you were
there, you were taking on terrorism, the next day you were going to
be successful,' he said. 'You would maybe get a score; you would
maybe come upon an incident where you would take a few of these
guys out. That's the truth of the matter. You were of the mind to give
as good as you got.'

In September 1972, Second Lieutenant Stewart Gardiner was shot
dead at Moybane, where Caie had been killed, while investigating a
report of a landmine. Private Taylor, the radio operator, was
wounded and in the haste to evacuate the area the Argyll and
Sutherland Highlanders left an SLR (self-loading rifle) at the scene.
Malcomson and McCleary, both in plain clothes, drove down in an
MG Midget to recover the weapon. When they arrived, they found

what appeared to be a command wire stretched across the road to a possible firing point in a field. This could have indicated they had found a landmine but to Malcomson the wire seemed in too obvious a place and he suspected it was a 'come on' designed to lure them into a trap. 'I remember gathering the wire up and thinking that I could find a practical use for it,' said Malcomson. 'It could have been used to detonate a landmine and yet I could use it for wiring up speakers in a car or something around the garden. You need to know me; I'm a hoarder from my earliest days.'

The mistake the two policemen made was to return to Crossmaglen by the same route they had come. Malcomson said:

> We had maybe three roads we could have used. But it was my then girlfriend's birthday and what was uppermost in my mind was we were going to a party that evening and going back along the Drummuckavall Road was saving at least half an hour. We were driving back and suddenly there was what I thought had been an explosion under the car. My whole body just reacted as if I had been speared through by a red-hot poker from left to right. That was the image in my mind. And I can remember thinking that we had been blown up into the air and I was bracing myself for the car to hit the road again. This was all in slow motion. But then that didn't happen. I realised the car was driving on, I heard shots and I can remember trying to pull the working parts of my Sterling sub-machine gun back. I tried to cock the Sterling because I realised that this was an ambush and I had been shot.

A fraction of a second before Malcomson was hit, McCleary had been shot by an Armalite bullet which passed through his trunk. Malcomson recalled:

> Albert looked over at me and he then just slumped over the steering wheel. I could see a little spurt of blood coming up out of his back through his corduroy jacket and getting bigger and bigger. I just assumed that he was dead. Then I thought: 'Right, I've got to survive this and I have to cock the weapon. The car's going to hit the hedge. I'm going to be sitting there,

somebody's going to come up to the side window or the windscreen and finish me off. At least that will be my last chance just to squeeze the trigger and take somebody with me.' Then Albert just twisted around, straightened up and said: 'I've been shot.' All this had happened in seconds but the car was still moving in a straight line and he just had the presence of mind to keep the car between the hedges.

Malcomson grabbed the wheel and between them the two wounded policemen managed to steer the car along the narrow country roads to Crossmaglen, two miles away. As they drove out of the ambush, they weaved across the road to make the car as difficult a target as possible. Malcomson said:

I had been hit with an SLR but there was no pain; survival instincts had taken over. When we got into the Square in Crossmaglen, we turned left to go up to the police station and Albert said: 'I can't stop the car, I've got no control.' His foot was sitting on the accelerator and we just drove into the gates of the police station. We'd only had the car for a week and this was a new regiment just in so we were bracing ourselves for the soldier in the sangar to open fire on us. Luckily, he didn't. I don't remember being lifted out of the car but I recall lying on the footpath beside Albert. By this time the pain was so great I was just screaming. I remember catching a young soldier by the trouser leg and begging him to shoot me. The Army medic rushed out and we got morphine injections. The local doctor then appeared and when he was asking if I had been given morphine, I was shouting: 'No, no, I haven't.'

According to Special Branch officers at the time, one of the two IRA men suspected of carrying out the ambush was Tommy McMahon, who was later convicted of the murder of Lord Mountbatten in 1979. The ambush had probably been mounted from a 'standby house' which, according to Volunteer M, would be set up at strategic points for IRA men to lie in wait for the security forces. 'There'd be a phone call or a car would drive into the street and one of the boys would say: "Right, there's a Brit patrol coming out of

Crossmaglen heading down the Monog Road,"' said Volunteer M. 'Immediately, the operations officer would say: "Look, I think they're heading there. Let's get there before them and have a reception committee waiting." It was a war of wits.'

By the time Malcomson and McCleary were shot, Volunteer G had fled across the border after blowing up the courthouse at Forkhill; wanted by the RUC for the bombing, he had joined a unit of IRA men on the run. He said:

> We slept rough in an old Austin A30 for a few days and then a group of us lived in a disused petrol station on the New-townhamilton Road. There were seven or eight of us and we were out on an operation together all day every day. We had operations at night too. One crew would come in and another would head out; the beds were never cold. There was no house we couldn't go to in our own area. You had three or four houses you knew was good and you'd go there in time for breakfast or dinner and you'd always get a good feed.

The volunteers were given £5 a week, the same as the wage paid to Michael Collins's volunteers in 1916. 'Guerrilla warfare is a great thing; it's just hit and run,' said Volunteer G. 'There was always a field or half a field between us and the Brits. We didn't really think of killing or being killed; in later years you might think about it but at the time it was all a high. There was a feeling of great exhilaration after an operation. We'd go back and wait for the news to hear the damage we'd done.'

In December 1972, Volunteer M and two other men were arrested by gardaí in a field at Courtbane after a cross-border gun battle with the British Army. 'They came in with two squad cars, jumped out and we were caught,' he said. 'It was against the rules to shoot the guards.' At the Special Criminal Court in Dublin, all three refused to recognise the court and sat with their feet on the edge of the dock during the trial. As they were led away after being convicted of possessing four rifles and 176 rounds of ammunition with intent to endanger life, one of them shouted 'Up the Provos' and they were cheered by supporters in the public gallery. 'There was no way I was going to stay in jail,' said Volunteer M. 'You took your chance to escape if you got it and I was always looking in that direction.' After an unsuccessful attempt to escape from the Curragh, Volunteer M and Kevin Mallon, from Coalisland in County Tyrone, masterminded the springing of 19 IRA prisoners from Portlaoise jail. Under fire from Irish Army soldiers on the roof, Volunteer M detonated a bomb that blew a hole in one of the inner courtyard walls of the prison. 'That took us into the small courtyard where the Governor's residence was and we'd blown all the glass out of the windows. This was just before midday on a Sunday and I can remember him standing looking out completely mesmerised wearing a pair of pyjamas and a jacket.'

It took Volunteer M three days to get back to South Armagh:

> Initially when I came out I was wearing a screw's uniform. That was part of the escape plan. But I discarded that and I liberated a pair of trousers and jumper off a clothesline somewhere around County Offaly. I also took a loaf of bread that some woman had baked freshly from her window sill. Her dog probably got a kick for it but it serves it right in a way because he just lay there. I had been given the name of a family to go to and there were two of them on the lane and the one I went to was the wrong one. But they were quite accepting when I explained I was an escaped prisoner. They fed me very well and gave me a flagon of cider and a whole loaf of tomato sandwiches . . . I eventually got home in a lorry. I think we went through 13 Garda checkpoints on the way and I was concealed in the back. I was back in Crossmaglen by the Wednesday and I just carried on where I had left off.

A fortnight later, Volunteer M was wounded in another gun battle; he had been holding his rifle in front of him when a bullet passed through both his forearms. Within six weeks, he had been shot again and recaptured after running into a Royal Marines patrol on the Dundalk Road in Crossmaglen while on his way to carry out a sniper attack with another volunteer. He was carrying a .38 revolver and a Winchester rifle fitted with a telescopic sight and loaded with armour-piercing bullets. 'I went to take a shot and the soldier ran when he seen we were firing shots at him,' he said. 'I could see the shots actually bursting in front of him and the white flash of aimed shots being fired back by him. I remember putting my rifle up and, before I could get him into my sight, the round entering the sleeve of the coat. That was it.' He was hit twice and the other volunteer managed to escape.

'I lay there weighing up all the options open to me and I realised I had none. I thought they were just going to shoot me in the head and finish me off. I made up my mind then to take one of the soldiers with me and I was lying there thinking I was going to shoot upwards in the gap beneath the flak jacket.' Volunteer M went for his revolver when the Marines reached him and it was kicked from his hand. 'Then the Marines gave me this awful beating, just kicked me to fuck. I was all bruises, my hands and everything destroyed, my knuckles were sticking out. I was not their favourite person, you know. I'm 45 now and I must say I still loathe the boy in command. Yet it was one of their medics who stopped them and probably saved my life. And I'm very thankful to him to this day and wish him good luck in everything he does.'

Volunteer M was taken by helicopter to Bessbrook Mill and then to hospital in Belfast. He recalled:

> The squaddies were sitting with their feet on me as I was being flown out and I knew I was near the fucking end, I felt myself going. It's a strange feeling but I was completely calm about it, it must have been the shot of adrenalin you get. But I couldn't get my mother out of my head. I knew I could hack the pain but I was fierce annoyed for the bother I was going to cause her. In the hospital they didn't know who I was. There was a female doctor who said in court that I was logged as a young man suffering from gunshot wounds, bleeding profusely, no history or name given. I can remember my legs losing strength, all these really bright lights and them scissoring the clothes off me.

In February 1975, Volunteer M appeared before a non-jury Diplock court in Belfast charged with possession of a rifle, a revolver and 44 rounds of ammunition. 'I took no part in the proceedings,' he said. 'Shot and caught a sniper boy. It lasted about two and a half minutes. No plea given, not guilty entered on my behalf, they went through the evidence and that was it. Bang. Ten years.' When he was released in 1979, Volunteer M was re-arrested at the gates of the Maze prison and extradited to the Republic to serve the remaining 18 months of his original sentence.

Volunteer G was charged with IRA membership in the Republic in 1975 but acquitted. 'I beat that charge and I was also arrested in Dundalk, Dublin, Kildare and Naas but I was never charged with anything. I'd be moving around meeting people involved in engineering [the design of bombs and weapons] and weapons supply.' He was listed as 'arrest on sight' by the security forces as late as 1982.

According to RUC intelligence records, Volunteer G was suspected of being one of up to 12 IRA gunmen who attacked a covert observation post at Drummuckavall in November 1975, killing three fusiliers and wounding a lance corporal. The four soldiers had walked in from Crossmaglen and set up the observation post at 2 a.m. the previous day in order to watch a bomb which had been discovered on the border. They were just 50 yards from some houses across the border and were spotted by a local who told the IRA of their position. At 4.20 p.m., just over 36 hours after the observation post had been set up, the silence was interrupted by heavy gunfire. Fusilier Peter McDonald, who was on watch armed with a light machine-gun, Fusilier Michael Sampson, who was finishing a meal, and Fusilier James Duncan, who was lying on his sleeping bag, were killed in the first burst of fire and McDonald's radio was disabled by a bullet. Lance Corporal Paul Johnson, who was unscathed and lying flat on the ground, heard one of the gunmen shout: 'Do you want to surrender?' He did not reply and there was a second, more prolonged burst and three rounds hit him in the back and upper arm. The surrender call was repeated again followed by more firing. Johnson then heard a shout of 'Up the Provos' and laughing and whooping as the gunmen ran across the border.

The gunning down of three soldiers by IRA men operating in broad daylight and with apparent impunity led Merlyn Rees to issue a statement that was to seal South Armagh's notoriety. It had been yet another nail in the coffin of the ceasefire announced by the Provisionals nine months earlier and honoured more in the breach than in the observance in South Armagh. In the statement, Rees said:

There has never been a ceasefire in South Armagh for a variety of reasons – the nature of the countryside and the nature of the people. It is an unusual area – there is little support for the security forces in South Armagh. The Government is not trying to buy off terrorism by the release of detainees as the numbers of terrorists arrested and charged shows. The release of detainees has nothing to do with the violence of the bandit country of South Armagh. There is wholesale gangsterism there.

Rees's label stuck, much to the resentment of nationalists, who regard it as a slur on the people of the area and republicans, who resent the implication that the IRA is made up of profiteers and criminals who can only operate because they are holding the local population to ransom. Volunteer M said he believed the term was deliberately used as part of the British policy of refusing to acknowledge that the conflict in Northern Ireland was a political one:

They had to label areas. They talked about gangsterism and rackets on building sites and money-laundering and even drugs but all that only really applied in urban areas. In rural areas they couldn't really hang that Las Vegas gangster tag on people so instead they came up with bandits: boys with little moustaches and big hats on them. It was gladly and greedily grabbed by the media. There were bandits down here whereas there were gangsters and godfathers in Belfast. It makes people down here puke but from a Brit perspective it's a great phrase. It works.

Rees, now Lord Merlyn Rees, has remained unrepentant. The term was accurate, he said, and deliberately used to portray the IRA in South Armagh as terrorists who would be shunned by all decent people:

It was a conscious decision to use that term, to try and show people who knew nothing about it the nature of it, that South Armagh was different. When I would go down there to Crossmaglen, I'd get out of the helicopter on a GAA field and run to the police station, which was heavily fortified. For my money, that's bandit country. It was a bit like the Wild West. South Armagh was a place unto itself. For God's sake, it reminded me of the American silent films I used to watch when I was a kid, with forts and the cavalry.

Despite Volunteer M's hatred of the term, some republicans in South Armagh view 'bandit country' as a badge of honour. When Alex Maskey, a Belfast Sinn Féin councillor, spoke at the Easter commemoration in Crossmaglen in 1996, he remarked that the volunteer who had preceded him was a 'hard act to follow' and was cheered when he added: 'But as one bandit to another bandit, I'll give it my best shot.'

Another product of what nationalists saw as the British propaganda machine was the story of Rats, a mongrel dog that had taken to accompanying Army patrols around Crossmaglen and eventually became resident in the security force base. Rats first came to prominence after he was injured in November 1978 when a radio-controlled bomb exploded in Castleblaney Street in Crossmaglen as a four-man 'brick' of Royal Marines and Grenadier Guards passed a derelict house. All four members of the brick were wearing Marine berets to disguise the fact that a new company was arriving; the early and final days of a company's tour were when soldiers were at their most vulnerable.

As Lance Corporal Kevin Kinton walked along the street, he noticed signs of fresh digging at the foot of a telegraph pole. Fearing a mine had been placed there, he kept close to a derelict house on the opposite side of the street. It turned out that the IRA had intended the patrol to notice the digging and had correctly predicted its members would avoid it. Two Calor gas cylinders containing 50 lbs of explosives had been hidden behind a low wall in front of the derelict house; the bomb was detonated, fatally wounding Marine Gareth Wheedon. Kinton, who was also wounded, later recalled that at the moment of the blast he had felt as if someone had jumped on his back. The breath had been blown from his body, his eyes burned and there was a sensation of fierce heat as if the door of an oven had been opened in his face. As giant flakes of soot began to fall to the ground, he heard Wheedon screaming and a dog yelping.

The dog was Rats, a brown and white corgi-Jack Russell crossbreed which had been badly cut and left a trail of blood in its wake as it ran back to the security force base. Three months later, Rats was 'wounded in action' once again. Kinton said in an interview with Max Halstock: 'I was very, very careful by now — particularly about parked cars, which I always gave a wide berth. If I saw a parked car I would deliberately take to the middle of the road. I knew, of course, that this might leave me open to a sniper — but, to be honest, I'd sooner be sniped at with a rifle than be blown up by a bomb. Besides, you always stand the chance of being missed by a sniper.' When he saw a car parked close to a derelict house in North Street, he instructed his brick to walk along the road and not go near it. The next brick was not so alert. As it passed along the same route, an incendiary bomb made up of petrol and explosives was detonated by radio control, enveloping Guardsman Lundy in a sheet of flames.

With his uniform on fire, Lundy ran along the street until Joe Cumiskey opened the door to his father's house and allowed the screaming guardsman to run into the bathroom. Lundy jumped into the bath and Guardsman Davis turned on the cold tap. For this act of mercy, Cumiskey, a relation of Eamon Collins, was threatened by the IRA and warned not to collaborate with the enemy again. Lundy suffered burns to a third of his body and spent several months in hospital but survived. The fireball also set alight the tail of Rats, who had been accompanying the patrol, leaving the dog with a three-inch stump to wag.

At the end of the summer of 1979, a BBC television crew discovered Rats and his story was soon picked up by Fleet Street. The Queen's Own Highlanders had lost five men during their tour, two at Narrow Water, one in Crossmaglen and two in a helicopter crash, and their morale badly needed a boost. The Army press office saw the attention on Rats as a way of promoting 'good news' stories about the military presence in South Armagh. Within weeks, newspapers were full of the credulity-stretching exploits of Rats jumping in and out of helicopters, growling to warn Army patrols of approaching danger and holding his own against the vicious dogs of Crossmaglen which had supposedly been trained to bite soldiers. By the end of the year, Rats had been flown to London to appear on *Nationwide* and received a gold medal from the Pro-Dogs charity engraved with 'Rats: Dog of War . . . For bravery, devotion to duty and the comfort you have provided to soldiers serving in Cross-maglen.' Up to 300 letters addressed to Rats began arriving at Bessbrook Mill each day and it was rumoured that the IRA had threatened to kill the dog.

Soldiers began to stop Rats going out on patrol with them because they were afraid the IRA would try to blow up the dog and get a soldier as well. Company Sergeant Major William Evans, of the Welsh Guards, told Halstock: 'I was always afraid he might come over the fence one night either dead or badly mutilated. You had to expect that kind of mentality for the opposition knew how damaging such a thing could have been to the men and there were previous cases where other Army dogs had been killed or tortured.' In early 1980, a dog that looked similar to Rats was run over by a Cross-maglen woman. 'It was quite deliberate and obvious that she only did it because she thought she was running over Rats,' said Evans.

Realising that Rats might have become a liability, the Army sent the dog to a farm in Kent shortly afterwards. Before he bowed out of the public eye, Rats travelled to Pirbright in Surrey for a ceremonial retirement from the Army and appeared on television beside Major Vyvyan Harmsworth at the Royal Tournament as the Welsh Guards company commander in Crossmaglen took the salute from the Queen Mother. Halstock wrote a book entitled *Rats: The Story of a Dog Soldier* while *Kennel News* was moved to describe the animal as 'a symbol of survival and friendship amidst the danger and hostility of Crossmaglen'. Rats died peacefully at the age of 17 in 1989 and in South Armagh is still regarded as something of a traitor to this day.

I f South Armagh was 'bandit country' then Dundalk would always be 'El Paso', the frontier town that had been taken over by fugitives from the law. After internment was introduced, scores of Official and Provisional IRA men fled to Dundalk and many of them remained for years. At first, they were greeted as political refugees but elements of the town began to turn against them when boredom soon led to drunken brawls and lack of money to a rash of bank robberies. In her memoir *To Take Arms: A Year in the Provisional IRA*, Maria McGuire, a former member of Cumann na mBan (the female section of the IRA), wrote that the northern volunteers thought 'they had come to paradise or Utopia' when they arrived in Dundalk. 'They played cards at the Imperial [hotel] with their revolvers left casually on the card-table beside their stake money, were often drunk, and fought among themselves. The most notorious incident came when they were watching an afternoon race meeting on the hotel's colour television. One of the volunteers was so enraged when the horse he backed lost that he shot up the television set.'

But the more eager volunteers used their time on the run to link up with the South Armagh units. On one celebrated occasion on 27 January 1972, Martin Meehan and Anthony 'Dutch' Doherty, who had both escaped from Belfast's Crumlin Road jail a few weeks earlier, took part in a four-hour gun battle at Dungooley. Some 4,500 rounds were fired by a detachment of the Scots Dragoon Guards across the border at Meehan and Doherty's unit. The only casualty was a farmer's prize pig but when Meehan boasted afterwards that 'we gave them a pasting', the Dublin government ordered the Garda to move. Meehan, Doherty and six others were arrested and charged with possession of an anti-tank gun, seven rifles and a carbine; the following month all eight were acquitted due to lack of evidence. On another occasion, Terence 'Cleeky' Clarke, from Belfast, was arrested by gardaí after he was pinned down in a farmyard by fire from the British Army. He was later imprisoned for his part in the killing of two corporals during a funeral in Andersonstown in west Belfast in 1988 and subsequently became Gerry Adams's chief bodyguard.

After his spell living in the disused petrol station, Volunteer G became part of the fresh influx to Dundalk when he went on the run after blowing up Forkhill Petty Sessions Court. He did not return to South Armagh until the IRA ceasefire of 1994 when it became clear that the Northern Ireland authorities were willing to turn a blind eye to such cases. 'The Belfast men didn't really fit in that well,' he said. 'They were city men in a country area and Dundalk wasn't big enough for them. They were lost. Most of them didn't stay that long.' Eventually, the IRA's GHQ Staff, embarrassed by the antics of its volunteers in Dundalk and keen to monitor their activities more closely, ordered that all IRA men on the run should reside no further north than Dublin unless directed otherwise. Dundalk remained of key strategic importance for the IRA in terms of the supply of arms to units north of the border, as a base for South Armagh men wanted by the RUC and as a place where meetings could be held away from the prying ears and eyes of the British security forces. For much of the Troubles, the IRA's North Louth unit was in charge of all operations in the Newry area. 'Never in all my time as an IRA man did I go to plan an operation anywhere but Dundalk,' said Eamon Collins. 'A lot of the people who were running the whole show were based in Dundalk.'

Some RUC officers would do almost anything to avoid being stationed in South Armagh. Constable E, who served in Forkhill and Crossmaglen in the 1970s, said: 'By this time they were stations where only single men would be sent because of the danger. There was one gentleman, who shall remain nameless but was always known in the depot as Wingnut because his ears stuck out, who was told he was getting transferred to Forkhill. Within a week, he had got married and I was given his post.' In December 1974, Constable E's room-mate, Constable Jim McNeice, was shot dead. He recalled:

> Jim had a great enthusiasm for anything he undertook. If your car was broken down, he would be under the bonnet for you. If you wanted an extra light in your bedroom, he'd be the one would wire it up for you. He was a tremendous character. It was a Saturday and Jim was supposed to have gone on his weekend off but the chopper hadn't arrived in time. A couple called Rafferty had rung in to say their house in Meigh had been burgled the previous evening. It wasn't Jim's turn but because he was still waiting for the chopper he said he'd answer the call. It was typical of him.

McNeice jumped into a civilian Mark III Cortina along with Rifleman Michael Gibson, an Army intelligence operative. According to a report into the incident: 'It was normal for one of the Intelligence Officers to always go with the police as this was an effective covert method of obtaining military intelligence'. Unknown to the Raffertys, the burglary had been carefully staged by the IRA; a tape recorder and some tapes had been stolen and McNeice duly took down all the details. The RUC man and soldier began to drive off but braked when Mr Rafferty, who was driving in front, noticed a tape lying on the street and stopped his car to get out. As the Cortina slowed down, three IRA gunmen stepped out and opened fire with an Armalite, a Garand rifle and a 9 mm pistol. At least 22 shots were fired, killing McNeice, who was hit eight times, and fatally wounding Gibson.

The Army had concluded that the IRA in South Armagh was a formidable foe. In a report into the shooting dead of Corporal Stephen Windsor and Private Brian Allen in Crossmaglen in November 1974, Lieutenant Colonel M J A Wilson wrote: 'Every attack is very carefully planned. The operating pattern of the Army is studied in detail. Secure firing positions, fields of fire and killing zones are worked out, and escape routes well thought out.' In the Crossmaglen area, five to six men were 'operating together as a fighting unit . . . a kind of uniform is worn for operations which includes masks and gloves.' This unit was tying down 34 soldiers in the Crossmaglen area: 12 on base guard duty, ten in base headquarters, six on standby and six at the Drummuckavall observation post. This left enough men to carry out just two six-man patrols. The colonel added that intelligence and operational records were not being put to full use. 'There is a tendency for each unit to start from scratch in an area, warned only by some of the most recent lessons of the past and an ill-digested mythology of other events. We should be much more professional in our analysis of terrorist tactics.'

The practice of forbidding soldiers to cock their weapons had probably led to the death of Private Allen, who had seen the gunman but had not been able to cock his weapon and fire in time. 'In recognised areas of danger such as Crossmaglen weapons carried on patrol should be made ready; not made safe,' Lieutenant Colonel Wilson wrote. But it was to be by no means the last time a soldier's life was to be lost because he was operating within a strict set of rules – designed to apply to situations of civil unrest within the United Kingdom – against an enemy prosecuting a war and recognising no rules in the process. The colonel's report ended by paying tribute to the courage of Private Allen, who had written the registration number of the IRA's getaway car on his hand as he lay mortally wounded.

In March 1976, Pat Thompson became one of the first IRA men from South Armagh to be convicted of murder. Eight months earlier, Major Peter Willis, the Green Howards company commander in Crossmaglen, and three bomb disposal specialists had been investigating a milk churn at Cortreasla Bridge in Tullydonnell when they walked through a gap in a hedge next to a signpost. As they did so, an IRA volunteer pressed a button which sent an electric current through a 396-yard-long command wire to activate a 70 lb bomb packed into a beer keg and buried into the earth in the gap. All four soldiers were killed instantly and another wounded by shrapnel. Five minutes before the explosion, Corporal Anthony Warriner, who was part of a Green Howards team hidden in undergrowth on a nearby hill, had looked through his rifle sight and seen a man running and vaulting over fences. In the aftermath of the blast, roadblocks were set up and at one, manned by Warriner, a 21-year-old man was stopped. Warriner recognised his clothing and curly hair and noticed he had scratch marks on his forehead, thorns embedded in his hands and grass stains on his trousers. The man was Pat Thompson and the next day he signed a statement confessing to being the 'button man'. He had been running towards the button position when Warriner had seen him.

Thompson's statement said that the Crossmaglen IRA unit had carried out the attack in retaliation for the shooting dead of Volunteer Francis Jordan, a close friend of Volunteer G, as he had been about to bomb a Protestant pub in Bessbrook. In 1995, a housing estate in Jonesborough was named 'Francis Jordan Park' in his honour but the more immediate commemoration of his death was the setting up of the Cortreasla Bridge landmine at a spot where helicopters often dropped off troops. Thompson said in his statement:

> I took it upon myself to watch the crossroads to see how often the Brits landed there. After a fortnight I decided that where I was watching from was a good place to blow the explosives and to bury them in the ditch at the side of the signpost. I reported back to the OC and he told me that this idea was okay. A few nights later along with a few other members of my unit I put the charge down . . . The reason I did this was because of my hatred for them and I wanted to be the one to press the button . . . When I blew the Brits up I meant to kill them. I am not a bit sorry for what happened.

Thompson claimed he was beaten and forced to sign the statement but was given four life sentences and five years for IRA membership with a recommendation that he serve at least 30 years. He was released in 1991 after serving 16 years and still maintains he was not involved in the attack. 'It was a forced confession,' he said. 'They dictated it. I'll never deny that I was a republican but I will deny that I was the man who caused that explosion.' But Monty Alexander, the RUC sergeant who gathered evidence for Thompson's trial, said: 'His statement was made quite freely, quite openly and he detailed every move that he made.'

For the security forces, to travel by road in South Armagh was to dice with death. In June 1978, Constable E was called to the scene of what had been reported as a car accident at Sturgan Brae, close to Camlough lake, one sunny Saturday afternoon. He said:

> When we arrived, there was a blue Austin Maxi car driven into the right hand ditch. The back of it was riddled with bullets. In the centre of the road was Constable Hughie McConnell. I only recognised him because he was the only man in the sub-division who wore slip-on boots; half his head had been shot away and his face was totally gone. It looked as if he'd been pulled out, dragged across the road and dropped before being pumped with lead again to finish him off. The other policeman – we always drove in twos – was gone. We later found out it was Billy Turbitt, who had been the front seat passenger. He'd been hit, had gone forward and there'd been an impact with the wind-screen which was cracked and smeared with blood. The top plate of his false teeth had come out and was on the dashboard. You could see where Billy had been trailed out. He had been wearing steel tips on his heels and there were two lines travelling down the road. Then they disappeared.

Turbitt's body was dumped a fortnight later at Drumlougher, just across the border from where the Docklands bomb was later mixed. A post-mortem showed that he had probably been killed at Sturgan Brae and the body later submerged in a bog for a lengthy period. Nearly eight years earlier, Turbitt had been the last person to see Constables Donaldson and Millar leave the station before they were blown up. He had also been in the field comforting the two men as they lay fatally wounded and had been haunted by the words of

Millar, who had said repeatedly: 'I'm dying, I'm dying. Ah Willie, I'm dying.'

An informer told an Ulster Defence Regiment source handler the names of the three men who had planned the Sturgan Brae ambush. 'These two Constables were not the target, it was a "high-up" man in the police and they were to take his body away,' he said. The 'high-up' policeman in question was Chief Inspector Harry Breen; both he and Turbitt had a full head of swept back, grey hair and they could pass for one another at a distance. Three gunmen with Armalites opened fire as the car slowed down at an S-bend, and 74 cartridge cases were found at the scene. The car used to take Turbitt's body away was later found abandoned; the rear window was missing and there were tools, straw, clumps of grey hair and human tissue in the back.

A Parachute Regiment report into the incident concluded: 'This was a carefully planned and particularly ruthless and efficiently executed ambush. It is thought that the Chief Inspector, Bessbrook RUC Station, may have been the intended target, as he drives a similar car and has in the past used the same route when travelling to FKH [Forkhill] . . . it will serve as a timely reminder of the need to avoid establishing patterns and of the dangers of taking unnecessary risks.' But the risk-taking continued. Eleven years later, the South Armagh Brigade was to ambush a car on a border road and shoot dead two senior police officers; one of them was Harry Breen.

By the end of the 1970s, the IRA had claimed the lives of 68 soldiers and seven RUC men in South Armagh. Within the security forces, Tom Murphy's unit had gained a fearsome reputation and even a measure of respect for its discipline, professionalism and effectiveness as a killing machine. Constable B, a member of the RUC's Bessbrook Support Unit, a specialist anti-terrorist squad set up in April 1979, said the South Armagh Brigade's superior fieldcraft marked them out from the IRA in other areas. 'IRA teams [in South Armagh] actually stood up and fought and skirmished back the same way the British Army did. And they're very hard to overtake when they are doing that. They always had covering fire so we kept our heads down. They weren't one-eyed jack shots any more. They would actually go out and stay. We flushed one or two bombers out who were putting bombs in the sides of the roads. They would get down and use the old gullies and get away.' As well as their intimate knowledge of the countryside and the close proximity of the border, the standard of the IRA's military training was clearly high. According to Volunteer G, former members of the British Army and some serving Irish Army soldiers had initially carried this out. A handful, including Murphy, had trained in Libya.

But in Constable B's view, the IRA's main advantage over the security forces in South Armagh was the overwhelming support of the local populace. 'We can work without the people whereas a unit like that can't,' he said. 'Same as Che Guevara or people like that, they have to have the people on their side for intelligence, safe houses, safe places for the weapons, cover if they were caught so someone could say: "Yes, he was with us all night". If we could get the people against the IRA totally, the IRA would be no use.' But the security forces were in a Catch 22 position, he added, because local people who were opposed to the Provisionals were powerless. 'There is nothing we can do if they support the IRA. But if they don't support the IRA, there is nothing they can do.'

Lieutenant Colonel Wilson's report into the shooting of Corporal Windsor and Private Allen in November 1974 had stated that it was 'clear the gunmen are operating with the acquiescence if not the active support of the majority of people in Crossmaglen'. Locals were often warned by the IRA when an attack was about to take place. Minutes before Private James Borucki was blown up in the Square in Crossmaglen in August 1976, a sign was placed on the Cullaville Road stating 'Bomb Ahead' while on the Castleblaney Road a volunteer stopped traffic. 'It is obvious that the locals had warning of the device but, in the Crossmaglen fashion, said nothing,' said one Army report. 'Source reports suggest that this warning was given 15 minutes before the device was detonated. Windows were opened to prevent blast damage.' The radio-controlled bomb, which contained 3 lbs of explosives, had been packed into a carbon dioxide gas cylinder and placed in the basket of a ladies' Raleigh bicycle which had been stolen from a yard in Crossmaglen two days earlier. Borucki, the second soldier in a seven-man patrol which had been sent out to check the area in preparation for the visit of a senior RAF officer, was blown apart when he stopped next to the bicycle, which was resting against a gable wall.

By 1978 it seemed to the soldiers in South Armagh that even the
local clergy were unprepared to help them in any way. On 21
December, Sergeant Garmory was leading his brick in staggered
formation past St Patrick's Church in Crossmaglen; Guardsman
Graham Duggan, behind him, was carrying a Light Machine Gun,
while Guardsmen Kevin Johnson and Glen Ling were across the road.
Although it was market day, Garmory noted that the road was
almost deserted. He said later in an interview with Colonel Oliver
Lindsay for a history of the Grenadier Guards:

> On coming round the bend near the Rio Bar, I saw 40 yards
> away what looked like a British Rail parcel delivery van
> parked partly on the pavement on the left facing away from
> us. It had an 18-inch tailboard with a roll shutter that could be
> pulled down. The van immediately struck me as highly
> suspicious because I saw what looked like cardboard boxes
> piled to the top in the back, all flush with the tailboard so they
> would fall out if the van moved off fast. I instantaneously put
> my magnifying sight to my eye and saw four firing slits, two
> above the other two, among the boxes. I immediately opened
> fire.

Garmory said he knew by experience that he was under heavy fire
from three Armalites and an AK-47. Two IRA men were probably
firing standing with two lying down. He continued:

> Bullets passed through the sleeves of my smock. I could see
> them hitting the pavement in front of me and also the wall just
> to my left. Having fired off a whole magazine I whipped back
> behind a wall, gave a quick contact report and saw my three
> Grenadiers had been hit. I ran back to Duggan who was still
> conscious although an Armalite round had penetrated his liver. I
> told him to hang on. I was still under fire . . . I fired off Duggan's
> LMG magazine from the hip in one quick burst which quietened
> them down a bit. I could see the van's rear must have armoured
> plating behind the boxes because every third of my rounds was
> tracer and I could see them ricochetting upwards off the plating.
> When the magazine was empty I ran across the road to Johnson,

moved his body off his rifle and fired more shots at the van as it careered off, partly hitting a telegraph pole just in front of it.

Staff from the nearby health centre tended to the three guardsmen but it was too late.

'Looking back on it, as I've done so often since, the terrorists were highly professional,' said Garmory. 'Their supporters' signalling presumably indicated to them that our armoured car [which had been accompanying foot patrols earlier that day] was being refuelled . . . Months later I heard I'd got the Military Medal. The Queen presented it to me at Buckingham Palace in front of my mother, father and fiancée. It was all very grand.'

In a report after the incident, Lieutenant Colonel Michael Hobbs, commanding the Grenadier Guards battalion in South Armagh, wrote:

> Five minutes after the incident, Guardsman Saunders saw a priest by the church. He went over to him and spoke to him saying that three soldiers were lying badly wounded. The priest made no comment and turned away. Ten minutes after the incident, a second priest walked from the Parochial House to the church. He made no move towards the bodies. On withdrawal, Major Woodrow was going towards the church and saw a priest 20 metres away. He called to him; the priest turned and walked away. Comment: St Luke Chapter 10 Verse 31 would seem appropriate.

The biblical quotation, part of the parable of the Good Samaritan, reads: 'Now by chance a priest was going down that road; and when he saw him he passed by on the other side.'

The Army was probably suffering from a degree of paranoia and underestimated the almost impossible position in which priests in South Armagh found themselves. Six months before the three Grenadiers were killed, Archbishop Tomás Ó Fiaich, head of the Roman Catholic Church in Ireland, had described the killing of Paddy McEntee, a Crossmaglen postman shot dead as an informer by the IRA, as 'an act of fratricidal slaughter, a crime committed by brother against brother' that sullied the ideal of Irish patriotism. 'South

Armagh has suffered enough in the past from foreign judges and executioners to allow itself to be subjected to the tyranny of a local group,' he said. The words of the archbishop, who had been born in the house in Cullyhanna now lived in by Peter John Caraher, hurt the IRA because he was a local man who was passionately committed to Irish unity.

An IRA statement which attempted to justify the McEntee killing carried 'a message for the priests in the parish' about their 'outpourings of condemnation' of IRA attacks:

> We also say to one priest in particular that he should adhere to his ecclesiastical duties rather than involving himself in politics and using the influence of his clerical garb in an intimidatory request to call off [IRA] activities in the area . . . Once again our last word to Crossmaglen Clergy: ACT NOW AND GET THE TOUTS OUT OF CROSSMAGLEN AND YOU WILL SAVE LIVES. Informers cannot be tolerated in the War of Liberation.

According to Jim McAllister, it was not just the lack of support from the local population which left soldiers at a potentially fatal disadvantage; their lack of familiarity with the countryside was another serious drawback. He said:

> If they come here for six months at a time, they are never going to really learn the area like people who were born and reared here. They might be watching everything and see farmer Joe go by with his tractor loaded with hay three days of the week but one day it's not farmer Joe but IRA man Joe and he's got something extra underneath his hay. They don't know that and that's why they'll never win this territory. It's to do with community, it's to do with history and it's even to do with the fact that South Armagh always had to live on its wits.

Although Army and RUC officers often assume that everyone in South Armagh supports the IRA, voting figures right up to 1998 show an almost even split between Sinn Féin and the nationalist Social Democratic and Labour Party, which has always been opposed to violence. Séamus Mallon, the SDLP's deputy leader, has been MP for the area since 1986. According to Pat Toner, an SDLP councillor in Crossmaglen and then Forkhill throughout the Troubles, it is fear that has prevented people speaking out against the IRA. 'People might be SDLP but the fear is always there,' he said. 'Most people have a switch off system: you don't tell nothing. That's the way it is.' On other occasions, he said, people would be afraid that the IRA was tapping their phone line. After the IRA had mounted illegal vehicle checkpoints, volunteers would sometimes walk into a pub clad in the distinctive clothing they'd been wearing when stopping cars. 'It was a way of testing loyalty and people know that if they fingered the IRA man they'd end up dead.'

Jim McAllister said voting patterns were misleading because support for the SDLP didn't necessarily preclude support for the IRA. He said:

> I have always believed that support for the IRA is higher than for Sinn Féin. If you have the IRA on some farmer's land and the British Army appears, it doesn't matter if the farmer is a Sinn Féin supporter or a SDLP supporter or doesn't care about any politicians. That farmer would always invariably make sure the IRA knew there was soldiers in the vicinity. If the soldiers were hidden on the land they would come and warn our boys. They wouldn't dream of telling the British Army that there was IRA on their land. It's that old basic natural human thing that my own people are my own people even if I don't always agree with them.

Pat Thompson said that the overwhelming support for the IRA was the factor that set South Armagh apart from other areas:

> The IRA stopped them using the roads here. We forced them into the air and it was a very successful campaign to achieve that. It's not something which will be accepted now but that early period will go down in history as being similar to Tom Barry and the flying columns in Cork during the War of Independence. British soldiers were just cannon fodder. The only difference between the British Army and Republican Army

is financially the British Army had everything at their disposal. They'd mega bucks, millions and millions to fight here . . . The IRA had good military brains and an efficient intelligence network. There was discipline and respect for leadership. We were well educated in guerrilla tactics and we learned very fast. If you didn't learn very fast then you were dead.

Most important of all, though, was having the backing of the local population, he added. 'The people were the IRA's eyes and ears. You cannot run a guerrilla campaign without the support of the people.'

There were exceptions. Monty Alexander, who was an RUC sergeant in Forkhill and Newtownhamilton in the 1970s, said the police had always been able to count on a degree of co-operation from local people:

> There was one guy I'd done a favour for one time, a decent man, who phoned me and said he had to meet me because he couldn't talk on the phone. So he came and seen me and he told me that a constable was going to be killed within the forthcoming week. He told me the day, he told me the time and he told me that this constable was going out with this female who lived in Forkhill. The constable always came on the same time on the same night and they were going to kill him the next time he came down. He said to me: 'Sergeant, I do not want this man's blood on my conscience. You're the only policeman that I know.'

Sergeant Alexander could not believe that any policeman could be so rash. The constable was summoned and he was asked if it was true that he was regularly visiting a girl in Forkhill. Alexander recalled:

> He says: 'Aye, yes. That's right.' I said: 'Are you going to see her this week?' He said he was, so I told him: 'Well, they're going to kill you this week.' He just said: 'Jesus Christ, how do you know that? Who told you?' Needless to say, I never told him who told me. I would have been signing someone's death warrant. But that man from South Armagh saved that police-man's life. That was never reported to my authorities. They would have demanded the name of my informant and maybe

tried to get more information out of him so I couldn't have felt happy telling anyone that man's name. I have never mentioned it to anyone until now. What the constable was doing was crazy but I suppose where there's women involved we all do some stupid things.

On 19 September 1975, a man telephoned the RUC Confidential Phone to tell them who was responsible for the beating up of two gardaí in Gartland's Pub in Kilcurry. He said that the beating had been carried out by a group of men from the Silverbridge area:

Micksey Martin was the ring leader and this gentleman I believe has been involved in the beating up of two other gardaí . . . They stole the helmets of the gardaí, they brought them down to Donnelly's pub there in Silverbridge and they hung them up there on the counter and they dared Donnelly to touch them or he would have been shot. Now this area has been terrorised by these people and I think you ought to pass this information on to the authorities in the Free State.

But such instances of co-operation from the public were all too rare. Pat Toner said that, in addition to the fear factor, many local people were alienated by actions of the Army at the start of the Troubles.

When there was an attack in Crossmaglen or Forkhill the reaction of the soldiers was to run out afterwards and baton charge the first person they see. Instead of trying to get support from the people they were turning the people completely against them. I would see it over the years, numerous times people ringing me at three and four o'clock in the morning, mothers about their sons being stopped by the security forces and stripped completely, being pushed around and abused. Often it wouldn't be admitted the next day when you complained but those things were happening. They were turning people into the arms of the Provos.

Whatever the level of active support for the IRA, only a tiny proportion of the people in South Armagh felt any allegiance to the

British authorities. Even if they detested violence and the IRA, they had effectively withdrawn their consent from the state and this made it almost impossible for the security forces to gain the foothold in the community which they needed. Opposition to outside authority had been a part of life in South Armagh for centuries and few were prepared to renounce the rebellious tradition of their forebears.

Chapter Three

Roots of Rebellion

'To the traveller it is not safe, as Tories and Rogues infest the woodes. Here it was that Captain Groves and ten of his men were done to death in the past year.'

(Sir William Robinson writing about
the main road through South Armagh, 1698)

'This unfortunate district of Crossmaglen has been to my own knowledge – having been in this circuit for the last 14 years – always a stain on the fair province of Ulster.'

(Mr Justice Lawson at the Crumlin Road
Courthouse Spring Assizes, 1883)

Big Charley Caraher, known as Cal Mór, was an outlaw who was sentenced in 1718 to be 'hanged, and be cut down before he was dead, his privy members to be cut off, his bowels burn'd and his quarters dispos'd off at the King's pleasure'. His crime was to have been a cattle thief in South Armagh but to Peter John Caraher, who believes the outlaw might have been an ancestor, he was a martyr who died for a cause in the same way as the republican hunger strikers did in 1981. 'There was men from this area hanged for their ideas for the past 300 years,' he said. 'The cattle Cal Mór stole were his neighbour's cattle that were already seized by the bailiff. He was informed on and those cattle were lifted off his people because they couldn't pay the exorbitant rent that was being put on them. It was a political execution.'

According to John Donaldson's *A Historical and Statistical Account of the Barony of Upper Fews in the County of Armagh,* published in 1838, Cal Mór had decided to live outside the law after being dismissed from his post as keeper of the Dorsey cattle pound for killing a cow. 'He and his confederates were a terror to this and the neighbouring counties, from the number of murders and barbarous acts they committed.' He was subsequently arrested and tried at Dundalk Sessions. On 18 February 1718, he was hung from the gallows at Dundalk jail and cut down while still alive. 'When the hangman was cutting off his privities he cry'd out,' said a contemporary account. 'The hangman could not do it readily for he strugled very much. His head was afterwards cut off. His chops open'd and shut tho' his head was a yard from his body. His carcass was divided into parts and set up in four special parts of the country. He died very obstinately . . . his head [was] set on the gaol two yards higher than any of the rest with his hat and wig on.'

To Peter John Caraher, Cal Mór and his comrades – like the Catholic Defenders, Whiteboys and Rightboys who fought the Protestant Peep O'Day Boys, Oakboys and Steelboys in the 18th century – were forerunners of the modern IRA man. 'The treatment Cal Mór got was so bad that it scared the life out of all belonging to him,' he said. 'Everybody denied any relationship. And there was never a Caraher called their son Charles from that day on.' In 1973, Peter John Caraher christened his fifth son Cathal (Irish for Charles) in honour of Cal Mór. For republicans in South Armagh, the IRA's campaign over the past 30 years is simply the latest manifestation of a rebellion stretching back centuries.

Abraham Brewster once told the Monaghan Assizes: 'From time to time, something like madness takes possession of a district, until it becomes a bye-word. Among the districts having attained this unenviable fame was the district of Crossmaglen, in County Armagh.' He was speaking in 1853 in his capacity as Attorney-General; the remarks could have been made by any British government official 150 years later or two centuries before. In South Armagh, conflict, intrigue and opposition to authority have always seemed part of the natural order. Underpinning this rebel tradition has been a powerful collective folk memory of tales passed down from generation to generation. Descendants of rebels or informers in the 18th century are still held in esteem or at arm's length because of the deeds of their forefathers. The sins of long-dead landlords are seldom forgotten while sheep-stealers whose lives ended on the gallows are remembered with honour for their sacrifice. The modern Troubles are viewed not as a series of isolated incidents since the 1970s but as part of a continuum with the past.

At the heart of this folk memory is Slieve Gullion, setting for many of the Celtic myths which first gave South Armagh its distinctiveness. According to the 12th century tales of the Ulster Cycle, it was on the slopes of Slieve Gullion that Cúchulainn, the mightiest warrior of the Celtic race, acquired his name. During the reign of Conor MacNessa in the 4th century, the king and his Red Branch knights were invited to travel to a feast at the home of a blacksmith named Cullan. Setanta, a boy who was being educated at Conor's court in Emain Macha, the ancient capital of Ulster, was to accompany the royal entourage but delayed his departure because he was playing a game of hurley with his companions. Conor and his followers arrived at Cullan's fortress, the site of which is said to be close to Mullaghbawn, as night was falling. They feasted on wild boar and drank mead while Cullan barred the gates and let loose his ferocious hound, a beast said to have a spring as fast as a stone from a catapult and teeth as sharp as daggers, to patrol outside.

Suddenly, above the sound of the laughter and music that filled the great hall, the hound could be heard baying as it saw a stranger approach. Conor had forgotten that Setanta was following behind. The hound sprang at the boy who, tossing aside his hurley stick and ball, caught it by its neck and smashed it against the gatepost with such force that its limbs were ripped from their sockets. Seeing the hound lying dead at Setanta's feet, Cullan gave thanks that the boy had survived but cried: 'My hound was shield and shelter for our goods and herds.' Setanta replied: 'Give me shield and spear and I myself will guard your house; no hound guarded it better than myself.' Afterwards, Setanta was renamed Cúchulainn, Irish for the Hound of Cullan, in honour of his pledge.

Cúchulainn later became the Defender of Ulster, standing guard over the province's border at the entrance to the Gap of the North, the pass between Black Mountain and Feede Mountain, which leads through the Ring of Gullion from Leinster to Ulster. As the only pass wide enough to force through an army while under attack, the Gap has been a main route for invasion throughout Irish history. In Cúchulainn's time, the invaders were the forces of Maeve, Queen of Connacht, who carried out the *Táin Bó Cúailnge*, or Cattle Raid of Cooley, a foray into Ulster to recapture the Brown Bull of Cooley, which she had once kept in the Cooley mountains. According to legend, it was Cúchulainn – whose home was at Dún Dealgan, which later became Dundalk – who emerged victorious.

Finn MacCool, the superhuman hero of the Ossianic Cycle, was also associated with Slieve Gullion. He and his *fianna*, or warband, lived in the open air rather than the king's court and survived by hunting through the summer months. One tale, preserved in poetry, describes how Finn – 'the Fair One' – was loved by Áine and Miluchra, the two daughters of Cullan the blacksmith. They were jealous of each other's beauty and when Miluchra heard Áine remark that she would never love a man with grey hair, she saw a means of securing Finn for herself. Some time later, Finn was pursuing a fawn on the top of Slieve Gullion when he came across a small lake and, sitting beside it, a beautiful woman weeping. When she explained that she had dropped a gold ring into the water, Finn plunged in to retrieve it. But when he presented it to the weeping woman she slipped into the lake and disappeared. Realising he had been enchanted and that the woman – Miluchra – was a witch, Finn stepped back onto dry land to find he had become a wizened old man.

A search party sent to look for Finn reached the top of Slieve Gullion and found the old man, who whispered the tale of his enchantment and identified the perpetrator as Miluchra, who lived in the nearby Fairy Mound. Finn's men began digging up the mound and after three days found a maiden holding a drinking horn of red gold. Finn drank from it and regained his former strength and stature but his hair remained silver-white until his death. Miluchra became known as Calliagh Berra and the small lake on top of the mountain is still referred to as Calliagh Berra's Lough.

From the heroic age of Cúchulainn and Finn, South Armagh was a frontier zone between warring tribes which became the borderland or marchland which marked the limit of the English Pale and the beginning of the Gaelic world. The Dorsey ramparts, two parallel earth banks more than a mile long which form an enclosure near

Cullyhanna, are believed to have been an early defence against cattle raiders. Archaeologists date the northern side to 150 BC and the southern to 95 BC. They appear to have been defensive lines, the second built to reinforce the effect of the first. Although once thought to have been a cattle pound, the Dorsey in fact takes its name form the Irish *doirse*, meaning 'doors' or 'gates'.

The Dorsey was built around the same time as Navan Fort in Emain Macha, which later became the city of Armagh, and is now thought to have been the gateway to the fort and the first line of defence from the barbaric south. With bogs, drumlins and small loughs to the west and the Ring of Gullion to the east, the Dorsey was the only direct route from Dublin through to Ulster's capital. It was probably linked to other linear earthworks known as the Dane's Cast or Worm's Ditch, to the north and west of Slieve Gullion, and the Black Pig's Dyke, which runs intermittently from Monaghan to south Donegal. The earthworks do not form a continuous border but were designed to plug the gaps in Ulster's defences in areas where the terrain did not offer natural protection.

The main route to castles in the north was through the Gap of the North and much of the land either side was either bog or wood in contrast to the arable farms of the Norman manors lying in the County Louth lowlands to the south. Faughart Hill, Ireland's southernmost drumlin, commanded the entry to the Gap. According to tradition, Cúchulainn had slain 14 men there and the hill had been known thereafter as *Focerd* or 'the Good Art' of killing. Edward the Bruce, brother of Robert and the last pretender to the Irish high kingship, was buried on the hill after he was killed by the forces of Sir John de Bermingham at the Battle of Faughart in 1318. In May 1999, the graveyard at Faughart was chosen by the IRA as the place to give up the first of the bodies of 'the Disappeared'. A new coffin containing the remains of Eamon Molloy, an alleged informer from Belfast who had been shot dead 24 years earlier, was left underneath a holy laurel tree, adorned with religious charms, beside St Brigid's Well.

St Brigid, an early Patron Saint of Ireland, is believed to have been raised at Faughart. Her father, a local chieftain who was born in 434, was said to have defended the area from invasion. A pillar stone at nearby Kilnasaggart, the oldest cross-carved stone in Ireland, marks an Early Christian cemetery while at Killeavy, five miles to the north, a convent was founded by St Moninna, said to be a sister of St Patrick, in the 5th century. Although reputedly plundered by the Vikings, monastic life continued at Killeavey for a thousand years and the graveyard there is still in use.

During the Middle Ages, South Armagh and North Louth were at the mercy of two competing power blocks: the Anglo-Normans, following their invasion of Ireland in 1169, and the O'Neills of Tyrone, who styled themselves the Kings of Ulster. In the 1180s, parts of South Armagh were granted to Bertram de Verdun and Gilbert Pipard thus making Gaelic-Irish inhabitants such as the Mac Mahons and the O'Hanlons the tenants of the Anglo-Irish. The Anglo-Normans built a ring of castles, including Castle Roche – 'Castle of the Rock' – close to the modern site of the Slab Murphy farm complex at Ballybinaby, in 1236. They were part of a defensive line that held firm for more than three centuries.

In 1444, some of the O'Neills of Tyrone moved south to attack and burn part of Dundalk and annex the Fews as their septland. Their descendants became the O'Neills of the Fews. South Armagh and North Louth remained a disputed land, a patchwork of semi-autonomous Irish and Anglo-Norman lordships similar to the marchlands on the English borders with Scotland and Wales. South Armagh effectively marked the border between pre-Renaissance and post-Renaissance Europe; to the south, wealth was measured in terms of land while to the north it was based on numbers of cattle.

This situation forced the inhabitants of the area to be independent; to survive they tended to ally themselves with whoever held sway at any one time. The O'Neills of the Fews, for instance, had aligned themselves with Hugh O'Neill and the O'Neills of Tyrone in the early 1590s but by 1597 were fighting with the English in the Nine Years' War. In 1599 they were back on the side of their former kinfolk although in 1604 Turlough McHenry O'Neill was sufficiently in favour at the English court to be knighted by James I and granted more than 9,000 acres of land. But while those in power in Ulster and in Dublin both exerted influence over the South Armagh and North Louth borderlands, neither block could ever gain complete control. Rents tended to be paid only when enough force was exerted to collect them.

By the 1550s, the native Irish in the area were judged sufficiently troublesome for Sir Nicholas Bagenal, former marshal of Henry VII's army, to build and 'settle' a fortified town at Newry to prevent incursions into the Pale. In 1576, the Earl of Essex was given the barony of Farney in County Monaghan to populate, thereby blocking another route into the Pale. In a letter to Lord Burleigh, the principal secretary of state in England, Sir Nicholas Malby described these measures as a means of stopping 'the murders of good subjects on the borders'.

But South Armagh was not an enticing prospect for potential tenants. In 1572, Elizabeth I granted the lands of Orion and the Fews to Captain Thomas Chadderton on the condition that he would bring settlers into the area within seven years but the grant was revoked when none came. Raids from across the Ulster-Leinster border were a continuing problem and steps were taken to pacify the area. In an account of Red Hugh O'Donnell's journey north of Dundalk after his escape from Dublin Castle in 1591, a native Irish chronicler wrote of the 'watches and ambuscades set by the English on the border in every remarkable pass and each road' to impede O'Donnell's progress. It was in this period that the line of the modern Irish border began to emerge with the completion of the shiring of Armagh in 1582. In effect, the modern border, based on the 16th century county boundaries, is the ceasefire line between the native Irish and the Anglo-Normans of the Pale.

In 1600, Lord Mountjoy defeated Hugh O'Neill and secured the Gap of the North, by then also known as Moyry Pass, for the English. But O'Neill did not relinquish the pass without a fight and he would regularly ambush the tail ends of Mountjoy's patrols; the English soldiers would be beheaded and sent back to Mountjoy with their bodies strapped to their horses. In response, Mountjoy burned acres of forest to deprive the woodkerne (Irish footsoldiers) of their cover. Mountjoy was the first invader to fight through the winter and to build permanent garrisons, which were the forerunners of the modern watchtowers; principal of these was Moyry Castle, built on the hill commanding the pass. The castle, the ruins of which remain, was a three-storey tower with rounded corners and gun-loups and was garrisoned by a constable and 12 men. Travellers negotiating the Gap of the North were at the mercy of robbers and highwaymen up to the 1820s and in 1989 Chief Superintendent Harry Breen, the most senior

RUC officer to be killed during the modern Troubles, and Super-intendent Bob Buchanan were shot dead in an IRA ambush there.

In a survey of his diocese in 1670, Archbishop Oliver Plunkett wrote that the people of South Armagh found it almost impossible to engage in trade because 'nobody would come to buy from them or sell to them for fear of bandits'. The archbishop, who sought refuge on Slieve Gullion from the English, was later hanged for plotting rebellion and became St Oliver Plunkett. Another early South Armagh rebel was Turlough O'Neill, in whose house at Lough Ross the plan for the 1641 rebellion was believed to have been drawn up.

The year 1605 saw the arrival of large numbers of Protestant settlers in Ulster but whereas the Plantation eroded the Gaelic-Irish nature of society in the rest of the province, in South Armagh it was accentuated. In *A Description of Ireland, c. 1598*, Edmund Hogan wrote that South Armagh was 'a very strong country of wood and bog peopled with certain of the O'Neills accustomed to live much on the spoils of the Pale'. The first half of the 17th century, when the majority of north-east Ulster was planted by the ancestors of the modern Unionist majority in Northern Ireland, saw an influx of native Irish into South Armagh. These were people who had been pushed out by the Protestant incomers arriving in richer lands to the north, often because they had been unable to pay the rapidly increasing rents.

Most landlords in South Armagh were absentees and neglected their estates. Thomas Ball, a Cromwellian lieutenant who took on land surrendered by the O'Neills of the Fews, was one of the few 'improving landlords' in South Armagh. In 1672, he tried to establish a market at Crossmaglen — named from the Irish *Crois Mhic Lionnáin* or 'cross of the son of Lennon' — to draw in trade from outside the area and build up the local economy. But land ownership was mainly fragmented and the influence of landlords minimal; this left a power vacuum because the landlord formed the basis of the governmental structure of Ireland. The Government ruled chiefly by appointing landlords to serve in the offices of sheriff, justice of the peace, and, at the lower level, parish constable. The absence of suitable candidates for these positions meant that law enforcement was poor and social control weak. It was to South Armagh that the bandits or 'tories' — taken from the Irish *tóraidhe* meaning a raider or persecuted person —

gravitated and a system of law and order was never allowed to develop.

The most notorious outlaw of the second half of the 17th century was Redmond O'Hanlon, a former footboy to Sir George Acheson, a landlord in Markethill in mid-Armagh. According to a 1682 pamphet entitled *The Life and Death of The Incomparable And Indefatigable Tory Redmon O'Hanlyn, Commonly Called Count Hanlyn*, O'Hanlon, who was born in 1640, had been a collector of the poll tax who specialised in 'the general squeezing and over-reaching of the poor country people'. He took up highway robbery after being persuaded by his kinsman Laughlin O'Hanlon of Killeavey to form 'an offensive and defensive league against the King, the laws and all honest people'. After being imprisoned and escaping from Armagh jail, he used Slieve Gullion as a refuge and hideout for his followers. According to tradition, in one of his most ingenious robberies he dressed as a respectable squire and travelled to Armagh city where he called at the barracks and requested a military escort back to Mullaghbawn as protection against Redmond O'Hanlon. The request was granted and at the end of the journey he handed a florin to each trooper, whom he had plied with wine on the way, and asked them to fire a volley in the air in celebration of his safe journey. This was the signal for O'Hanlon's men to leap out of a thicket and strip them of their helmets, muskets and possessions.

In May 1679, the landlords of Armagh, Down and Monaghan paid each member of a force of 30 men nine pence a day to hunt down O'Hanlon. The following year £100 was offered for his head. But O'Hanlon was cunning enough to evade capture and it was only by recruiting a traitor that the Government got their man. William Lucas, a young army officer from Dromantine near Newry, persuaded Redmond's bodyguard, Art O'Hanlon, to turn against his foster brother and leader. On 25 April 1681, Art O'Hanlon shot Redmond as he lay asleep. The outlaw's head was placed on a spike outside Downpatrick jail and a contemporary document records a payment 'To Art O'Hanlon for killing the Torie, Redmond O Hanlon, £100'. According to Kevin McMahon, the Cullyhanna schoolteacher who was interned in 1971 and later became the foremost historian of South Armagh, many of the tories were the sons and grandsons of men who had lost their lands in the Cromwellian confiscations and had decided to hit back.

The authorities were determined to bring order to South Armagh and in 1706 Blackbank Barrack, later to become Fews Barrack, was built near Cullyhanna. In 1710, John Johnston, a Scottish former army officer who had served in Flanders and Holland, was sworn in as Constable of the Fews. His determined pursuit of the tories and ruthless suppression of the local Catholic population was to gain him a notoriety that survives today in the verse:

> Jesus of Nazareth, King of the Jews
> Save us from Johnston, King of the Fews

An entry in the Service Book of Colonel Nassau's Regiment of Foot for 28 April 1716 bears testament to Johnston's methods and effectiveness: 'Sergeant Wilde of this Corps stood for duty with six men at the redoubt of Blackbank, in the fewes . . . and, at the command of Mr Johnston, the Constable of that wild country, struck fear in the natives, who call for the Popish Pretender . . . We razed their cabins to the ground and whipped the curs, who cursed us in their Irish jargon . . .' Johnston believed that the backgrounds of his Scottish soldiers made them better suited than the English to fighting in South Armagh, a sentiment which was to be expressed by officers of Scottish regiments more than 250 years later. 'Thank the Lord, at last I have Scottish soldiers, instead of those damned English swine, to guard the Fews,' Johnston wrote in a letter to Dublin Castle in 1724.

Johnston encouraged local landlords to invite Presbyterian planters to settle on their estates and cleared the way by evicting Catholic tenants. A Presbyterian Meeting House was built at Freeduff near Cullyhanna in 1734 but burned down by Catholics nine years later. In a letter to the Duke of Devonshire, Lord Lieutenant General of Ireland, after the fire, 'the principal Proprietors & Inhabitants of the barony of Fews' called for a reward to be offered which 'would not only discover the authors of the present Horrid Fact but deter others from such future attempts and greatly conduce to the increase of Protestants in that Barony'. The Fews 'was formerly so uncultivated that it became a refuge for thieves and Rapparees but by care of the proprietors by giving proper encouragement to Protestants it of late is greatly civilised and improved . . . but the said Meeting House was . . . burnt down by Papists, which has intimidated any more Protestants to come and settle there and we greatly apprehend will drive the present Inhabitants away.' The Government offered a free pardon and £100 to anyone who could supply the identities of the arsonists.

The office of Constable of the Fews was occupied by Johnston for some 49 years and he was paid handsomely for the tories he captured or killed. His most prized scalp was that of Séamus MacMurphy, the poet and outlaw, who was hanged in Armagh some time between 1750 and 1760. MacMurphy's people had been the chiefs of the Fews before the arrival of the O'Neills and among his band of followers was Peadar Ó Doirnín, a poet whose school at Kilcurry had been broken up by Johnston. According to a proclamation by Johnston, Ó Doirnín was 'a person ill-disposed to the King, a favourite of the Pretender, who stirs up the people to rebel by his treasonable composition'. MacMurphy and Ó Doirnín are said to have held a large meeting at the top of Slieve Gullion in 1744 to prepare for the possible arrival of Bonnie Prince Charlie, the Young Pretender, in Ireland.

Like Redmond O'Hanlon before him, it was treachery that led to MacMurphy's downfall. Both avid drinkers and womanisers, Mac-Murphy and Ó Doirnín would frequent a shebeen on Flagstaff mountain run by a man called Patsy MacDacker, which gave the rapparee leaders a commanding view of the countryside. Another attraction for MacMurphy was Mollie MacDacker, Patsy's daughter, a raven-haired beauty whom he had seduced. But Mollie was also lusted after by Arty Fearon, one of MacMurphy's lieutenants, and he tried to tempt her away from his master by telling her of his infidelities. Angered by MacMurphy's promiscuity, Mollie plotted revenge. One night, she plied Ó Doirnín with drink and persuaded him to pen a lampoon on Johnston. The next day, she took the verse, entitled 'The Heretic Headcutter', to Johnston and told him who had composed it. Johnston offered her £50 for the outlaw's head and Mollie used the lure of the money to enlist the help of Fearon and her father. One August Sunday morning, the trio let Johnston's yeo-manry into the shebeen as MacMurphy lay comatose after a night's drinking. He was manacled, taken away and executed at Gallow's Hill in Armagh city the following year. Tradition has it that Patsy

MacDacker dropped dead from exhaustion while carrying his blood money from Armagh and Fearon was killed on his way back from the execution. Mollie MacDacker is said to have drowned herself in Carlingford Lough because she could not live with the shame of what she had done.

The 18th century saw a marked increase in sectarian strife as the social, economic and cultural differences between North Armagh and South Armagh were exacerbated by religious factors. By the 1780s, Catholics had begun to compete with Protestants for small farms and jobs in the rapidly expanding linen industry in the county. In 1786, John Ogle, Sheriff of County Armagh, reported that the name 'Break-a-Day Boys' was being used for the gangs which were 'ransacking the houses of Papists' at dawn and seizing arms. More commonly known as Peep O'Day Boys, they were a forerunner of the modern Orange Order that was formed in 1795 after a faction fight at Loughgall near Portadown in the north of the county. One of their grievances was the eviction of Protestant tenants in favour of Catholics willing to pay higher rents. In response to the proliferation of these gangs, Catholics began to organise themselves into groups of 'Defenders'.

The Defenders soon became an agrarian secret society organised throughout County Armagh and parts of North Louth. A document found in the possession of a suspected Defender leader arrested near Jonesborough – founded early in the 18th century by Colonel Roth Jones – had been signed by 51 Defenders at Drumbanagher in County Monaghan and was dated 24 April 1789. It outlined for the benefit of a new Defender lodge in County Louth the oath members had to swear and the rules they had to follow. These rules included: observing strict secrecy about Defender affairs; refraining from drunkenness, profanity or loud talk at lodge meetings; each Defender supplying himself with a gun and bayonet; and Defenders only going 'to a challenge' with the permission of three members of the committee. According to a 1792 pamphlet called an *Impartial Account of the Late Disturbances in the County of Armagh* published in Dublin by a J. Byrne, the suspected Defender leader was released due to lack of evidence. Byrne wrote that 'it seems that this state-prisoner has learned so much of the law in the metropolis, that he has got a certain sort of an itching to recover damages, &c. &c.'

*   *   *

I t was in the parish of Forkhill that the sectarian and agrarian clashes were most savage. Byrne described the inhabitants of the area as 'very illiterate, from their mountainous situation, that scarcely affords them potatoes and goat's milk, of course the English language in many families is scarcely known'. Richard Jackson, the landlord of the Forkhill estate, had died in 1787 and left a will that was to be administered by the Reverend Edward Hudson, the local rector. In Byrne's words, the will laid down 'that whenever a Papist's lease was expired, they should be banished their rocky habitations, and Protestants reinstated into the land of their fathers'. Hudson enforced these terms zealously and also dismissed the local teacher, nicknamed 'Mr Knowledge', replacing him with Alexander Barclay, who was resented because he was the brother-in-law of James Dawson, Hudson's hated bailiff.

'Mr Knowledge it seems, promised to learn 40 children the popish prayers in Irish,' wrote Byrne, 'which made these poor people have a heart-love for him . . . Mr B—y would not learn the Popish children any thing but the Protestant prayers'. In a letter of 7 December 1789 to the Earl of Charlemont, Hudson wrote that the Defenders would gather in large numbers and stated that 'many traces of Savage life still remain amongst us — the same laziness and improvidence — the same unrelenting ferocity in their Combats, the same love of intoxication, the same hereditary Enmities handed down from generation to generation — add to this they are all related to almost every other in it.'

On 17 December 1789, Hudson's horse was shot and killed as he was riding it and on Christmas Day the following year Father Cullen, the Catholic priest in Forkhill, was attacked at Carrickasticken in apparent retaliation. The priest's chalice was destroyed and his vestments slashed; local Catholics blamed the bailiff Dawson who was said to have enlisted the help of two English soldiers and a group of Peep O'Day boys. The attack, wrote Byrne, 'set all the Defenders in that quarter, into a sort of mad rage'. In January 1791 matters came to a head when a number of Defenders rapped on Barclay's door and demanded entry. Hudson, in a letter dated 29 January 1791 to Francis Dobbs in Dublin, wrote that when Barclay opened the door 'in rushed a Body of Hellhounds — not content with cutting & stabbing him in several places.' He continued:

They drew a cord around his neck until his Tongue was forced out — It they cut off and three fingers of his right hand — They then cut out his wife's tongue, and some of the villains held her whilst another with a case knife cut off her Thumb and four of her fingers — There was in the house a Brother of hers about fourteen years old on a visit to his Sister — his Tongue those merciless villains cut out & cut off the calf of his leg with a sword.

Barclay's sister subsequently died in Dundalk Infirmary and three of the trustees of the Jackson Estate, including Hudson, reported to the Bishop of Dromore in 1791 that Defenders were 'parading around the roads with torches' and that the Barclay incident was 'publicly exulted in in the parish'. Several Defenders were arrested and Peter Murphy was hanged on Forkhill Bridge on 3 May 1791 after being convicted of taking part in the crime. The Barclay incident was one of the most infamous in 18th century Ireland and is still recounted by loyalists, who sometimes embellish the tale by stating that Barclay's sister had her breasts cut off. In 1976, in the wake of the Kingsmills massacre, the Reverend Ian Paisley, the hardline Democratic Unionist Party leader, used it to argue that sectarian murder was endemic in South Armagh.

The unrest continued right up to the 1798 rebellion by the United Irishmen. In 1795, a military barracks was built at Belmont in Mullaghbawn. The United Irishmen in Forkhill and Mullaghbawn would meet at the Market Stone on the pretext of trading linen. The stone remains and a rough yard measure chiselled on the side can still be seen. In the spring of 1797, Ensign Thomas Goodwin of the Royal Dublin Militia, stationed at Newtownhamilton, wrote that South Armagh was in a 'very ugly and dangerous situation'. Lord Blaney formed a 'flying camp' and resorted to drastic measures in an attempt to put down the rebels. 'I went the other night to a place called Cross [Crossmaglen] and Creggan,' wrote Blaney. 'I burned 22 houses and one man I had strong reason to suspect as returning from those associations, so rode up and cut him down . . .' In June 1797, Blaney burned the house of a man named Donaldson, said to be a rebel leader. Tradition has it that the Donaldson homestead is at Freeduff; the building later became known as the 'Ambush House' after the IRA killed a policeman and a postman there in 1921.

On 28 March 1797, Colonel John Ogle, commander of the Forkhill

Yeomanry, wrote to Colonel Sankey in Dundalk that he had 'received information that a rebel force was in the act of assembly on a mountain near here called Slieve Gullion, under their Commander Shaun O'Neial, well known for his seditious activities in these parts.' According to local tradition, Ogle's informant was Betty O'Neial, wife of Shaun O'Neial, who was referred to as 'the cuckoo' in the ballad *The Boys Of Mullaghbawn*. In the ballad, the boys of Mullaghbawn are transported on the orders of a 'vile deceiving stranger' and reflect that they will never again see South Armagh:

> The trout and salmon gaping as the cuckoo left her station
> Saying fare thee well Killeavey and the Boys of Mullaghbawn

The poem 'The Market Stone' mentions that 'traitors they were busy' and that a man called Duffy was also an informer. Weapons gathered in preparation for the 1798 Rebellion were hidden in caves in Slieve Gullion and other hideouts 'as in forty-one before', a reference to the 1641 Rebellion.

Another poem, 'The Carrive Blacksmith', tells the tale of Thomas Lappin, a blacksmith, who was betrayed by yet another informer and captured by the Ancient Britons who were commanded by Captain Farnan and based at Belmont Barracks. People in South Armagh still speak about the injustice of Lappin being tied to a cart and flogged for four days because he refused to name his comrades. He was left to die in a road next to the barracks henceforth known as 'Whipping Lane'. According to the poem, Lappin had made pike heads at his forge for the rebels:

> But a traitor watched his actions
> And for cursed English gold
> To notorious Captain Farnan
> He his information sold

Local tradition has it that the informer who turned in Lappin lived in Tullydonnell and was seized by his neighbours and burned in his own kitchen fire. Another blacksmith — 'brave, honest Tom McArdle . . . famed for mirth and innocence, and never charged with crime' — is also remembered in a ballad. McArdle, from

Crievekieran near Cullaville, was hung from a high ash tree on suspicion of making pike heads during the 1798 Rebellion:

> It was in the year of '98
> That year of blood and sin
> That they hanged brave Tom McArdle
> Near the town of Crossmaglen

James O'Callaghan, a Cullaville man and one of the South Armagh rebels in 1798, escaped and fled the country to France where he carried on his fight against the English by becoming a colonel in the French Army during the Peninsular War. By a curious twist of fate, his men captured Blaney whose 89th Foot regiment had mounted a raid on Spain from Gibraltar. O'Callaghan then insisted on Blaney being held as a ransom for some of the United Irishmen in English custody.

Between 1835 and 1855, there were at least 25 murders in South Armagh. A number of the killings were sectarian and in 1847 Joshua Magee, a coroner speaking at Armagh assizes, described the people in the area around Newtownhamilton as 'undereducated, wild and fierce in their disposition' and 'divided into two hostile factions, Orange and Catholic'. One victim was George McFarland, a 77-year-old Protestant landowner who had served nearly eight years in the British Army. On 27 December 1837, he was sitting with his granddaughter, Elizabeth Johnston, 15, in the kitchen of his farmhouse at Roxborough, near Cullyhanna, when more than two dozen men armed with guns and sticks burst through the door. Elizabeth Johnston told the police afterwards:

> They said: 'It is a fine night.' They then came up to the fire and struck my grandfather and myself. Several men struck us with sticks . . . A man took me by the arm and brought me to show him where the arms were. I went with him to the far side of the kitchen. 'Damn your soul, keep your blood off me,' the man then said . . . The arms weren't there, and the dog went to bite one of the men that was holding me. They lifted up the candlestick and knocked out the dog's brains.

After breaking the windows and smashing up the kitchen, the men left McFarland dying, his head split open by a turf-hatchet.

McFarland's killers had called at the farm hoping to find John Johnston, his son-in-law and a former member of the local yeomanry. In 1815 Johnston had allegedly been involved in an attack on the house of Hugh McMahon, a Catholic man, during which Edward Hanlon, another Catholic, had been shot dead. Ribbonmen were suspected of killing McFarland. The *Newry Telegraph* reported: 'It is an alarming fact that a Ribbon Inquisition is established in the County Armagh. Several persons saw the sanguinary band going in the direction of Roxborough, and they heard them returning, they heard them fire a shot, cheer and huzza. Why? Because they had dipped their hands in the blood of their fellow-creatures. And these people all go quietly to bed. The next neighbour within ten perches of Johnston's heard nothing at all of the matter.' The situation became so bad that in 1852 the Government convened a Crime and Outrage Committee in London to consider what might be done. Major Henry Brownrigg, the Deputy Inspector General of the Irish Constabulary, told the committee: 'Crossmaglen, I believe, is probably the worst part of the country.'

William Steuart Trench, a land agent who started work on the Marquis of Bath's estates in County Monagahan in 1851, painted a colourful picture of the violence and lawlessness associated with Ribbonmen in his *Realities of Irish Life*.

The temper of a portion of the peasantry at this time around Carrickmacross, and on the borders of the counties of Armagh and Louth, was very bad indeed,' he wrote. 'Mr Mauleverer, a gentleman residing near Crossmaglen, had been most barbarously murdered a short time before [on 23 May 1850]. He was a magistrate and a land agent, and of a bold and fearless disposition; but mere boldness without caution is an unsafe protection from the stealthy attacks of the Ribbonmen. Mr Mauleverer was going to meet the train at Culloville station, only a short distance from his house; and thinking that there could be no danger during so short a journey, he put his pistols in his hat-box and locked them up, intending on his return to have them ready for use and to be well prepared . . . just as he came to a lonely part of the road, two men leaped out with bludgeons in their hands. Mr Mauleverer instantly snatched at his hat-box to get his pistols; but his arms were suddenly seized,

and he was held down by a false ruffian upon the car, he was
brutally murdered, and his brains dashed out upon the road.

Few were convicted of these murders because they were approved
of by perhaps a majority of the Catholic population and the
remainder were too frightened of reprisals to co-operate with the
authorities. A landlord who escaped death was Meredith Chambré, a
French-born magistrate who lived at Hawthorn Hill on the road
between Killeavey and Meigh. On 20 January 1852, he presided at
Forkhill Petty Sessions Court before setting off for home in a side-car
with his brother and butler, who were both armed with pistols. As
they approached the top of Drumintee Hill, two shots were fired, the
first knocking Chambré's hat off and the second taking off part of the
left side of his face. Francis Berry was arrested and convicted after his
sister brought him food wrapped in part of a newspaper that had
been used as wadding in the blunderbuss fired at Chambré. Berry's
boot-prints were found at the scene of the crime and he admitted
taking part in the plot but he maintained that he did not fire the shots.
In South Armagh Berry, who was hanged at Armagh jail, is still
mourned while Chambré, who survived, is viewed as the villain of the
piece. There is even some residual embarrassment that the job was
left unfinished and Chambré lived until old age. Michael J. Murphy, a
collector of folklore in South Armagh, recalled a stranger to South
Armagh teasing locals with the gibe: 'Whatever we done in our
country, we never half shot a landlord.' In July 1999, a memorial to
Berry was unveiled outside his former home in Adavoyle Road in
Jonesborough. Several republicans attended, including the Surgeon
and Danny O'Rourke, who served part of a ten-year jail sentence for
the manslaughter of Captain Robert Nairac, the undercover Army
officer, in 1977.

At the Crime and Outrage Committee hearings in 1852, James
O'Callaghan, a landlord whose estate included Courtbane and Shelagh, said the identity of many murderers was known but that drastic
measures would be needed to convict them. 'Nothing but martial law
will put it down, in the first instance. No juries are to be got to do their
duty . . . We know that these murderers go about to public-houses and
their Ribbon lodges are perfectly well known.' When the Attorney
General asked Maxwell Hamilton, another landlord, if there was 'any

part in the whole circuit in which Ribbonism is worse than at a place called Crossmaglen', Hamilton replied: 'I think it impossible it can be worse anywhere than at Crossmaglen.'

Crossmaglen became even more notorious in 1883 when 13 local men stood trial for plotting to murder two landlords, Robert McGeough and Henry Brooke. They were also charged with conspiring to overthrow the Queen's Government by becoming members of an unlawful organisation and taking an oath '. . . to establish an Irish Republic by force of arms.' The case became known as the 'Crossmaglen Conspiracy' but in South Armagh it is still maintained that the only conspiracy that took place was one concocted by Dublin Castle against the men in the dock. The 13 were said to have been among those who formed a new society called the Irish Patriotic Brotherhood with branches in Crossmaglen, Cullyhanna and Mullaghbawn. Made up of members of the Ribbon society, the Bogmen and the Rednecks, the brotherhood was believed to have been inspired by Patrick Burns, a visiting American, who had worked for Jeremiah O'Donovan Rossa. O'Donovan Rossa was a Fenian leader who had gone to America after being released from prison in 1871 and spent the period 1881 to 1885 directing the first Irish republican bombing campaign in Britain.

The Crown called evidence from no fewer than seven informers. One of these, Edward O'Hanlon from Mullaghbawn, told Belfast's Crumlin Road Court:

> The man joining the Ribbon Society held the flag of America in his left hand and the book in his right hand and went down upon his knees and said that he would keep secret all orders and demands of the Society. Should it fall his lot at any meeting to murder any man or injure horses or cattle, that he would carry it out, and not keep company with any police or any Government servant.

A man identified only as 'Informer A' gave evidence that three South Armagh men, James Malin, Terence McCabe and John McBride, had been supplied with a brass blunderbuss, double-barrelled revolving pistol and American Eight Shooter to murder Major James Blair, a magistrate in Castleblaney. 'A young man named Brennan from Castleblaney was present at the meeting and said that Mr Blair was one of the greatest devils that ever got leave to live and said also that it was a sin to let this tyrant to live any longer'.

Twelve men were convicted of taking part in the Crossmaglen Conspiracy and all but two were sentenced to ten years' penal servitude. Delivering sentence, Mr Justice Lawson ridiculed them. 'Who are the people that have banded themselves together to overthrow the British, blow up Dublin Castle, murder landlords, drive tyrants out of the country?' he asked. 'A few small farmers, tailors, labourers and National schoolmasters. These are the men by which the country is to be regenerated by a process of murder and assassination.' The case became a nationalist *cause celebre*; in 1915, the *Irish Volunteer* newspaper described it as a 'campaign of calumny' in which 'the landlord and capitalist moulders of public opinion contrived to keep up the notion that Crossmaglen was a constant centre of bloodshed and murder'. Informer A fled to America but justice, it is said, caught up with him when he was shot dead by an assassin in a saloon in Nebraska.

In South Armagh, the belief that the Crossmaglen conspirators were framed by the state remains part of a potent sense of historical injustice. In 1998, Eamon Collins said:

> As I was driving out of Newtownhamilton with a local woman the other day, she says: "There's supposed to be an old barracks of the Johnstons' around here, they were a notorious family that hung and killed and they were like a Protestant yeomanry". What that encapsulates is that it is still within the memory of people in South Armagh: the man whipped to death in Mullaghbawn, Johnston of the Fews, the Crossmaglen Conspiracy when innocent men were taken and charged. That's still within the memory and it has left mistrust.

Peter John Caraher said that Michael McVerry, the IRA man killed in 1973, once told him that every house in his parish had a relation who had taken up arms at one time or another. 'Michael could tell of battles fought by the Ribbonmen, the White Boys, the rapparees and other bands of freedom fighters. One of his own relations was Neal Quinn who was hanged in Monaghan jail on the evidence of an informer.' Quinn had been convicted of the murder of Thomas Bateson, a bailiff, in 1851. In his poem 'On Slieve Gullion', Michael

Longley characterised the British soldier in South Armagh as being weighed down by the burden of the past:

> He draws a helicopter after him,
> His beret far below, a wine-red spot
> Swallowed by heathery patches and ling
> As he sweats up the slopes of Slieve Gullion
> With forty pounds of history on his back

By the time the 20th century dawned, South Armagh had already developed a sense of isolation and fierce independence. Its violent history continued to be relived each day and laid the basis for what was to come. Even before the partition of Ireland and the historical accident of South Armagh's proximity to the border, it was a place apart.

Chapter Four

A Place Apart

'Now when first the border started and 'twas seen that smuggling paid
King George he ordered out his men to try and stop the trade
"But don't," says he, "pass Silverbridge, you might not come back again,
For there's not a cop would ever stop the boys from Crossmaglen." '
(Traditional ballad *c*.1940)

'The Platoon at FORKHILL was visited. They are surrounded by
Southern Sympathisers. Persons loyal to the Northern Government
appear to be quite the exception in the Southern portion of Armagh.'
(Report by Lieutenant Colonel W.M.Sutton,
secretary to the Border Commission, 1922)

D arkness had fallen across the Square in Crossmaglen as two
Grenadiers on lookout duty in Golf Five Zero watchtower
spotted a red tractor towing a muckspreader chug past and
turn onto the Cullaville Road. The time was 6.28 p.m. and such a
routine sighting did not merit an entry in the logbook for 12
November 1992. But suddenly the tractor began to reverse back
towards the watchtower, named 'Borucki sangar' after the paratrooper who had been blown up 16 years earlier by the bomb hidden in a
bicycle basket. As the muckspreader came to a stop, it shot out
streams of petrol, dousing the sangar from top to bottom. Seventeen
seconds later, a small gunpowder explosion ignited the petrol. A
30-ft-high fireball fuelled by an estimated 1,100 gallons of petrol

engulfed the structure for a full seven minutes, sending the temperature inside soaring.

Fearing they would suffocate or be cooked alive, the lance corporal and three guardsmen inside radioed for help and took turns to stand in the shower to cool down. Six soldiers were sent from Crossmaglen security force base to rescue their comrades but were beaten back by the heat. The lives of the four Grenadiers were saved by Sergeant David Adkins, who grabbed the keys to a Saxon armoured personnel carrier and threw them to a driver. 'I stood in the turret of the Saxon,' Adkins recalled later in an interview with Colonel Oliver Lindsay. 'It was very dark and raining. I screamed at the driver to ram the tractor away from the sangar. I could see locals coming out of the pubs to watch. I was worried about secondary explosive devices and assumed that the four Grenadiers were all dead, asphyxiated. But then I saw four faces poking out and a thumbs up. All was well.' Although only the seventh attack on the sangar since it had been built in 1977 it was the fifth in 11 months. Adkins was mentioned in dispatches for his bravery and military analysts assessed the attack, a carbon copy of one carried out during a Scots Guards tour the previous year, as yet another example of the ingenuity and gift for innovation of the Provisionals in Crossmaglen.

In fact, the tactic was more than 70 years old and had first been used by the IRA when Newtownhamilton barracks was destroyed in the early hours of 9 May 1920. Having taken over the village with more than 200 men, the IRA's 4th Northern Division pinned down Sergeant Traynor and five constables with gunfire before breaching the day room of the barracks by blowing up the wall of Paddy McManus's pub next door. The leader of the IRA men used a megaphone to call on the police to surrender. 'Never,' replied Sergeant Traynor, followed by a fusillade of shots from his men, who were resupplied with ammunition by his wife, who crawled along the floor from the back room where she had left their two children. 'Then the Sinn Feiners brought potato sprayers into operation,' the *Newry Reporter* detailed two days later. 'With these they soaked the front of the premises with petrol and paraffin, and set it alight. Soon the building was a mass of flames, but still the gallant policemen kept up the fight and it was only when the roof was about to collapse that they grudgingly effected a further retirement to the barrack yard and out-buildings.'

The man with the megaphone who had planned and led the

operation – the first major attack in South Armagh during the Irish War of Independence – was Frank Aiken, a 22-year-old from Camlough. Three years later, he was to become the IRA's Chief of Staff, the only South Armagh man to hold the post until Tom Murphy took over from Kevin McKenna in October 1996. Aiken, who had been helping to manage his family's farm since the age of 13, brought a rural cunning and ruthlessness to IRA operations in South Armagh which left a legacy that was still being drawn on more than half a century later. As leader of the 4th Northern Division, which covered South Armagh, North Louth and parts of County Tyrone and County Down and comprised several hundred men, Aiken remained resolutely opposed to the Anglo-Irish treaty of 1921, which partitioned Ireland and led to South Armagh remaining under British rule.

Jim McAllister, the former Sinn Féin councillor from Crossmaglen, is still fond of pointing out the spot just outside Cullyhanna where the IRA claimed its first victim in South Armagh. 'Sergeant Holland was shot dead here by the IRA on 6 June 1920,' he said with undisguised pride. 'Anyone who says this all started in South Armagh in the Seventies is talking bullshit.' Sergeant Timothy Holland, 42, of the Royal Irish Constabulary, had been in charge of Crossmaglen barracks, where he lived with his wife and four children, when an attempt was made to seize police weapons. He had been sitting on a wall with two constables as the crowds left an Irish festival in Cullyhanna when seven or eight men moved towards them and shouted: 'Hands up!' When the officers refused, one of the volunteers opened fire, fatally wounding Holland in the stomach and abdomen. Holland fired seven shots from his revolver, killing Peter McCreesh, 29, a farmer from Aughanduff, who was hit in the lung.

Six months later, Aiken led an attack on Camlough barracks in which up to 300 IRA men laid siege to the building with Sergeant Beatty and six constables inside. As with the Newtownhamilton attack, the roads were blocked by felled trees, and a group of volunteers gathered on the Egyptian Arch, a 100-ft-high railway bridge just outside the village, and dropped bombs on top of the troop reinforcements as they arrived from Newry. A hand grenade was used to blow open the steel shutters in front of one of the windows of the barracks and the police had to barricade it with beds and tables to prevent the volunteers swarming in. The reinforcements eventually fought their way through and relieved the besieged barracks. B-Specials then burned nearly half of Camlough in reprisal.

The next morning, the Aiken family home in the townland of Carrickbracken was burned down, the first of ten houses belonging to the family to be set alight by the B-Specials or Black and Tans. Aiken was forced to go on the run among what he would describe as 'our loyal allies, the hills' but stepped up the number of attacks against Crown forces. In January 1921, police escorting Patrick Kirke, a postman and former soldier, from Crossmaglen to Cullyhanna were ambushed by 50 volunteers at a house at Freeduff. Constable Philip Boylan was wounded in the arm and chest and Kirke was killed as Aiken crouched behind a stone gatepost, firing a rifle to cover the retreat of his men. When more police arrived from Dundalk to look for Kirke they too were ambushed and Constable William Compston was mortally wounded by a bullet in the groin. The house is still known as 'the Ambush House'. A week later, Aiken and his men opened fire on a police patrol from the ruins of his family home, wounding three constables.

Aiken, who became Commandant of the 4th Northern Division in March 1921, was soon one of the most wanted men in Ireland. One Sunday in April 1921, 16 IRA volunteers cycled to Creggan, held up members of the Protestant congregation arriving for the midday service at the parish church and placed them under armed guard in McConville's pub. Minutes later, five B-Specials cycled over Creggan bridge, as they did each Sunday. As they approached the church, Special Constable John Fluke, who was the lead man, saw three men run into the pub. The policemen dismounted to search the building but found the door closed.

Special Constable Samuel Dougald said afterwards: 'Constable Fluke knocked at the door and asked for admission. The door was then partly opened and a bomb came from the opposite side of the road, striking the ground almost where the five of us were standing. Part of the bomb struck Constable Fluke as it exploded. The rest of us separated and as we did so three more bombs were flung at us in quick succession.' IRA men then opened fire with rifles and revolvers from behind a five-foot-high wall, killing Fluke and hitting Special Constable Edward Linton twice in the leg.

Civilians also suffered at the hands of the IRA in South Armagh during the War of Independence. Five days after the Creggan ambush, John McCabe, a former soldier who lived in Crossmaglen, was dragged from his bed in the early hours, subjected to a brief 'trial' before a Sinn Féin court and sentenced to death. He was shot in the leg, head, chest and back, and left with a notice pinned to his stomach which read: 'Convicted spy, I.R.A.' McCabe managed to drag himself to a stable where he was found at dawn and taken to hospital under a police escort. Miraculously, he survived.

Another person punished for allegedly colluding with the authorities was Francis Lappin, a postman in Mullaghbawn from 1913 to 1920. Lappin had appeared as a witness for the Crown during a court hearing of a compensation claim brought by two Royal Irish Constabulary (RIC) officers who had been attacked and beaten by members of a Gaelic football team at Camlough. In a letter to District Inspector Parkinson Cumine at Bessbrook in August 1928, Lappin wrote that in 1920 he had been 'kidnapped by armed Sinn Feiners, was blindfolded and gagged and taken to an unknown destination where I was tried by a drum head Courts Martial and charged with being on friendly terms with the enemies of the Irish Republic namely the Royal Irish Constabulary'. His evidence in court, he said, was the reason he had been abducted:

> Ever after this incident I was considered a very dangerous man by the Sinn Feiners . . . as they claimed that I went to Bessbrook to give information to the Police I was found guilty of all charges and was sentenced to be shot which was afterwards commuted to deportation out of Ireland but to be shot at sight if found in Ireland inside of 24 hours, so I had no other alternative but to leave quickly and I have arrived back after an absence of 7 years and 9 months . . . I am unemployed and will soon be without visible means of support as the people in this district will not give employment to an informer.

District Inspector Cumine decided that Lappin was likely to be killed if he remained in South Armagh and arranged for him to be given a job as an auxiliary postman in Benburb in County Tyrone. 'Mullabawn is a very wild and disloyal area, and I believe that Lappin is running a very considerable risk in being there at all,' he wrote. Apart from testifying against republicans, there were also dangers in consorting with or being related to policemen. In January 1921, three girls were seized on the Dublin Road outside Newry and driven towards an isolated area. One of them was accused of 'keeping company' with a constable and ordered at gunpoint to get on her knees as her hair was cut off. Five months later, Lizzie Hyde of Ballintemple near Newtownhamilton was held up in her home by two armed men who blindfolded her and chopped off her hair with a blunt knife. They then rubbed an irritant into her eyes and told her she would be shot if she looked at them. They added that they bore no ill will towards her, only her 'bastard of a brother' who was a B-Special.

By the middle of 1921, it had become clear that Ireland would be partitioned. On 22 June, George V opened the new Northern Ireland Parliament after arriving in Belfast on board the Royal Yacht *Victoria and Albert* and being taken to the City Hall in a carriage flanked by a mounted escort of the 10th Royal Hussars. Opening the new assembly, the king said: 'I pray that my coming to Ireland today may prove to be the first step towards an end of strife amongst the people, whatever their race or creed. In that hope I appeal to all Irishmen to pause, to stretch out the hand of forbearance and conciliation, to forgive and to forget, and to join in making for the land which they love a new era of peace, contentment and goodwill.' It was neither the first nor the last time such hopes were uttered in vain.

The next day, Frank Aiken and a group of his men lay in wait next to the railway track at Adavoyle near Jonesborough as a train approached the Gap of the North on the main Belfast-to-Dublin line. It was carrying 113 men, more than a hundred horses and four officers of the 10th Royal Hussars under the command of Captain Lord W.W. Montagu-Douglas-Scott MC. Armed IRA volunteers had earlier 'arrested' men working on the line and placed bombs between the sleepers. They exploded beneath the luggage van, derailing the carriages and 18 wagons containing horses and toppling them over a 15 ft embankment. Sergeant Dawson, who had been manning a Hotchkiss machine-gun, Trooper Harpur, Frank Gallagher, the guard, and 63 horses were killed while Trooper Telford died later in hospital. Shots were fired by soldiers at local men who were said to have failed to stop when challenged. One of them, Patrick McAteer, died of his wounds. As with the Hyde Park bomb of July 1982, for which Danny McNamee of Crossmaglen was sentenced to 25 years for killing four bandsmen and seven horses, it was the dead animals rather than the dead soldiers who elicited most public sympathy. The Army made men living nearby help to clear the wreckage and bury the horses; a week later, soldiers returned to order the men to dig up the rotting carcasses and bury them deeper.

The War of Independence in South Armagh then degenerated into a series of reprisals and counter-reprisals. The fringes of the area, where substantial numbers of Protestants lived, were fertile killing grounds where long-festering sectarian hatreds led neighbour to kill neighbour. In January 1921 John Doran, a prominent IRA man, was dragged from his father's home in Camlough and shot dead. Five months later, Special Constable George Lynas was killed by gunmen as he searched a Catholic house and James and Owen Magill, both Catholics, were shot dead by B-Specials. In June 1921, four Catholics, Peter Quinn, Peter McGennity and brothers John and Thomas Reilly, were taken from their homes at Altnaveigh near Bessbrook and shot dead by the roadside. Many of the killings of Catholics were believed to have been carried out by B-Specials who gained access to their victims by pretending to carry out police raids on their homes.

On 9 July 1921, a truce was signed which effectively brought the War of Independence to an end. By December, Michael Collins, who had led the IRA's negotiating team at Downing Street, had signed the Anglo-Irish treaty, which established the 26-county Irish Free State. Although one of the terms of the treaty was the setting up of a Boundary Commission to make the border 'conform as closely as possible to the wishes of the population', for the moment County Armagh was among the six counties making up the new entity of Northern Ireland. Aiken bitterly resented what he saw as a betrayal by Collins, who subsequently became commander-in-chief of Free State forces. But Aiken was determined not to take sides in the almost inevitable civil war, believing that Irishmen fighting Irishmen would only serve the interests of the British. Collins appointed Aiken head of a secret Ulster Council of the IRA, which was supposed to receive weapons from the Free State so that the fight would continue in Northern Ireland. It is doubtful whether Collins ever intended these plans to come to fruition; they were probably just a way of pacifying Aiken while negotiations with Winston Churchill and James Craig, the Northern Ireland prime minister, continued.

The killing in South Armagh did not stop. In March 1922, Aiken led an attack across the newly drawn border, thereby exploiting the difficulties for the Northern Ireland and Free State authorities of mounting a response in two jurisdictions. This was later to become a standard tactic of the Provisionals in South Armagh. Dozens of armed IRA men crossed the stream that divided County Armagh from County Monaghan and lay in wait on the northern side of the border at Cullaville. At around 11.30 a.m., a patrol of seven B-Specials led by Temporary Sergeant Patrick Early came into view. Special Constable James Wallace told the subsequent Court of Inquiry at Crossmaglen:

> Fire was opened from a hill; we got under cover and replied to the fire. T/Sergt Early went into the field on the right of the road. We were forced to retire owing to the fire of men posted on the side of the hill and in front. These men were dressed in trench coats and bandoliers and wore civilian caps; I saw about 30 of them. The firing died down and I went forward again. I found Sergt Early lying wounded in his left side, apparently by a bullet.

Special Constable John Blevins told the inquiry that the leader of the attack, presumed to have been Frank Aiken, spared his life. 'As we went down Sergt Early was hit, he fell into the hollow and crawled along on his hands and knees a few yards and lay there,' he said. 'Constable Harper and Constable Dougald [who had been wounded in the Creggan ambush] were also hit.' He then saw four men with a machine-gun in a ditch about 200 yards further up the road. 'I could not see very clearly how they were dressed. There then appeared about 12 men, some on the road close up to where we were. Others from behind me took my rifle and ammunition and those of Constable Harper who was dead and of Sergt Early and Constable Dougald who were wounded.' Early died later.

Blevins continued:

> One of the men who came up was dressed in a dark green uniform, the others in civilian dress mostly with trench coats; they appeared to be taking orders from the man in uniform. I was told to put my hands up by one of the men who then asked me if I was wounded. I was then asked if I were a Roman Catholic and if I had any arms or papers on me. I told him I was not a Roman Catholic whereupon he said to the man in uniform:

"Shall I put a bullet into him". He replied that he was not out for shooting men who were disarmed. Shortly after, they ran off down the road in the direction of Castleblaney. They appeared to carry two men either dead or wounded with them.

But Aiken was to show no such compunction about shooting unarmed Protestants on subsequent occasions. In June 1922, he issued a directive calling for the destruction of enemy property, the property of Orangemen and the shooting of spies and informers. Reprisals for the murder of Catholics were to be carried out on a ratio of six to one. During the early hours of the morning of 17 June, Aiken's men claimed the lives of six Protestants and a policeman — the greatest loss of life in South Armagh on a single day until the Kingsmills massacre in January 1976. The carnage began with the ambush of a 14-strong B-Special foot patrol mounted from McGuill's public house at Drumintee, later the site of the Three Steps pub from which Captain Robert Nairac was abducted in May 1977.

About 50 IRA men opened fire from in and around the pub which, according to police documents, 'was being used as a meeting place for Dromintee Company IRA'. Special Constable Thomas Russell was shot in the head and killed and Special Constable George Hughes wounded. Two special tin mines, a mine exploder and coils of fuse were later found on the road. County Inspector W.S. Moore reported that the publican, James McGuill, who had been a Sinn Féin county councillor, 'was for some time a prominent IRA man' and that the ambush had been planned to divert Crown forces away from Altnaveigh where the sectarian killings were to take place. He added: 'McGuill's house commanded the road from Forkhill to Newry for about a mile and was built on a short steep hill with a turn which would necessitate a considerable slackening of speed in cars coming from Forkhill and was therefore well situated for an ambush. I had it burned, and the walls knocked down as a matter of military necessity.'

The Altnaveigh killings all took place after 2.30 a.m. and lasted about an hour. Landmines were used to block the main roads to delay the police and the houses selected for attack were all remote. John Gray and his family were the first to be woken when the windows of their house at Lisdrumliska were smashed. He and his wife, four daughters, five sons and two cousins were ordered downstairs. 'If you are not all out before five minutes you will be burned out,' one of the IRA men shouted. The house was set alight while the family huddled together outside. Mrs Gray asked one of the men why the attack was taking place and was told: 'It is being done for the Roman Catholics of Belfast.' Ordering the Grays to remain where they were, the raiders moved on to the Heslip household next door. Finding John Heslip, 54, his wife and two sons, Robert, 19, and William, 16, hiding in a stable, they pulled them out and made them stand with their hands up as the house was burned. After a few minutes, the leader of the group asked how many men there were and was told there were two men and a boy. John and Robert Heslip were then taken from the stable to the lane outside and shot dead. Four or five more shots were fired into the bodies. The IRA men then returned to the Gray house, picked out Joseph Gray, 20, and shot him five times; he died a few hours later.

At 3 a.m., the same IRA group arrived at the house of Thomas Crozier, an elderly farmer, and his wife Elizabeth. One of their daughters was woken by shooting followed by battering on the door and a loud explosion. When Mr Crozier opened the door he was heard to say 'Don't do anything like that, Mick' to a man wearing a navy-blue coat, policeman's cap and cloth bandolier who was standing outside. He was then shot and, mortally wounded, fell back into the arms of his son. Mrs Crozier then came out of the house and said: 'I didn't expect that of you, Willie.' She was shot twice and died 45 minutes later. According to her children, her last words were: 'Keep together and look after the little child.' The raiders exploded a bomb in the parlour before making off.

A second IRA group raided the Little and Lockhart households some distance away. William Lockhart was woken by his dog barking moments before shots were fired at the house and the windows smashed. He, his wife and their only son, James, 25, were told they had half a minute to get out before the house was burned. They were then lined up outside with their neighbours, the Little family, as the IRA men had a brief conversation a few yards away. Mr Lockhart, his son James and John Little were then ordered to walk down the road. Mrs Lockhart protested and when her son turned to speak to her he was grabbed by one of the raiders who told him he had disobeyed orders and shot him dead at his mother's feet; his father and Mr Little were spared. Five other Protestant houses were also attacked and burned by the IRA that night. The horror of Altnaveigh has remained deeply embedded in the Unionist psyche in Northern Ireland. Several of the victims were Orangemen and during the modern Troubles two more members of the local Orange lodge have been killed by the IRA. The Altnaveigh Orange Hall has frequently been attacked by nationalist arsonists. In May 1995 it was destroyed by fire; just over two years later, the new hall was set alight.

Two weeks after the Altnaveigh massacre, William Frazer, 48, a Protestant publican from Newtownhamilton, disappeared after being held up in his lorry by three armed men as he drove to Newry. Lieutenant Colonel W.B. Spender, secretary to the Northern Ireland Cabinet, wrote later that officials in Dublin had been 'able to confirm the information that Frank Aiken is probably responsible for his [Frazer's] capture.' Nothing more was heard until 1924 when the RUC received information that Frazer's body was buried in a bog on the Ballard Mountains, about four miles from Camlough. Using grappling irons, they dragged Frazer's skeleton to the surface. The police report stated: 'The skull, two leg bones, lower jaw bone, teeth and chest with putrid flesh attached, was all of the remains that was recovered. No portion of the remains with the exception of the teeth (which were large and prominent) and a small portion of hair on the skull, could possibly be identified.'

The Irish Civil War began on 28 June 1922 when the Irregulars, or anti-treaty faction, were attacked at their headquarters at the Four Courts in Dublin. Aiken was opposed to the treaty and his links with Collins were now broken but he tried to remain neutral and keep the 4th Northern Division united. Johnnie Faughey, an uncle of Jim McAllister, was one of Aiken's section leaders. In an interview in 1975, he said: 'At first we didn't believe it. We couldn't believe that Collins had done it. If partition was to be, which we didn't want at all, we could not believe that they had put us in the North. People were confused by it all and demoralised. Now it was our own fighting our own.' Faughey left for America in 1923 and lived there for 40 years before returning to Crossmaglen. An ardent admirer of the Provisionals, he told the interviewer: 'I wish I was 18 again with a Webley in my fist.' He died in 1982.

Aiken was dragged into the Civil War against his will on the morning of 16 July 1922 when he woke in Dundalk to find two Thompson guns pointed at his head. He and 120 of his men had been placed under arrest for refusing to recognise Collins's Provisional Government of the Free

State. But nine days later Aiken was free. As OC of the IRA prisoners in Dundalk jail, he ordered that all his charges take physical exercise at 6.30 a.m. each day. At the same time, he gave the governor a long list of items required by the prisoners to make their sojourn tolerable, as if to indicate they had no plans to leave. But arrangements had been made for his adjutant, John McCoy, who had not been arrested, to blow the prison wall from the outside on the sounding of a whistle. When Aiken blew his whistle at a prisoner who had deliberately failed to get into line, McCoy exploded a 60 lb charge and all IRA prisoners bar the handful who had slept in that morning escaped.

In his autobiography *Dublin Made Me*, Tod Andrews, father of David Andrews, Irish foreign minister when the Good Friday Agreement was signed in April 1998, described how he had been billeted in a safe house with Aiken on the eve of an attack on Dundalk barracks on 14 August 1922. 'The elderly woman of the house gave us tea with home made bread and butter before we turned in,' he wrote. 'Aiken never uttered a word. We rose very early next morning and got more tea and bread and butter with boiled eggs for breakfast. Still no word came from Aiken.' The next day, the two men drove to a farmhouse in silence. It was guarded by armed IRA sentries and in the farmyard was a large group of volunteers filling petrol cans with explosives and priming their caps with detonators. Another IRA unit arrived, making about 60 men in all. They were armed with rifles or Thompson guns and revolvers and about a dozen carried petrol tins and rolls of electric cable.

At midnight, they all moved silently towards Dundalk with Aiken taking what Andrews described as 'textbook precautions to protect a body of troops on the march'. It was three or four miles to Dundalk and the main body was preceded by an advance guard and protected on each flank. Boats were in position to get the men across the river to the barracks. Once across, a group of ten men, five armed with Thompsons and five carrying petrol-tin mines, went to the southern gate and a similar group to the northern side. Each group was backed up by a party of riflemen as the mines were let off simultaneously, blasting open both gates. Machine-gunners ran through the entrances and opened fire while mines were thrown through the windows. The barracks had been taken over by dawn and more than 200 anti-treaty prisoners released. Five members of the Free State forces were killed and ten wounded while Aiken lost just one man. 'As a guerrilla operation, his recapture of

Dundalk was by far the most spectacularly efficient carried out by the IRA,' wrote Andrews. 'Had it been directed against the British it would have had a larger place in the mythology of the period than even [Tom] Barry's famous ambush at Kilmichael. In Civil War, alas, there is no glory; there are no monuments to victory or victors, only to the dead.'

In 1998, Joe Farrell, blind and at the age of 95 one of the last surviving members of the 4th Northern Division, described Aiken as one of the greatest republican leaders of the century. 'I don't know anyone who could say so much in so few words,' he said. 'He didn't send men out, he went with them and he was looked up to by everybody. When the Civil War came, the 4th Northern was the one division in the country in which none of its members went Free State. They were all still thinking of Ireland as a Republic and that was due to Frank Aiken's leadership.' Farrell had joined the Fianna na hÉireann — the junior wing of the IRA — in Dundalk after the Easter Rising in 1916. He ran messages for the IRA and during the Civil War carried out sniper attacks on Dundalk jail. 'We'd be keeping them on their toes at night time,' he said. 'They had a sentry on the four corners and we'd take them away and make sure they couldn't see. We were prepared to die for Ireland.' Shortly before the Civil War ended, Farrell was arrested and charged with taking up arms against the Free State.

Both Farrell and Aiken joined the Fianna Fáil party and were elected to the Irish Parliament. Aiken rose to become Minister for External Affairs in the Dublin government and then deputy prime minister from 1959 to 1969. He died in 1983 and was buried in Camlough just a few yards from the grave of Raymond McCreesh, the IRA hunger striker, who had died in the Maze prison two years earlier. In March 1988, Joe Farrell's cousin Mairéad Farrell and two other volunteers were shot dead by the SAS in Gibraltar while preparing to blow up an Army band. 'She believed in what she was doing,' said the veteran of the old IRA. 'The British government was guilty of murder. They should have arrested her.'

M any of those who joined the Provisionals after 1970 were the sons and grandsons of men who had fought in the 4th Northern Division in the War of Independence and Civil War and the same surnames on security force lists in the 1990s appear on government files from the 1920s. According to District

Inspector McFarland of Bessbrook RIC, writing in September 1922, Edward Moley, a 42-year-old farmer from Cregganduff, was a 'notorious organiser of crime' and was 'believed to have been concerned in ambushes in the Crossmaglen area, and particularly with recent ambush at Culloville resulting in the death of Sgt Early and another'. Another internee from South Armagh was Michael Carragher (the anglicised spelling of Caraher), who was described by the authorities as: 'Boy officer 4th Battn IRA, prominent IRA man. Leader of Sinn Fein in Cullyhanna. Believed to have taken part in ambush of police at Cullyhanna. June 1920.'

Jack McElhaw, a relative of Aiken's who lived in Camlough, was interned from 1925 to 1926. A file on him states: 'Was a prominent IRA man and associated with Frank Aiken. Took part in attack on Camlough Barracks in 1920. Was found in possession of arms in Free State and interned there. Is an organiser and is likely to resume his activities if allowed to.' McElhaw's son, Joe McElhaw, served in the US Marine Corps and was interned from June 1973 to July 1974 for suspected IRA activities. Joe McElhaw, for many years a publican in Camlough, is an uncle of Dessie, Declan and Conor Murphy, among the most prominent republicans in the village. Both Conor, who was elected to the Northern Ireland Assembly as a Sinn Féin representative in June 1998, and Declan have served sentences as IRA prisoners.

The fathers of Peter John Caraher and Eamon Larkin, of Republican Sinn Féin, were members of the 4th Northern Division. Caraher said:

> My father fought against the Black and Tans and was arrested and was in the jail in Newbury in County Kildare in 1921. There was a mass escape. He couldn't see and he struck a match. The sentry saw him and opened fire on them; some got away, some, like my father, tried to get back into the tunnel. When they came back up on the side of the prison, the Black and Tans were there and they battered them with rifle butts. My father was very badly injured and he developed epilepsy. He died in 1944 at the age of 45. There were dozens of old men round here — they are nearly all dead now — who fought in the 4th Northern Division. South Armagh was always republican and was one part that should have been in with the Free State. Not that that would have made us any better or made us any happier; we'd likely still be republicans.

Larkin said that his grandfather, Thomas, had been a Fenian and his father, James, a member of the Irish Republican Brotherhood. 'I was born into it. The man that took me into the republican movement at the age of 17 was Peter McAteer from Faughiloutra, Jonesborough, my father's company captain from the 1920s. That tradition was in families.' Part of the legacy of the Civil War period was a deep suspicion of the Free State, the term still used by republicans to refer to the 26 counties that became the Republic of Ireland in 1937. 'The Free State forces were brutal in their establishment of authority on the North Louth area and they showed no mercy for the people of South Armagh. So there would be a distrust for the Free State. The people of South Armagh would never see the Free State as their guarantors.' Larkin, who lives next to Moyry Castle in the Gap of the North, was arrested in 1998, questioned about Continuity IRA activities and released without charge. The arrest, he said, was 'political harassment' and designed to discredit Republican Sinn Féin.

Each year, Tom Murphy attends a commemoration for an IRA volunteer who was shot dead not by British but by Irish troops. Barney Morris, 23, a former merchant seaman from Cullaville, was killed by Free State soldiers on 1 April 1923 on Larkins Road. Sergeant Martin Daly, a Free Stater who had formerly commanded an IRA flying column in County Monaghan, also died in the engagement. Daly had been in command of a 19-strong cycling column sent to Ballybinaby to arrest a number of wanted men after information had been received that they would be holding an IRA meeting under the cover of attending a barn dance. As the soldiers wheeled their cycles up Larkins Road, they saw Morris and ordered him to halt; he tried to run away but was shot when he slipped in a potato pit. The cycling column was then attacked with a Thompson gun and hand grenades by the dead man's comrades. One of the grenades exploded as it struck a gatepost and blew off the right side of Daly's skull. When Morris's body was examined, he was found to have been wearing a trench coat and a bandolier with 40 rounds of .303 rifle ammunition in it. The modern Sinn Féin cuman (branch) in Crossmaglen was named after Barney Morris and a banner with his name on it is carried at all republican rallies in the area.

Aiken brought the Civil War to an end on 30 April 1923 when, as IRA Chief of Staff, he called a ceasefire. A month later, he ordered his men to dump their arms and abandon their fight. For the next three years, the people of South Armagh were convinced that the Boundary Commission would transfer them from Northern Ireland to the Free State.

The Northern Ireland authorities shared that view and regarded South Armagh as an unwelcome possession that could not be relinquished too soon. A complaint from Sarah O'Hanlon that B-Specials had wrecked her public house in Mullaghbawn during a search in November 1922 was treated with contempt. A police report noted:

> Mrs O'Hanlon has seven sons, two of which were arrested by Free State troops and are at present in custody. 'A third son is a cripple having lost a leg in the fight between Free State soldiers and Irregulars last May at Dungooley, the remaining four sons are only quite young. She also has two daughters, the eldest — Bessie — was suspected of carrying dispatches from Frank Aiken and [John] McCoy — the Irregular leaders in this locality — and was seen frequently coming from the Free State.

The one-legged son was Patrick O'Hanlon, father of Paddy O'Hanlon, who became nationalist MP for South Armagh in the old Stormont parliament and a founder member of the SDLP in the early 1970s. Patrick O'Hanlon's leg was buried in Dundalk cemetery and each year on the anniversary of the incident he would travel there to pay his respects to his limb before spending the evening in a local bar commiserating its loss.

O'Hanlon's pub had been noted as a stopping off place for Aiken and had been searched after two men in trench coats were seen disappearing inside. District Inspector McFarland wrote: 'She would not bother writing this complaint only that she now realises that the police are "top dog" on Sinn Féin in South Armagh.' County Inspector Robert Dunlop added: 'Mrs O'Hanlon and her family are bitter Republicans. Their house, up till a year ago, was a meeting place for the blackguards of Mullabawn and Forkhill . . . The Police are of the opinion that this lady is anxious to get anything she can from the Northern Government before she finds herself transferred to the Free State.'

But neither Mrs O'Hanlon nor anyone else in the area was to be transferred to the Free State even though the Border Commission, the Northern Ireland element of the Boundary Commission, had decided that South Armagh should be given up. A Border Commission report of June 1922 alluded to the military difficulties involved in keeping South Armagh within Northern Ireland. Lieutenant Colonel W. M. Sutton, Border Commission Secretary, wrote: 'The South Armagh Platoons (Middletown, Keady, Newtown Hamilton, Crossmaglen and Forkhill) would all be unfortunately situated if fighting took place, owing to being surrounded by Southern Sympathisers, to the difficulty of communication with their Headquarters or with each other, and to all roads into the Free State being open.' Public meetings held to select representatives to appear before the Border Commission rejected British rule. A police report on a meeting at Newtownhamilton stated that 'it was the unanimous wish of those present that they should be transferred to the Free State, and they pledged themselves to use every legitimate means in their power to attain that end'.

The Boundary Commission concluded that a more rational border should be drawn up, tidying up the meanderings which cut loughs and parishes in two and divided farmhouses down the middle. The length of the border would be reduced from 282 to 231 miles with 12 main pockets of population being affected; eight would change sides from North to South and four would go the other way. The largest of these pockets was to be in South Armagh, where Crossmaglen, Forkhill and Jonesborough were to be transferred south. The result in South Armagh would have been to make 13,859 Catholics and 817 Protestants into citizens of the Free State.

There was uproar when these proposals were leaked to the London *Morning Post* in November 1925. Nationalists were furious that Northern Ireland's land area was to be reduced by just four per cent. They had wanted all of Tyrone and Fermanagh, South Derry, South Armagh and South Down to be transferred because those areas had Catholic majorities. The furore led to the shelving of the commission's report and London, Dublin and Belfast agreed that the territory of Northern Ireland would remain that set out in the Government of Ireland Act of 1920. South Armagh's sense of abandonment and isolation was complete.

The eccentricities of the border remained. The settlement on the southernmost extremity of Northern Ireland was split in two; it was called Cullaville north of the border and Culloville to the south. To the south of Jonesborough, the border ran along the middle of the

Kilnasaggart Road; this meant that in 1983, Liam Campbell, an IRA suspect excluded from Northern Ireland, was liable to be arrested if he crossed the road outside his front door. Campbell's elder brother Sean was one of two IRA volunteers blown up by their own bomb at Killeen in 1975. The border separated South Armagh from its natural hinterland of North Louth and Monaghan and parishes were split in two. 'My wife came from about a mile up the road,' said Jim McAllister. 'She was born in County Louth, the same parish as me. Crossmaglen parish, two different countries. To get married we had to go through a whole rigmarole.' Despite the inconvenience of border crossings and the almost comical system of having to display tin discs on all vehicles – including carts and bicycles – crossing the border the people continued to look south. Teenagers would, and have continued to since, travel frequently to dances in Dundalk, Castleblaney or Carrickmacross but seldom venture into Newry for a night out.

Decades later, many figures in the British establishment were to rue the decision to ignore the Boundary Commission's recommendations; if South Armagh had been placed south of the border, they reasoned, the lives of scores of British soldiers might not have been wasted. Merlyn Rees said he considered the possibility of transferring South Armagh to the Irish Republic in the mid 1970s:

> I used to look at the map and think: 'Why on earth don't we give it to the Republic? Why should we waste our time with it?' Well, the answer was it gave a defence in depth in the movement of arms. You give South Armagh back to the Republic and the IRA and their arms caches are that much nearer to Belfast. Militarily it would have been a mistake. I looked at the re-drawing of the border and bothered myself by reading about the Boundary Commission and concluded that neither the British nor the Irish government was very interested. The Republic wouldn't have wanted South Armagh either. It wasn't just a bad place from a British Army point of view, it was a bad place from an Irish point of view.

Harold Wilson, Prime Minister during that period, was apparently of the same view. In January 1976, during a debate on the situation in Northern Ireland following the Kingsmills massacre, David James, Tory MP for Dorset North, asked Wilson whether he would 'consider the real possibility of approaching the Government of the Republic to see whether it is possible to do an acre-for-acre swap of the southern end of Armagh, which is totally republican in character, with the northern end of Monaghan'. Wilson replied: 'I am not at all certain that the Republic of the south would be all that enamoured of the honourable Member's proposal that they should be given large tracts of South Armagh. Should the Government of the Republic show enthusiasm, it is a matter that we should not be slow to follow up, but I think that it is most unlikely.'

Throughout the 1970s, successive Army commanders argued that the border should be re-drawn or at least treated differently. One proposal was that there should be a 'neutral zone' in which both Irish and British forces could operate; another was that an 'artificial border' be drawn some 2,000 yards inside Northern Ireland to force the IRA to come forward and stop them being continually presented with sitting targets. Such proposals were fraught with political difficulties, not least because Unionists bridled at the prospect of any UK territory being ceded to the Republic. In March 1984, Margaret Thatcher, Conservative Prime Minister from 1979 to 1990, secretly asked Robert Armstrong, her Cabinet Secretary, to commission a study into changing the border. 'My instinct was that there might be political and security gains from getting rid of the anomalies, in the event that our talks with the Irish came to nothing,' she wrote in her memoir, *The Downing Street Years*. The continuing talks with Dublin that led to the Anglo-Irish Agreement in November 1985 prevented this being developed any further.

While the imposition of a border that put lifelong friends and members of the same family in different countries was seen in South Armagh as an impertinence and an inconvenience, it also opened up new possibilities. Price differentials between the two jurisdictions and the existence of dozens of 'unapproved' roads without customs posts meant that smuggling could be a profitable sideline or, for some, a principal occupation. Jim McAllister said:

> When the border came in people took to smuggling like ducks to water because it was lucrative and, if you don't respect the border and your government, there's no shame and no crime in it. Everything would be smuggled at one time or another. It would just depend on what was cheaper where. It might be as simple as

razor blades now and in a couple of months' time it could be potatoes, alcohol, anything. The people round here don't look at smugglers as criminals. The only question is: are they good smugglers? If they're good, fair play to them; if they're bad, God help their wit. After the EEC there was a lot of actual smuggling by paper, different subsidies for travelling to a foreign country with our beasts and that kind of thing. Again, it would be classed as fair game: if you can get a few bob off them go ahead.

Those families whose land straddled the border were ideally placed to smuggle. Among them were the Murphys of Ballybinaby, who had been landowners in the area for more than a century; in 1839, a house, offices, corn mill, kiln and lands in Ballybinaby belonging to a Thomas Murphy had been assessed as having an annual rateable value of £3 and 12 shillings.

For more than 30 years, the presence of the border prompted little more than a simmering resentment and a refusal to acknowledge that the police and customs officials were anything other than part of a force of foreign occupation. But a handful of families, among them the Carahers, kept the republican tradition alive. Tom Caraher, a cousin of Peter John Caraher's father, had been an IRA commandant in Monaghan during the War of Independence. In August 1942, 20 IRA men were billeted in Tom Caraher's loft in Donaghmoyne in County Monaghan in preparation for the day Tom Williams, a Belfast IRA man, was to be hanged for shooting a policeman. In his memoirs *Harry*, ghosted by Uinseann Mac Eoin, Harry White, then a young IRA volunteer, described how they were to mark Williams' execution. 'Crossmaglen barracks would be heavily shot up that morning, and if things went well, we hoped to capture a British officer and hang him,' he related. The boys had rifles, there was at least one Thompson, and a Lewis gun. Many of the lads wore Easter lilies, with peaked caps pressed tightly on their heads. He continued:

> By eight o'clock, we were on the road heading for the tiny northern hamlet of Cullaville. It was on the same route north of there towards Crossmaglen, a mile away, that we were passed by an RUC car with two occupants. They braked sharply on the gravel surface, as did we, then they swung around and within seconds, firing burst out on

both sides . . . The noise of the Thompson demoralised the police, one of whom had been cut with splintered glass, and they surrendered. One of our lads also was hit in the back and later had to be rushed to Carrickmacross hospital. What were we to do with the sergeant and the policeman? I know what would happen these days but at this time we had not been battle-conditioned. We rendered their car immobile, we disarmed them, but we left them their uniforms. In the circumstances, we could not pursue the attack.

Minutes of the Crossmaglen branch of the Anti-Partition League, a post-war nationalist group, reveal a defiant streak of independence. During the Berlin blockade, its chairman wrote solemnly to Clement Attlee, the Labour Prime Minister, to inform him that he would not be able to rely upon Crossmaglen's support in the event of a Third World War breaking out. In 1950, the branch called on the Dublin government to 'provide facilities for volunteers from the Six Counties to do a three months' course of military training'.

But there was little stomach for armed resistance and the IRA's Border Campaign of 1956 to 1962 was desultory. In South Armagh, one policeman was killed and a few transformers and customs posts blown up. In November 1957, the IRA suffered its worst single loss since the Civil War when four volunteers and the owner of an isolated cottage he was letting them use were killed in a premature explosion at Edentubber in North Louth. Owen Craven, from Newry, Paul Smith, from Bessbrook, George Keegan and Patrick Parle, both from Wexford, and the cottage owner Michael Watters are still commemorated each year as the 'Edentubber Martyrs'.

Owen Caraher, a younger brother of Peter John Caraher, was one of just two South Armagh men sentenced during the campaign. He described how, at the age of 20, he cycled across the border with his friend Mick Daly to a secret location to swear the Oath of Allegiance that made them IRA volunteers. Weeks later, he and Daly were on their bicycles again, this time taking a bomb to a transformer just outside Crossmaglen. He recalled:

We trained a little bit with explosives and how to use a Thompson machine-gun. But the bomb was made up for us and we just cycled up there with it in one of the baskets and put it there. It was on a timer and it went off ten minutes later. It cut off all the electricity in Crossmaglen but even then people realised that the IRA did it and they didn't say too much about it. We also set fire to a bus. The aim was to disrupt and cause a bit of financial embarrassment. Looking back, it was a very small blow to strike but it was a way of keeping things going.

Both men were arrested and spent the next four years in Belfast's Crumlin Road jail. The RUC, as well as the IRA, was still using two-wheeled transport in South Armagh. Constable Henry Ross was cycling along the road near Forkhill shortly after Caraher and Daly had been arrested when a landmine exploded; he died from his injuries a day later.

Peter John Caraher was devastated by the failure of the Border Campaign and the decision by the IRA in 1962 to dump its weapons and stand down all volunteers. He said:

My brother was in jail; I was in this house and I was putting an architrave on the back of a door when it was on the news that it had been called off. And I sat down in the chair and I cried. But I knew that it was just the end of another phase. And if that phase had failed there'd be another phase and another phase and another phase until the Brits decided to leave Ireland and then we'd have the peace we wanted.

By the time the modern Troubles erupted, Unionists were bemoaning the British government's failure to act on the recommendations of the Boundary Commission. Today, most Unionists do not consider South Armagh to be part of Northern Ireland in anything other than a technical sense. When Ian Paisley declared at a mass rally in Belfast's Ulster Hall in October 1997 that he would take his message to 'every hamlet, village, town and corner of this province', one supporter got a big laugh when he piped up: 'Even Crossmaglen?' John Taylor, deputy leader of the Ulster Unionist Party, told the author in 1998: 'South Armagh is not really part of the United Kingdom. What a pity the Boundary Commission report was not enacted. We'd have lost Crossmaglen and Cullyhanna in return for somewhere nice like Letterkenny.' Perhaps, he could have added, it might have prevented some of the bloodshed of the past three decades.

Chapter Five

'A Long-Awaited Day'

'The Green Army is a waste of time in South Armagh. It's the moving target.'

(Major C, former SAS officer,
on the need for undercover soldiers, 1998)

'Nil military casualties, 1 x enemy Killed in Action . . . The dead terrorist has subsequently been identified as SEAMUS HARVEY aged 20 years of 21 Drummuckavall Rd, Crossmaglen (GR 928136) a carded member of the PIRA.'

(Army incident report by Major Michael
Rose of the SAS, January 1977)

After more than 31 hours in position, four SAS men crouched silently in the undergrowth behind a wooden hut as they heard a van approach. It was 2.15 p.m. on a cold January day in 1977 and a thin carpet of snow covered the yellow Ford Granada they were staking out at a clearing in Coolderry, about half a mile from the Slab Murphy farm complex. The IRA had left the car there several days earlier. The SAS men made their weapons ready and listened intently as the van doors slid open, two men got out and a voice said: 'Check the exhaust and the tyres.' One of the men walked back towards the van, which then drove away. Soldier B edged forward to see Volunteer Séamus Harvey wearing a balaclava, olive green anorak and combat trousers with a shotgun cartridge belt around the waist. Harvey went over to the car and prodded the tyres before getting into the driver's seat and trying to start the ignition.

According to the Army account of the events that followed, Soldier B, backed up by the staff sergeant commanding the SAS team, broke cover to arrest Harvey. He then threw himself to the ground as a previously unseen gunman with an Armalite fired six or seven rounds at him from the other side of the clearing ten feet away. As Soldier B fired two shots back, Harvey slid out of the Granada and crawled along the ground to the back of the vehicle. Soldier B shouted that the man by the car had a shotgun; the soldiers opened fire with their SLRs, hitting Harvey 13 times and killing him before he could fire a round. The man with the Armalite was wounded by at least one bullet but managed to escape across the border 200 yards away. Beside Harvey's body, lying in a pool of blood behind the Granada, was an Ithaca 12-bore shotgun loaded with four cartridges. The engagement had lasted three minutes.

It was confirmed officially that the four men had been members of the SAS when inquest papers listed the main witness to the incident as 'Patrol Commander, 22 SAS Regiment, Bessbrook'. The first version of the Army account was contained in an incident report signed by Major H.M. Rose at 6 p.m., less than four hours after the shooting. At the end of the report, Rose, later to become General Sir Michael Rose and commander of United Nations troops in Bosnia from 1994 to 1995, recorded his appointment and unit as 'OC D Coy 1RHF'. In fact, he was commanding officer of the SAS's D Squadron, which had arrived in South Armagh six weeks earlier. At midnight, a signal sent from Bessbrook Mill to the 3rd Infantry Brigade head-quarters stated: 'A LONG AWAITED DAY. 1420 COOLDERRY . . . A PATROL SAW ONE MAN ACTING SUSPICIOUSLY AND ATTEMPTED TO ARREST HIM . . . DEAD MAN SEAMUS HARVEY.' The drinking in the SAS bar on the top floor of Bessbrook Mill lasted into the early hours as D Squadron celebrated the first successful Special Forces ambush of an IRA unit in Northern Ireland.

But scepticism about the Army account has lingered. Soldier A stated that Harvey 'was requested to surrender and then I opened fire on him' and Soldier C that they had 'opened fire as he did not surrender'. There was no mention in the incident report of a call to surrender and SAS men privately concede that it was highly

The SAS had just returned from a six-year counter-insurgency campaign in Dhofar in southern Oman fighting against rebels trying to overthrow the Sultan. Their fighting skills were second to none but they were given little preparation for South Armagh, which was a very different theatre of operations. Wilson's decision to send the regiment in was essentially a response to the public outrage in Britain over the wave of sectarian killings and its soldiers were not accustomed to operating under political constraints. Major C, a member of A Squadron who arrived in South Armagh in April 1977 and went on to win a Military Cross during the Falklands War, said: 'We were used to firing first and checking afterwards.' Staff Sergeant P, a member of B Squadron who had operated out of Bessbrook Mill in the second half of 1976, described the SAS's role as one of fighting fire with fire. He said: 'I think the score, the tally by 1976 was 49 British soldiers shot dead to two terrorists and so our job was to equalise the tally and, of course, to stabilise the province.' It is doubtful whether these two objectives were compatible.

In April 1976, the SAS claimed its first victim when Volunteer Peter Cleary was shot dead after being arrested while he was visiting his fiancée Shirley Hulme at her sister's home near Forkhill. The couple had been due to be married the following week and the Army had put in a four-man SAS team after receiving intelligence that Cleary was likely to go to the house. Two SAS men were hiding in undergrowth 120 yards east of the building while their colleagues occupied a support position a further 300 yards away in the same direction. They had been in place for more than three days when Cleary arrived and went inside; Soldier A, the officer leading the SAS team, decided to move in to arrest him. Soldiers A and B covered the front of the house while Soldiers C and D prepared to go in through the back door. But as they did so, one of a group of men tinkering with a car at the front of the house shone a torch into the bushes and spotted two figures with blackened faces and wearing camouflage gear. Realising they had been compromised, Soldier B fired a shot into the air with his submachine-gun and ordered everyone to line up against the front of the house. Soldier A jumped on Cleary as he ran out of the front door in an apparent attempt to make a sprint for the border, which was 60 yards away. He was frisked and then taken for questioning to an outbuilding where he insisted his name was Eamon

McCann even though the soldiers had already identified him as Cleary from photographs.

Hulme claimed afterwards that as Cleary was taken away from the house, Soldier A had said: 'Which one of you is Shirley? You are, aren't you? It won't be long till the wedding now. I have news for you. You are not going to have one.' According to Soldier A, he took Cleary to a field to await the Puma helicopter he had just requested while the other three SAS men prepared to guide the aircraft towards the landing site. A Scout helicopter fitted with a searchlight to illuminate the area was also on its way. In a statement read out at the inquest into Cleary's death, Soldier A said he had made the IRA man lie on the ground while he stood over him with a rifle.

Soldier A said that when he could see the helicopters, he ordered Cleary to stand up.

> As the Puma started to close in, but before the searchlights were turned on, Cleary hurled himself at me. I was aware of his arms stretched in front of him directed towards my throat. This was an unprovoked attack. It was dark, the moon still being obstructed by the cloud. I was alone with a known IRA man who had just attempted to escape 30 minutes earlier. I believed him to be a killer, who might be heavier and stronger than I was and who would not hesitate to kill me and make his escape . . . As he lunged at me, my instinctive training as an SAS soldier took over; I released the safety catch on my SLR and started shooting and continued to fire until the danger to my life was past, and that was when Cleary was on the ground. I had no chance to warn him.

Brigadier Morton, who was listening in to the radio net when the incident took place, said that the first he knew of the shooting was when Soldier A told Bessbrook Mill to 'have a bodybag waiting on the LS [Landing Site] for us when we arrive'.

The statement raised more questions than it answered and was almost certainly not a truthful account. Cleary, from Belleek, was a shy young man with a pronounced stutter who had been drawn towards the IRA after he was beaten by paratroopers in 1973. He was not well built and should have been no match for an armed SAS man with three colleagues nearby. The autopsy, moreover, found that the three shots that passed through Cleary's chest had not been fired at close range. Mention of Soldier A's story usually prompts a wry smile on the face of an SAS man. One senior NCO who spent nearly 20 years in the regiment was unequivocal: 'Cleary ran because he was allowed to run. So he was shot. As simple as that.' Constable E, who was based in Forkhill at the time, said he would 'hazard a guess' that Cleary was not killed in self-defence. 'Perhaps he did make a run for it and they took the easy option,' he said. 'Or it was already agreed this man would not be brought in and at that time, the powers that be were maybe trying to redress the balance, trying to win back public opinion, trying to reassure the public by saying: "Look, there's a dead IRA man. We're doing our job."'

Both former and serving SAS men told the author that in the 1970s and 1980s members of the regiment had deliberately crossed the border into the Irish Republic for specific operations. One of the first occasions was in March 1976 when Sean McKenna, 23, an IRA man wanted for attempted murder and a string of other offences, was woken from his bed in a house in Edentubber at 2.45 a.m. 'They came through the kitchen and tried to open my bedroom door,' McKenna said in a statement written in jail. 'I had a chair against it but they kicked the door down. One of them put a short against my head; it was a 9 mm Browning; he told me not to move or he would blow my head off . . . I dressed and one of them said: "I want to explain the case to you. Do you realise that I could have shot you? If you want to put up a struggle or if you don't want to come, say so. I will have no hesitation about shooting you now." I said that I would go with them.' McKenna was taken into Northern Ireland and arrested at Killeen. The Army denied the SAS had taken McKenna from his home and said he had been arrested while drunk and wandering around just north of the border. Two months later, he was sentenced to 25 years' imprisonment. Republicans claim that there were other instances of the SAS attempting to snatch suspects from the Irish Republic. In September 1981, Anthony 'Red' McShane, a 25-year-old from Crossmaglen, said that undercover soldiers had tried to abduct him from a farm at Rassan in County Louth some 200 yards south of the border.

But the most notorious border crossing incident, and one which provoked a major diplomatic row, was probably the result of a genuine error. The haphazard nature of the border meant that inadvertent incursions into the Irish Republic were frequent; there were 121 in 1974, 68 in 1975 and 55 in 1976. The normal procedure was for the Irish government to lodge a formal protest through the British Embassy in Dublin in return for an official explanation of the circumstances from the British defence adviser. After the controversies over the arrest of McKenna and the shooting of Cleary, however, there were members of the Garda Síochána who were determined to prevent SAS squads from entering the Republic.

This was the background to the chain of events which began at Cornamucklagh, 700 yards south of the border, on 5 May 1976 and ended in the Special Criminal Court in Dublin ten months later. The first incident was at 10.40 p.m. when Troopers Ilisoni Ligari, one of a number of Fijians in the SAS, and John Lawson were arrested after being stopped in a Triumph 2000 at a Garda-Irish Army checkpoint. They were in plain clothes but a Sterling submachine-gun and Browning pistol were in the car. Lawson said they were off duty and denied they were SAS members; Ligari refused to talk about 'the mission we were on'. It emerged later that they had been intending to drive to the Flagstaff Hill area to collect two other SAS men, Staff Sergeant Malcolm Rees and Corporal Ronald Nicholson, who had been carrying out surveillance of two border crossings.

Back at Bessbrook Mill, there was growing concern when Rees and Nicholson radioed to say they had not been picked up. Fearing there had been an IRA ambush, four plainclothed SAS men, Troopers Niall McClean, Vincent Thompson, Nigel Burchell and Carsten Rhodes, were sent out to investigate. At 2.05 a.m., a Hillman Avenger with Thompson and McClean in the front seats was stopped at the same checkpoint. In the back were Rees and Nicholson, who were still in uniform after having been collected from Flagstaff Hill a few minutes earlier. Two Brownings, a Sterling, a Remington pump-action shotgun and 196 rounds of ammunition were in the car. Behind the Avenger was a Vauxhall Victor with Burchell and Rhodes, each carrying a Sterling, inside. Rees said to the gardaí: 'Let us go back. If the roles were reversed we would let you go back. We are all doing the one bloody job.' But he was forced to order his men to hand over their weapons when Irish soldiers surrounded the vehicles and aimed their rifles at them.

At their trial in March 1977, the eight SAS men, who had been freed on bail, were each fined IR£100 for possessing arms and ammunition without a firearms certificate. Although it seemed improbable that two sets of experienced SAS men could have made the same apparently basic map-reading error on the same night, Brigadier Morton later explained how this could easily have happened. On the 1:63,000 scale map the soldiers were using a T-junction was marked just north of the border; in fact, as the 1:20,000 map showed, there was no T-junction. When navigating in the dark, the mistake, while a severe embarrassment to the SAS, was a relatively simple one to make.

One typical early SAS operation was a raid on the Three Steps bar in Drumintee in the autumn of 1976. An informer had tipped off his handler that Francis Hughes, a County Derry volunteer living on the run in Dundalk, would be meeting someone there that evening. A 'close target reconnaissance' had been carried out in the early hours by two SAS troopers who had been dropped by an unmarked car a mile away before walking across fields to the pub. 'They wore night goggles and made a detailed sketch map of the place,' said Staff Sergeant P. 'They noted all the measurements of the doors, what locks were there and whether they could be picked, what state the windows were in and whether they could be smashed with a hammer, and established that there were no security cameras or dogs.' As darkness fell, Staff Sergeant P and seven other SAS men were driven from Bessbrook Mill in an armoured minibus and left close to the Three Steps. One of them was Staff Sergeant P. He recalled:

> The two guys at the front had Remington pump action shotguns and the rest of us had MP5s and 9 mm Browning automatic pistols. The shotgun guys had pistols on the back of their belts. We had the sketch map so we knew the set-up at the back of the pub. We kicked the door down and went in through it to the crowded bar. The first two guys blasted a volley of shotgun rounds into the ceiling and shouted: "Get your fucking hands on the table". They fucking shit themselves when the plaster came down on them. We'd chosen those two guys to go in first because they were Irish and the accents confuse the locals. My job was to search the room once it had been dominated by the shotgun guys and the two back-ups. They kept an eye on everybody's hands and then me and the other three came in and fed around the room, searching and

checking IDs for Hughes. Unfortunately, the bird had already flown.

Hughes was captured in 1978 and died on hunger strike three years later.

There were also SAS operations directed against the Slab Murphy farm complex, some of which led to the arrests of farm workers who were not connected with the IRA. During an SAS swoop on the farm on 6 July 1977, Michael 'Legs' McLoughlin, his brother Jim and a young volunteer from County Tyrone called Gerry McGeough were arrested and flown to Bessbrook Mill for questioning before being released without charge. During the fracas, Tom Murphy's brother Francis ran across the border into the Republic and an Alsatian dog belonging to their mother was shot dead by the SAS team.

But most of the SAS man's time was spent waiting in covert OPs or, occasionally, ambush positions, which were later known by the euphemism 'reactive OPs'. Staff Sergeant P said most OPs would be in large blackthorn hedges:

> We'd move in at night, get into the middle of the hedge and put hessian camouflaged netting up around us. With us we'd have a high-powered telescope, a camera with a big lens for taking long-range pictures and a tape recorder for logging movements. And we'd shit into plastic bags that would be taken out with us so we didn't leave any sign we'd been there. If you buried it you'd get dogs coming along, sniffing around and digging it up. Dogs barking or being nosy were a big problem so we had this syringe dart that you could fire to tranquillise them. We just whacked the dog with that and it was out for the count. In severe cases we would kill the dog with steak laced with poison, drag it in and keep it in the hide with us. South Armagh was a very dangerous place for a dog.

Locals would use dogs to check for undercover soldiers. The SAS team which carried out the Séamus Harvey ambush had nearly been compromised when a farmer arrived at the derelict houses ten yards from their position with his collie and Alsatian dogs; he then walked through every room of each building. On that occasion, the staff sergeant commanding the team had deliberately avoided the most obvious covert OP position even though it would have provided better cover. Hunter also remembered animals as one of the SAS man's occupational hazards. 'Cows were a bastard,' he said. 'They'd sense you and come over and start having a chat with you. And of course the farmer would see that straight away.'

The SAS was a finite resource and was soon being used throughout Northern Ireland so there was a need for regular soldiers to be trained to operate covertly. This led to the establishment of Close Observation Platoons (COPs) by Major General Dick Trant in 1977. The philosophy behind them was to select 30 of the best soldiers from each battalion and teach them covert observation techniques. Many COP-trained soldiers subsequently joined the SAS or other undercover units and the British Army's covert observation expertise is now generally accepted as the best in the world. As well as carrying out surveillance, COPs – which are tasked by RUC Special Branch rather than by the Army – have also been used in South Armagh to mount ambushes. Although all 'residential' battalions spending two years in Northern Ireland were also allocated COPs, it was only in South Armagh that a battalion on a four-month tour had one.

The COPs had some success. At 1 a.m. on 6 May 1981, three four-man teams from the Royal Green Jackets COP assumed ambush positions close to the border to the east of the main Belfast-to-Dublin road. Intelligence had been received that the IRA planned to hijack vehicles or mount an illegal roadblock to mark the death of Bobby Sands, the IRA hunger striker. After 40 hours in position, one of the COP team commanders spotted three IRA men with rifles moving along the line of a river about 15 yards away. He shouted a challenge and opened fire. The three gunmen fired back and ran but only one, who was wounded, managed to escape. Volunteer Kevin Donegan, from Drumintee, was arrested while his brother, James, got across the border but was pinned down by fire from the Green Jackets and arrested by the Irish Army. The 12 COP soldiers fired a total of 689 rounds.

Two months later, the IRA exacted its revenge when it mounted a clever counter-ambush. This time, 18 soldiers from the Green Jackets COP were driven into the Glasdrumman area at 11 p.m. and divided into five ambush teams in and around McElroy's scrapyard just along the border from the Slab Murphy farm complex. Again, it was expected that an IRA roadblock was going to be set up and the aim was for the 'trigger' team to initiate the ambush while the other four teams – Alpha, Bravo, Charlie and Delta – covered the possible escape routes. The Bravo and trigger teams were hiding in old vans in the scrapyard. The events which followed were later used by Army instructors to emphasise the importance of selecting the right ambush positions, the dangers of locals acting as the eyes and ears of the IRA, and the need to withdraw all COP teams if it was suspected even one had been compromised.

On the first day, the commander of Alpha team believed his position might have been spotted by a passer-by but decided to remain where he was. The following afternoon, Delta team withdrew after it was seen by a woman; at the same time, Charlie team observed an old man beating hedgerows with a stick. That evening, a farmer spent three hours cutting his hedges and the Alpha team commander, now certain he and his men had been compromised, decided to pull out. Moments later, the van containing the three members of Bravo team was riddled with more than 250 bullets fired from six or seven gunmen using an M60 belt-fed machine-gun and Armalites from behind a hedge 160 yards away and across the border. Lance Corporal Gavin Dean, the Bravo team commander, was killed and his two riflemen wounded. Army investigators concluded that Dean's team had been seen on the first day, allowing the IRA to carry out detailed reconnaissance of the area and select a firing position. Bravo's van had been used two weeks earlier by another COP team, which had left cigarette butts there.

The incident illustrated the danger of undercover operations in South Armagh where anything out of the ordinary was likely to be spotted and passed on to the IRA. Hunter said:

> Farmers would go round their land every morning and night and they'd be beating hedges, looking for anything to indicate that troops were on the ground. They would never give an indication that they'd seen you unless the IRA had told them to. They would clock you, go back and pass the information on. Then the IRA would decide whether they could ambush you on it. The other problem was that there were only so many places you could use for cover. The South Armagh people know that ground. The Army had been there for so long that the locals

knew what was sort of place was used for an OP and the same places did get used again and again.

In December 1979, Private Peter Grundy, a member of an eight-man Parachute Regiment COP team, was blown up in a derelict house at Tullydonnell after just over two days in position. Soldiers had been seen occupying the building before and the IRA had hidden a baby monitor in the corner of the main room to warn of any activity there. As Grundy crouched over a hexamine stove brewing some tea, a command-wire bomb packed into a milk churn and buried under the peat floor was detonated from several hundred yards away. A sergeant and a lance corporal who were lying in sleeping bags in the same room survived.

The small, tight-knit communities in South Armagh meant it was almost impossible for undercover troops to remain unseen or pass themselves off as locals. 'Any Q [unmarked] cars or anything like that were immediately clocked,' said Hunter. 'It is like a white man going into the middle of a Malyasian jungle and going into a village – he would stand out, and it's exactly the same in South Armagh. You cannot disguise yourself, all you can do is limit what they think you are. It is very difficult country to operate in.'

After Dean was killed, some Army commanders concluded that it was not worth risking the lives of soldiers to prevent an IRA roadblock being set up. As well as a means of hijacking vehicles for use in attacks, the roadblocks were designed to ram home the message that the IRA controlled the roads in South Armagh. A 1979 intelligence report concluded that 'it would be reasonable to assume that these IVCPs [Illegal Vehicle Checkpoints] are organised and mounted by Thomas "Slab" Murphy (RC, PIRA, 27/01/44, Ballybinaby)'. The skill with which they were being set up was illustrated in November 1979 when a Beaver aircraft carrying out a reconnaissance mission spotted an armed man wearing a balaclava standing in the middle of the road just north of the border. Next to him was a dark-coloured van blocking the road and a car that had apparently been stopped. When the pilot descended to 200 feet to take photographs, the Beaver came under heavy fire and was hit six times; the plane withdrew and the van could be seen driving slowly into McElroy's scrapyard while the car disappeared across the border.

The photographs taken by the Beaver gave the Army a valuable insight into IRA tactics. They showed two gunmen in the open and at least seven others covering them from defensive positions, which were all well-chosen with arcs of fire covering at least 200 yards in all directions. Those not firing at the aircraft had the discipline to resist any temptation to look up. Their weapons included an M60, an Armalite, a Garand and an M16 carbine. It was suspected that one of the gunmen was Frank McCabe. Photographs of the illegal checkpoint have been used for instructional purposes and the border crossing point has been known as 'Beaver junction' by the Army ever since.

The RAF pilot of a Wessex helicopter flying 'top cover' for the Beaver and containing an Airborne Reaction Force (ARF) from the Welsh Guards decided not to pursue the van. He had just received a radio message that there were casualties at Ford's Cross, where one guardsman had been killed and another fatally wounded in a bomb explosion; he was also afraid of being hit by gunfire. The slow speed of the van might have indicated a 'come on' designed to draw the Wessex into an attack from another position. Although the pilot was not disciplined, Army commanders were furious that the van was not engaged by the gunner in the rear of the Wessex. An Army signal report stated:

AT FIRST SIGHT THIS INCIDENT SEEMS TO HAVE BEEN AN OPPORTUNITY OF INFLICTING SEVERE CASUALTIES ON THE OPPOSITION WHICH WAS LOST. HOWEVER, ALL ATTENTION WAS FOCUSSED ON THE CASUALTIES AT FORD'S CROSS. ALSO, HAD THE ARF BEEN LANDED TO INTERCEPT THIS VAN AND ATTEMPTED TO DO SO WITHOUT KNOWING ABOUT THE SEVEN HEAVILY-ARMED OCCUPANTS, THE VICTORY MIGHT WELL HAVE BEEN PYRRHIC.

The incident showed the IRA's willingness to take on helicopters and the reluctance of some elements of the security forces to engage the IRA.

Two years after the COPs were introduced, an undercover RUC group called the Bessbrook Support Unit was set up. It comprised around 30 men and was the brainchild of Sir Kenneth Newman, then RUC Chief Constable, who intended it to be the rural counterpart of E4A, the undercover police unit that operated in urban areas. Commanded by Inspector Earl McDowell, BSU officers operated in plain clothes and civilian cars and mainly performed surveillance tasks. Constable B, a former BSU member, said he and his colleagues would often dress so they might be mistaken for IRA men. He said:

> As far as the authorities were concerned you did go in police uniform but we would carry our police jackets in our rucksacks and put on our combat jackets and bush hats. When we were in the field we did dress as we expected the enemy to be because . . . if you were come across by PIRA they would pause for two or three seconds thinking. That would give us some time to react. We never patrolled roads. We patrolled fields and behind hedges and, if need be . . . we'd then set up a hard base, we'd stay in the hedge, wait for the car to come down, we'd then pounce on it, possibly stop it.

Many people in South Armagh mistook them for the SAS. Constable B said:

> It was the English ones that actually spoke in the BSU so they wouldn't know we were police. We were as tough physically and mentally as a paratrooper. We could stay on the ground up to three weeks self-contained, which is about the limit of a para-trooper. I could have said up to the standard of the SAS but you never would be . . . they [the SAS] work by fear. They are trained to do whatever needs to be done to get a job done. They have no concept of time. If they're there for two weeks, they'll stay for two weeks. But you can't expect mercy from them. If they're told that this man's away, then this man must be put away.

The success of the BSU, said Constable B, enabled the uniformed RUC to operate in South Armagh for the first time in many years. 'We actually cleared them [the IRA] out within a mile of the border in South Armagh, which has never been done before.' But when Sir John Hermon succeeded Newman as Chief Constable, he decided the BSU's duties were too far removed from ordinary policing and in the spring of 1980 he ordered that it be disbanded.

According to Major C, the 'Green Army' was little more than a 'moving target' in South Armagh. He said: 'One guy is expected to get slotted every tour and when he does there's almost a sigh of relief and a feeling of "Thank God it wasn't me." ' By the 1990s, an SAS man could expect to be engaged in undercover work in South Armagh for more than half of the total time he was in Northern Ireland. Members of 14th Intelligence Company — usually referred to as 14 Int, 'the Det', short for detachment, or, in its early days, 'the unit' — are also deployed there in strength. 'At first, we didn't really understand what was going on down in South Armagh, we were chasing our arses and stumbling around,' said Major C. 'But things gradually evolved and technically we got much more sophisticated. The unit would do the watching and listening and it was our job to provide the reaction. They were passive and our guys were more aggressive. In South Armagh, an undercover soldier is worth ten uniformed people. What the IRA hates is when it doesn't know what is going on.' While an infantry battalion might be able to keep the IRA at bay, only Special Forces units have had the potential to inflict any real damage on the South Armagh brigade.

Almost as soon as a soldier arrives in South Armagh, a chart of 'number of days to go' will go up beside his bunk. In Crossmaglen, in particular, this is also a 'days to survive' chart with the likelihood that someone in the company will be leaving early in a bodybag or bound for hospital with his career and possibly his life in ruins. John Hockey, a sociologist at Lancaster University, spent several weeks with the King's Own Border Regiment in Crossmaglen in 1980 and drew on his observations in a PhD thesis later published as *Squaddies: Portrait of a Subculture*. He found that serving there brought soldiers together, enabled them to improve their military skills and gave them a chance to escape the 'bullshit' and routines of barracks in Britain or Germany. In South Armagh, they were better motivated than anywhere else because remaining alert meant remaining alive.

Failing to move across a gap between two houses quickly enough or neglecting a designated arc of fire could be fatal. Members of each brick would eat, sleep and work together. Their team spirit often showed itself in brick nicknames such as 'Kelly's Heroes' or 'Charlie's Angels', named after the patrol commander, 'One-Two-Fuck-Up', from the brick callsign, or 'the Rat Pack', because of the brick's crew cuts.

During Hockey's period in Crossmaglen, the deaths of Private John Bateman, killed by a sniper's bullet, and Private Sean Walker, from burns caused by a blast incendiary bomb, only strengthened the determination of the others to survive. Black humour was a way of coping with the reality of death and soldiers frequently joked about appropriating one another's possessions if someone was killed; claims were put on boots, watches and even parcels from home. After the company commander ordered his troops to wear camouflaged trousers because Private Walker's burns had been least severe where he had been wearing them, there was much laughter when one private exclaimed: 'Fucking hell, fancy going to identify a pair of legs!' Officers were happy to allow non-standard items of kit, such as waterproof orienteering boots, and the scrawling of football slogans on flak jackets. A blind eye was also turned to practices like taping open the cocking-handle of the SLR so the weapon could be fired more quickly or using civilians as cover from IRA attack. The latter activity was explained by one soldier thus: 'PIRA are callous bastards but they're not stupid enough to take out their own just to get a few of us.'

Brigadier Morton had worked on the same principle in 1973 when he would drive his old minivan in and out of Crossmaglen – a highly unorthodox thing to do even then. 'I used to do things like trail the school bus or I would always be very close to the car in front so that the IRA chap sitting on the hill couldn't separate me from the other vehicle,' he said. Some regiments deliberately antagonised local people. In 1985, a captain in the King's Own Scottish Borderers was protected by a dozen of his troops as he paraded around the Square in Crossmaglen playing *The Sash*, an Orange marching tune, on the bagpipes to mark his company's departure. 'It was a big two fingers at them because we didn't lose anyone in Crossmaglen,' he said. But the line would be drawn at soldiers taking out their frustrations violently. In 1976, Morton sentenced a private who had crept out of the security force base to saw down a goalpost on the Crossmaglen Rangers GAA pitch to 28 days' detention and discharge from the Army. Others were tried by the courts. In October 1986, four Black Watch soldiers were fined at Belfast Crown Court for kicking, punching and stabbing a Crossmaglen man with a screwdriver after announcing during a drunken party that they would mark the end of their tour by leaving the base to 'do over a local'. Such incidents were not uncommon.

Some soldiers were prepared to go even further. In 1973, Guardsman Frank Gillan, of the Scots Guards, came close to shooting an unarmed man after a landmine blew up the Land Rover he had been travelling in. He said:

> It was about four in the morning and there were eight of us patrolling in two vehicles down one of the wee back roads near Bessbrook. It was pitch black and all of a sudden my jeep was blown up 15 or 20 feet in the air and we were thrown out of the back. I couldn't see or hear anything for a few seconds and then there was shouting and debris flying about. The windscreen had come through into our driver's face and he was screaming about his eyes. We got the driver down on the ground and we all took up fire positions. I had a night-sight on my rifle and I could see a car driving off towards the border. I opened fire and got about 20 shots off but it was soon across the border and away. A couple of minutes later, this little Ford Zephyr comes driving along with four guys in it leaning out of the windows shouting "Up the IRA" and "Fuck the British Army". We stopped the car and pulled them out and one of them turned out to be a well-known face. We'd been after him for years but just couldn't get enough proof on him. He was giving it lots of shouting and telling me I couldn't touch him because he was an Irish citizen. I just lost it and hit him with my rifle butt and he was lying on the ground giving me even more verbal. So I pulled this guy up onto his knees and put my rifle against his forehead. He just looked at me and said: "You're not going to shoot me you Brit bastard." I thought: "That's it. Enough." I took the safety catch off my SLR and was just about to shoot him when the sergeant jumped on my back and pulled the rifle out of my hands. I was put to one side and told to calm down while the other guys gave the four in the car a few slaps and told them to piss off. In those days, we could have got away with it. We could have wasted the four of them and torched the car and it would have just been put down as another sectarian attack. But I suppose the sergeant did the right thing stopping me.

During his time in Crossmaglen, Hockey noticed a high degree of fatalism among the soldiers, who would often describe themselves as 'number 11s', after the man-sized targets used on firing ranges, or 'bullet-catchers'. They would repeat such dictums as 'if you're going to be a loaf of bread [dead] that's the way it'll be', or 'if your name's on a round, that's it'. There was also a feeling of complete isolation both from the community in South Armagh and from the Army hierarchy. One private told Hockey he was angry about the official line they had been given as they prepared to deploy to South Armagh. 'The trouble is before we came here we were told that we were coming to help the civvies,' he said. 'Well you can stuff them, they wouldn't piss on you if you were on fire. They're all for PIRA.'

An illustration of the hostility the soldiers faced was the tale of how a doctor had apparently refused to come to the aid of Private Bateman until a cocked rifle had been levelled at his head. Like the experience of the Grenadier Guards with the local clergy in 1979, this was used as an example of just how 'on its own' the Army was. It was also felt that little help was forthcoming from the authorities. One private felt that the constraints placed upon him were unrealistic and could potentially cause his death. 'We'd have had the mess cleared up now if it wasn't for that fucking Yellow Card [the rules about when to open fire],' he said. 'Instead of lift [arrest] on sight, it'd be shoot on sight. Get rid of some of these cunts, instead of like now when we can't do anything.'

This sense of frustration and impotence mirrored the feelings of many in the Protestant community in the northern parts of South Armagh where 11 off-duty part-time UDR men, four former UDR or RUC members and 19 Protestant civilians were killed by IRA members between 1972 and 1978. During the same period, loyalists killed 11 Catholics in South Armagh in sectarian attacks. Most of these took place in the 'mixed' areas around Newtownhamilton, Bessbrook and Keady, where there were and continue to be substantial numbers of Protestants. When the Troubles broke out, Protestants and Catholics, often living in adjoining farms, turned against each other and a full-scale sectarian conflict broke out. Protestants, many of whom were members of the locally-recruited security forces, saw it as their duty to resist what they now describe as 'ethnic cleansing' by the IRA. UDR men would carry shotguns on their tractors as they went about their land and, as in the 1920s, lived in fear of the rap on the door in the middle of the night.

William Frazer, a distant relative of the Newtownhamilton publican of the same name who was abducted and killed by the IRA in 1922, was 15 in 1975 when his father, Corporal Bertie Frazer, was pulled out of his car at a neighbour's farm and shot dead by three IRA gunmen. The Frazers were one of only two Protestant families in the staunchly republican village of Whitecross. William Frazer said:

> My father's friend Willie Meaklin had been tortured and killed two weeks earlier and I'd taken it very badly. After the funeral my father took me aside and he said to me: 'Willie you're going to have to grow up pretty soon. You're going to have to go to a lot more funerals in the future.' He knew he was going to be killed. The week before he was shot, he put all his Army gear away in a kitbag and civilian clothes in a suitcase and just kept out one set of combats, a suit for going to church and a pair of overalls to work in. He knew he was going to die but he believed he had to stand his ground while the government got its act together and started dealing with the terrorists.

Bertie Frazer was the second of seven members of an intelligence-gathering unit based in Newtownhamilton to be killed by the IRA. None hid their bitter opposition to republicanism and some, including Bertie Frazer, were suspected of being members of the UVF. 'On the second night of my father's wake,' said William Frazer, 'there were up to 14 gunmen seen in the field behind our house. The Army was called and they ran off when the lights and sirens went on. The following night, they did the Tullyvallen Orange Hall.' On the night of 1 September 1975, a group of Orangemen were finishing a meeting at which they had decided it would be too dangerous to use the hall again. Its position a few hundred yards from the Monaghan border and three miles north of Cullyhanna made it an easy target for the IRA. As the Orangemen prepared to leave, two gunmen burst in and opened fire; at the same time, the windows were smashed by gunfire from outside. Four were killed and four wounded, one mortally, and the gunmen only fled when a lodge member who was an off-duty UDR man returned fire with his pistol. Anthony

McCooey, from Cullyhanna, who was convicted of the murder of the five Orangemen, later signed a statement in which he told police he had driven the gunmen to Tullyvallen after he had been told by a man in Dundalk that there was 'a job on, shooting Protestants'.

McCooey was also convicted of murdering Corporal Robert McConnell as the UDR man walked from his cousin's home to his farmhouse at Tullyvallen in April 1976, and Private Joe McCullough at his farm at Tullygeasy. McCullough had been living away from his farm for his own safety after the Tullyvallen Orange Hall killings and was in the habit of returning at last light to feed his dog. In February 1976, he parked his car outside the front door and changed into his wellington boots. As he entered the farmhouse, he was overcome by intruders who stabbed him in the stomach and neck and then dragged his body out to the front gate. In his police statement, McCooey said he had driven a group of men to McCullough's farm because he was told there was 'a bastard we have to get'. Afterwards, one of the men, who had a bayonet in a pouch by his side and was 'cheering and laughing', told him: 'I got the bastard. Pity there was not another cunt there, I would have cut his throat too.' Nearly 22 years later, a former Provisional who had recently joined the Real IRA described McCullough's killing to the author in a pub in Dundalk. 'We slit the old man's throat from here to here,' he said, as he drew his finger from his left ear to his right. 'He was passing information to loyalists and was involved in the Dublin and Monaghan bombings [in which 33 people were killed in May 1974]. He deserved everything he got.'

The sectarian killings spiralled out of control towards the end of 1975. On 19 December, three Catholics died in a loyalist gun and bomb attack on Donnelly's bar, which, according to unfounded local rumour, had been one of the places where Meaklin had been taken before he was killed. On New Year's Eve, a group calling itself the 'People's Republican Army' – a cover name for the INLA – killed a Catholic woman and two men when they bombed the Central Bar in Gilford in County Down. After loyalists shot dead three of the Reavey brothers, who were believed by local Protestants to be IRA sympathisers, at Whitecross and Joseph O'Dowd and his two nephews at their home in Gilford on 5 January 1976, republicans decided to respond with even more brutality.

Séamus Twomey, then IRA Chief of Staff, authorised a major sectarian attack on a group of Protestants after Brian Keenan, later to be one of the seven Army Council members who sanctioned the Docklands bomb, argued that it was the only means of preventing more Catholics being slaughtered. 'Keenan believed that the only way, in his words, to put the nonsense out of the Prods was to just hit back much harder and more savagely than them,' said Sean O'Callaghan, a former head of the IRA's Southern Command who was also acting as an informer for the Garda. 'Twomey and Keenan did not consult with the Army Council on it and there was a lot of shit about it afterwards. Gerry Adams wasn't happy about it and said something like: "There'll never again be another Kingsmills."'

The Kingsmills massacre, the incident which was to lead to Harold Wilson sending in the SAS, took place the evening after the Reavey brothers were killed. Sixteen mill workers in the village of Glenanne, north of Newtownhamilton, piled into a red Ford minibus after work. On the way home, the talk was largely of football with the occupants of the van dividing into two camps, not of Catholics and Protestants but of Manchester United and Leeds United supporters. At Whitecross, four Catholic workers got out leaving 11 Protestants and one Catholic to continue the journey to their homes in Bessbrook. As usual, each was sitting in a particular seat so that the man to get out next was at the back door while the last man was beside the driver. As the van headed through the darkness and drizzle along the deserted Ballymoyer Road, the outlines of a group of 12 armed men, one of whom was waving a red torch, appeared ahead.

Assuming they were being stopped and searched at an Army checkpoint, the men filed out and lined up against the side of the minibus. It was only when the name of Richard Hughes, the only Catholic, was called out and he was ordered to step forward that they began to realise that something was wrong. Walter Chapman feared they had been stopped by loyalist gunmen and squeezed the hand of Hughes, who was standing next to him, and whispered that he should stay where he was. But Hughes responded when the order was repeated; the leader of the gunmen then told him: 'Get down the road and don't look back.' As Hughes walked away, the IRA gunmen turned on his 11 workmates, cutting them down with bullets from

Armalites, SLRs, a 9 mm pistol and an M1 carbine, riddling the bus with bullets as a total of 136 shots were fired.

That evening, the text of an Army incident signal read: '1742 HRS. GRID REF 014308. A REPORT RECEIVED FROM RUC THAT THERE HAD BEEN AN AMBUSH AT KINGSMILLS NEAR WHITECROSS . . . 1746 ARF IN PUMA MOUNTED IMMEDI-ATE FOLLOW-UP WITH RUC. ON ARRIVAL AT THE AREA THE SCENE WAS ONE OF COMPLETE DEVASTATION WITH 10 OCCUPANTS DEAD, 1 SERIOUSLY INJURED AND 1 UN-INJURED.' On the road, which was gouged with bullet marks, lay lunch boxes, Thermos flasks, rain-soaked sandwiches and the top half of a set of dentures. The bodies had been lying there for nearly 20 minutes before Hughes, who was so shocked he could barely speak, had managed to hitch a lift and raise the alarm at Bessbrook RUC station. One car had driven past the minibus without stopping before a man and his wife travelling in another had got out and begun to pray beside the bodies.

As they prayed, the man heard a faint moan from behind the van. Alan Black, the last man out of the vehicle, was still alive, his head in the gutter and a trickle of ditch-water keeping his face cool. While they waited for help, Black, who was convinced he was going to die, gave instructions about his will and how his wife and children should be looked after. Minutes later, an ambulance arrived and Black, who was drifting in and out of consciousness, was soon on his way to hospital in Newry. Later, he recalled how the ambulance driver had been radioing the hospital to tell them that there seemed to be ten 'black' (dead) and one badly injured. He could not understand why they were saying ten Blacks when he was the only Black in the ambulance.

As Black's overalls and leather jacket were being cut off him at the hospital, Father Henry Devlin, a Catholic chaplain, came forward and asked quietly if the injured man was a Catholic, so he would know whether to administer the Last Rites. Black said: 'I'm not, but I could do with a prayer anyway.' The priest took the injured man's hand and said the Our Father as he was wheeled into the operating theatre. Elsewhere in the hospital, relatives had arrived from Bessbrook to identify the dead. Danny Chapman, who had lost his two nephews, was taken into the morgue where the bodies of two of the Reavey brothers had already been laid earlier in the day. 'I cried before I went in,' he said. 'I expected the worst and it was the worst. They pulled down the sheets and there they were, dead like dogs with their teeth showing.' Somehow, Black, who had been hit by 18 bullets, survived. He and Richard Hughes still live in Bessbrook.

Both the Tullyvallen Orange Hall and Kingsmills massacres were claimed by the 'South Armagh Republican Action Force'. The intelligence assessment was that this was a cover name for a group of Provisionals based in South Armagh and North Louth who were operating outside the normal IRA command structure. Ballistics analysis showed that several of the weapons used at Kingsmills had also been used at Tullyvallen and in a series of previous IRA operations. Some of the guns were in almost constant IRA use for the next two decades; one of the Armalites was fired at the SAS team during the Séamus Harvey incident a year later. In April 1990, two Armalites were discovered hidden in a dry stone wall at Sheetrim near Cullyhanna during an Army search. Between them, they had been involved in 17 killings stretching back to 1974, including the Tullyvallen Orange Hall and Kingsmills massacres; the killing of the three fusiliers at the Drummuckavall ambush in 1975; and the killing of Constables Turbitt and McConnell in 1978. It was worked out that the Armalites had been used so frequently and in so many of the same incidents that they were likely to have been in the possession of the same two IRA men for more than 15 years.

No one was ever charged in connection with the Kingsmills massacre, although the security forces drew up a long list of suspects, including three men who grew up in Bessbrook and knew many of those killed. Two others lived in Whitecross and the massacre was thought to have been planned by a man who had grown up and received military training in America before moving to Northern Ireland. Another of the gunmen was believed to be a Belleek man who later became involved with the left-wing French group *Action Directe* and helped them carry out a major Securicor robbery in Paris in the early 1980s. Police files record that Micky McKevitt, who was later to become leader of the Real IRA, had been one of 14 volunteers who attended an IRA meeting at the Road House on the main Belfast-to-Dublin road on New Year's Eve at which Kingsmills was thought to have been planned. The RUC Special Branch collator's index recorded McKevitt thus: 'MCKEVITT, Michael H. DOB 4/9/49. 270 Greenacres, DDK [Dundalk]. Planned attack 2 x RUC Sturgan Brae 17/6/78 [Turbitt and McConnell]. OC PIRA 79.'

South Armagh republicans pride themselves that their struggle against the British state was never sullied by the sectarianism which infected the IRA in Belfast. Kingsmills, they argue, was an aberration, a desperate measure in the aftermath of past Catholic slaughter and the fear of more to come. According to the Reverend Mervyn Kingston, the Church of Ireland minister in Creggan parish, which includes Crossmaglen and Cullyhanna, sectarianism in the southern portion of South Armagh is rare because the number of Protestants is so small that they present no threat. They also, he said, tend to 'keep their heads down' and keep their Unionist views largely to themselves. There are currently 17 Protestant families in the parish and he admitted his congregation was in 'terminal decline'. At the start of the Troubles, he said, one family moved because their hayshed was burned and a couple of others because they had relatives in the security forces. In August 1969, the windows of Loane's drapers and outfitters, the only Protestant business in Crossmaglen, had been broken during a riot. But the Rev Kingston said that 'in no sense whatsoever can one say there has been any either general or particular intimidation of Protestant people in these parts'. He added: 'It is true that Protestants are tolerated in South Armagh so long as they don't inform but the same could be said of Catholics.' In the southern part of South Armagh the only Orange hall still in existence is at Adavoyle, near Jonesborough; it has been a burnt-out shell since it was set alight by the IRA in March 1922.

Volunteer M said that IRA members were ordered by their leadership to carry out the Kingsmills massacre. 'It was a gut reaction and a wrong one,' he said. 'The worst time of my life in jail was after Kingsmills. It was a dishonourable time and I'm not in any way criticising or knocking the people who done it, just the mindset which caused it. But I know in my heart that I was never motivated, and most of my comrades were never motivated, by sectarianism.' Volunteer G, too, emphasised that he 'never agreed with Kingsmills' and was bitterly sorry it ever happened. But Peter John Caraher, who in 1980 provided an alibi for Anthony McCooey in an attempt to prove he could not have been present at Tullyvallen, gave what appeared to amount to a justification for the massacre. 'We can mix with our Catholic and Protestant neighbours,' he said. 'We have no qualms and we never think about Protestant or Catholic.' But those responsible for the Kingsmills massacre, he argued, were the loyalists who had shot the Reavey brothers. 'It was sad those people [at Kingsmills] had to die but I'll tell you something: it stopped any more Catholics being killed.'

Among the RUC officers present at the aftermath of Kingsmills was Constable Billy McCaughey, a member of the Special Patrol Group based in Armagh city. 'The sides of the road were running red with blood and it was the blood of totally innocent Protestants,' he said. Unknown to his superiors, McCaughey, who had extreme loyalist views, had already made contact with UVF leaders in Lurgan and Portadown. He was one of a number of RUC officers who were prepared to take the law into their own hands to defeat an enemy whom they believed included all Catholics. 'Our colour code was Orange and it was Orange by nature and several of us were paramilitaries,' said McCaughey. 'Our proud boast was that we would never have a Catholic in it. We did actually have a Catholic once, a guy called Danny from Dungannon. The day after he joined we had him dangling out from the back of a Land Rover with his chin inches from the road. He lasted a week.'

McCaughey, who described himself as a 'freelance terrorist', and his colleagues progressed from passing intelligence to the UVF and UDA to taking part in killings. In April 1977, McCaughey, along with Sergeant John Weir and two loyalist paramilitaries, shot dead William Strathearn, a Catholic who ran a grocery store in his home village of Ahoghill in County Antrim. He was also prepared to carry out similar actions in South Armagh. 'On UVF operations occasionally police undercover cars were driven in front of UVF cars with bombs and guns in them,' he said. 'If you hit an Army roadblock then the UVF car had a chance to turn and get away. We gave them quite a lot of support that way. We got away with things, we just had that kind of courage that was really recklessness.' Some senior members of the RUC and Army, he claimed, turned a blind eye because they 'didn't mind a wee bit of terror being spread'. In June 1978, McCaughey heard that RUC Special Branch expected Dessie O'Hare, a notorious IRA man known as the 'Border Fox', would be in the

Rock Bar in Keady on a particular Saturday night. McCaughey and three other SPG members, Constables Laurence McClure, Ian Mitchell and David Wilson, decided to kill him by 'spraying' the bar with gunfire and letting off a 10 lb gelignite bomb. McCaughey recalled:

> The bomb had been made some days previously and we stole a car from the Ritz Cinema while we were out on patrol. On our tea break we took the stolen car out into the country half way to Keady and loaded it up with guns and the bomb. We then had an hour for lunch and took an unmarked police car to the pub as a getaway vehicle. After doing the job we were to burn the stolen car and come back in the police car. The plan was for the machine-gun men to go in first and spray the customers and then the bomb was to be thrown in as we left. I was the first into the bar. There was an outside door and an inside door and when I reached the inside door there was a man coming out. We were masked and armed so he quickly caught on and tried to bang the door shut. I managed to get hold of him and pulled him out. I told him to get the fuck out of the road but he insisted on grappling with me so I blasted him a couple of times in the chest. The bomb didn't go off and the whole operation was messed up. We went away rejoicing because we had got away from the Army. Some of the others were back in the police station in time to get the emergency call.

The man McCaughey had shot survived.

McCaughey was later convicted of the murder of Strathearn, the attack on the Rock Bar and the kidnapping of a Catholic priest. He served 16 years of a life sentence and was released from the Maze, where he had completed an Open University degree in Education and Social Science, in 1994. The years when McCaughey and the other SPG men were at large represented the only period when loyalist paramilitaries made forays deep in South Armagh. In November 1975, Thomas McNamee, the father of Danny McNamee, later convicted of the Hyde Park bombing of 1982, died nearly a year after a blast outside McArdle's pub in Crossmaglen. RUC members were also suspected of masterminding the bombing of Donnelly's bar the following month. McCaughey claimed that a large number of policemen and UDR soldiers were active members of loyalist groups operating in South Armagh. The most significant of these, he said, was Corporal Robert McConnell. 'He was shot a UDR man and buried a UDR man. But he was very senior UVF and also deeply involved in military intelligence. I knew 24 or 25 RUC officers who were involved with loyalist paramilitaries at some level or another.'

Billy Wright, the Portadown UVF and Loyalist Volunteer Force leader who was shot dead in the Maze by the INLA in December 1997, said shortly before his death that the Kingsmills massacre had prompted him to join the UVF. From the age of six, when his parents had separated, he lived in a children's home in Mountnorris. 'I was 15 when those workmen were pulled out of that bus and shot dead,' he said. 'I was a Protestant and I realised that they had been murdered simply because they were Protestants. I left Mountnorris, came back to Portadown and immediately joined the youth wing of the UVF. I felt it was my duty to defend my people and that is what I have been doing ever since.'

William Frazer, a childhood friend of Billy Wright, said that the end of the sectarian murder campaigns was brought about not by the SAS but by a deal between the UVF and IRA. He explained: 'The IRA agreed: "We'll leave the ordinary Prods alone if you leave the Catholics alone." But the price of that was that Protestants had to behave themselves and keep quiet. That's the way the IRA has got this community. Although there are Protestants still living here they're not really living they're only surviving. Any member of the security forces or anyone that was a threat was killed or made to move out of the area. The people left are only Protestant in name. As my Da used to say: "You can live in Rome and not be a Roman as long as you abide by the Roman law." ' In this situation, Protestants had to stand together if their heritage was to be preserved. 'When a Protestant farmer dies, the other Protestants will club together and buy his land to ensure it doesn't go to the other side of the house,' he said approvingly. 'It's the same with the Roman Catholics. There was a Protestant who was given a beating recently because he put a bid in for some Roman Catholic land.'

William Frazer described the killing of William Meaklin as one of the pivotal events of his life and McCaughey used it as one of the justifications for his actions. 'They held him for four days,' said Frazer.

'His private parts were cut off and the only way he could be identified after they'd finished with him was by the colour of his hair. The tattoos had been cut off him and there were holes all over his body where they had beaten him with a lump of timber with six-inch nails at the end of it. One arm was pulled completely out of the socket and the other was tied behind his back with barbed wire. His teeth were missing. His fingernails were missing plus he had been pumped full of drugs so he would remain conscious and see what they were doing to him.' Frazer named a doctor and a nurse, both Catholics still living in South Armagh, who were supposed to have taken part in torturing him.

In fact, Meaklin died as a result of laceration of the spinal cord and lungs caused by a dozen or more .357 calibre bullet wounds to the head, neck and chest. The pathologist concluded that 'the deceased was subjected to a very severe beating or kicking before being shot' but there was no evidence Meaklin was tortured by the IRA and the events described by Frazer never took place. The post-mortem photographs show the body intact apart from bullet wounds, bruising and abrasions. But such myths have proved more enduring than the truth and the virulent sectarianism passed from generation to generation in parts of South Armagh has shown no sign of abating.

Chapter 6

'We got 18 and Mountbatten'

'It was military precision. It was thinking about what the British Army would do after the first bomb went off. It was classic . . . If the British Army had an intelligence officer of that capability then he'd go right to the top.'

(Pat Thompson, IRA member, on the
Narrow Water massacre of 1979)

'Mr Breen got out of the car and waved a white handkerchief; one of the gunmen walked up to him and shot him in the head. Mr Buchanan was despatched in the same manner.'

(RUC report into killings of two senior police officers, 1989)

N arrow Water Castle, which juts out into the mouth of Carlingford Lough, was one of a series of tower houses designed by the Elizabethans to defend the east coast of Ulster. Four centuries later, a cartographer's invisible line dissected the waterway separating the castle in Warrenpoint in Northern Ireland from Omeath and the Cooley peninsula in the Republic just 50 yards away. From Flagstaff mountain, where Séamus MacMurphy was betrayed, the view of the castle commanding the lough entrance against the backdrop of the Mournes is one of the most beautiful in Ireland. And so it was one summer bank holiday afternoon as the warm sunlight caught the lapping waves and a handful of tourists milled around the shore. In the lay-by next to the castle, an old trailer piled high with bales of barley straw had been parked.

The date was 27 August 1979, and Brendan Burns and Joe Brennan were looking down on this scene from their vantage point among the ferns next to a disused railway track on the Omeath side. The two young IRA volunteers watched in anticipation as a Land Rover and two four-ton trucks containing 26 members of the Parachute Regiment's 2nd Battalion turned off the Warrenpoint roundabout and onto the dual carriageway, the last leg of their journey from Ballykinler to Newry. In the line of sight from the position in the ferns to the hay trailer was a Victorian navigation tower, which the IRA had selected as a marker. At 4.40 p.m., as the truck at the rear of the convoy crossed the line of sight, Burns pushed a button that sent a radio signal to a fertiliser bomb hidden underneath the straw bales in the trailer.

A ball of flames enveloped the trailer as the 700 lb device, packed inside milk churns and surrounded by petrol cans, exploded. 'All I can remember is a flash and a rumble,' said Tom Caughey, an 18-year-old private who was keeping lookout with his rifle from the back of the truck. 'Then there was a sensation of flying, of losing vision. I remember lying on the road and then sitting up and looking about. There was bits of bodies around me, some of them on fire, but I couldn't see anybody moving. There was this terrible silence, then it suddenly clicked that my legs were on fire.' Nine paratroopers from A Company were in the truck and only Caughey and Private Paul Burns, the other 'tail-end charlie', survived. Hearing the explosion nearly two miles away in Warrenpoint, a detachment of Royal Marines and Royal Engineers in six vehicles rushed to the scene. A Wessex landed a medical officer and an eight-man Quick Reaction Force while a four-man Airborne Reaction Force circled overhead in a Scout helicopter. Lieutenant Colonel David Blair, commanding officer of the Queen's Own Highlanders battalion based at Bessbrook Mill, landed in a Gazelle helicopter with his signaller. Minutes later, Major Peter Fursman, officer commanding A Company, arrived in a Land Rover and it took him about 20 seconds to walk to the gatehouse opposite the castle where an initial control point had been set up.

At 5.12 p.m., just as Fursman got to the gatehouse, a Macgregor receiver/decoder device in a tupperware lunchbox was activated, setting off 1,000 lbs of explosives contained in milk churns lined up along the front wall inside. The building was completely destroyed and its granite blocks hurled hundreds of yards. The gatehouse bomb had been 'armed' with a memo park timer set for half an hour and started by a second radio signal sent by Burns moments after the trailer bomb had exploded. In planning the attack, which had been intended to catch Royal Marines based in Newry, the IRA had studied how the Army had reacted to previous incidents beside the castle. Three years earlier, a group of Marines had discovered an unexploded bomb there and taken cover in the gatehouse. It was calculated that 30 minutes after the first blast would be the optimum time for killing as many soldiers as possible. Caughey recalled:

> I'd been loaded onto the Wessex on a stretcher and we had just taken off when the second bomb exploded. There was another flash and a rumble and it was the same nightmare again. It blew the whole tail end of the chopper off course but somehow the pilot managed to keep it up and get us to Bessbrook. I was drifting in and out of consciousness and I remember looking over and seeing the other guy was Paul Burns, who wasn't a particular friend, and saying to him: 'Of all the people, it had to be you'.

Colonel Blair and ten others were killed by the second bomb; Major Fursman, who had been closest to the blast, was vaporised and initially listed as 'missing presumed dead'. One police report said it was suspected that an additional substance such as coal had been added to both bombs to give them extra 'woomph'. In the confusion after the smoke cleared, the surviving soldiers started shooting towards Omeath, firing 112 rounds. Michael Hudson, an Englishman whose father was a coachman at Buckingham Palace, was killed and his cousin, Barry Hudson, wounded; the pair had gone down to the lough shore out of curiosity after hearing the first explosion. The RUC later concluded it was highly unlikely the IRA had opened fire; the paratroopers had probably panicked when they heard ammunition exploding in the burning Land Rover.

The memories of the day have continued to haunt Caughey. He said:

> The hardest bit is the guilt that I survived and others didn't. Ten minutes before the first bomb went off, I'd swapped places in

the wagon with Gary Barnes. I still have trouble talking about this. We were going to go to his sister's wedding in the September. Afterwards in hospital I asked if Gary had been killed and they said yes. Up until then I was doing well and my mum said I just slid downhill again. I can't remember any of it but his mum and dad came up, people I never met before, and spent a week with me just talking to me. It was Chris Ireland's lance corporal's stripe that killed him. Before we set off that day, he came up and said: 'Is there any NCOs in the back of this wagon?' We told him there wasn't any need for any. But Chris says to Steve Taylor: 'Can I get on?' It was just his vanity that he had to be there because he was an NCO. That killed him and Steve Taylor survived. Years afterwards it's those wee things you think about. There was a lad, Pete Grundy, who had just been posted to A Company two weeks before it happened. He survived Narrow Water but he said afterwards: 'This Company is spooked, I want out of it.' So they posted him to C Company and about three weeks later he was blown up in a derelict house in South Armagh and A Company never lost another guy.

Narrow Water had been a devastating blow to the Army. Sixteen paratroopers had been killed, the regiment's heaviest casualties on a single day since the Battle of Arnhem in 1944; the Queen's Own Highlanders had lost their commanding officer, the most senior soldier killed by the South Armagh Brigade during the Troubles. Nor was it the only IRA attack of the day. That morning, another radio-controlled bomb constructed in South Armagh had claimed four more lives. Earl Mountbatten of Burma, the 79-year-old uncle of Prince Philip and cousin of the Queen, had been holidaying at Classiebawn Castle in County Sligo in the Irish Republic. After a late breakfast of mackerel, Lord Mountbatten and six others had set out in his boat *Shadow V* to pull in lobster pots and fish in the bay. Five minutes from the shore, a 50 lb bomb placed in the bottom of the boat exploded, killing Nicholas Knatchbull, Lord Mountbatten's grandson, and Paul Maxwell, the 15-year-old boatboy. Lord Mountbatten's legs were blown off and he drowned in the water; the Dowager Lady Brabourne died in hospital the next day.

The man who had put the bomb together and driven it to Mullaghmore was Tommy McMahon, who had been behind a string of landmine attacks in South Armagh in the 1970s. Intelligence documents name him as the man who made the landmine that killed Corporal Harrison and Lance Corporal Brown near Newtownhamilton in March 1973; he was also suspected of being one of the gunmen who shot Sam Malcomson in 1972. McMahon and Tom Murphy were close friends who had been trained together by the Libyans; Murphy had attended McMahon's wedding in Carrickmacross.

Murphy, by this time a senior member of the IRA's Northern Command which co-ordinated operations north of the border, had acted as 'intelligence officer' at Narrow Water. Although the blowing up of Mountbatten had been an operation organised by GHQ staff, he had played a key role in the planning. That August day had made his reputation within the IRA and marked him out as a future Chief of Staff. For the republican movement, it had been revenge for Bloody Sunday in 1972 when members of the Parachute Regiment had opened fire during a riot after a civil rights demonstration in Derry, killing 13 people. Tom Caughey, who suffered 35 per cent burns at Narrow Water and might still lose his legs, said: 'I hope they're proud. I suppose there would have been a good party. In Newry afterwards, the graffiti went up: "Bloody Sunday not forgotten, we got 18 and Mountbatten". Fair enough. It was a good op, it was thought out well and they knew where we would go for cover. But the dice were on their side and all they had to do was press buttons.'

Two paratroopers were decapitated with one of the heads being later recovered from the lough by a police diver; three could be identified only by their shoe sizes and blood groups because the top halves of their bodies had disintegrated. After Humphrey Atkins, the Northern Ireland Secretary, had visited the scene, a paratrooper held up a plastic bag to a reporter and said: 'This is one of his soldiers.' Constable B, one of three RUC men from the Bessbrook Support Unit who were detailed to clear the area, said:

> You're talking about three or four hundred yards . . . bits of leg, bits of arm. It got to the stage that the fourth day, you had to have a handkerchief on your mouth. We were picking up bits with sticks. People wonder why people are always blown up that way. It's because when a bomb goes off, the air inside the body has to

get out somewhere and the easiest way out is the joints. We found a hand embedded in a tree about 50 yards away.

The Narrow Water attack, and Tom Murphy's planning of it, is a modern legend within the IRA. Pat Thompson, who had been in jail for four years at the time, said:

> It will go down in British Army history as one of the most sophisticated operations in a long, long time. It was military precision. It was thinking about what the British Army would do after the first bomb went off. It was classic. The brains behind it was second to none. If the British Army had an intelligence officer of that capability then he'd go right to the top. And I'm sure that they must have thought at the time that whoever that individual was I'm sure they would have fancied having him on their side. It was a co-ordinated effort for two operations on that day and they were planned to perfection.

Of the killing of Lord Mountbatten, he said: 'I don't glorify death but I had personal pride in what happened because it was a military operation and they took him out.'

Four IRA volunteers were arrested that bank holiday Monday but only one convicted of murder. Burns, 20, and Brennan, 21, were stopped by gardaí outside Omeath as the second bomb exploded. They were riding a Suzuki 100 motorcycle without registration plates; a hollow compartment had been cut into the seat to carry the radio transmitters but it was empty. On their clothes and hands, there were traces of firearms residue and ammonium nitrate, which had been used in both bombs. Empty lemonade bottles and a Major cigarette butt, the brand smoked by Burns, had been left at the firing point while the ferns there matched those on the clothes of the two men. Two elderly ladies who lived near the firing point said they had seen the motorcycle there but after initially co-operating with gardaí changed their minds and refused to sign their statements; it was suspected republicans had threatened them. Detective Inspector Eric Anderson, who led the Narrow Water inquiry and was later to be in charge of the investigation into the Omagh bomb of 1998, concluded in a report: 'In effect we can connect the motorcycle with Burns . . .

The Garda can connect the motorcycle and the two suspects with what is thought to be the alleged detonation point on the Southern side.' But proving it was another matter. Burns and Brennan were both charged with motoring offences and released on bail.

McMahon and Francis McGirl, a County Leitrim volunteer, had been stopped by gardaí in County Longford more than two hours before the bomb that killed Mountbatten exploded. They were arrested and remained silent in custody until McGirl blurted out: 'I put no bomb in the boat.' Sand from Mullaghmore and traces of nitro-glycerine and ammonium nitrate were found on the clothes of both men while McMahon's shoes and socks had picked up flakes of paint from *Shadow V*. McMahon was sentenced to life imprisonment. McGirl was acquitted and in March 1995 was killed when the tractor he was driving toppled over and crushed him.

The investigation into the Narrow Water massacre was the most wide-ranging in Northern Ireland's history and involved the questioning of more than one thousand people across the UK. The York trailer was traced to Bartley Fearon, a scrap metal dealer from Cloghogue, who told the RUC he had exchanged it with Brian McLoughlin, a neighbour of Tom Murphy, for several bags of potatoes. McLoughlin, a brother of Michael 'Legs' McLoughlin, worked for Murphy and regularly drove one of his articulated lorries. After lengthy questioning by the RUC, McLoughlin admitted he had given the trailer to Tom Murphy after being approached by him at the end of a Gaelic football training session one night and asked for it. He said that it was 'more than my life is worth' to include Murphy's name in any statement.

The motorcycle was traced to a man in Bessbrook who had sold it to Michael Conlon, the 16-year-old brother of Tom Conlon, Murphy's Gaelic football team-mate, two days before the attack. Burns had told gardaí he had bought the motorcycle himself. Michael Conlon burst into tears when he was questioned by detectives and then told them what had happened. A confidential signal sent from Bessbrook Mill on 14 September said: 'CONLON HAS COME CLEAN. BURNS GAVE HIM 130 POUNDS AND ASKED HIM TO GO TO BBK TO BUY THE MOTORBIKE FOR HIM. BURNS COLLECTED IT LATER.' The statement Conlon signed also implicated Tom Murphy by revealing that Burns had told him to leave the motorcycle outside the Slab Murphy farm complex for collection. There was also circumstantial evidence to link Tom Murphy to Narrow Water. Burns worked as a lorry driver for the Murphys and in February 1980 he and another man were arrested by gardaí at Ballybinaby and held under the Offences Against the State Act. Brennan was a diesel salesman for the Murphy oil companies. Detectives who worked on the investigation believe that the trailer bomb had been loaded with explosives at the Slab Murphy farm complex the day before the Narrow Water attack.

As if the death of 18 soldiers was not enough for the South Armagh Brigade, there was an unexpected bonus when the man known as the Undertaker – later to become Tom Murphy's second in command – was suddenly released from custody shortly afterwards. In another IRA operation two weeks before Narrow Water, he had been arrested at his family's farm complex outside Crossmaglen. An Army Electronic Countermeasures (ECM) device had detected a signal from a radio transmitter of the type used to detonate bombs. Seven likely firing points were identified, one of them the Undertaker's farm; covert units were then used to cut off possible escape routes and a Wessex containing Colonel Blair flew in from Bessbrook Mill to observe from the air. Shortly after the Wessex arrived overhead, a man later identified as the Undertaker ran from the road to join his brothers, who were 13 and 11, and was spotted by Colonel Blair placing a green plastic bag in a hedge. A milk churn bomb attached to a radio receiver in a tupperware lunchbox was discovered nearby and the plastic bag found to contain a transmitter. The Undertaker was taken to Gough barracks for interrogation, charged with attempted murder and remanded in custody.

Volunteer M said that what happened subsequently showed why IRA men should admit to nothing during questioning:

> One chap had been in charge of something and the only evidence against him was that Colonel Blair said he seen him doing something from a helicopter. He was going down the chute for it but he shut his mouth and said nothing. His battery pack or something was found in a hedge and he said: 'It's not mine, I know nothing about it', even though Blair's evidence was he had seen him putting it in there. He could have decided to say: 'Well, okay,

much to my regret I did do this' but he didn't, he shut up, then Blair was killed at Narrow Water and he had to be let out.

Before Narrow Water, Colonel Blair had enjoyed a run of extra-ordinary good luck. On 11 July 1979, two volunteers, Eugene O'Callaghan and Eugene Byrne, had been arrested on Lough Ross in a cabin cruiser loaded with radio-control equipment, including five Macgregor devices. A third volunteer was shot in the leg and escaped across the border, which runs through the lough. O'Callaghan and Byrne were later convicted of possession of bomb-making materials. It was thought they had been testing the boat before placing a bomb into it, guiding it by remote control to a Royal Navy patrol vessel on Carlingford Lough and detonating the device. Colonel Blair's staff officers described the arrests of Eugene O'Callaghan and Byrne as a 'fortuitous success' and the capture of the Undertaker as 'a bold plan which surprised even us by its complete success'. Two days before the Narrow Water massacre, Colonel Blair had a close escape when a helicopter that had just flown him to Bessbrook Mill crashed killing two of the three soldiers on board. In a signal he sent to Brigadier David Thorne after the arrest of the Undertaker, Colonel Blair had remarked: 'THIS SUCCESS FOLLOWS ON THE SUCCESS OF THE LOUGH ROSS INCIDENT AND SOME REACTION MUST BE EXPECTED.' He could hardly have imagined how bloody that reaction would be or that his good fortune would end so abruptly.

Brendan Burns's luck was also finite. After being freed from custody, he and Brennan joined the legion of IRA men on the run in Dundalk. Undercover army teams dug in close to their homes in Crossmaglen but they were not detected even though Burns was almost cavalier in his attitude to the risk of being captured. Jim McAllister recalled:

Brendan was known as a gung-ho chap, the life and soul of a party. He was at home all the time even though he was supposed to be on the run, if you know what I mean. He was in his own house one day when the Brits came looking for him. He picked up a bucket, walked right past them and went out to feed the cattle in the field. He started calling to the cattle "go on walk, walk" and he just walked them over the hill and away. They all thought that it was just a farmer. They assumed that an IRA man wouldn't be feeding cattle.

By the time he took part in the Narrow Water attack, Burns was already an accomplished bombmaker whose skills had been nurtured by Tommy McMahon. Four months earlier, he had been the 'button man' who detonated the radio-controlled 500 lb bomb which killed four RUC officers driving along the Millvale Road in Bessbrook in a Land Rover. Burns killed five more soldiers in April 1981 when a 1,000 lb landmine he had set up in Camlough blew up an Army Saracen. The attack was timed to mark the death of Raymond McCreesh; the Camlough volunteer had lapsed into a coma and two days later became the third IRA hunger striker to die. That evening, Bik McFarlane, OC of IRA prisoners in the Maze, added a postscript to a 'comm' to be smuggled out to Gerry Adams and the IRA leadership on the outside. 'Have just heard about that cunning little operation in S. Armagh,' he wrote. 'Oh, you wonderful people!! Far from home they perish, yet they know not the reason why! 'Tis truly a great shame. They kill and die and never think to question. Such is the penalty for blind folly.'

The words of Father Brian McCreesh, Raymond's brother, are used to this day to commemorate the dead hunger strikers; a sign placed next to ten crosses beside the Dundalk-to-Cullyhanna road reads: 'My Brother is not a Criminal.' In Courtbane, outside the Naomh Malachi clubhouse where Tom Murphy regularly socialises with his former Gaelic football team-mates, there is a stone memorial honouring 'the ten hunger strikers who died in 1981 and for all those republicans who gave their lives for Irish freedom'.

McFarlane was to meet Burns in May 1983 after he and six other IRA men made their way on foot to South Armagh after the Maze escape. 'Seamus [McElwaine] scampered down the embankment and read the signpost – Camlough 3 miles,' wrote McFarlane ten years later. 'This was it. Time to get off the tracks and head into God's Country, as the South Armagh lads always called it . . . We had smashed the H-Blocks wide open and were now with true friends and comrades celebrating the victory along the narrow winding roads of South Armagh. This was freedom.' In all, 18 of the 19 escapers who were not recaptured immediately eventually made their way to South Armagh where Burns and Volunteer Brendan Moley were in charge of picking them up and transporting them to safehouses. Burns was arrested in Dundalk in February 1984 after a request from the RUC that he be extradited for questioning about the murder of the five soldiers in Camlough in 1981 but was freed after a mistake was found on an extradition warrant.

At 11.39 a.m. on 29 February 1988, Burns was loading a bomb onto the back of a Talbot van next to a barn in Creggan when it exploded, killing him and Brendan Moley. Inspector Paul Murfitt was among the first on the scene.

> The fragments were so small you couldn't say for certain they were parts of a body. It had almost totally disintegrated. Burns must have been right on top of the bomb. His ribcage had been blown into an adjoining field and it was as if it was part of a carcass that the butcher dealt with; the bones were virtually clean. We found an ear lying by the road and part of a foot but they were the only real indications that the remains were human. There was no blood or intestines. Anything soft or moist had been obliterated.

The next day, as a snowfall held up the clearance operation, wild animals ate much of what was left of Burns's body. Apart from McCreesh and Peadar McIlvenna, an Armagh city man who had been shot dead while on the run, Burns and Moley were the first South Armagh volunteers to die for more than 11 years. The security forces and hardline Unionists were delighted. 'I welcome this own goal,' gloated Sammy Wilson of Ian Paisley's Democratic Unionist Party. 'We don't ask for an inquiry or an explanation, just a repeat performance as soon as possible.' Brendan Moley's body was not found in the follow-up search by the Army but three days later was apparently discovered under a pile of straw in the barn by his brother, Séamus, also a volunteer. The Army and RUC concluded that the body had been taken away after the explosion and returned.

Narrow Water threw the security forces into confusion and drove a wedge between the Army and the RUC. Two days after the attack, Mrs Thatcher, who had been Prime Minister for less than four months, flew to Northern Ireland to be briefed on the security crisis. Brigadier Thorne told her he doubted whether the IRA in South Armagh could be contained if the RUC continued to take the lead role in security matters. Pulling a lieutenant colonel's epaulette from his pocket, he held it up and said: 'Madam Prime Minister, this is all I have left of a very brave officer, David Blair.' Lieutenant General Sir

Timothy Creasey, General Officer Commanding Northern Ireland, told her that cross-border liaison should not be left to the RUC and that internment should be brought back. His staff had prepared a priority list of the names of 20 people who should be arrested and held indefinitely without trial; at the top was Tom Murphy.

But Sir Kenneth Newman, the RUC Chief Constable, was adamant that the policy of 'police primacy' introduced by Merlyn Rees should remain in all areas, including South Armagh. The Army's decision not to travel by road in South Armagh was wrong, he argued, because it gave the IRA too much freedom. At this time, senior Army officers were advocating closing security force bases in Crossmaglen and Forkhill and conducting all operations from Bessbrook; Newman believed this would be disastrous and it was he who won the argument. The RUC retained its primacy although South Armagh remained a 'black' area in which the police could do almost nothing without Army support.

Even more serious than the friction between the RUC and the Army over how to deal with South Armagh after Narrow Water was the rift between the RUC and the Garda Síochána. Liaison between the two forces had always been problematic, and in his report on the Narrow Water attack, Detective Inspector Anderson noted: 'It is a fair assessment of that liaison that the Garda showed a degree of reticence in co-operating with us, at official level anyway . . . at local level with established contacts in Newry RUC Station there appeared to be a more congenial relationship and at least a little more assistance was forthcoming.' The Garda had refused to supply the RUC with a copy of the results of the forensic analysis of what had been found on Burns and Brennan after Narrow Water although this was 'obtained by Newry CID via the unofficial channel previously mentioned'.

Sir John Hermon, who enraged Garret Fitzgerald, the Irish premier, in May 1985 when he stated that the Killeen bomb had emanated from the Republic, said: 'The Republic was very sensitive about having it suggested that anything happened in the South. The Garda did as much as their government allowed them to do.' The Army had established that the Killeen device had been detonated from high ground in the Republic, which overlooked the road where the trailer containing the bomb was parked. In his draft statement to be read at the inquest into the deaths of Constable Doak and her three colleagues, Arthur Orr, the then coroner for South Down, wrote: 'It is clear to me that the device was detonated in the Irish Republic. The fact that no evidence has been forthcoming from the Garda Síochána of any command wire or other detonating device places grave doubts upon the Irish government's sincerity in its claim to have stepped up border security and also upon the undertaking given by the Garda Síochána of co-operation with the Royal Ulster Constabulary and upon the vigilance of its officers and personnel.' Before the inquest, he scored through this section of remarks, perhaps anticipating the political storm they would have caused.

Volunteer G said gardaí would usually apologise to him when he was arrested and they allowed him and other volunteers to make their escape after cross-border gun battles. 'There was one time at Dungooley when two of our lads had been wounded. The guards arrived and said they'd give us an hour to clear the stuff and get out.' When apprehended in the Republic, IRA men were often sentenced to just six months in prison for possession of a weapon. Much to the frustration of British Army officers, the Irish Army has always refused to take part in any scheme of cross-border co-operation. Although some 800 men of the Irish Army's 27th Infantry Battalion at Dundalk would be available for border duties in North Louth, there were no joint operations carried out with the British Army. When Colonel Louis Hogan of the Irish Army was asked in a BBC interview in 1976 whether there should be cross-border co-operation with the British Army, he replied: 'I don't see the point of it. We have a mission to perform, presumably they have a mission as well. What their mission is I don't know and I don't wish to know.'

The Garda would only deal with the British Army through the RUC. This meant that valuable minutes would often be lost as a company commander in Crossmaglen contacted his RUC counterpart to ask him to request that a border crossing point be sealed off by gardaí. While there are arrangements for British Army helicopters to cross the border for a limited distance in certain circumstances, there is no facility for 'hot pursuit' into the Republic by ground troops. On numerous occasions, IRA men were pursued to the border where the British Army stopped and watched them disappear. Captain Nick Lewis, the Coldstream Guards officer who served in South Armagh in 1996, said:

> The IRA in South Armagh will never be defeated militarily while the border is porous for the terrorist and a brick wall for

the security forces. I would like to see cross-border chains of command and two-way hot pursuit. We should be on the same radios as the Garda and the Irish Army and both sides should be able to task the other. It is also pretty frustrating to have Army officers come up with a plan to apprehend a terrorist being made to wait to react to something until the duty RUC constable has made his mind up. The RUC does a great job and many of its officers are of high calibre. But they have the priorities, the sense of urgency and the thought processes of policemen.

Although the Garda delivered a series of blows to the Real IRA in the months before the Omagh bomb in 1998, its stomach for fighting the Provisionals has always been questioned by the security forces in Northern Ireland. An RUC Special Branch officer said: 'After nearly 30 years of protests from the guards that we were asking too much of them on the border, when the BSE crisis came there were suddenly vehicle checkpoints every night of the week and more security than ever before. A very good source who was also a smuggler told us that in the 20 years he had been operating until BSE broke out he had no problem and then suddenly he couldn't move for guards.'

The most serious blow to RUC-Garda relations came on 20 March 1989 when Chief Superintendent Harry Breen, whom the IRA had intended to abduct at Sturgan Brae in 1978, and Superintendent Bob Buchanan were shot dead on the Edenappa Road, near Jonesborough. They were killed a few yards into Northern Ireland in the Gap of the North, where so many English soldiers had perished centuries before. Senior RUC and Garda officers told the author they were certain that information passed by a Garda officer enabled the IRA to ambush them as they returned from a meeting with Chief Superintendent John Nolan at Dundalk Garda Station. The subject of the meeting was Tom Murphy's smuggling activities. Tom King, then Northern Ireland Secretary, had ordered the RUC to investigate how Murphy could be reined in after he had been told in an intelligence briefing that a stream of lorries carrying smuggled grain had been seen driving down Larkins Road by soldiers in Golf Three Zero watchtower at Glasdrumman. 'King had blown a fuse and told Hermon he wanted action taken and that was the reason Harry

Breen was travelling to Dundalk that day,' said an RUC sergeant who was one of the last to see Breen alive. Breen was uneasy about the meeting and had confided to the sergeant that he was concerned about one Garda officer, identified here as 'Garda X', whom RUC Special Branch believed might be working for the IRA.

Breen was head of the RUC's H Division, covering County Down and County Armagh, while Buchanan was in charge of cross-border liaison with the Garda Síochána. The meeting had been arranged by telephone three hours beforehand and scheduled for 2 p.m. Buchanan had been making the journey regularly in his private car, a red Vauxhall Cavalier. RUC officers crossing the border are not permitted to carry weapons for fear of infringing the Republic's firearms laws and the only precaution Buchanan took was to vary his route back across the border between the Edenappa Road and the main A1. On the day they were shot, Buchanan had driven down to Corry Square station in Newry from Glengormley near Belfast and was met there by Breen, who had travelled from Armagh city. Although it is likely that on previous trips Buchanan's registration number had been noted, he had never before left from Newry to go to Dundalk and it is highly unlikely his arrival or departure that day would have been noted by the IRA.

Subsequent events indicated that the IRA must have found out about the visit some time between 11 a.m. and 2 p.m., when the two officers arrived at the station after having driven down the A1 and into the town. At 2.30 p.m., a beige van arrived at the Edenappa Road and stopped outside a derelict house. Two armed IRA men dressed in full combat gear and wearing camouflage cream went into the house. They had chosen a perfect ambush position: in dead ground (an area which cannot be seen) from Romeo Two One watchtower on Jonesborough mountain at a point where the road hit a sharp rise and was sheltered by trees.

An IRA man with a CB radio was watching the two officers as they left Dundalk Garda Station at 3.35 p.m., drove through the town and turned onto the Edenappa Road. A beige van, which was in CB radio contact with one IRA team at the derelict house and another at a point near the A1, was waiting at the junction and fell in behind Buchanan's Cavalier at 3.45 p.m. The IRA was taking no chances and the car would have been ambushed whichever route it had taken. As Buchanan, who was a slow driver, headed north, the two gunmen at the derelict received a radio message from the beige van that the policemen had chosen the Edenappa Road and would be arriving at the ambush point in a few minutes. The two gunmen then stopped three cars travelling south towards Dundalk and ordered the occupants to get out and lie face down on the grass verge. They were careful to leave the cars on the road so that there was space for only one vehicle to get past.

Seeing men in combat gear ahead, Buchanan began to brake, thinking he had reached an Army checkpoint. As he did so, the beige van overtook them and stopped in the space next to the three cars so that the road ahead was blocked. The back doors of the van burst open and four IRA men in combat gear jumped out and opened fire with Armalites and an AKM assault rifle. Buchanan slammed the gearstick into reverse but he was hit in the head with a 7.62 mm bullet and the car skidded and crashed into a dry stone wall; his right foot was still pushed down on the accelerator when he was later pronounced dead. Breen grabbed the hand microphone attached to a radio transceiver in the glove compartment but then dropped it when he realised it was too late to summon help. Already wounded, he staggered out of the passenger seat and waved a white handkerchief as one of the gunmen walked up to him and shot him in the head with a Ruger pistol, blowing off the top of his skull. The gunman then leaned through the open passenger door and fired another shot into the head of Buchanan's body, which was still strapped into the driver's seat. Before the gunmen fled back across the border, they pulled out the pockets of the dead officers, taking wallets and diaries, and removed their briefcases from the boot, which they unlocked with the ignition key.

Within two days, RUC CID investigators had concluded that Buchanan's visits to Dundalk had been noted previously and an ambush planned with meticulous care. The 10 or 15 IRA men involved had almost certainly been placed on standby but it had not been known Buchanan was planning to travel that day and the volunteers who took up position at the derelict would have needed at least an hour's notice to do so. Analysis of video footage from cameras outside Newry station and along the A1 all but ruled out the possibility that IRA dickers had monitored the car on its way to Dundalk. There was also technical information which confirmed that the IRA had been contacted by someone within Dundalk station. RUC Special Branch then received intelligence that a Garda officer had telephoned an IRA member to tip him off. This sequence of events was confirmed by Detective Inspector L, a former member of Garda Special Branch, who said: 'I'm afraid the leak came from a guard. Bob Buchanan was a lovely, lovely man and those murders were an absolute tragedy. The fact that one of my colleagues was involved made the whole thing tens times worse.'

The implications of two senior RUC men being set up by a member of the Garda Síochána who was in league with the IRA were far-reaching and Sir John Hermon, the RUC Chief Constable, took immediate steps to quash speculation about the matter. 'We can categorically deny the betrayal of these officers from within the Irish police,' he said at a press conference the following day. Hermon, however, had not received a full briefing from his CID officers beforehand. Years later, he blamed Buchanan's belief in predestination for his failure to take basic security measures; the superintendent had been a lay preacher and member of the Reformed Presbyterian Church. 'The reason they died was so simple,' he said. 'There was no advance preparation, they just went. Bob Buchanan was a very devout Christian and he did not believe in taking precautions because God was in control. He did not follow basic, elementary security procedures. I still don't understand why no one spotted he was going down there so casually. By the time they left Dundalk, the place was swarming with IRA men and there was no way they were going to get back.' An RUC Special Branch officer, who was able to name the Garda officer who had told the IRA about the meeting, said: 'Hermon stamped on that story but it was blatantly true. [Garda X] was a well-known republican sympathiser. The question is: what else did he tell the IRA?' Garda X was later involved in laundering money for the IRA but fell out of favour after being accused of creaming off part of the profits.

The RUC believed the ambush of Breen and Buchanan had been conceived, planned and led by the Surgeon, the young OC of the South Armagh Brigade whose clinical and ruthless approach inspired fear among his own volunteers as well as members of the security forces. He had not been seen between 10.35 a.m. the day before the ambush and 12.33 p.m. two days later. Although just 27, he was already an IRA veteran. Ten years earlier, he had taken part in his first major IRA operation when he had been one of the two dozen volunteers who loaded the explosives for the Narrow Water attack. By 1998, RUC

Special Branch estimated that the Surgeon had been at least partly responsible for the deaths of up to 70 people. Another volunteer was believed to have taken part in the Kingsmills massacre in 1976, the Narrow Water attack in 1979 and the Omagh bombing in 1998. This meant he had been involved in killing 57 people in just three incidents.

Although arrested a dozen times under anti-terrorist legislation and charged twice, the Surgeon has never been convicted of a criminal offence. His first arrest was on 19 October 1981 when he was questioned about the kidnapping of Ben Dunne, the heir to the Dunnes supermarket chain, three days earlier as he drove to Newry to open a new store. Dunne's black Mercedes 500 had been blocked at Killeen; four masked men placed a hood on his head and bundled him into a car hijacked earlier on the Concession Road in Cullaville. While the Surgeon was in custody, RUC Special Branch received information that a ransom of £500,000 had been handed over in Crossmaglen. On 22 October, Dunne was released outside St Michael's Church in Cullyhanna.

A year later, the Surgeon married Annette, the daughter of a Scottish policeman who had moved to South Armagh to take up a job as a primary school teacher. They set up home first in Jonesborough and later in Drumintee, where they now live with their two sons. The Surgeon runs the family farm complex in Jonesborough and when not engaged on IRA business spends his time tending his sheep and cattle. Following a reorganisation of IRA units in South Armagh in 1983, the Surgeon was appointed OC of the North Louth-Camlough unit. After he was arrested that November, *An Phoblacht*, the republican movement's newspaper, reported that it was the fifth time in two years that the 21-year-old had been taken into custody: 'Last year he was held for five weeks in Crumlin Road jail on trumped-up charges of possession, charges which a judge was forced to throw out of court.'

At 1.35 p.m. on 31 January 1984, Sergeant William Savage and Constable Thomas Bingham were killed when their armoured Talbot Horizon was blown off the road as they drove between Drumintee and Meigh. The bomb had been detonated by command wire from a firing point 700 yards from the Surgeon's house where, according to his wife, he had been working at the time of the explosion. Army investigators found that the command wire, 670 yards of flex, had been dug into a field using a turf cutter and then inserted into a narrow groove in the road which had then been covered by tarmac laid by the District Council. The RUC identified an IRA member who worked as a council labourer as the person who had supervised this. A hedge had been trimmed to provide a clear line of sight to the top of a gate, which was used as a marker.

The investigation report noted that 'a high degree of accuracy was displayed by the firer of the bomb' and that this split-second timing against a moving target 'argues an experienced and steady bomber'. It concluded:

> This bears many similarities to the Sturgan Brae attack (23 May 83) when a similar device narrowly missed its target . . . That last attack was attributed to [the Surgeon] and members of the North Louth-Camlough PIRA. Given the style of the attack, and the assessment that [the Surgeon] needed a successful attack to hold his authority over his newly-formed grouping, it seems probable that this attack should be attributed to the same team . . . it emphasises the danger of regular vehicle movement in South Armagh, whether by covert vehicle or not. Very little could have been done to prevent this attack, which has blooded the new North Louth-Camlough grouping.

The Surgeon was absent when the Army and RUC went to his home to arrest him but his wife was noted as being friendly and offered the soldiers cups of tea. He was eventually arrested on 26 February and held in Gough barracks but he refused to answer any questions about the landmine attack during seven days of interrogation and was released without charge.

Another Drumintee man, Paul Hughes, who is closely related to the Surgeon, was arrested in woods on the Dutch-Belgian border in June 1990 and charged with the murder of Nick Spanos and Stephen Melrose, two Australian tourists mistaken for off-duty British soldiers, in Roermond in Holland the previous month. He was acquitted and extradited to Germany where he was charged with the murder of Major Michael Dillon-Lee, who had been shot dead a fortnight before Hughes and his alleged comrades Donna Maguire, Gerard Harte and Sean Hick had been arrested. All four were acquitted but Judge Wolfgang Steffen said: 'It is clear they are members of the IRA and trained as IRA volunteers. It is also clear they were members of an active service unit.' On the final day of his trial in Holland, Paul Hughes had told the court that it was inexcusable for a 'liberation army' to make mistakes. 'All death is regrettable but civilian death is even more horrific,' he said. The AK-47 assault rifle used to shoot Dillon-Lee had also fired the bullets which killed Mick Islania, an RAF corporal, and his six-month-old daughter in Wildenrath in Germany in October 1989.

One of the key areas within the Surgeon's domain was 'bomb alley' – the three-mile stretch of the A1 between Cloghogue and Killeen which had claimed the lives of 24 people between 1971 and 1992. The victims of IRA operations masterminded by the Surgeon and carried out there included: Constable Doak and her three colleagues killed in the Killeen bomb in May 1985; Lord Justice Sir Maurice Gibson and his wife Cecily, blown up in April 1987; three members of the Hanna family, blown up in July 1988; and Detective Constable Louis Robinson, abducted and shot in September 1990. As well as his own men from Jonesborough and Drumintee, the Surgeon would often also bring in members of Len 'Hardbap' Hardy's Newry unit for attacks close to the A1. Like Paul Hughes, Hardy had been active during the IRA's continental campaign; after being arrested in July 1989 with Donna Maguire, whom he later married, he was sentenced to five years for possession of explosives.

By the mid-1980s, the Customs post at Killeen had long since been shifted five miles north into Newry; instead, patched tarmac and trees scarred by bomb blasts marked the frontier. Army patrols only ventured into this no-man's-land after carrying out a detailed reconnaissance and with helicopter support. For the IRA, there was great symbolism in controlling the road linking the two seats of power based in Belfast and Dublin. Killeen was also the spot where the occasional extraditions of IRA suspects from the Republic to Northern Ireland took place. Successful attacks mounted there, moreover, invariably soured relations between the British and Irish authorities. For the same reason, up to the 1980s the South Armagh Brigade regularly bombed the Belfast-to-Dublin railway line, which passes through the Ring of Gullion and the Gap of the North. The Gap, as Frank Aiken had found in the 1920s, was also ideal for mounting train robberies. Frank Keating, a sports journalist, took the train south to watch the Ulster team play Australia in 1984. 'At the border, the train was ambushed by the IRA, balaclavas and sten-guns,' he recalled in an article 15 years later. 'They axed open the mail van and stole a cache of used banknotes. Then they allowed us to proceed. The rule seemed to be: if raided thus, the buffet-bar was open and gratis to all for the remainder of the trip. We all rolled into Dublin, scared no longer and blind drunk – on miniatures.'

Three years later, Nigel Carr, David Irwin and Philip Rainey, members of the Ulster team which had played against Australia that day, were injured at Killeen when a Ford Escort was blown up as they drove down the A1 for a training session in Dublin with the national side. Lord Justice and Lady Gibson, the occupants of the Escort, were killed and their bodies burned out of recognition when the vehicle burst into flames. One of the main factors in their deaths was Lord Justice Gibson's disregard for basic security procedures. Despite being a prime IRA target whose house was guarded around the clock by RUC officers, he had booked his Devon holiday and made his ferry reservation using his own name and title along with a description of his car and its registration. The elderly judge had insisted on returning to Ireland on the Liverpool-to-Dun Laoghaire ferry because he and his wife wanted to attend a Gang Show at the Grand Opera House in Belfast that night; catching a ferry to Northern Ireland would have meant they would arrive too late. They were accompanied by a Garda car as they drove north but followed by the IRA en route and details of their progress telephoned and radioed ahead to the South Armagh Brigade.

Shortly before 8.30 a.m., the Gibsons reached the border and were left by the Garda car to drive the three miles to Romeo One Five, the Cloghogue checkpoint. Less than a mile into Northern Ireland, a 500 lb car bomb packed into a blue Ford Cortina stolen in Jonesbor-ough a month earlier was detonated by radio control from a point 150 yards to the west of the road using a telegraph pole as a marker. The device was believed to have been made by Brendan Burns. Although the car would normally have been seen by soldiers in Romeo One Four watchtower on Cloghogue mountain, visibility was limited because of a heat haze. This, coupled with the fact that the bomb had been driven into position only a short time before the Gibsons crossed the border, made it a comparatively easy attack to mount. As a result, a 'Control Zone' between the border and

Cloghogue was declared, within which it was forbidden to leave a vehicle unattended.

A little over a year later, the IRA struck again barely 200 yards from the same spot, once more taking advantage of the weather conditions to plant a bomb. At 5.50 a.m. on 23 July 1988, soldiers in the Cloghogue mountain watchtower reported a car stopping close to the road just north of the border; a man was seen to get out, do something by the roadside and then drive away five minutes later. Low cloud and poor light meant that neither the type of car nor its registration number could be seen. Shortly beforehand, a brown Ford Cortina, driven by an IRA man from Bessbrook, had been sighted by a patrol in Drumintee. At 9.15 a.m., a 12-man Royal Welsh Fusiliers patrol was sent out from the Cloghogue checkpoint, to investigate the suspicious activity. Fifty-seven minutes later, when the patrol was 150 yards from the point where the unknown car had stopped, there was a massive explosion. A passing silver and metallic blue Mitsubishi Shogun jeep was virtually destroyed and its occupants, Robin Hanna, a heating contractor from Hillsborough in County Down, his wife Maureen and their six-year-old son, David, blown to pieces. A 1,300 lb bomb had been packed behind a wall next to a derelict cottage and detonated by radio control. It had been placed there to kill Mr Justice Ian Higgins who was due to cross the border in a silver Nissan Sunny at the same time.

The fact that the judge's car was completely different from that of the Hannas indicated that the IRA volunteer standing to the east of the road had probably set off the device after panicking when he saw the Fusiliers approaching. Both the Hanna and Higgins families had travelled on the same flight from Florida to Dublin and it was also possible a mistake in identifying the correct car had been made. The Higgins family had been due to be escorted across the border by a Gazelle helicopter flying overhead but had been held back by gardaí in Dundalk while their route was checked. The Hannas were literally blown to pieces and had to be identified from passports and their holiday photographs taken in Disneyland a few days earlier. In a field next to the A1, search teams found Mrs Hanna's left foot, the toenails painted with red nail varnish. Her son's right hand and forearm and her husband's left foot, still wearing a Reebok trainer, were lying nearby. When the Surgeon was arrested in November 1988 and questioned about the murder of the Hannas, he once again remained silent.

The limitations of the Cloghogue checkpoint and the watchtower on the mountain above it were again illustrated in September 1990 when a white Mercedes van containing five prison officers and Detective Constable Robinson slowed down just north of the border when they saw what appeared to be a military checkpoint. The group had just spent a week on a fishing trip in Dingle in County Kerry and, in contravention of security guidelines, had used a van registered to the Maze Social Club. Soldiers manning the Cloghogue mountain watchtower could not see what was happening because their view was obscured by McKevitt's BP garage and a hedge. As they slowed down, the occupants of the van discussed whether it was a British or Irish Army checkpoint. 'It must be Irish Army, he's got an old Armalite,' said Ernie Crawford. The 6-ft-tall figure who stopped the van was dressed in smart combat uniform, camouflage cream and light brown beret. He spoke with an English accent and asked the driver, Sam Humphries, where they were coming from. 'Dingle Bay,' Humphries replied. 'We were fishing. Do you want some?'

The van doors were then pulled open and there were shouts of 'Get out' and 'On the ground you bastards' as six or seven gunmen wearing balaclavas appeared. Realising they had driven into an IRA roadblock, James Girvan pushed one of the gunmen, knocking him off balance, and he and Ferguson jumped out. A shot was fired as the pair ran away and flagged down a car to take them to the Cloghogue checkpoint to raise the alarm. Ernie Crawford was left with the van as the three men with beards – Robinson, Humphries and Harold McClurg – were each ordered into the boot of a car and driven away. Robinson and Humphries were in the boot of the same car and at one stage the detective managed to pop it open. The car halted abruptly and the two captives were told they would be 'blown away' if they tried to open the boot again. Half an hour later, the car stopped once more and Robinson was thrown a hood to put on before being led away.

McClurg was pulled out of the other car, a seat cover placed over his head and he was spread-eagled in a field. With a gun pushed against his temple, he was asked his name and occupation. 'Harold McClurg and I am a fitter by trade,' he replied. 'We'll try again,' said the IRA man, believed by the RUC to have been the Surgeon. 'What do you work at? You could die tonight.' McClurg said in a statement afterwards:

When he said that there, I thought he knew what I worked at and I said I was a prison officer at the Maze. He replied: 'You're the black bastard [policeman] we're after, you're Louis Robinson.' I heard another commotion and someone being dumped on the ground close to me, to my right. He seemed to be getting a battering. I heard him speak and it sounded like Louis. He told them he was a painter and decorator and that he wasn't working at the moment . . . He was asked for a telephone number to contact his wife. He told them he was separated. They asked about kids and he said there would be nobody home. The reply they made was: 'That's fucking convenient.' The man then said that one or possibly two was going to die tonight and I'd better tell the truth. He then said: 'I think you're the black bastard.' I replied: 'I'm not in the RUC, I'm a prison officer, I'm a prison officer.' I think I was stood up and moved about five to six yards from where I was lying. The same boy that done all the talking to me came back to me again and asked me for my home telephone number. I told them my wife was deaf and it would be one of my kids that would answer the phone. I think at this stage he called me Harold and told me that I was going to be taken back to where I had come from, that they were sparing my life because they had no grudge against prison officers in the Maze but a few would be dealt with in the Crum [Crumlin Road jail]. Another person then said to me that if he had anything to do with it he'd blow me away now. They undone my wrists. I was still on the ground and one of these men stood on my right arm which had a tattoo of an Ulster flag on it.

A few minutes after Robinson had been taken from the car boot, Humphries was dragged out. Humphries said:

I was asked who I was. He said: 'You are Louis the policeman. That other man says you're the policeman.' He then asked me was the fellow Louis who was in the boot with me the policeman. I said he was. He then asked me what rank the policeman was and I said I didn't know. He then punched me violently in the stomach and repeated the question. I said again that I didn't know his rank.

McClurg was put in the boot with Humphries and the two prison officers were driven to a priest's house in Belleek and dumped on the road. 'Harold McClurg, you're a lucky man,' said the volunteer who had interrogated him earlier. 'You are going to live and see your wife and kids. If you're ever in the Crum, don't be beating up our men.' The pair were then kicked in the stomach and chest, Humphries sustaining two broken ribs, before the car drove away.

Two days later, Robinson's body was found lying on a farm track off the Foxfield Road in Crossmaglen. He had been shot three times in the head with a .38 Webley pistol and his mud-caked socks showed he had been forced to walk the last few yards to his death. His hands had been tied in front of him with baling twine and a bag placed over his head. There were marks on his face and bruising to his chest, apparently from punches. It later emerged that Robinson, a CID officer nicknamed 'Louis the Lip' and based at Belfast's Mountpottinger station in the unit which looked after supergrass witnesses, had been introducing himself as 'Detective Inspector Robinson' in a bar in Dingle. If the IRA had known he was a mere constable it is unlikely such a complex operation to abduct him would have been mounted. Robinson was a heavy drinker who suffered from stress and depression and had been off work for the best part of two years. Before his body had been found, his wife Anne had pleaded with the IRA to release him because he needed to take his tablets for high blood pressure and rheumatism.

The man who could have put the Surgeon's IRA career on hold for ten years – and possibly saved the lives of the Gibsons, the Hannas and Robinson in the process – was Eamon Collins. After taking part in a series of IRA operations in Newry that had gone wrong, Collins, weighed down with family pressures, was becoming increasingly disillusioned with the republican movement. At 6.37 p.m. on 28 February 1985, just after he finished his shift at Newry Customs and Excise office, he heard a series of explosions in quick succession. The IRA was firing nine Mark 10 mortar bombs at the RUC's Corry Road station from a range of 190 yards; eight overshot the station but the ninth scored a direct hit on a portakabin housing a temporary canteen, killing nine officers. It was the largest number of RUC officers killed by the IRA during the Troubles but only the first time in 89 mortar attacks that more than a single casualty had been inflicted.

Among those killed was Chief Inspector Alex Donaldson, the

brother of Constable Sam Donaldson who had been blown up outside Crossmaglen in August 1970; their cousin, Jeffrey Donaldson, later became an Ulster Unionist MP. Hitting the canteen had been a stroke of good fortune for the IRA, although had the firing point, known as the mortar 'baseplate', been 40 yards further away six bombs would have landed in the station itself, causing substantially more casualties. The attack had been led by the Surgeon and carried out jointly by the South Armagh Brigade and Hardy's Newry unit.

The South Armagh Brigade had developed an unparalleled proficiency in mortars over the years since one was first used in the area against Crossmaglen security force base in 1974. Most of the ten mortar variants identified by the security forces up to 1985 and the eight identified afterwards were built and fired for the first time in South Armagh. An intelligence report written in 1985 noted: 'XMG PIRA have a considerable amount of mortar attack expertise. They are known to "export" their knowledge and expertise throughout N. Ireland.' The Newry mortar attack was launched from the back of a red Ford flatbed lorry which had been hijacked by two gunmen at Drummuckavall around 1 p.m. that day. A volunteer had driven it into the town, slipping on a Ronald Reagan mask as he crashed through a set of locked gates and parked it on waste ground, using the radio mast above the Corry Square station for alignment. On the back of the lorry, concealed underneath a plastic tarpaulin and between wooden pallets, were nine mortar tubes, each containing a gas cylinder packed with 45 lbs of homemade explosives.

The only tell-tale mark which could have been detected as the lorry drove through the town was a pipe punched into the back of the lorry cab to carry wires from their firing mechanism to the mortar frame, which had been bolted to the back. As with other Mark 10 attacks, the mortars were launched in a ripple one after another to prevent the frame buckling. The propellant used was a black powder mix, a combination of potassium nitrate and sulphur, which had been tested in a single-tube Mark 10 attack on Crossmaglen security force base in November 1984, also from 190 yards away, which had probably been a practice firing for the Newry attack. The use of black powder made it possible to calculate the range more accurately.

Collins was arrested the night of the Newry attack and, under intense pressure on the sixth day of his interrogation at Gough barracks, agreed to make a statement. Among the 20 men he implicated in IRA activities was the Surgeon, who was arrested and charged with conspiracy to murder members of the security forces and IRA membership. But the RUC's euphoria at having the Surgeon behind bars and a new supergrass on their books was short-lived. After his wife Bernie pleaded with him not to betray his comrades, Collins withdrew his statement and the Surgeon was released; charges against all the other suspects, apart from those who had incriminated themselves by making admissions, were dropped. A military intelligence report written at the time noted: 'The deaths of nine RUC officers in one fell swoop was of immense propaganda value to them. The Newry supergrass Eamon Collins, who was arrested after the attack, has since retracted his statement of evidence – cause for more jubilation within the PIRA ranks.'

Collins himself was eventually freed after Mr Justice Higgins – the IRA's target in the attack which killed the Hanna family – ruled that there was a possibility he had been assaulted while in custody. But Collins was a marked man and, after a terrifying 'debriefing' by members of the IRA's 'internal security' squad, was ordered to leave Newry in disgrace and live south of Drogheda. It was this treatment which caused him to turn against the Provisionals.

Despite his break with the IRA, when discussing Tom Murphy and other senior IRA men, Collins continued to refer to them in admiring terms. The Undertaker, he said, was 'a very tough, resilient man, extremely shrewd, a good soldier and, like the Murphys, a dedicated patriot and a great businessman'. He added: 'In different circumstances, they could have been fucking diplomats.' Describing the Surgeon, he said:

> He is really dedicated. Very nice, very plausible, very careful. Will not let you know anything that you shouldn't know. Not a fucking chance. And he was brave. If he was in the British Army he would be rated as a first class soldier. People like him would be what the British Army would say is SAS material, top soldier gear. Apart from that, I would say that he would have given me the benefit of the doubt and mercy when others wouldn't.

The Surgeon had trusted him, he said, and had gone ahead with future operations which Collins had been involved in planning because he knew that he would have remained silent about them. One of these was the Killeen bomb which killed Constable Tracy Doak and her colleagues in May 1985. Shortly before his death, Collins revealed that he had come up with the original idea for the Killeen attack and had begun to plan it with the Surgeon. 'If I had remained in the IRA I would have finished with Newry and I would have operated with [the Surgeon], that's for sure. I had the brains to get really good operations and I had a good intelligence network built up and he had the whole machinery and access to the equipment and the manpower to carry them out. We would have been devastating.'

More than 15 years after the Narrow Water massacre, its legacy continued to cast a shadow over RUC-Garda relations. In 1994, when Joe Brennan was convicted of taking part in a mortar attack on Golf Three Zero watchtower at Glasdrumman, the RUC re-opened the inquiry with a view to charging him with the murder of the 18 soldiers. But it transpired that the motorcycle used by Burns and Brennan had been thrown on a skip during a clear-out at Dundalk Garda Station and that the cigarette butt found at the firing point — which could have been tested for DNA — had been destroyed. 'It beggars belief that that sort of vital evidence in such a significant case could be disposed of,' said a senior RUC officer. There was also criticism from within the RUC of the Director of Public Prosecutions in Northern Ireland when he decided not to prosecute Brennan even though, the loss of the Garda evidence notwithstanding, there was a powerful case against him. The IRA ceasefire had just been declared and there were suspicions that it had been judged that it would not have been politic to have revisited Narrow Water.

Concerns about individual Garda officers also lingered. In 1998, one serving and one retired sergeant were arrested on suspicion of helping the IRA to acquire at least six false passports; one had previously been based at Hackballscross and the other had served in Dundalk. They were both released without charge and a file sent to the Director of Public Prosecutions in Dublin. Although the political agenda in Northern Ireland was often dominated by allegations of 'collusion' between the British security forces and loyalist paramilitaries, discussion of links between the Garda Síochána and the IRA remained strictly off limits.

Chapter 7

Arms and the Man

'The incident at Slab Murphy's has implications for cross-border security. No effort was made by gardai to search Slab Murphy's barns . . . It appeared that they were intimidated by the presence of the Murphys.'
(Army incident report, 1986)

'At the preparatory meetings with Tom, the latter insisted I should buy a German Shepherd dog and offer it to Nasser from Joe Cahill.'
(Adrian Hopkins on Tom Murphy's preparations for shipping arms from Libya, 1987)

T he Irish Sea lapped around Tom Murphy's knees as he waded out in the moonlight towards a rubber dinghy, its outboard engine idling in the water, and held out his arms for the gift he and the IRA had long dreamed of. On the wooden box he was handed, the words 'Libyan Armed Forces' were stencilled in black lettering; inside were four Russian AK-47 assault rifles. Out in the bay off Clogga Strand on the County Wicklow coast was moored the *Casamara*, a British-registered 65-ft yacht. She had sailed from Malta a few days earlier on 6 August 1985 and taken on a deadly 10-ton cargo during a rendezvous with the Libyan ship *Samra Africa* off the island of Gozo.

It was the first of four arms shipments with a cargo courtesy of the Libyan government to be landed by Murphy in Ireland. On board the *Casamara* as it dropped its anchor were 300 boxes of weaponry including AK-47s, Taurus automatic pistols from Brazil, seven Soviet-made RPG-7s and three Russian DShK 12.7 mm heavy machine-guns. Murphy had driven down the beach on a tractor to supervise the unloading along with Kevin McKenna, the IRA's Chief of Staff; such was their eagerness to get their hands on the weapons that they rolled up their sleeves and helped the young volunteers load the boxes onto the trailer they had brought. Within a few hours, the consignment had been landed, broken up into lorryloads and transported to farmhouses and underground hides throughout Ireland.

By 1985, Murphy had been appointed to the IRA's GHQ Staff and his training in Libya in the mid-1970s made him a logical choice to oversee the delivery of arms from Tripoli. He was re-introduced to the Libyans by Joe Cahill, a former IRA Chief of Staff who had won a reprieve after being sentenced to hang for the murder of a policeman in 1942. He had been convicted of running guns from Libya in 1973 and had assumed overall control of the IRA's finances after his release from jail. Murphy's main contact was Nasser Ashur, who had been sent to London by Colonel Gaddafi in April 1984 after WPC Yvonne Fletcher had been shot dead outside the Libyan embassy. Although ostensibly a diplomat working to rebuild relations with the British government, Ashur was also a high-ranking Libyan intelligence officer whom Gaddafi had tasked with re-establishing contact with the IRA.

Adrian Hopkins, who was employed by Murphy as skipper for all four voyages, later described Ashur in a statement to the French police: 'He spoke English with a very distinguished accent. He never looked you in the face, likes to parade, has small feet, wears Italian shoes, drinks whisky but does not smoke.' On one occasion, the Libyan offered Hopkins a box of grenades as a present. Ashur and Murphy must have made an unlikely pair but they agreed to do business. Hopkins also 'met two other individuals in a house in Northern Ireland', according to his statement. 'The names of the latter are Tom [Murphy] and Kevin [McKenna]. Tom is tall, about 1.85m, thin but well built, he has a mat complexion and dark hair and has a slight stoop . . . We organised the voyage but I noticed that they had a very poor knowledge of geography. They were not very confiding and refused at that time to tell me where the loading would take place.' Murphy paid Hopkins £100,000 in wads of notes stuffed in plastic bags after the *Casamara*'s cargo was safely landed.

Another shipment, again picking up ten tons of arms off Gozo and ·landing them at Clogga Strand, was arranged for October 1985. This time, Hopkins registered the yacht under the Panamanian flag and renamed her the *Kula*. 'Regarding my second voyage for the PIRA, I was again contacted through [Henry] Cairns [the IRA's go-between] and met Tom and Kevin to finalise details,' said Hopkins. 'I again had the boat brought to Malta . . . For the *Kula* mission I received a total of £100,000 in £20 and £50 notes. This money was handed to me by Tom when I met him in Dundalk. I then deposited it in the Bank of Ireland [in Newry] with instructions to transfer it to my account in Jersey.' Gaddafi's determination to help the IRA's fight against the British state was redoubled when American F-111s based at Upper Heyford in Oxfordshire bombed Tripoli.

Two weeks later, on 28 April 1986, Murphy flew into Athens on a false passport to see three senior IRA men. He met Gabriel Cleary, the IRA's 'director of engineering', James Coll and James Doherty in the lobby of the Hotel Grande Bretagne, where in 1944 Winston Churchill had narrowly escaped being blown up by Greek communists who had planted a ton of TNT in a sewage tunnel. The next day, Murphy flew to meet Ashur. Sitting on a boat off a Greek island, they discussed the third shipment, which was later to be landed at Clogga Strand with a 14-ton cargo which included, at Murphy's request, two Russian-made SAM-7 missiles.

The fourth shipment was to be the biggest arms consignment ever landed by the IRA. At the beginning of October 1986, 30 Libyans took two nights to load the *Villa*, a converted Swedish oil rig replenisher, with 80 tons of arms including seven RPG-7s, 10 SAM-7s and a ton of Semtex-H, a Czech-made plastic explosive. Before the collapse of the communist regime in Czechoslovakia, more than 1,000 tons of Semtex, a brown, putty-like substance, were exported to Libya. Manufactured at Pardubice, 90 miles from Prague, it is odourless and cannot be detected by X-rays. Semtex will not explode even when exposed to a naked flame but when used with a detonator can produce a blast many times more powerful than a fertiliser-based explosive. Since late 1986, virtually every bomb, rocket and mortar made by the IRA has incorporated Semtex brought into Ireland on board the *Villa*.

The estimated 650 AK-47 assault rifles landed in the four shipments also continued to be used right up to the end of the
millennium. Invented in the Soviet Union by Mikhail Kalashnikov
in 1947, the AK-47, which has a distinctive banana-shaped magazine,
was first issued to the Red Army and has since been used by guerrilla
organisations throughout the world. Reliable, robust and easy to
keep in working order, it can fire a hundred rounds per minute and is
effective to a range of 300 yards. In the vast majority of IRA
operations since the Libyan shipments, at least one volunteer has
carried an AK-47 or an AKM, the improved and lighter version first
produced in 1959.

The *Villa* was too large to anchor off Clogga Strand so her cargo
was landed instead at Roadstone Pier nearby and tractors lent by
farmers were used to help unload. According to Hopkins:

> The delivery of the load went off smoothly. On land there were
> two trucks which brought the cargo to another place unknown
> to me . . . Tom told me several times that nothing would be
> circulated until we had delivered the whole stock. According to
> conversations I had with Cairns and Cleary, I think they
> envisaged a massive attack in South Armagh and on Long
> Kesh [the Maze] prison. I received $500,000 given to me in the
> White Horse pub in north Dublin.

In 1986, Murphy made at least seven trips to the Mediterranean to
meet Libyan officials. The fifth shipment was to be even bigger and
Murphy was keen to show the IRA's gratitude. 'At the preparatory
meetings with Tom, the latter insisted I should buy a German
Shepherd dog and offer it to Nasser from Joe Cahill,' Hopkins told
the French police. In September 1987, Hopkins sent a telex to the
Maltese veterinary authorities. 'I wish to have a dog transferred from
a reputable kennels in Germany to a Panamanian-registered vessel
presently being repaired in Malta,' it said. 'This vessel will depart for
various African ports about 19 September. I wish the dog to be
despatched by air from Frankfurt on 17 September to a quarantine
kennels in Malta and from there transferred direct to the vessel
immediately before she sails.' Murphy also authorised the purchase of
a double bed, a large clock and two cans of olive oil, which were

picked up at a factory near Valetta, as gifts for Nasser. The gifts, including the dog, were transported to Tripoli on board the *Eksund*, an ageing 237-ton freighter which Hopkins had fitted with a crane on deck.

Fifty Libyan soldiers were on the jetty at Tripoli to help load 130 tons of weaponry over two nights. Hopkins later recalled: 'According to the agreed code, I transmitted a message to Tom via a shipping company . . . in London. I used the codeword Stockholm which indicated the unloading date, October 29th 1987.' Murphy had been given the codename Halliday. But as the *Eksund* left Libya, she was already being monitored by MI6 and the French intelligence services and tracked by a Royal Navy hunter-killer submarine. When the crew saw a spotter plane overhead as the vessel was five miles off Roscoff, Hopkins sent the following message to Murphy: 'Pender to Halliday. The unloading of cargo date plus 17.' This told him that the *Eksund* and its cargo were about to be scuttled. By the time French customs officers had clambered on board, the vessel's forward ballast tanks had already been filled with water and she was beginning to sink from the bows. The crew were wearing diving suits and preparing to climb into dinghies.

Two tons of Semtex, a thousand Romanian-made AK-47s, a thousand mortars, 600 Soviet F1 grenades, 120 RPG-7s, 20 SAM-7s, 10 DShKs, two thousand electric detonators, 4,700 fuses and more than a million rounds of ammunition were found in the *Eksund*'s hold. Hopkins, Doherty, Coll, Cairns and Cleary were all arrested and later jailed but Murphy remained at large. On 28 May 1989, he flew into Split in Yugoslavia to meet Ashur once again to discuss further shipments; he is also believed to have travelled to Eastern Europe on arms-buying missions.

The Libyan shipments transformed the fortunes of the IRA and Murphy's role won him promotion to the IRA's Army Council, where there was now an increasingly clear division between Gerry Adams and Martin McGuinness, who favoured the dual strategy of the Armalite and the ballot box, and out-an-out militarists like McKenna and Murphy who feared Sinn Féin was diverting valuable resources from the IRA.

McKenna had lived in Smithborough in County Monaghan since fleeing from his native Tyrone after shooting dead Francis Caddoo, an off-duty UDR man, at Aughnacloy in May 1973. He would often meet Murphy to discuss IRA matters during cockfights or games of road bowls at Hackballscross, a crossroads near Ballybinaby named after a Paddy Hackball who had once owned a pub there. Vincent McKenna, an East Tyrone volunteer who was based in Monaghan in the 1980s, remembers meeting Tom Murphy and his brother Patrick before the funeral of Seamus McElwaine in Scotstown in County Monaghan in April 1986. McElwaine, one of the Maze escapers who had found sanctuary in South Armagh in 1983, had been shot dead by the SAS while planting an 800 lb culvert bomb near Rosslea in County Fermanagh. 'Everybody was at McElwaine's funeral and everybody with status was at the family house,' said Vincent McKenna. 'Adams, McGuinness, the whole IRA command staff was there. I came out of the house about midday and Jim Lynagh and Kevin McKenna were standing talking to a man beside the garage.' Lynagh, a senior IRA man who had just been released from Portlaoise jail, was later among the eight volunteers and a civilian shot dead in an SAS ambush at Loughgall in County Armagh the following year. Vincent McKenna said:

> After they'd finished talking, Jim asked me if I knew who the person was. I said I didn't and he told me he was Tom 'Slab' Murphy. I had heard Kevin McKenna mention his name before when we were talking in the Sinn Féin office in Monaghan. I knew Tom was a big player, major league status and that he was on equal terms with Kevin. Tom seemed to have an established authority. He spoke in a very slow country-type manner and was saying that this would need to be done this way and this was the way forward. Lynagh was in desperate need of commercial explosives. Kevin would have been saying there was a need for 'stuff' — explosives — to be brought in and Tom would have been explaining to Kevin the complexities of getting hold of it.

Lynagh was a great admirer of Tom Murphy because he commanded what Lynagh described as a 'liberated zone' in South Armagh. Having studied Mao's writings during his five years in Portlaoise and an earlier spell in the Maze, Lynagh believed that the

IRA's aims could be achieved through the creation of a series of liberated zones which would be secured by attacking remote security force bases in mainly-nationalist areas and then pushing out the few remaining Protestants. Tom Murphy admired Lynagh's military prowess but had little time for his theorising. Vincent McKenna said:

> Jim Lynagh was into Maoism and all that sort of shite because he'd had time to read in jail. The likes of Tom Murphy and Kevin McKenna had probably never read a book in their lives. They were ordinary fellas who left school at 14 with no educational qualifications and learned everything they knew on the ground. There was no big philosophy, no desire to have high-falutin meetings or anything. They looked like farmers tramping about. Kevin saw the politics as a veneer. He would laugh at Adams and say: 'Ah, look at that fucking idiot. Just stick him up on a platform and let him talk, that's all he's good for.' That was the sort of banter there was.

Murphy's attitude was little different. Sean O'Callaghan, head of the IRA's Southern Command from 1984 to 1985, remembers him attending one meeting of the IRA's Revolutionary Council in 1983 and two GHQ Staff meetings the following year. The Revolutionary Council, a republican think tank set up to discuss long-term strategy, was held in a republican home in Charlestown in County Mayo. Like most IRA meetings, it involved people arriving at different times and by different means. The participants would often not know exactly where they were as they would have been picked up and spent the last leg of the journey in the back of a van. Other meetings were held in cars, pubs or under the cover of a Sinn Féin conference. Among those attending the Revolutionary Council meeting were: Adams; McGuinness; Pat Doherty, the IRA's adjutant general and vice-president of Sinn Féin; Danny Morrison, Sinn Féin's director of publicity; and Martin Ferris.

As well as being a senior IRA man, O'Callaghan was an informer who regularly passed information to his Garda handler; the following year, O'Callaghan was responsible for Ferris being arrested on the *Marita Ann*, a trawler loaded with seven tons of American weapons. 'Tom Murphy was there representing South Armagh,' O'Callaghan said. 'I cannot remember him saying anything and he gave the clear impression that he would rather have been in South Armagh than at any meeting.'

One of the GHQ Staff meetings took place at Heath House, a Georgian mansion in County Kildare owned by Uinseann MacEoin, the historian who had worked on Harry White's memoirs. MacEoin had allowed his home to be used by republicans although he was not made aware that an IRA meeting would be held there. Kevin McKenna, as Chief of Staff, was in overall charge and others present included Doherty, McGuinness, Séamus Twomey and Gabriel Cleary. O'Callaghan said:

> Before the meeting, there seemed to be a sort of ritual between Doherty and Murphy where Doherty introduced him by saying: 'So, how are we going to win the war, Tom?' Tom replied: 'We'll bomb them to the conference table and then booby-trap the table.' It was all very jokey and Doherty said: 'What about the Sinn Féin delegation?' Tom came back: 'In South Armagh, we never tell people where we put our booby-traps.' It was all said in jest but it seemed to sum up Murphy's attitude towards the political side of the movement. He left nobody in any doubt that he believed South Armagh was the best area in IRA terms and he was obviously very proud of that.

It was the South Armagh Brigade's very success that had led to moves within the IRA leadership to limit its influence. O'Callaghan recalled attending an IRA meeting in Bundoran in County Donegal in 1980 or 1981:

> At that time the Belfast Brigade was literally paying for the Army Council, GHQ, England and Southern commands, everything except South Armagh which was self-financing because of the money being got from smuggling. The IRA was broke, it was raising £2 million a year and that just about kept its campaign going. Smuggling was in its heyday and one of the big hopes of the meeting was exploiting the huge financial potential in South Armagh.

From this point on, South Armagh began to play a much bigger role in IRA finances. This meant that there was less pressure on Belfast to raise cash and therefore Gerry Adams had the flexibility to divert resources towards electioneering. O'Callaghan said:

> Up to then, South Armagh were quite happy, they didn't give a fuck. They financed themselves, they didn't need any money from anybody but they weren't contributing any money. From the point of view of the IRA leadership, there was always a slight wariness about Tom. There was a lot of money floating around South Armagh and there was a sense that Tom was too parochial. Tom was effectively told by Martin McGuinness to get off his arse, that the IRA wasn't just South Armagh. It wasn't a suspicion that Tom was dishonest, just that personal activities in South Armagh all mixed in with the IRA and the rules of discipline didn't really seem to apply down there. Tom would very quickly excuse the boys getting pissed in Dundalk and fighting with the cops because they were his boys. So by channelling this into helping finance the rest of the IRA, Adams was being clever because he was freeing money for Sinn Féin and reining Tom in at the same time.

By raising more money for the wider movement, Tom Murphy was inadvertently helping to undermine both the military campaign and South Armagh's long-term influence.

As early as 1984, there was concern within the South Armagh Brigade that the IRA was taking a back seat to Sinn Féin for the first time since the formation of the Provisionals. Eamon Collins described how he was summoned to a safe house outside Dundalk to meet the Undertaker and Jim McAllister:

> He [the Undertaker] told me they were worried about the emerging ascendancy of Sinn Féin to the detriment of the army [IRA] and my opposition to this had been noted. He said Sinn Féin was the IRA's Achilles heel and the Adams leadership was either inept or was trying to end the military campaign by stealth. I was to join Newry Sinn Féin immediately and start running it totally to the advantage of the IRA, using it to get recruits and safe

houses and gather intelligence. McAllister told me I would be put
forward as a Sinn Féin candidate for the council elections.

Collins did as he was asked, but his candidature for the elections was
blocked by Sinn Féin in Belfast. Collins said: 'South Armagh was saying
that here was a hardline militarist, somebody who was pretty intelligent
and was capable of arguing the toss with those smart fuckers from
Belfast. That was their attitude. But Belfast was not stupid. They would
have said to themselves that this cunt was going to become a thorn in
their side so they said no.' On another occasion, he said, the Undertaker
'went fucking ape-shit when he found out I was dealing with Belfast
people over safe houses for the "nutting squad" [the South Armagh
Brigade's interrogation unit]. He said to me: "I don't give a fuck who told
you to deal with them: I don't trust them and we're going to do our own
thing."' The suspicion between the Belfast leadership and South
Armagh was mutual. In 1986, Paddy McGrory, Collins's solicitor
and a close friend of Adams, told Collins that he would not be safe
if he returned to Newry after his acquittal. The solicitor said this was
because the Sinn Féin president had told him that South Armagh was 'a
notorious area where they would kill their own granny if they had to'.

Adams's concern about the power of South Armagh mirrored that
of the security forces, which in the mid-1980s launched a two-
pronged strategy to clip Tom Murphy's wings. Mindful that Al
Capone had been jailed not for murder but for tax evasion, the
authorities on both sides of the border began to look at ways of
curbing Murphy's smuggling activities and uncovering irregularities
in his business dealings. At the same time, a direct challenge to the
IRA's freedom to carry out operations was made by Margaret
Thatcher in the form of a multi-million-pound building programme
to establish a ring of military watchtowers.

The 12 Golf and Romeo towers, as the Army calls them, have
become a motif for the Troubles in South Armagh, a symbol of the
area's defiant abnormality. Built as part of a basic military philosophy
similar to that propounded by Mountjoy when he constructed stone
towers in South Armagh nearly 400 years earlier, the watchtowers
were to become the Army's most significant assets in the area. They
have continued to limit severely Tom Murphy's capacity to mount
attacks in much of his domain. But for the local population, they are

manifestations of imperialist oppression which have which helped to reduce to almost nil what little tolerance there was of British rule.

In 1986, Lieutenant Colonel Tim Spicer, whose activities as a 'military consultant' in Papua New Guinea and Sierra Leone were to prompt controversy a decade later, was a major and company commander of the Scots Guards in Crossmaglen. 'Before the towers went in they almost had complete freedom of movement and could pick the time and the place,' he said. 'They had a number of aces in their hand, and our intention was to try to take the initiative from them through total surveillance combined with unpredictable patrols.' Spicer's job was to oversee Operation Condor and Operation Magistrate, the codenames given to the massive troop movements needed to bring in the raw materials and equipment to construct the watchtowers. These operations, which were later repeated periodically when the watchtowers or bases were strengthened and upgraded, involved extra battalions of troops effectively closing down South Armagh to the IRA for weeks on end.

Operation Rectify, the rebuilding of Crossmaglen security force base beginning in April 1994, involved the largest British air-mobile operation since D-Day. More than a thousand troops descended on the town and 1,400 tonnes of building supplies were moved by the Royal Logistics Corps in huge vehicle convoys along secured routes; another 30 tonnes of equipment were moved by air. The work on the base was carried out by 180 Royal Engineers using 39 pieces of heavy plant, including seven cranes which were double-crewed to enable work to continue 24 hours a day. There were five IRA attacks within the 10 weeks it took to rebuild the base; on one occasion, a sapper was injured by a mortar bomb but work was underway again within two hours.

Starting as little more than huts perched on flimsy scaffolding structures, the watchtowers developed into much more substantial installations housing sophisticated equipment such as video and still cameras, computers, telescopes, communications aerials and helicopter-refuelling facilities. Although watchtowers were also erected in other border and some city areas, only in South Armagh was there such a concentration. Their genesis lay in the early Army practice of setting up static observation posts (OPs) on high ground to monitor the routes between Crossmaglen and the border. The first was established at Drummuckavall – named after the Irish *Dromach a'Bhfal* or 'ridge of the great dyke'. These OPs were exposed and extremely vulnerable to attack, particularly as soldiers had to be flown in and out by helicopter every few days. They were not always manned and in August 1974 Corporal Dennis Leach and Marine John Southern were killed when a 100 lb radio-controlled bomb buried underneath the Drummuckavall OP was detonated as they arrived to occupy it.

In May 1986, Major Andrew French, Spicer's predecessor as company commander in Crossmaglen, and two RUC officers were blown up as they stepped across a gap in a dry stone wall during a search of Cornoonagh Hill, less than a mile from the Slab Murphy farm. The search, codenamed Operation Overcount, was being conducted at the request of RUC Special Branch as part of the task of protecting the Golf Three Zero watchtower at Glasdrumman, named after the Irish *An Ghlasdrommain* or 'the green ridge', which was under construction. A few weeks later, Privates Carl Davies and Mitchell Bertram were blown up by a 1,000 lb van bomb at a sandbag sangar set up to guard the Royal Engineers who were constructing it. Tom Murphy later applied for compensation for damage to his property which he claimed had been caused by the blast. Brendan Burns was believed to have been the driver of the van and Brendan Moley one of his accomplices. Burns and Moley, commemorated in song as *The Two Brendans* by South Armagh republicans, also took part in four mortar attacks on Golf Three Zero before they blew themselves up in 1988.

An Army intelligence officer said:

> Although there were all sorts of factors involved in the siting of the watchtowers, you could boil it down and say that Glasdrumman was chosen because of its proximity to Tom Murphy at Ballybinaby and Drummuckavall because of [the Undertaker] at Courtbane. The tragedy about Glasdrumman is that five men died protecting it as it was built but the design was disastrous and the thing was waterlogged and unusable within weeks. The engineer officer in charge was sacked and we had to go through the whole process again. The new design incorporated a submarine-like structure underneath the ground containing a gym and accommodation for 32 soldiers.

In May 1989, Corporal Russell McGonigle was blown up by a bomb attached to a telegraph pole as he led his brick along the Silverbridge Road during an exercise to secure the route for heavy vehicles to drive south with equipment for refurbishing three watch-towers.

On 28 October 1986, Semtex from the Libyan shipments was used by the IRA for the first time in seven Mark 6 mortar bombs fired at a 12-man team protecting the Drummuckavall watchtower. The South Armagh Brigade was determined to score a direct hit on a watchtower and Mark 6 mortars were used again just over a month later against the watchtower itself. Nine mortar bombs landed and exploded to the west of the structure; one of them crashed through a sandbag-and-corrugated-iron roof into the kitchen area but did not detonate. The firing position was next to Glasdrumman School, where Tom Murphy had been educated, and five IRA men were seen from the Glasdrumman watchtower jumping into a red Escort and escaping across the border towards the Slab Murphy farm complex. Major Spicer rushed to the Lynx on the helipad in Crossmaglen security force base and was airborne within four minutes.

Spicer recalled:

> We believed there was a red car involved and we had a report that it had gone into Murphy's so we landed literally on the road outside and blasted into the farmyard in hot pursuit just as it was getting dark. As we went in all the arc lights in the yard came on and I thought: 'We're in real trouble because if we have cornered them then we're silhouetted.' I had six men in the ARF, me and a signaller but if you've cornered them and they've got an M60 it's quite tricky. I'm still pretty clear in my mind that they were in there somewhere but they had the good sense not to take us on. If they had, we'd have got away with firing on them, even if they were in the South.

Spicer ordered his men to cock their weapons and search the sheds, which had the border running through them. Lance Corporal Robinson saw two figures at the end of one of the sheds; he ran towards them − and into the Irish Republic − and came face to face with

Francis Murphy and another man. They grabbed him and he lashed out with the butt of his rifle. Hearing the commotion, gardaí who had just arrived on the southern side of the border went into the shed and saw the men holding Robinson. To Spicer's frustration, the gardaí arrested Robinson for being in possession of an illegal firearm and, despite all protestations, took him away to their patrol car. 'The sensible thing to have done would have been to just shove him back across the border,' said Spicer. 'He had done nothing wrong except run in pursuit of what he believed to be armed terrorists. He was a young guy and it was not as if he had deliberately done it. But Murphy made an issue of it.'

According to an incident report written by the Scots Guards operations officer, the gardaí 'indicated they were concerned' that Tom Murphy would see them return the soldier to Northern Ireland. 'The gardai had not searched the buildings and made no attempt to enter his [Tom Murphy's] yard or houses. Their main reason for being in the farm was now forgotten and concern for a minor border incursion took over.' Spicer was told he could not speak to Robinson and the lance corporal, still carrying his rifle and radio, was driven to Dundalk Garda Station. After negotiations between senior RUC and Garda officers, Robinson was handed back to the Army at Killeen; he had spent six and a half hours in custody. The Scots Guards report stated he had been treated well in Dundalk. 'He was taken into a room, given coffee and left alone,' the report said. 'Eventually he was taken to a conference room and given sandwiches. No charges were made against him and they [the gardaí] joked about him being in the Republic of Ireland . . . they never asked him any formal questions. They seemed very concerned about [Tom] Murphy.' The operations officer concluded laconically that there was 'room for improvement' in the area of cross-border co-operation.

Although often seen simply as surveillance platforms, the watchtowers are also patrol bases which allow Army commanders to put men out on the ground without immediate recourse to helicopters. Brigadier Roger Brunt, commander of 3 Brigade from 1997 to 1999, said: 'The towers were designed principally to defend the soldiers in Forkhill and Crossmaglen who are in a very exposed position. They give us depth, another line of defence which allows us to react to cut off escape and approach routes to and from the border. Of course, our methods have evolved over time but the fact the towers have been put to other uses such as surveillance is secondary.' The watchtowers are run and manned by the Army although the intelligence gained is passed to RUC Special Branch.

Almost a third of the troops in South Armagh are stationed in the watchtowers. Golf Four Zero at Croslieve, which has the air of a small shanty town, comprises two surveillance platforms, which look out over Forkhill to the east and Silverbridge and Tullydonnell to the west, and a helicopter landing pad. The accommodation is contained in corrugated-metal crates lifted in by a Chinook helicopter and the only recreation facilities are a television, video and a small weights room decorated with nude pin-ups; at other watchtowers, dogs, cats and even chickens are sometimes kept as pets. There is enough fuel, water and food stored on site to last several months. The soldiers are told to move quickly between the crates because they are within range of sniper fire. Lines of barbed wire surround the perimeter fence.

The extensive use of watchtowers in South Armagh has been a controversial subject within the Army. The former SAS officer Major C said: 'I suppose the towers are a visible sign of deterrence but they are a bad thing because they have become a Maginot Line and allowed a siege mentality to develop. The French were great ones for watchtowers; they did it in Vietnam and Algeria but all they did was tie down a lot of men and material and achieve the square root of fuck all. The same has happened in South Armagh. It would have been much better to have used those resources for putting in covert OPs so you could go in, hit them and then disappear.' An IRA volunteer told the author that the organisation had made detailed 'dead ground studies' of South Armagh and worked out exactly where they could and could not be seen; he estimated the towers could see no more than 35 per cent of the land area and this could be reduced dramatically in certain weather conditions.

Colonel Spicer said:

> I'm generally opposed to static operations because all they do is act as areas for the enemy to avoid or magnets to attack. On the

other hand, the balance is to have fixed patrol bases with a minimum number of troops and you make them hi-tech. You've got to have enough troops to protect yourself if you are going to operate 24 hours a day, but with the bulk of your force manoeuvring around them, they are no bad thing. What you don't do is get into a defensive mentality but using them as patrol bases to be proactive and aggressive makes sense. And obviously the standing surveillance platform 20–30 feet high is not bad. There are good optics up there and you can also use them as communications platforms to overcome the problem of all the undulations. Watchtowers can act as a third dimension. Patrols are two-dimensional and you need something above them.

This meant that the patrol commanders could talk to the watchtowers and be guided by what they could see and hear. Anything unusual could then be investigated by a patrol. 'For example, there could be a JCB moving down the road where you don't normally see one,' said Spicer. 'The towers get very familiar with the pattern of life: "We don't know this JCB, we've never seen it, check it out." Then you go straight up the road, bang, grab it and it might have a bomb in it.'

A modern mythology has built up about the capabilities of the gadgets contained in the all-seeing, all-hearing watchtowers. Tales abound of speedometers being read inside cars driving past a watchtower and conversations taking place eight miles away being monitored. Privately, the Army admits that their equipment is not quite as spectacular as this and it suits the purposes of the security forces for capabilities to be over-estimated. In a crude form of psychological operations or 'psyops', mysteriously shaped boxes and fake aerials have been placed at some sites to keep the IRA guessing about what they might be. 'No one is going to discuss exactly what's in any of the towers but you can rest assured that some of the most sophisticated equipment in the world is there,' said one Army intelligence officer. 'The cameras are state of the art, the sort of gizmos that David Attenborough uses to film a cheetah giving birth several miles away.'

The Army acknowledges that the downside of the watchtowers is that they reinforce the feeling among the local population that the Army is a force of occupation and that their presence can be an important factor in a young man's decision to join the IRA. Opposition to the watchtowers is almost universal, uniting the old lady who believes the radio masts on the towers interfere with her television reception, the housewife who considers them a blot on the landscape and the hardline republican. Despite dubious evidence, groups such as the South Armagh Farmers and Residents' Association have blamed the watchtowers for leading to deformities in cattle and sheep, leaking human sewage and causing skin cancer, brain haemorrhages and physical handicaps. The security forces believe that the organisation with the greatest interest in removing the watchtowers is the IRA for the simple reason that they hinder their operations and threaten their domination of South Armagh.

South Armagh has become one of the most heavily monitored parts of the world. The Army uses its 'Vengeful' computer system to check car numberplate details which are manually inputted in watchtowers and at checkpoints. On the 'Crucible' system, there is a map and photograph of where each suspect lives plus details of his associates, criminal record and IRA activities. In 1997, a hundred automatic numberplate registration cameras, codenamed 'Glutton', were mounted across Northern Ireland and ports in England; the heaviest concentration was in South Armagh. Artificial intelligence is being harnessed with systems called 'Caister', 'Calshot' and 'Mannequin' all being trialled; the aim is to cross-reference all intelligence information to enable comprehensive details on an individual to be accessed within seconds. Helicopters fly a daily route to observe the places where leading IRA men live and key locations for mounting attacks. Listening devices are used extensively in South Armagh; republicans take it for granted that their telephones are tapped. The Army also has the technology to carry out 'jarking', the placing of tiny tracking devices on weapons in arms caches so their movements can be followed.

The Cloghogue checkpoint, Romeo One Five, has proved the most vulnerable link in the ring of watchtowers and fortifications in South Armagh and the IRA's attack on it on 1 May 1992 illustrated the potency of the threat to soldiers manning any static position. At 11.45 p.m. on 30 April, four masked IRA men burst into a house just north of the border in Killeen, held hostage Gerard McEvoy and his wife Joanne and stole the JCB parked next to their house. The JCB was then driven two miles north to Killeen Bridge where a Renault Master van, stolen a fortnight earlier in Dundalk, was waiting next to the road; packed into the van was a 2,200 lb bomb. The JCB was used to knock down a stone wall by the A1 and the stones and pieces of wood were used to build a ramp leading up to the railway line. As the ramp was being built, the van was fitted with specially constructed wheels designed to run along the railway line; a steel bar had been welded to the edge of each wheel to ensure it would be kept flush with the edge of the tracks.

The JCB was then used to lift the van on to the railway line so it could be driven by a volunteer 800 yards further north along the tracks to Rogers Bridge. A firing pack was attached to one end of a twinflex command wire more than a mile long; the van bomb was at the other end. At the same time, the IRA set up roadblocks north and south of the Cloghogue checkpoint to divert vehicles away from the A1, the southern one manned by volunteers dressed as gardaí and using Department of Environment signs. The van was then put into first gear and pushed so that it ran downhill along the tracks towards the checkpoint as the command wire paid out behind it.

At 2.04 a.m., Lieutenant Peter Allanach, commanding a Royal Regiment of Fusiliers patrol 300 yards south of Cloghogue, heard the sound of metal on the tracks and reported that a slow-moving train was approaching the checkpoint. Looking through a telescope mounted on the Cloghogue mountain watchtower, a soldier realised that the 'train' was in fact a dark transit van with its back doors open and a line of twinflex trailing behind. A driver's light had been left on in the front so that a volunteer with a CB radio could tell the 'button man' back at Rogers Bridge when the van reached the Army checkpoint. At 2.05 a.m., as the van drew level with the east sangar, Fusilier Andrew Grundy, who had been on duty in the sangar for just ten minutes, shouted into his intercom: 'Proxy bomb. Rear gate.'

A second later, the bomb was detonated, ripping the sangar off its mounting and hurling it 12 yards. The force of the blast flung Grundy against one of the metal corners of the inside of the sangar; his skull was fractured, lacerating his brain, and he died within seconds. The operations room, portakabins, washrooms and kitchen, together with the vehicle search bay, corrugated screen, blast wall and gates, were all destroyed. The only part of the checkpoint left unscathed was the hardened concrete cube which contained the accommodation block. The cube, which was near the epicentre of the explosion, was so effective at protecting the block that several soldiers slept through the blast. At the start of his posting to Northern Ireland eight months earlier, Grundy had decided to have an Ulster flag in the shape of Northern Ireland tattooed onto his left arm. Around it was written: 'N. Ireland Tour of Duty No Surrender 1991–'.

A report into the incident concluded: 'This was a well-planned and well-executed attack indicative of the imaginative, innovative and capable nature of South Armagh PIRA. The attention to detail and sophistication of the attack is a mark of the technical capabilities of the terrorist.' The attack, one of the most ingenious of the Troubles, led to a fundamental rethink by the Army about the wisdom of having a checkpoint at Cloghogue. Many senior officers believed it unnecessary to risk lives to check vehicles on the A1 when anyone transporting bombs or weapons across the border could use one of the 'unapproved' crossings to the west.

Eighteen months earlier, Ranger Cyril Smith had been killed when a 1,500 lb proxy bomb packed into a van exploded at the Cloghogue checkpoint where he was on duty in the early hours of the morning. The van had been driven there by James McEvoy, a 65-year-old garage owner who had been taken blindfolded from his home in Newry by the IRA an hour before. His wife and seven children were held at gunpoint and he was told two of his sons would be shot if he did not co-operate. He was put into a yellow Toyota Hiace van, which he was told contained a bomb, his blindfold was removed and he was ordered to drive to Cloghogue checkpoint and stop there. As he drove, a group of volunteers followed in a car with its lights switched off. At 4.09 a.m., McEvoy reached the checkpoint, jumped out of the van and shouted out that there was a bomb inside which he had been told would go off in 40 minutes. Ranger Smith ushered him to safety before returning to the road to warn his colleagues to take cover. As he did so, a volunteer standing to the east of the checkpoint set off the bomb by firing a radar gun which sent a high frequency signal to a modified radar detector connected to the bomb's detonator. The van blew up, killing Smith and injuring nine other soldiers and Mr McEvoy; Smith was later awarded a posthumous Queen's Gallantry Medal for his actions. Mr McEvoy's 'crime' in the eyes of the IRA had been to allow members of the security forces to buy petrol from his garage.

After the 1992 attack, it was decided that a new checkpoint should be built on the opposite side of the A1 so it could cover both the A1 and Forkhill Road; it cost more than £7 million to build and was designed to minimise the chances of major loss of life by holding only a small number of troops at any one time. Between 1996 and 1998 the new checkpoint was dismantled and removed completely.

The Lance Corporal Robinson incident was not the first time Colonel Spicer had visited the Slab Murphy farm complex. On 18 November 1986, he had helped lead a joint Army and RUC operation to raid the complex as part of an investigation involving Scotland Yard, the RUC and the Garda into a trailer and bulk grain carrier fraud believed to be worth more than one million pounds. As the person who owned and controlled the complex, Tom Murphy was known to be the man behind the fraud. The intention was to search the Murphy land on the northern side of the border and seize documents from the farm offices. Earlier in the investigation, the body of a smuggler called John Kearney had been found in a fume-filled car in Omeath forest. He had been due to meet a Scotland Yard detective to discuss offering information about Tom Murphy. Although he had written notes saying goodbye to his wife and son, there was a strong suspicion that his death was not a straight-forward suicide.

Spicer said:

> We couldn't touch him [Tom Murphy] but the powers that be wanted to investigate the farm and vehicles. We had a number of helicopter assets, we put in a cordon and we were told the gardaí were going to be on the other side of the border. And in we went. It took a while to get in and [Tom] Slab Murphy left down the road in his silver Granada as we were coming in. He was stopped by the Garda, let through and disappeared. I suppose you could say he drove out of his house in the South and there was nothing we could do about it. We would have

very much liked to have found him in the North but it wasn't to be.

Francis Murphy and another man remained at the farm as the search began and demanded to see the search warrant, Francis filmed the proceedings with a Panasonic colour video camera owned by his brother Tom. 'He started to video all the members of the security forces, particularly the RUC and he was doing it in a belligerent way and making a point of doing it,' said Spicer. According to the RUC, Francis Murphy had strayed across the border into Northern Ireland and Inspector Richard Russell, the senior RUC officer there, told him he was committing an offence under the Northern Ireland Emergency Provisions Act 1987. He continued to film and Russell decided to arrest him. 'They jumped him, grabbed him and took the camera,' said Spicer. 'He's a big chap and it took two or three of them to subdue him and take the camera off him. He was arrested, put on a helicopter and taken away to Bessbrook.' In the struggle, the video camera was dropped and broken and Detective Constable David Dunwoody received a gash to the head that later required seven stitches. The videotape, which belonged to Tom Murphy, was discovered to contain propaganda footage of IRA men with an M60 machine-gun.

Francis Murphy was later interrogated at Gough barracks but remained silent throughout and was released without charge. According to RUC interview notes:

> We asked Murphy if he had any Wilcox trailers and we told him we suspected he was involved in the handling of stolen trailers on behalf of PIRA. He made no reply . . . We asked if he had bought any equipment recently and he made no reply. We asked if he knew John Kearney from Kilcurry and he made no reply. We told him Kearney had committed suicide about a month ago in Omeath forest and he made no reply, looked at us, appeared to be thinking and shrugged his shoulders. We mentioned smuggling and asked various questions about his personal life but he would not engage in conversation.

In 1988, Operation Amaizing was launched by the RUC and Garda to investigate the smuggling of cattle, grain and oil across the border. The first case to come to court involved the smuggling of 24 tons of maize and enormous resources were devoted to examining the Murphy oil businesses. The RUC's part of the investigation was called Operation Dung and involved observation of the Slab Murphy farm complex by undercover soldiers and police between 3 June and 23 July 1990. At the end of the period, the RUC searched the complex and seized enough documents to fill a room. A report prepared by Detective Inspector Paul Hamlin proposed that Tom Murphy and three other men be charged with conspiracy to defraud the exchequer of the Irish Republic of IR£260,000 in June 1990 and IR£210,000 in July 1990. Hamlin proposed that all four men be arrested in connection with providing funds for the Provisional IRA. 'The evidence against each of them is that at varying times each was seen actively concerned with the dealing of the fuel within the complex of 71 Larkins Road, Crossmaglen and can be individually identified from videotapes taken by police officers.'

Despite Detective Inspector Hamlin's recommendations, no charges were brought. Instead, an attempt was made to force Tom Murphy out of business through an Act of Parliament. On 1 August 1990, the Newry and Mourne Regulation Hydrocarbon Traffic Order, made by Peter Brooke, then Northern Ireland Secretary, came into force. It had been drawn up under the Prevention of Terrorism Act and stated that 'any vehicle constructed or adapted for the use of hydrocarbon oil' was banned from Larkins Road unless written permission from the local sub-divisional commander of the RUC had been obtained. The High Court in Belfast had been told that the order was needed to prevent the IRA from raising funds by using Larkins Road to smuggle oil.

On the same day, a new company called Gilgan Limited was set up by Mícheál Caraher, who applied for a judicial review against the order. He swore an affidavit which said: 'In the early summer of 1990 I formed the view that diesel oil and petrol was profitable and decided to go into that business . . . In or about the month of July 1990 I heard that [there were] oil tank and pumping facilities at Larkins Road. I went to see the premises and found them suitable and as a result Gilgan Ltd took a lease . . . By reason of Gilgan's inability to use Larkins Road . . . the premises are rendered useless. No alternative premises found.'

After Tom Murphy was told the legal application had little chance of success, he ordered Caraher to drop it and for the next eight years the order was responsible for cutting revenue from oil smuggling to a fraction of what it had been. Caraher was the latest in a long line of IRA men employed at the Murphy complex. Brendan Burns and Joe Brennan, Patrick Casey, convicted of explosives offences in 1975, Micky McKevitt, later to become leader of the Real IRA, and Micksey Martin all worked as lorry drivers for Tom Murphy at different times. Others employed at the Slab Murphy farm complex had no involvement with the IRA.

The authorities in the Irish Republic were also concentrating on Tom Murphy's oil business. As part of Operation Scorpion, a joint investigation with Irish customs in 1989, James Livingstone, head of the special inquiry unit of the Revenue Commissioners, discovered that Murphy had set up a company called Cowan Oils which he used to smuggle petrol across the border and supply to outlets in the Irish Republic. After building up a list of Murphy's customers, Livingstone set about recovering the unpaid revenue from each of them; the customers then stopped buying from Murphy and his income from oil decreased.

On 6 April 1989, a Cowan Oils tanker carrying 9,200 litres of smuggled oil and 2,300 litres of kerosene was seized by customs officers. The following evening, two customs officers, Seamus Colgan and Denis Byrne, were driving north along Larkins Road as part of a routine border crossing inspection. They had intended to turn around in the Slab Murphy yard and head back to Dundalk but a car was blocking the yard entrance. Colgan decided to drive across the border 50 yards further on and turn at the crossroads there but as he did so they were blocked by a car; Colgan immediately radioed for Garda assistance.

A large, powerfully-built man grabbed the keys but during the ensuing scuffle Colgan managed to snatch them back and start the car up. Byrne jumped out of the car to open a gate which had been closed to stop the car getting back down Larkins Road. Tom Murphy then appeared and hurled a lump of concrete which hit Byrne on the arm. Francis Murphy pulled out the car radio and began swinging it by its cable while the powerfully-built man smashed the driver's window, punched Colgan and told him he would be 'taken to Cross to be fixed'. At that moment, a Garda car arrived and Tom Murphy and the others ran off. Charges of assault were considered, but were not brought because the offences had taken place in Northern Ireland.

When the case dealing with the seized tanker came to court at Carrickmacross, a man describing himself as manager of Cowan Oils told the court that the company had had a turnover of nearly IR£1.5 million during a six-month period that year. Cowan Oils lost the case but Tom Murphy never paid what was owed to the Revenue Commissioners. He immediately lodged an appeal, put Cowan Oils into liquidation and set up a new and identical company called Trillfield; the appeal was then abandoned. In 1997, Ray Jackson, who had been appointed official liquidator for Cowan Oils five years earlier, reported to the High Court in Dublin that the only asset he had been able to trace to the company was the sum of IR£869. After being pursued by the Revenue Commissioners for unpaid VAT, Trillfield was wound up and Tom Murphy set up Ace Oils, the sixth oil company he has run from Larkins Road. He had named one of the previous companies West Star, after an oil company in the television series *Dallas*.

Larkins Road had always been considered dangerous territory for the forces of law and order. In 1984, an oil tanker driving south across the border had rammed a Garda patrol car blocking its way. A car then blocked the patrol car, allowing the tanker to drive away. Two weeks later, a house being built by Garda David Shannon, who had been in the patrol car, was burned down.

It was not just customs officers and gardaí who were placing themselves in danger by prying into the business affairs of Tom Murphy. During Operation Scorpion, Austin Rowan, a senior investigator, was transferred to Brussels when an incendiary bomb was found in his car. Some time later, James Livingstone received a threatening letter accusing him of putting lives at risk by passing information to the Northern Ireland authorities. In December 1992, Livingstone's wife, Grace, was found murdered at their home in Malahide, north of Dublin. She had been beaten, tied up in the bedroom and blasted with a shotgun kept in the garage by her husband. Livingstone was arrested and questioned about the crime but released after two days; senior Garda officers later admitted he could not have been the killer. Livingstone told detectives that the murderer, who had tried to frame him, was probably someone he had investigated. He produced the names of three men he believed might have been responsible; Thomas 'Slab' Murphy was one of them.

Chapter 8

Spies and Informers

'It is said that if you raped your next-door neighbour it will soon be forgotten: if your grandfather had been an "INFORMER" you would be an outcast.'

(*Talking to People in South Armagh*
by Captain Robert Nairac, 1977)

'It would appear that he was made to kneel at the scene, shot from behind and dragged onto the side of the road. He had minor lacerations to the chin and nose, consistent with being dragged face down.'

(Army report into shooting of Séamus
Morgan, alleged informer, 1982)

The anonymous caller spoke no more than a dozen words before the line went dead. 'Go to Lough Ross Road in Cullaville, Father,' he said. 'Something's been left there.' Father Donal Sweeney put down the receiver and walked slowly towards his car. He had already grasped what the IRA's messenger was referring to and his only course was to follow the instruction. Such was one's priestly duty in the parish of Crossmaglen. In a ditch close to the main Concession Road from Dundalk to Castleblaney, and some 500 yards north of the border, was the corpse of a large, well-built man, wearing just a pair of grey slacks and white socks. The hands had been bound in front of the body with blue baling twine and a blood-soaked yellow polyester blanket tied around the head.

Three bullets had been fired from an Armalite at point-blank range into the back and side of the man's head. Fragments of human skull later found embedded in the bottom of the ditch showed he had been shot after being ordered to kneel at the roadside. The bullet exit wounds had left a gaping hole where the left eye had been; the head, legs and torso showed signs of having been beaten with a heavy blunt object. Father Sweeney anointed the body and said prayers for the dead man.

Two days earlier, at about 11.20 p.m. on 16 July 1989, John McAnulty had been leaving the Rosewood Country Club in Ravensdale after enjoying a drink with his ex-wife when he was pounced on by a group of men dressed in black and wearing balaclavas. A pistol was pointed at Helen McAnulty's head and she was told she would be shot unless she left the car park. Her 48-year-old ex-husband used all his six feet three inches and 16 stones to resist being taken away and was only subdued by being beaten on the head with a wooden baton. Mrs McAnulty ran into the country club to raise the alarm only to find that all telephone lines to the building had been cut. When she returned to the car park it was empty apart from McAnulty's bloodstained wedding ring, which had been wrenched off during the struggle and was lying on the tarmac. Within hours, he had been interrogated in a farm outbuilding on the Cooley peninsula, pronounced guilty and sentenced to death.

Shortly after McAnulty's body was found by Father Sweeney, a statement was issued by the Provisional IRA which said the long-time grain smuggler had been an informer and named an RUC officer whom he had met regularly in the Downshire Arms in Banbridge to pass on information. Suspicion had fallen on him when he had been arrested by detectives involved in Operation Amaizing and freed without charge while others had remained in custody.

Although nicknamed 'the Big Note' because of his habit of carrying a wallet stuffed with £50 and £20 notes, McAnulty had been in financial difficulties. His firm, Cambrook Farm Feeds, had been liquidated and he faced a divorce from his second wife, Peggy, and proceedings brought by a firm which claimed he owed them £350,000. In the early seventies, the RUC had suspected him of helping the IRA transport arms from the continent. But it was his cross-border smuggling activities, which had brought him into contact with

Tom Murphy and other IRA men, which now made him of potential use to the security forces. The prospect of payments which could alleviate his financial situation and a blind eye being turned to his smuggling led him to agree to pass on information. It seemed a good deal but he was effectively signing his own death warrant.

McAnulty's body was the twelfth of an alleged informer to be dumped near the border after a summary execution carried out by the South Armagh Brigade. Interrogations could take place in safe houses or barns away from the watchtowers and Army patrols; the body would then often be used to draw the Army and RUC into danger by attaching booby-traps next to it or planting a bomb nearby. Around half of the victims, who totalled 18 by the time the July 1997 ceasefire was called, were local men suspected of having been 'turned' by RUC Special Branch, British military intelligence or MI5. The others were mainly volunteers from further north who had been handed over to the South Armagh Brigade's nutting squad.

Eamon Collins, who was briefly part of the nutting squad, said: 'We were interrogating people in Knockbridge and Inniskeen, the hinterland of South Armagh, and we were spoilt for choice for interrogation centres. South Armagh provide the set-up for in-depth interrogations: the houses, the personnel, the whole lot. And the body is dumped in the North. The forensics are in the South and then the people who have to investigate that murder are the RUC. It fucks up their investigation.' A body on a lonely border road would also strike fear into anyone who was considering passing information to the security forces. Officer D, a recently retired MI5 'source handler' responsible for recruiting and managing informers or 'agents' in South Armagh, said:

> Television footage of a body on the border is very bad news for recruiting sources. South Armagh is a difficult enough nut to crack even without that. But MI5 has never lost a source in Northern Ireland. We've had to relocate a few people – take them out of circulation, give them a new identity and set them up somewhere else – but all the dead sources have been RUC or Army. The main problem is the initial approach and for every one that succeeds there are several that fail and there's always the danger that you've been compromised.

Once a source has been recruited, he or she is allocated a number and their true identity limited to a tiny circle of people. 'Some sources have more than one number so it is impossible to trace them by piecing together all the information they've given,' said Officer D. It has always been more difficult to arrange a meeting with a source in South Armagh than in any other part of Northern Ireland. 'Sometimes they are not in control of their own time so arrangements have to be made at very short notice,' said Officer D. 'The handler will have a false identity, occupation and "cover story" about why he or she is in the area. There's almost no limit to our interest in South Armagh. We are always looking to recruit sources and there are any number of different ways to do that. But safety is the watchword; the IRA would love to hit one of us but we're very, very careful.'

In July 1977, the IRA in Crossmaglen mounted illegal roadblocks and handed out statements warning of 'loose talk about IRA activities' and giving any 'guilty parties' seven days to leave the area. 'We wish to make it clear that we regard the behaviour of these people as tantamount to passing information direct to the enemy forces and consequently they are now classified as INFORMERS.' The following month, 60-year-old William Martin was dragged from his home in St Joseph's Place, Crossmaglen by two masked men as his wife looked on. His body was found dumped on the Castleblaney Road outside the town a day later.

Paddy McEntee, a Crossmaglen postman and former Army sergeant who had been tarred, feathered and shot in the knees by the IRA five years earlier, suffered a similar fate in 1978. He had never been afraid to be seen talking to the security forces. Recalling his time as a constable in Crossmaglen, Sam Malcomson said: 'McEntee would have given the odd wee bit of information if he thought it would save somebody's life. I remember some of my colleagues talking about meeting up with him while he was on his post round.' An IRA source in Crossmaglen said that the postman had been identified as an informer by a British soldier who had deserted and become involved in the Troops Out movement. 'At first we couldn't believe it,' he said. 'So we showed this guy a photograph of the Armagh Diocesan visit to Lourdes and asked him to identify the man he was talking about. He pointed to McEntee.' There were obvious dangers in treating the former soldier's words as conclusive evidence and the killing of McEntee prompted an unprecedented wave of anger in Crossmaglen.

Jim McAllister said that local opinion changed when people were told the full details of McEntee's activities:

> An informer is a despised creature. There'd be a feeling of sympathy for the family but in South Armagh the worst thing a person could be is an informer of any type — whether it's to do with smuggling, somebody doing the double, anything at all. In an area where people have had to live on their wits for generations against outside authority, informers were always seen as beyond the Pale. Everybody learns as time passes, including those that are being targeted [by the authorities] as informers. It happens all the time and it's still happening. But because there was a couple of informers shot, now when somebody's put under pressure they will almost always come and explain to a republican what's happening because they know they would be caught eventually. Then the whole thing can be sorted out and there's an end to it. So you could say that initially it was a contest between British intelligence and IRA intelligence and IRA intelligence basically won by catching a few and shooting them.

The crime of being an informer outweighed all other considerations; one man was said to have been killed after his wife told the IRA she suspected he was passing information to the security forces. Jim McAllister said: 'There was one guy shot, Anthony Shields, and I would have classed Anthony as a friend of mine. We had manys a pint over there in Keenan's bar down the years and I was sorry for Anthony; he was a hail-fellow-well-met kind of a character but he got sucked in, so . . . it's a tough call.' Shields was a middle-aged bachelor who was slightly retarded as a result of contracting meningitis at the age of 12. In 1980, he was dragged from his car by four gunmen at Drummuckavall as he returned from a pub in Dundalk and his body was found on the border next to McElroy's farm at Glasdrumman two days later. A plastic meal sack had been placed over the head and two bombs placed nearby. For four days the body lay in the heat while Army bomb disposal experts made the area safe. As with all those whose bodies were found dumped, the final indignity for Shields came when a rope was tied to his body, which was then dragged along the road by the Army to set off any booby-traps. He was buried in St Patrick's churchyard in Crossmaglen, just a few yards from the republican plot where on Easter Sunday a masked IRA volunteer had told the crowd: 'We regret to say that as a result of several warnings being unheeded, we now have to execute another informer in this area. Announcing this may shock many people but we are left with no alternative in the present war situation.'

It seems unlikely that Anthony Shields could have known anything of great value to the security forces. At the time this was advanced as a reason for supposing that he could not have been an informer; in fact it was probably more an indication of the low grade nature of most of the intelligence being passed on and an illustration of the desperation of the Army and RUC to gain a foothold in the Crossmaglen area. Brigadier Morton said the Army's intelligence picture was 'pathetic' in 1973 and had hardly improved by the end of the decade. 'We didn't know much at all,' he said.

Much of the information contained in military intelligence source reports of the 1970s was little more than a mixture of rumour, triviality and statements of the obvious. A 1974 report stated that a source had revealed that a particular IRA suspect 'was seen in McArdle's shop in Newtownhamilton buying meat and received preferential treatment'. After the IRA volunteers Sean Campbell and Jim Lochrie had been killed by a premature bomb explosion in 1975, a handler recorded that his source had told him: 'Campbell was not a bad man but Lochrie was mad, just like Sean McKenna. He was a real republican but a header [nutcase].' In 1981, a Crossmaglen informer revealed: 'The Provos in South Armagh are desperate for funds just now. There was an H-Block concert in Fintan Callan's [pub, in Hackballscross] on Sun 25 Oct 81. It cost £1 per head to get in.' Each source report was annotated with a lengthy comment from the handler and then solemnly forwarded up the line to Brigade headquarters to be analysed further. The information gathered by intelligence officers was often little better. After observing an Easter commemoration in Mullaghbawn in 1978, an Army captain wrote a report stating that a man called Michael was unemployed and 'worth watching as I have seen him in dubious company before'; another participant, Patrick, was 'a particularly evil-looking man who was drunk'.

Given the type of information being passed by the likes of Martin, McEntee and Shields, it seems that a decision to 'execute' an informer was as much to do with maintaining the IRA's grip on South Armagh as it was preventing operations being compromised. Punishment beatings and kneecappings were another means of stopping people from stepping out of line. On 6 June 1972, Michael McVerry and Brian Hearty were among five masked and armed volunteers who abducted Cyril McKay, 23, from his farmyard near Dundalk and drove him to a shed to be interrogated.

After being questioned about cattle stealing and his giving court evidence against three republicans accused of brawling in the Fair-ways Hotel, McKay was punched in the face and body and asked to choose to be shot in the head or the legs. 'I said I would prefer to be shot in the legs,' he told the judge during Hearty's trial. 'At one time they put me kneeling on the ground and told me to say an Act of Contrition.' He was put up against a wall, stripped to the waist and a gallon of tar was poured over his head. McVerry then shot him once in the right knee and twice in the left. McKay lay where he had been shot until he was found by a farmer the next morning. Hearty was sentenced to eight years despite protestations that he and McVerry had spent the night in Donnelly's bar in Silverbridge.

Petty offenders have often been dealt with by IRA kangaroo courts to show the people of South Armagh that it is the republican movement and not the RUC that protects them. On 17 August 1975, four youths were seized outside a carnival dance at Shelagh by men wearing black hoods. They were taken in a Ford transit van to a disused farm building where they were beaten and questioned about car stealing, hay theft and an alleged rape. Up to ten IRA volunteers were involved. The youths were kept there until dawn when a man they referred to as 'the Judge' arrived to 'sentence' each of them. One youth, who was accused of raping his 15-year-old sister, was ordered to leave Crossmaglen within a week and never to return. Three of the youths had their heads shaved and were tied up in Crossmaglen and Creggan with signs saying 'RAPIST PUNISHED by the 2 Bn [2nd Battalion] IRA' and 'PUNISHED by the 2 Bn IRA for Crimes' hung around their necks. They were ordered to stay where they had been tied up for two hours and wear the signs at a dance at Carrickmacross that night and at Mass in Crossmaglen on the Sunday. Such forms of public humiliation were used by Chairman Mao's Red Army in China during the Cultural Revolution.

Anyone attempting to enforce the law of the land in South Armagh is treated with intense suspicion. 'You would be wary of anyone with a briefcase,' said Jim McAllister. 'Even now, somebody will come and say: "There's strange boys up there in a car, I don't know what they're doing." They could be anything from television licence men to dole men but people notice them straight away and tell everybody they're around. Even enemies would tell each other.' Referring to an incident in November 1997 in which two television licence inspectors had been held up at gunpoint by the IRA while masked men smashed up their van, Jim McAllister protested that it was wrong to describe such acts as 'thuggishness or banditry'. He said: 'It's actually the fact that people like that would never have dreamt of coming near South Armagh pre ceasefire. But they're coming now. It isn't over the bloody TV licences. It's authority again trying to stamp itself on this area.' When interviewed by detectives in 1997, Bernard McGinn said his IRA activities had included threatening a woman called Callaghan in the Ardross estate in Crossmaglen. 'Frank McCabe sent me there,' he said. 'She had been fighting and going mad and afterwards the problem stopped. The IRA treats itself as a police force.'

The practice of dumping bodies on the border has undoubtedly increased South Armagh's notoriety within the wider republican movement. In January 1990, Sandy Lynch, an IRA volunteer who had been passing information to the RUC, was rescued by the police as he was being interrogated in an IRA safe house in Lenadoon in west Belfast by members of the nutting squad. According to Lynch's court testimony, an interrogator called Fred Scappatici told him he would prefer to carry out the questioning in South Armagh, which he called God's Country. 'He [Scappatici] said that if I didn't admit to being a tout, I'd get a jab in the arse and wake up in South Armagh and he'd be able to talk to me the way he wanted, hung upside down in a cattle shed,' said Lynch. 'He said it didn't matter about me screaming because no one would be able to hear.' As Lynch resigned himself to a terrible death, the RUC raided the house and rescued him. Among those arrested was Danny Morrison, Sinn Féin's director of publicity, who was known within the IRA as the 'Lord Chief Justice' because he was the man who held the power of life or death over an informer. Fred Scappatici was acquitted due to lack of evidence.

In January 1999, Dublin's Special Criminal Court heard that John Quinn, an IRA volunteer accused of arms offences in connection with the murder of Detective Garda Jerry McCabe during a botched robbery in County Limerick three years earlier, had told detectives he would be killed if he talked. After agreeing to make a verbal statement, he said: 'I'm a dead man . . . I was told I'd be found in South Armagh with a bag over my head.'

The threats were very real. On 30 June 1992, the bodies of Gregory Burns, John Dignam and Aidan Starrs, three Portadown volunteers, were dumped in South Armagh after they had been shot dead following interrogations lasting more than a week. Starrs had been tortured with a red-hot poker which had been pressed into his flesh and cigarettes had been stubbed out on Burns's thigh. Although lurid tales about the torturing of informers have become common-place, this was the only case in South Armagh of an informer's body showing more than bruising. Burns, Dignam and Starrs had all passed information to the RUC or Army; they had also used IRA weapons for robberies to line their own pockets and had strangled and beaten to death Margaret Perry, Burns's former girlfriend. Perry's body had been found buried in a wood on the Classiebawn Castle estate close to where Lord Mountbatten's fishing party had been blown up nearly 11 years earlier.

Just before he was killed, Dignam was told he could write a letter to his wife. Part of it was read out at his funeral:

Dear Claire, love,

I am writing this letter to apologise for all the pain and heartache I have caused you. I have only a matter of hours to live my life. I only wish I could see you and the kids one last time but as you know, this is not possible. I have done nothing but think of you, and Claire, believe me, I've shed some tears for you, Sean and Ruairi, sometimes uncontrollably. You are going to have some bad times ahead of you but never drop your head and keep your chin up. I wish you all the best with our new baby which I'm not going to see. I'll never know if I had a daughter or not. Tears are streaming down my face. There is only one thing I can say to you now, that I love you and cherish you and the kids until I die, and after if possible. Tell your family and my parents and sister I love them also. Pray for me, look after my grave and visit when you can. Your life is ruined. I hope you can piece it together again. Cherish this lock of hair and letter for the rest of your life. Tell the kids I will always love them and cherish them.

Your loving husband,
John

Dignam's naked body was found wrapped in two bin bags and dumped on a roadside at Lislea. He had been shot with two .357 Magnum bullets; one had lodged in his brain after being fired through his right nostril, the other had entered the back of his head and exited through the left side of his forehead. The body was discovered by Father Oliver Breslan, a local priest, who covered it with a pink blanket before offering prayers for the dead man. Shortly afterwards, Claire Dignam gave birth to a baby girl.

Only a handful of people have lived to tell the tale of an interrogation at the hands of the South Armagh Brigade. One of these was Private Richard Lewis, a part-time UDR member from Omagh who would deliver soft drinks in South Armagh once a month for his employers, Cantrell and Cochrane. At 2.30 p.m. on 26 November 1991, he and Private Ken Newell, a full-time UDR man who occasionally helped out with a delivery run, arrived at O'Neill's garage near Cullaville on the Concession Road. Jim O'Neill, the 52-year-old garage owner, asked them to wait outside while he rang their headquarters in Belfast to complain that they could not deliver spirits. The Concession Road, which runs from Dundalk to Castleblaney passing from the Republic into Northern Ireland and back into the Republic again, had been a strategically important area for the IRA since the beginning of the Troubles; vehicles needed for IRA operations were regularly hijacked there. When plans were drawn up in 1983 for another petrol station and a shop to be built there, the contractors were visited by local IRA men telling them to abandon the idea. Letters from the 'Second Battalion IRA, Crossmaglen' stated that the Provisionals didn't want any more traffic on the road, as it was a key route for their 'military operations'.

In his statement to the RUC afterwards, Lewis said:

> I was reading the paper and I think Ken was going through the dockets when I heard a screech of tyres and the sound of a car coming from the direction of the border. It was a red, four-door car in bad condition. I looked into the mirror and saw four boys get out of this car. All four of them were wearing balaclavas. Two men went to each side of the lorry. One man pulled me out of the lorry and put me on the ground; the man that was with him had what looked like an AK-47 with him. My hands were tied behind my back while I was on the ground and I was put into the boot of the red car.

The car sped away across the border; 20 minutes later it turned off the road into a lane and reversed into a hayshed. As the doors were closed behind the car, Lewis heard Newell being taken out of the back and questioned. 'I heard them asking him about other members of the security forces that live in the same housing estate as Ken,' said Lewis. 'I heard him name Kenny Sproule and Alan Shankland.' From the boot, Lewis could hear cars passing on the main road and a bulldozer working nearby. 'I think they had the sports bag that we had our lunchboxes in as I heard one of the men ask if Ken minded them finishing off his lunch,' he said. Lewis was then pulled out of the boot and a wet suit they had found in his bag was tied around his head.

The IRA men took it in turns to ask him questions. Lewis recalled:

> They asked me if my mate was in the UDR; I said he worked for Cantrell and Cochrane like myself. Ken was not beside me and I didn't know what he had said so I didn't say too much . . . One of them kept punching my shoulder and telling me I was lying. He knew my nickname was Beano; I felt a gun at my side. I just kept to the same story, that I wasn't in the UDR, that if I was it would be stupid to come up to this area every month. The

questioning went on for hours; they seemed to be writing down my answers and going over and over again to see if I was giving the same answers.

The South Armagh Brigade had been supplied information by the IRA in Omagh. As well as Lewis's nickname, they knew he had applied to join the UDR when he was 18 and that his brother had served in the regiment. After several hours of questioning, the IRA man in charge, believed to have been the Surgeon, told the interrogation team that they had spent too long in the shed. Lewis was told to get back in the boot and he and Newell, who was in the back seat, were driven into a shed full of cows. After further questioning, Lewis was certain he was about to be shot dead:

> One of them came up to me and pushed a gun into my arm. He asked me if I knew what it was. I said no and he said that it was a rifle. He was moving the cocking handle about and he asked me if I knew what that was and then told me that it was the cocking handle. He told me to get down on my knees and asked if I wanted to say a prayer. I said no. I felt the rifle barrel at the back of my neck and heard it being cocked. I closed my eyes and thought I was going to be shot.

There was a silence as Lewis waited for the rifle to be fired and then the IRA man walked away.

Another interrogator warned Lewis that it was his last chance to speak. 'He asked me if I would take a bomb into the Army camps and I said I would do to get out of here tonight,' said Lewis. Again the interrogators decided that they had been in the same place for too long and Lewis and Newell were driven to a third shed and questioned again. 'They said they knew we were Prods but that that was okay, the only ones they were interested in were Special Branch men,' said Lewis. As he was being put back into the boot, Lewis heard Newell ask where they were being taken. Some time later, Lewis was pulled out of the boot and, still blindfolded, told to walk away from the car. This time he was certain he was going to be shot. 'Then they said that they were not sure of me but that if they found out I was lying they would come back for me,' he said. 'They told me never to darken this country again.'

The car then sped away towards the Cregganduff Road near Crossmaglen where Newell, who had his hands tied behind his back with brown parcel tape, was forced to kneel by the side of the road before being shot twice in the back of the head with an AKM rifle. The fact that Newell had been allocated to the job just ten minutes before they set off probably saved Lewis's life. The South Armagh volunteers were expecting only one UDR man to be in the drinks lorry and were confused when Newell admitted almost immediately that he was in the UDR. They knew nothing about Newell and if he had denied he was in the UDR he would almost certainly have been spared and Lewis killed instead. Jim O'Neill did not contact the RUC that day and waited until 7 p.m. before he called Cantrell and Cochrane to tell them their lorry was still at his premises. He was charged with withholding information about the kidnappings and the case against him was later dropped.

Lewis showed a rare presence of mind. According to Eamon Collins, himself later abducted and killed by the Provisionals, most victims would tell their captors exactly what they thought they wanted to hear and beg for their lives. In 1982, Thomas Cochrane, a part-time UDR sergeant, was knocked off his motorcycle with a spade handle as he rode to work at Glenanne Mill; his body was found at the foot of Sugarloaf Hill in Lislea a week later. 'A man called Kieran told me that the poor bastard volunteered everything,' said Collins. 'He just pissed himself. They wanted information, they got it. They wanted to know the names of other personnel, he told them. But they still shot the guy dead.'

The fear also extended to the South Armagh community. In 1979 and 1981, Gerry Evans and Charlie Armstrong, who both lived in Rathview Park in Crossmaglen, disappeared without trace. Evans, who was last seen hitching a lift back from Castleblaney, was listed by the Army as an IRA member. Armstrong was a quiet family man with no connection to the republican movement who vanished after setting off to Cullyhanna to drive an elderly woman to Mass; his car was found outside the Adelphi cinema in Dundalk the following evening. In 1999, Anna McShane, Armstrong's daughter, said: 'A blanket of silence came down in an area where everybody knows everything.' For nearly two decades afterwards, fear prevented the Armstrong and Evans families even discussing the two disappearances.'You wouldn't even talk about it within these four walls,' said Mrs Evans. In 1995, her husband Gerard was found floating in nearby Kiltybane Lough on his 63rd birthday. 'He took it very badly,' said Mrs Evans. 'For years I was trying to save him and that meant I carried the lot myself. There was no life for us after Gerry was taken away.'

At least two of the IRA men abducted, interrogated in South Armagh and shot dead as informers had not been working for the security forces. One of these was Paddy Flood, a Derry bombmaker who disappeared from his home in June 1990. 'The next night a man knocked at our door,' his wife Elizabeth Flood said in a statement. 'I answered it and it was dark, he was wearing a duffle coat with the hood up and dark glasses. I couldn't see his face. He told me to turn out the lights in the hall. He said he was a friend of Paddy's and that Paddy would be away for a while. He asked for a set of Paddy's clothes. I gave them to him – a jumper, shirt, trousers, vest and pants, shaving gear.' On 26 July, Flood's body, bare-footed and with the hands tied behind the back, was found lying beside the Coach Road at Tullyvallen by a Mrs Hopkins who lived nearby. Dressed in just a blue boiler suit, the body was still warm; the blood-sodden head was bound over the eyes with brown plastic tape and wrapped in a black bin liner. Flood had been allowed to wash and shave that morning before being shot once in the back of the head with a 7.62 mm bullet which blew away part of his brain and the right side of his forehead.

The Derry volunteer had maintained his innocence for seven weeks before 'admitting' what his interrogators had accused him of. In a taped 'confession' later sent to Flood's family, he said he had been recruited by RUC Special Branch officers after they had threatened his wife. 'The police were always reminding me about my wife,' he said on the tape. 'They could bring her in at any time. They would break her like a plate. She would go down for a long, long time. It was really the big hold they had over me.' The IRA's Derry Brigade had been searching for an informer for months after a series of compromised operations and the finger had been pointed at Flood when legal documents received by two Derry republicans held on remand revealed that a booby-trap bomb he had made had not been fitted with batteries.

An Army intelligence officer said that he believed the IRA had been tricked by RUC Special Branch into thinking Flood was an informer.

> The Branch is always very careful about what it tells us but it seems that their thinking was that Flood was a known bomb-maker so there would be few tears shed if he was removed from the scene. If he was thought to be the tout then it would also divert attention away from the person who really was touting. The detail about the missing batteries was deliberately slipped in so that the IRA would lift Flood.

A senior RUC Special Branch officer would not be drawn on whether this was the case but indicated that Flood had never been an informer. 'Eventually the sheer fear and exhaustion got to him and he confessed to something he hadn't done,' he said. 'Every man has his limit and in the end he just told the boys what they wanted to hear.' Army and RUC documents list Tom Murphy as the man who supervised Flood's interrogation. A year later, Martin Hogan, a senior Derry IRA man, disappeared from his home as his comrades prepared to question him about their suspicions that he was an informer. It was later confirmed that he had indeed been working for the RUC but no one from the security forces would comment on whether Flood had been set up to protect him.

One of the most notorious abductions of the 20th century was that of Captain Robert Nairac, who was taken from the Three Steps pub in Drumintee in May 1977. For Nairac – a Grenadier Guards officer who worked from Bessbrook Mill as the liaison man between 3 Brigade headquarters, the SAS and RUC Special Branch – South Armagh had become an obsession. Shortly before his death, he wrote an Army paper entitled *Talking to People in South Armagh* (Appendix B) which was a mixture of originality, sensitivity to the nature of republicanism and naivety in almost equal measures. The paper outlined how it might be possible to gather information in South Armagh despite the age-old stigma attached to informing. There were 'ways around these taboos' and 'among fringe PIRA (or even active terrorists) there are those who might be "turned" by the right approach'.

Nairac had been one of the early members of 14 Int and by the end of 1974, he had concluded that the Army could not defeat the IRA militarily. The 'war', he argued, had to be fought on the basis of intelligence and would not be won by 'out-ambushing or out-shooting' the IRA on their home turf, he wrote in an internal report. 'We are up against a sophisticated enemy and we must prepare accordingly.' The IRA in South Armagh, and particularly in Cross-maglen, was more professional and more successful than the IRA in any other part of Northern Ireland. 'It is true that little of the Crossmaglen ideas or expertise have seeped through to the rest of the IRA. This is because of both the insularity of the unit and the thick-headedness of the rest of the IRA,' he wrote. 'However, it is extremely dangerous to assume that they won't take root in the future. Once this happens it is too late.'

The report recommended that soldiers who served in South Armagh should be specially trained and hand picked; everything they did should be directed towards establishing local contacts and amassing low-level intelligence. As a result, a dossier could be built up on every man, woman and child in the area even if they had no link to the IRA. 'It must be made quite clear to each soldier that the worst crime he can commit — worse than buggery, rape or shooting another soldier — is to compromise a source.' Nairac added that an Army intelligence officer should be assigned to South Armagh; he would need to be 'reasonably brave' and possess qualities of imagination, determination and adaptability. 'I would put his chances of surviving his tour at less than 50 per cent.' Nairac was effectively writing his own job description and within 18 months he had been appointed to this new liaison officer's role. He was determined to make a mark.

Robert Laurence Nairac had the background and many of the attributes of a successful Guards officer. Born in 1948, he was the fourth and youngest child of Dr Maurice Nairac, an ophthalmic surgeon, and his wife Barbara, and was educated by Benedictine monks at Ampleforth, Britain's leading Catholic public school, where he excelled both academically and on the sports field. When he was

14, his brother David, a doctor, died suddenly of a mysterious illness and Robert was left to carry the hopes and ambitions of his parents and older sisters Rosamund and Gabrielle. In 1968, he won a place at Oxford University and went up to Lincoln College to read History. There he resurrected the near-defunct university boxing club and won a Blue.

But Nairac also displayed an unorthodox side at Oxford and was constantly seeking to test himself. He kept hawks in his college room and would try to strengthen his nerve by putting a small piece of raw steak on the bridge of his nose and allowing one to swoop and take it. At one raucous summer party held on a college barge, he and his friend Julian Malins, who later became a QC, provided the entertainment by engaging each other in a bare-knuckle fist fight. Nairac joined the Army while still an undergraduate and took his Finals in his Grenadier Guards uniform; he needed an extra year of study to secure a Third Class degree but his thoughts had already moved on to his military career. Twenty years later, Malins recalled: 'The Oxford class of '68 was good-looking, confident and unlike any previous generation since the 1930s. We came after austerity and before the shadow of stress had fallen on the young. The sun shone and the girls were sensational. Robert stood out. He had a terrific aura.'

Nairac already felt he had an affinity with the Irish. 'He used to go there for lots of holidays as a boy to stay with people and to fish,' his sister Gabrielle said. 'He just loved it long before he even thought of joining the Army.' Nairac was determined to squeeze all he could out of life but his self image as a swashbuckling Boy's Own hero was more suited to Oxford than South Armagh. Séamus Murphy, a former leading Official republican from South Armagh said:

> He drew immediate attention to himself. He would be on patrol in Crossmaglen with the regular British soldiers but he would be wearing a cowboy hat and trainers. He'd talk to whoever he could and I remember him proudly showing me his Remington Wingmaster shotgun which had 'Law Enforcement Agencies Only' stamped in the metal. Nairac was clearly intelligent and always probing. He'd ask people for a light to test out their reactions and find out a bit about their character. He was a

good-looking fellow who would even try to chat up the girls in Cross and spin yarns about how his mother was from Galway. He also knew his Irish history and was keen to discuss politics. You could say that he cut a dash.

He told Séamus Murphy of his 'pipeline theory' about the IRA. There was an inflow of idealistic young volunteers into the IRA pipeline and an outflow of people who were too tired or felt the struggle was futile and drifted away. 'We're always concentrating on the middle of the pipeline when we need to concentrate on cutting off the inflow,' Nairac would say. They also discussed the theories of Brigadier Frank Kitson contained in *Low Intensity Operations*, the Army's unofficial handbook on revolutionary warfare and counter-insurgency. In what appeared to become something of a personal crusade, Nairac would try to talk to every young person who was brought into Crossmaglen security force base or Bessbrook Mill.

It seems clear from *Talking to People in South Armagh* that Nairac's method was to sympathise with the concerns of local people and try to get them to trust him. This was partly to gain information but also to persuade them that someone in the Army cared more for their welfare than the IRA did. This approach left him open to the charge of naivety; when combined with the full scope of his activities, it also endangered his life. Major C, who arrived with the SAS's A Squadron a few weeks before Nairac was abducted, said:

Nairac was our SB Liaison Officer. It was early days for us and Nairac was quite useful to the squadron because he knew the Special Branch boys and could find his way about. But he was playing a bigger role than that. Basically he was doubling up as an undercover man and a source handler. One day he would go on patrol with the Green Army in Crossmaglen with long hair and a shotgun and the next he would be in Forkhill or Newry in civilian clothes. It was all pretty amateurish and you just can't combine an undercover role with an overt role. As an operator with 14 Int he had done a good job but he couldn't let go. He was trying to do everything. There was already a Nairac myth growing up after his time in the Det and his work with G Squadron before us. A couple of us warned he was going to get his head shot off and tried to get him removed but the powers that be wouldn't have it.

There were also signs that Nairac's romanticism was perhaps colouring his view of republicanism. He cultivated a passable Belfast accent and his singing of rebel songs in Paddy Short's bar in Crossmaglen earned him the nickname Danny Boy. When his room at Bessbrook Mill was cleared out by Major C after his abduction, he discovered that Nairac had been learning Irish. 'He was a Catholic, he almost believed in the cause,' said Major C. 'His room was an absolute shit tip and amongst all the rubbish was a collection of Gaelic language tapes.'

Staff Sergeant P, who was a corporal in B Squadron SAS in late 1976, got to know Nairac well and respected him as a fine officer:

The SAS had the top floor of Bessbrook Mill and we turned it into the best drinking bar in South Armagh. It served draught Guinness on tap, 24 hours a day, and the only outsiders allowed in were people from 14 Int and Bob Nairac. He was a Guinness drinker and so am I, so we got on famously. At first I wondered who this guy was – he'd got a broken nose as bad as mine. Then after a few pints it all started coming out, the extent of his work and the fact that he was operating alone, totally without back-up. He had his own little source circle and he would go out and feed little titbits into the intelligence machine. It was a bit of bravado with him: 'I get down there and entertain the locals, you know. I'm well in with them.' It was this sort of patter.

But before long, he became concerned about the Guards officer's *modus operandi* and was not surprised when he later heard he had disappeared:

I remember I had to do a job with him, a drop off. I was a driver and he was going to do something and he wouldn't tell me what it was but my job was to take him down to Newry in an unmarked car and drop him off there. I said to him, 'Hey Bob, where's your pistol?' He said: 'Oh, I don't need a pistol, I've got this,' and on the seat beside him was a shotgun in a leather carrying case. So off we went down the road and dropped him off, him with his shotgun in a leather case, over his shoulder and off he goes on his own, wandering up the street with no back-up, which the SAS would always have had. Bob was a rogue knight and how his cover was never blown earlier, I'll never know. But he was a brave bastard.

There was at least one occasion when Nairac was compromised. Séamus Murphy, alleged by the authorities to have been a leading Offical IRA man, spotted him at a cattle market in Newry. 'Nairac was wearing a dirty old overcoat and was swigging from a bottle of whisky,' he said. 'When he saw me looking at him he turned away and within a few minutes I was surrounded by RUC men and soldiers; Nairac just slipped away.' It was as if the danger was part of the fix for the young officer. He once sat up until 3 a.m. in the mess in Bessbrook Mill talking to another officer about his prospects for the future. 'I've got this feeling that I'm going to get the chop here,' Nairac said. 'They are after me. They realise I am getting through to the young people and they know – or think they know – who I am.' His only worry, he added, was that someone would look after Bundle, his pet Labrador.

When Nairac attended an Oxford reunion in the autumn of 1976, he regaled contemporaries with tales of his undercover work. Malins was surprised and worried. 'A child could tell from 50 paces that Robert was Ampleforth, Oxford and the Guards,' he said. 'There never walked a man less capable of any deception.' A picture taken at a social evening at Bessbrook Mill hosted by the SAS shows a very different Nairac from the clean-cut Guards officer who had passed out of Sandhurst. His undercover image was one of slightly affected scruffiness: moustache, patched jeans and long, bushy hair. Constable E, based at Forkhill at the time, was also at the function. 'Nairac was playing a guitar and dressed in this strange attire,' he said. 'He was very sociable and obviously talented. And he was blending in, which obviously was what he had aimed to make his forte. He was trying to be a chameleon. Unfortunately he didn't have enough stripes.'

At 9 p.m. on Saturday 14 May 1977, Nairac slipped on a shoulder holster and picked up his 9 mm Browning pistol and two magazines. The pistol had been adapted for undercover use; it had a filed-down butt and the standard safety catch had been replaced with a larger one. The holster enabled the gun to be carried under the left arm so it would not be detected by someone brushing past. He was wearing jeans, an anorak and workman's boots and carrying a driving licence in the name of Danny McErlaine, an Official IRA member from Belfast. Before leaving, Nairac went into the operations room and told Captain David Collett, the SAS operations officer, that he was going to Drumintee and would be back by 11.30 p.m. At 9.25 p.m., he left Bessbrook Mill in a red Triumph Toledo, an Army unmarked car fitted with a microphone under the seat and a high-powered radio. Using the callsign '48 Oscar', Nairac radioed the ops room three times during his journey to Drumintee before making a final call at 9.58 p.m. reporting that he had reached his destination.

That destination was the Three Steps Inn, a known haunt of Provisionals on a site long associated with resistance to British rule. There had been a soup kitchen there during the Great Famine years in the mid-19th century. The same building became McGuill's public house and was burned down by the RUC in 1922. By 1977, it was known to be a gathering place for Provisionals. In January 1975, an Army intelligence officer recorded that Jim Lochrie, blown up by his own bomb later that year, had been 'sourced as being a member of Drumintee and Jonesborough PIRA who meet in the Three Steps pub, Drumintee'.

It was Nairac's desire to recruit an informer that sowed the seeds of his demise. 'He was desperate to get a source because he'd had no success while we were there,' said Major C. 'He had gone to the Three Steps for a meet.' Nairac had already visited the pub the previous night after making contact with a man outside Newry courthouse earlier in the day and arranging to meet him there. The man, it seems, failed to turn up and the following day there were two calls put through to the operations room in Bessbrook Mill from a man with a South Armagh accent asking for Bobby. But Nairac was not there; flouting Army rules, he had crossed the border to spend the day fly-fishing in the Republic. It seems probable that when he returned at teatime, Nairac took a third call from the man and arranged once again to meet him in the Three Steps. The fact that he had not been detected in the bar the night before led him to take another gamble and turn down Collett's offer of SAS back-up.

Nairac had invented a cover story that he was Danny McErlaine, a

'Stickie' — Official IRA member — from Belfast who had fled to the border because things had got too hot. He decided that if he were questioned further he would say he was in the bar to meet Séamus Murphy, believed by the Army to have once been the Official IRA leader in Drumintee area and was wanted in the Republic for possession of a weapon. Murphy had renounced violence and been co-opted to the local council as a Republican Clubs member; Nairac had met him several times at Murphy's advice centre on the Square in Crossmaglen. But the cover story was never likely to stand up to scrutiny. The bar was a Provisional rather than an Official IRA haunt. Although his brother Frank, who was not aligned with either faction, was in the bar at the start of that night, Seamus Murphy had been warned to stay away and no longer drank there.

The John Murphy band from Creggan was playing in the Three Steps that night and up to 200 people were crammed into the bar. Nairac first drew attention to himself by asking people if they had seen a packet of Major cigarettes that had disappeared from the bar. He seemed perturbed about losing them; it was thought afterwards he might have written a telephone number or message on the packet for it to be picked up by his contact. Nairac ordered pints of Guinness at the bar and went to the gents several times and it was there that he was challenged by two Jonesborough men, Kevin Crilly and Danny O'Rourke, and asked who he was. He told them in his Belfast accent that he was Danny McErlaine and that he had come to meet Séamus Murphy.

But there were a number of people who had come the 12 or so miles from Crossmaglen with the band; Nairac might not have been seen in uniform around Drumintee or Jonesborough but many in Crossmaglen would have recognised him as an Army officer. From this point on, Nairac's every move was being watched by a group of men at the bar; they included Crilly, O'Rourke, Terry McCormick, a Larne man who had recently moved to Jonesborough, Pat Maguire, Gerry Fearon and Thomas Morgan, all from Jonesborough, Michael McCoy, from Forkhill, and Owen Rocks from Killeavey. At 11.15 p.m., Charlie Quinn, a band member, announced that there was a special request for Danny McErlaine who had come 'the whole way from Belfast'. Nairac got up and sang *The Broad Black Brimmer* — including the words 'But when Ireland claims her freedom, The men she'll chose to lead 'em, Will wear the broad black Brimmer of the IRA' – and *The Boys of the Old Brigade*, both maudlin songs about the War of Independence.

It was McCormick, a heavily built former boxer, who next confronted Nairac. Eyewitness reports are conflicting but it seems that McCormick asked the stranger outside for a fight; there was no struggle in the pub. Morgan told the RUC later: 'The dance band was loading up and about five minutes later I saw McCormick go over to the SAS man [Nairac] and say something to him. The SAS man then walked out of the pub and through the front door.' Rocks claimed that McCormick had told him: 'We think that fellow at the bar is an SAS man. We're going to take him outside and give him a good hiding.' At Oxford, Nairac's boxing had been governed by the Queensberry rules; McCormick was not interested in a fair fight. As he stepped outside the bar behind Nairac, McCormick pulled a red-and-white scarf over his face and Maguire blocked the pub door so no one else could come out. Crilly, McCoy and Rocks were already in the car park while Morgan and Fearon had just returned after scouting the road in Morgan's car to see if any Army patrols were in the area.

Even at this stage, Nairac had a chance of escaping but he chose to take McCormick on. Both McCormick and Maguire laid into him with feet as well as fists and Nairac's Browning pistol flew out if its holster and onto the tarmac. McCormick grabbed it, placed it against Nairac's head and warned: 'Don't move you fucker or I'll shoot you.' The Guards officer was then pulled by his hair into a bronze Ford Cortina which Crilly had driven into the car park. McCormick and Maguire sat either side of Nairac on the back seat while O'Rourke jumped into the passenger seat. Crilly drove the car, which was followed by Fearon and Morgan. McCoy and Rocks were left behind and, despite knowing that Nairac was almost certainly being driven to his death, decided to continue drinking and headed for the Fairways Hotel in Dundalk.

It took about seven or eight minutes for the two cars to drive across the border to a small bridge over the River Flurry next to a field just off the A1. After Nairac was pulled out of the car by McCormick and Maguire, Crilly and O'Rourke drove on to Dundalk to find Liam Townson, an IRA man from Meigh who was on the run and living at the home of Liam Fagan, a senior Provisional, at Proleek next to

Ravensdale Forest. Townson was found in the Cabin Inn in Bridge Street in the town; he had been drinking most of the day but agreed to come with them when O'Rourke told him they were 'holding some boy out the road' who was believed to be an SAS officer. On the way back, Townson told Crilly to stop the car so he could pick up his .32 revolver, which was hidden in a stone wall near Kilcurry.

When Townson arrived, Nairac was propped up against the bridge being questioned by McCormick while Maguire pointed the Browning pistol at his head. Townson began to drag Nairac into the field; he tried to break free and was kicked and punched again before being questioned by Townson and pistol-whipped with the Browning. Townson later told the Garda: 'I told him to get up, that we were heading for the North and that he would not be coming back. When we were coming to a ditch, he grabbed his own gun from my hand and I shouted: "Come quick, he has the gun". The two of us fell on the ground. Pat [Maguire] came forward and lifted a paling post and hit him a number of times across the head.'

Nairac had now almost lost consciousness and knew he was about to die. Townson said in his statement:

> I shot the British Captain. He never told us anything. He was a great soldier . . . I had a lot of drink taken. I asked the Captain who he was and he said he was a Stickie. I asked him who he knew and he said Séamus Murphy from Drumintee. I told him I didn't believe him, that he was a British soldier and I had to kill him. I hit him on the head with my fist and then the butt of my gun. He said: 'You're going to kill me, can I have a priest?' He was in a bad state . . . Terry [McCormick] came over and I said: 'Let on you are a priest and see can you get any information from that man.' He knelt down over him and blessed himself and we all stood back away out of the road. Terry talked to him for a few seconds. I do not know what he was saying. I took him away then and shot him in the head. The gun wasn't right that I was using, so I clicked it a few times and then it went off.

Morgan said that Townson had screamed 'Fuck you, it's only blanks' at Nairac as the gun misfired three times before the fatal shot was fired.

Back at Bessbrook Mill, Collett became concerned when Nairac did not report back. At 12.05 a.m., he told his commanding officer that Nairac was missing and then sent two SAS men in an unmarked car to drive past the pub. At around 1 a.m., an SAS trooper was put out on the ground to see if there was anything suspicious; he saw Nairac's car with a wing mirror broken and cigarettes and coins around it, which indicated there had been a struggle. 'The guy had left us in a quandary,' said Major C. 'We weren't sure what he had been doing. He could have been screwing some lady, all sorts of things could have happened. There was very little we could do before first light because it might have been a come-on or the car could have been booby-trapped. We were left high and dry and Nairac actually endangered the lives of a lot of our guys.' At 5.45 a.m., the RUC was informed that Nairac had probably been abducted and a full-scale air and ground search began on both sides of the border. At Bessbrook Mill, there was concern that Nairac's filofax-type diary was missing. He invariably carried it with him and it was crammed with information about his work. It was never found.

A Provisional IRA statement claimed that 'we arrested him on Saturday night and executed him after interrogation in which he admitted he was an SAS man' but of the nine men involved in killing Nairac, only Townson and Fearon were in the IRA. No one in the Three Steps had known precisely who Nairac was and his abduction was not a planned IRA operation. Constable E, who was involved in the murder investigation, said:

> Nairac didn't cost anybody's lives because he wasn't properly handled by the thugs that had him. Townson was drunk and he turned out to be the main man but all he did was to ask a few simple questions and then shoot him. If he had been compos mentis himself and had he taken cognisance of the fact that this man was probably military, he had hardware on him and a false identity etc., he would have been stashed away, tied up, guarded and handed over to more senior IRA men. They would have had a field day with him both in terms of propaganda and extracting information.

Townson was arrested by the Garda at Liam Fagan's farm while O'Rourke, Fearon, Morgan, McCoy and Rocks were brought in by the RUC. McCormick had been questioned by Constable E and another officer but fled across the border with Maguire and Crilly before they could be arrested. It later transpired that McCormick, who had been sweating profusely during questioning, had been suffering from a bullet wound to the stomach sustained when Maguire accidentally shot him as Nairac tried to escape.

In December 1978, Townson was convicted of murder on the basis of his statements and sentenced to penal servitude for life. After his arrest, it emerged that his English father, a sanitary inspector with the Department of Health, was a former soldier who had served in Northern Ireland during the war and settled in Meigh after marrying a local girl. Morgan was tried in Northern Ireland and also convicted of murder while O'Rourke received ten years for manslaughter, McCoy five years for kidnapping and Rocks two years for with-holding information. Townson was the last to be freed from prison when he was released in August 1990. He remained in the republican movement and was among Conor Murphy's canvassing team in Drumintee during the assembly elections of June 1998. He lives quietly in St Moninna Park, a council estate in Meigh, with his girlfriend, Eileen Winters. O'Rourke is a prominent Sinn Féin member and pillar of the local community in Drumintee where he is chairman of the GAA club. Rocks, McCoy and Fearon all still live in the Drumintee and Jonesborough area. Morgan was released from prison in 1986 but was killed a year later when his car collided with a cement mixer on the same A1 road he had used to drive to the field by the River Flurry on the night Nairac was killed. McCormick, Maguire and Crilly remain on the run either in the Republic or North America. McCormick was last heard of in New Jersey where he was in trouble with the police for breaking a patrolman's jaw; one of his relatives now runs a boxing club in Jonesborough.

Danny McErlaine, the Belfast motor mechanic whose identity Nairac had used in the Three Steps and on his false driving licence, was shot dead by the IRA in June 1978. His maggot-infested body, the hands tied with nylon binder twine, was dumped on the Edenappa Road, less than a mile from the Three Steps. McErlaine had been on the run since 1974 and had moved to South Armagh before Nairac's death; the IRA said he had been 'executed' for using their weapons for unauthorised criminal activities.

In February 1979, it was announced that the Queen had approved the posthumous award of the George Cross, the highest honour for gallantry in peacetime, to Captain Robert Nairac. The citation said: 'His quick, analytical brain, resourcefulness, physical stamina and above all his courage and dedication inspired admiration in everyone who knew him . . . he was subjected to a succession of exceptionally savage assaults in an attempt to extract information which would have put other lives and future operations at serious risk. These efforts to break Captain Nairac's will failed entirely.' *An Phoblacht* took a rather different view. In a cartoon strip by Cormac, entitled 'Captain Nervewreck' and published eight months after Nairac's death, the officer was portrayed as an upper-class buffoon in a 'stirring tale full of action, adventure and the gross stupidities of the Brits'. An example of his attempts to mimic an Irish accent was: 'Hoots mon, would you ever be giving me a pint of bitter, begorrah, the noo? And where would you be thinking I was from old man – I mean, bejapers, och aye!' The story ends with Nervewreck being asked by a pub customer: 'Excuse me, would you mind stepping outside?' Pat Thompson, who had been in jail for two years when Nairac was killed, said: 'He believed his own propaganda and he paid with his life, didn't he? Very stupid man. He probably thought he was Jack the lad and all the natives were thick paddies. It was very, very unprofessional. Some of his superiors must have been doing their head in.'

More than 22 years after his death, Nairac's body has still not been found. According to both republican and security sources, the most likely explanation for this is that the body was destroyed by the IRA either to avoid negative propaganda or because of the severe injuries he had received. Liam Fagan is believed to have been entrusted with disposing of the body; he became a member of Republican Sinn Féin after the split in the republican movement in 1986 and died three years later. The secret of what happened to Nairac's body probably died with him.

A year before Nairac's abduction, five people who objected to planning permission for an extension to the Anglo-Irish Meat Company plant in Ravensdale received death threats in a note delivered by three masked gunmen to their homes. 'Withdraw your objections to the factory extension or a member of your families will be dead in 24 hours,' the note said. In 1983, Eamon Collins stayed in a safe house in Dundalk owned by one of the men said to have put Nairac's body through a mincer in a meat factory. Unknown to the factory owners, a number of IRA men had been working there on a short-term, casual basis. Another IRA man told Collins that the body had been left in a pit near the factory and then taken in and dealt with like any other carcass. 'They scalped him, cut out his innards, then turned him into meat and bone-meal,' the IRA man said. 'I think they must have burnt the scalp and the giblets.'

Exactly seven years after her brother's death, Gabrielle Nairac travelled to South Armagh to see for herself the car park where he had been bundled into Crilly's Cortina and the field where Townson had shot him. 'We had been very close and the time just seemed right to go there,' she said. 'Robert certainly stuck his neck out. He was a bit dotty like that. He thought he could get away with it but in a way we all do. As a small boy he had read Bulldog Drummond so you can imagine his approach. It was very romantic and he just thought he could do something to make a difference.'

In the two decades since Nairac's final visit there, the Three Steps, a bungalow built in the early 1970s, has changed little. On the walls there are paintings depicting peasants hunting near Killeavey, Cúchulainn playing a hurling game, Art McCooey penning an epic poem to mourn the death of O'Neill of the Fews and the chieftains of the Fews plotting the rebellion of 1641. Behind the log bar, there are certificates of good management and a collection of willow pattern crockery. The Surgeon drinks there regularly and in 1998 the pub car park was the scene of vicious brawls between Provisionals and Real IRA members in the weeks after the Omagh bombing. When the IRA finally agreed to release details of the whereabouts of some of 'the disappeared', the names Charlie Armstrong and Gerry Evans were missed off the list. No information about these bodies would ever be given, the statement intimated.

One Sunday afternoon in June 1999, a body was found dumped on the Carrowmarron Road near Belleek, a bloodstained sheet wrapped around the head. The victim was Paul 'Bull' Downey, a drugs dealer from Newry who had been abducted outside the Canal Court Hotel in the town 15 hours earlier. He had been stripped to his underpants and socks before part of his forehead was blasted off with a shotgun. It was the first such killing by the IRA for more than five years but few dared to hope it would be the last.

Chapter 9

'Taking the War to England'

'We mixed the explosives for Baltic Exchange in a shed in South Armagh. I can't remember what shed, it could be any one of a dozen . . . I have done between 15 and 20 mixes ranging from 200 lbs to 10 tons.'
(Volunteer Bernard McGinn to RUC detectives, April 1997)

'In recent years, South Armagh has been a major source of the strategic planning, logistics, engineering, assembly and development aspects of the PIRA campaign on the mainland.'
(Assistant Commissioner David Veness,
Metropolitan Police, October 1998)

'Make me an offer I can't refuse,' said Bernard McGinn as he lifted his head up, opened his eyes and placed both hands on the formica table in front of him. The two detectives in the Gough barracks custody room could hardly believe what the IRA man had just said. He had refused to answer questions during eight interview sessions conducted in the 51 hours since he had been arrested in a hayshed near Crossmaglen along with three other South Armagh Brigade volunteers. Now he was offering to become an informer. 'You know what I mean,' he said. 'I want out. I want my freedom.' The following morning, he dropped another bombshell. 'Do you want to stop another Canary Wharf?' he asked the detectives. 'I can tell you how it happened and how it was planned. I can tell you what is going on in South Armagh.'

Initially, the RUC had not even known their prisoner's name and had thought he might be a Belfast volunteer living on the run in Dundalk. His face had been badly bloodied after being punched and kicked by the SAS men who had detained him but he appeared composed and ready to face seven days of interrogation in Gough barracks. At first, he would stare at a fixed point on the wall or pretend to be sleeping. If he was hearing the questions put to him, he showed no inclination to answer them. But gradually he began to listen and then respond. In the fifth interview, on the evening after his arrest, he had told them his name and a few details about his family; it turned out that Caoimhghín Ó Caoláin, elected as Sinn Féin's sole member of the Irish parliament two months later, was his brother-in-law. After asking for a deal involving immunity in return for his co-operation, McGinn began to talk about his son and wept at the thought of him growing up while his father was in jail.

McGinn was cautious, telling the interviewers they could not write down what he was telling them. The detectives, in turn, were walking a tightrope for they knew that if they kept him talking then lives would undoubtedly be saved but any false promise of immunity could lead to charges being thrown out by a court. But over the following five days he made confession after confession and implicated more than two dozen South Armagh men in IRA attacks in Northern Ireland and Britain. He told the detectives he had joined the IRA 24 years earlier at the age of 15 and had 'shot a wee lad in Keady' when he was 18. His accomplice on that occasion had been Dessie O'Hare, the IRA's 'Border Fox', whom Constable Billy McCaughey had tried to kill in the Rock Bar in Keady two months earlier. O'Hare and McGinn had watched Gilbert Johnston as he drove into Keady with his girlfriend, Kathleen Trimble, and stopped at McGennity's store to buy some crisps and ice cream. As Johnston got back into his Fiat, O'Hare and McGinn, clad in balaclavas and green combat uniforms and wielding Armalites, jumped out of a blue van and fired 18 .223 calibre rounds into the car, killing him instantly. IRA supporters had fingered Johnston as a UDR man but he had left the Army four years earlier after his elder brother Samuel was shot and badly wounded at the family farm at Tullyvallen.

After returning the guns to an arms dump at Clontibret in County Monaghan, McGinn vomited as he recalled the sight of Johnston's bullet-riddled body. A year later, he was arrested at a disused farmhouse as he arrived to pick up a car containing a milk churn. He jumped bail and was sentenced in his absence to 10 years in jail for possession of explosives. After several months on the run, McGinn was re-arrested when he gave himself up at the end of a 27-hour siege at a house in Dundalk. He had been holding a family hostage with a pistol and a hand grenade from which he had removed the pin; this episode earned him the nickname 'the Pin' within the IRA. He was sent to Portlaoise jail, where he met Frank McCabe, who regaled him with tales of the exploits of the South Armagh Brigade. McGinn was released in 1987. 'I went back to the Castleblaney unit but they were no good so I tried to join the South Armagh unit,' he told detectives. 'But it took a long time before they would trust me. I was only accepted after about four or five years.'

Although Castleblaney is just seven miles north-west of Cross-maglen, McGinn was viewed as an outsider by republicans in South Armagh. Their initial reluctance to involve him in operations turned out to be well founded because now, 17 years after he first met Frank McCabe, he was giving detectives the most important insight into the activities of the South Armagh Brigade since the Troubles began.

McGinn revealed that the IRA had been plotting to bomb Birmingham. The plan, he said, had been discussed in Peter John Caraher's kitchen in February 1997 with McGinn, Frank McCabe, Micheál Caraher and one other present. 'We discussed where the mix for the Birmingham bombing would be made,' he said. 'The Major's shed at Cullyhanna or the same place as Canary Wharf was mentioned but nothing was decided . . . old Caraher was not present but knew it was an IRA meeting.' The shed, which was in fact situated off the Monog Road outside Crossmaglen, had once been owned by Major Michael Wright, formerly of the Royal Hussars, whose family had lived in South Armagh since 1720. He and his wife, who were both Protestants, had lived there peacefully until 1979. The man who bought the shed from them lived some way away and had not known the IRA was using it.

McGinn said the Birmingham bombing was to be similar to that of Manchester in June 1996 with the explosives being shipped out by freight through Dublin and loaded onto a vehicle bought in England. But the plan had been shelved when an IRA man from 'the Dundalk-

Newry end' reported that he 'reckoned he had tails' from the police or MI5 when he visited Birmingham to decide where the bomb should be planted.

McGinn confirmed that the South Armagh Brigade had been providing the main impetus for the IRA's England campaign since the early 1990s. Having supplied the majority of the large bombs used to blow up towns in Northern Ireland in the late 1980s, it had seemed logical for South Armagh to 'export' similar devices across the Irish Sea. The Baltic Exchange bomb of April 1992 was the first large fertiliser-based device to be exploded in England; the bomb's power had been enhanced by Semtex-based detonating cord being wrapped around the explosives. Baltic Exchange also marked a shift in IRA tactics towards economic targets. By blowing up the City of London, the republican movement was warning the Government of the consequences of resisting Sinn Féin's demands. After Baltic Exchange the 1990s saw bombs made in South Armagh explode three times in London and once in Manchester. Another South Armagh tactic, the use of mortars to attack heavily protected targets, was also exported to England during the same period.

The Baltic Exchange bomb was mixed in a shed in South Armagh under the supervision of the Surgeon. McGinn, who was part of the mixing team, said the shed was one of a dozen made available to the IRA for grinding explosives. After the mix had been completed, the explosives were put into clear plastic bags and loaded onto a trailer, which was then towed away by a tractor. The explosives were shipped to England where the bomb was assembled and loaded into a white Ford Transit van sold for cash by a Home Counties couple to two Irishmen on the morning of 10 April 1992. At 9.25 p.m. on the same day, the van, which had been parked in St Mary Axe, opposite the Baltic Exchange, in the heart of the City of London, exploded, killing three people and resulting in an insurance payout of about £350 million.

The IRA's reasoning behind stepping up its England campaign was that military casualties in Northern Ireland were not putting enough pressure on the Government. Soldiers were becoming much more difficult to kill and their deaths hardly registered on the political Richter scale. But bombing England, and particularly economic targets in London, kept Northern Ireland at the top of the news agenda. In February 1993, a member of the IRA's GHQ Staff told Owen Bowcott of the *Guardian*:

> Last year saw 46 bombs, £1,200 million worth of damage, the collapse of insurance cover and the introduction of armed roadblocks in London. There were 1,060 occasions when commuter traffic and businesses ground to a halt. It's a crisis in the heart of the British capital which has demonstrated that so long as interference in Irish affairs continues then the consequences of that conflict will spill over and be visited on the national territory of the occupier.

McGinn said he had been part of 'basically the same outfit', led by the Surgeon, which had mixed up to 20 bombs. 'When the mixes were done, if they were for the six counties we didn't know exactly where they were for,' he said. 'We knew about the English ones because it was talked about.' But he did remember making a 2,500 lb bomb which was abandoned near the Army's Drumadd Barracks on the outskirts of Armagh city in November 1996. He said:

> The big bomb outside Armagh . . . was mixed at the same place as the Canary Wharf bomb. It was for an Army patrol. Myself, Frank McCabe, McArdle, Micheál Caraher, and [the Surgeon] mixed it in the shed. The mix was fertiliser and sugar. One ton was mixed and put into a twin axle trailer . . . [the Surgeon] towed the trailer away with a big red car. It was dirty and I don't think it was his own car . . . The fertiliser and sugar are just bought at normal outlets. I have nothing to do with buying.

According to Sean O'Callaghan, the South Armagh Brigade had only ever been on the fringes of the England campaign in the 1970s and 1980s:

> They ran some training camps for the England Department in places like Ravensdale. They manufactured timers for the England people. On some occasions they arranged for guys going across to England on the backs of lorries. But they didn't play a huge part. It was from the very late 1980s that South

Armagh got stuck into England on a big scale. All through the IRA campaign in England they had been planting relatively small bombs. Once they began to use big fertiliser bombs they needed transportation and stuff and that's when South Armagh came straight into it. They then essentially had a stranglehold on the England department. The IRA also became more dependent on South Armagh because the RUC was getting on top of it everywhere else. South Armagh was the one safe base area they had.

As well as making the bombs for England, the South Armagh Brigade also began to supply volunteers to be based there. One of these was Jimmy Canning, a bombmaker and quartermaster who was sent to England by Tom Murphy in 1990 after the IRA suffered a series of setbacks in England. In December 1988, the Clapham bomb factory had been discovered and Nicholas Mullin, its quartermaster, arrested. A year later, two IRA men, Liam O'Dhuibhir and Damian McComb, were captured at St Bride's Bay on the Pembrokeshire coast as they loaded Semtex, guns and ammunition into their car to be taken to a rented flat in Luton. Canning was sent to London to plug the gap.

Although his heavy drinking and gambling made him an unusual choice for 'active service' in England, Canning's Scottish accent and regular trips across the Irish Sea to take up labouring jobs meant that he was more likely than most to escape detection. He was known to the security forces as a trusted and experienced IRA volunteer but he had had no convictions or reputation outside anti-terrorist circles to set him apart from scores of other unemployed South Armagh men who would travel regularly to Britain to look for work.

Canning's hatred for British rule had been fuelled by beatings he had received from soldiers in South Armagh, where he had lived since the age of 11 after moving from Glasgow when his parents' marriage split up. A few days after the Narrow Water massacre in 1979, he had been dragged out of a friend's car at an Army checkpoint in Forkhill and abused by members of a Queen's Own Highlanders platoon. His Glasgow accent and known IRA activities meant Scottish regiments often singled him out. Incensed by what he saw as unwarranted harassment, Canning's friend grabbed a soldier's rifle and threatened:

'If you don't leave him alone, I'll stick this up your fucking hole.' As the pair drove off at speed, Canning, who was expecting the car to be riddled with bullets at any moment, curled himself up in the well of the passenger seat. The next day, Canning's friend went to the security force base in Forkhill to complain about the way they had been treated and was confronted by the officer who had been in charge of the platoon. 'There are three things you should remember,' said the officer. 'First, some of my men are very young and they are very frightened of being in South Armagh. Second, their commanding officer and 17 soldiers were blown up last Monday. Third, if you ever again tell one of them that you'll stick a rifle up their "fucking hole" then I'll shoot you myself.'

Nearly twelve years later, 'Wee Jimmy', as Canning was nicknamed, was in the saloon bar of the Adam and Eve pub on the Uxbridge Road in Hayes in Middlesex during a singles night when he spotted Audrey Lamb, a 60-year-old divorcee. She had split up with Andy Masters, her boyfriend of 22 years, some months earlier and they had sold the greengrocers they had run together in Northolt. Masters continued to pay the mortgage at their bungalow but Lamb, rather than return to a home empty of all but her memories, would sometimes book into a guest-house for the night. She often spent her days sitting in the local launderette chatting aimlessly to anyone who would help her while away the hours. In a further blow to her sense of self-worth, she had undergone a mastectomy after discovering a tumour in her breast. Reflecting bitterly on her relationship with Masters, who was 17 years her junior, she had written in her diary: 'I had served my purpose and he left me.' Another entry read: 'What am I? I am old, I am fat, I have got nothing left.'

Canning, who was 37 and staying in a bedsit in Hayes, began to woo Lamb with tales of his loneliness in the capital. Lamb was flattered by the attention he paid her; she could not quite believe that this man had appeared to rescue her from her despair. He moved into her bungalow at 15 Islip Gardens, a tree-lined cul-de-sac in Northolt, in May 1991, just a month after they had met. For Canning, however, Lamb's only purpose was to provide a cloak of suburban normality to cover his IRA activities. Lamb, who had two grown-up children, knew nothing of Canning's English wife Sue and their four young children who lived in a council house in Fairview Park next to

Forkhill's security force base. For the past decade, he had spent long periods working in England and on one of his early spells there had met his future wife and persuaded her to join him in a mobile home in Forkhill. His trips to England continued and he would sometimes only return home for a fortnight in the summer, most of which he would spend getting drunk in the Welcome Inn in the village and blowing his wages by buying rounds of drinks. In the meantime, Sue Canning would struggle to manage the family and house on her social security benefits.

Within a month of meeting Lamb, Canning could be seen busying himself with odd jobs around the house, gardening and wheeling a trolley around the supermarket as Lamb selected the groceries. They owned a cat called Sylvester, Canning took up golf and a Neighbourhood Watch sticker appeared on their sitting room window. Lamb thought she had found a new happiness and over the course of a year she showered him with gifts worth £10,000, one of them a battered Ford Granada with a 'Jimmy/Audrey' sticker across the top of the windscreen. The couple exchanged rings in a ceremony at the Adam and Eve and she hoped they would soon marry.

Lamb's emotional dependence on Canning became so strong that when she discovered he was an IRA man she agreed to remain silent rather than risk losing him. But their relationship was stormy and they could often be heard arguing, once after another man had patted Lamb on the bottom in the Adam and Eve. Canning's periodic absences in Ireland were another source of friction and Lamb began to suspect he was seeing another woman there. In October 1991, desperate to win him back, she persuaded her friend Anne Hanmore to travel to South Armagh with her to track Canning down and persuade him to return to London. They eventually found him at the Welcome Inn in Forkhill. He had no choice but to tell Lamb about his wife, by this time expecting their fifth child, but promised to go back with her. Lamb was so besotted that neither his wife nor his IRA activities shook her faith in the relationship. Afraid Canning would drink or gamble away the money the IRA had given him to pass on to other volunteers in London, she offered to look after it.

In January 1992, Canning used his Ford Transit van to move weapons and explosives into Islip Gardens. He built an arms bunker underneath a flowerbed next to a rabbit hutch in the garden and used it to store AK-47s. Hundreds of rounds of ammunition, timing and power units, under-car mercury tilt switch bombs, incendiary devices and detonators were secreted around the house. Blocks of Semtex were stored underneath the bed the couple shared and they slept with a loaded .357 Smith and Wesson revolver under the pillows.

Canning was involved in at least a dozen IRA attacks across London in 1991 and 1992. His primary role as quartermaster was to prepare, maintain and supply bombs to other IRA men; some of the devices, however, he planted himself. There were four fire-bombs left in Brent Cross shopping centre in December 1991 and another at the National Gallery, Trafalgar Square the following day. In January 1992, he left a bomb in Whitehall Place, close to 10 Downing Street, and in February a similar device in Parliament Street in Whitehall. There were also bombs at Clapham Junction and London Bridge stations, outside the offices of the Crown Prosecution Service and on two trains at Ilford. When Lamb heard a radio report of a bombing, she would ask Canning: 'Was that one of yours?'

A speck of dust was probably responsible for Canning's eventual capture and conviction. Shortly after 9 p.m. on 27 June 1991, just over two months after he had met Lamb, he left a brown canvas holdall containing nearly 30 lbs of Semtex outside the Alfred Beck Theatre in Hayes. The bomb had been set on an hour-long timer designed to detonate it just as the 27 members of the band of the Blues and Royals, part of the Household Cavalry, were completing their performance in front of nearly 300 people. The timer worked but tests later carried out at the Defence Research Establishment in Kent established that a micro-switch had failed, possibly because a particle of dust or fluff had stuck to it. Canning had chosen his spot carefully; the bomb had been hidden from view by a grassy bank and close to an air vent, 50 ft from the stage, which would have channelled the blast into the building. The bomb was twice the size of the one that had gone off at the Royal Marine School of Music in Deal, Kent in September 1989, killing 11 bandsmen. Had the micro-switch worked, the bomb would probably have brought down the roof of the theatre and killed members of the audience as well as musicians.

Within a week, the Metropolitan Police had established that Canning was the bomber. His finger and palm prints, which had been left on the holdall, matched those held by the RUC; he was claiming unemployment benefit under his own name and was swiftly traced to Islip Gardens. The police rented a bungalow opposite and began Operation Catnip, a programme of round-the-clock surveillance of the house. Canning was codenamed 'Snowstorm' and Lamb 'Scarlet Globe'. At 6.50 a.m. on 6 April 1992, three days before the general election, Canning, wearing a suit and Barbour jacket and carrying a black briefcase, was photographed leaving the house as Lamb, in her dressing gown and slippers, blew him kisses. An undercover police officer followed him as he walked towards Northolt tube station to join the commuter throng. At 7.18 a.m., another officer saw him get off the Central Line at Shepherd's Bush and catch a bus to Westminster Bridge Road near Waterloo station. At 7.58 a.m., he caught another bus to Lower Regent Street and then went into a Burger King restaurant at Piccadilly Circus.

Canning used anti-surveillance techniques, which are taught to IRA men operating in England, such as pretending to board a bus and then doubling back at the last minute. But by the time he went into Burger King he was being tailed by five undercover officers. Inside the briefcase, which he had bought at a car boot sale, was a small Semtex bomb on a one-hour timer. Lamb had watched him as he put the device together in her sitting room the day before. Canning went into the Burger King lavatories, spent four minutes activating the timer and left. At this point, he appeared to panic; either he could not find the target for the bomb or he had spotted one of the undercover officers. He dumped the briefcase in Bridle Lane in Soho, where it exploded shortly afterwards, shattering the windows of surrounding offices but causing no injuries.

Rather than arrest Canning as he left Burger King, Met officers had taken a calculated risk that they would be able to keep track of him and evacuate whichever area the bomb was left in. Fortunately, Canning himself had decided to leave it in a place where it was unlikely to cause loss of life; the intended target was never known. Two days later, Canning, wearing yellow rubber gloves, was filmed putting a collection of holdalls and binbags into his Granada. He was followed along the A40 to Uxbridge, where he unloaded everything into a lock-up garage. Operation Catnip was compromised when police interviewed the estate agent who had rented out the garage without realising he was a regular at the Adam and Eve. Fearing Canning might be tipped off, the Met decided to move in and arrest the IRA man and his mistress. Their last night together was spent, as their relationship had begun, at the Adam and Eve. After closing time, they called a minicab and were being dropped off at Islip Gardens when armed officers emerged from the shadows to surround and arrest them. Canning tried to get away but was wrestled to the ground and his face gashed on the kerb. His Smith and Wesson, which was loaded, was tucked into the waistband of his trousers.

At the garage in Uxbridge, police found 76 lbs of Semtex divided into 14 blocks, six Romanian-made AKM rifles, 651 rounds of ammunition, three car bombs, eight detonators and several mercury tilt switches. Ballistic tests revealed that the AKM had been used to fire 15 shots during the attempted assassination of Air Chief Marshal Sir Peter Terry, a 63-year-old former governor of Gibraltar. He had been hit nine times in the face and body during an attack at his home in Staffordshire in September 1990 but survived. Semtex, timers, fire-bombs, detonators and a Honda motorcycle fitted with false number plates were found in a second lock-up garage which Canning had rented in Southall.

Lamb broke down during questioning and told detectives: 'I am not a member of the IRA and I do not support what they do. I did wrong in loving a man and I know I did wrong in what I did. I never planted or made any bombs. I will help the police by giving as much information as I can to help catch these cruel people.' She added: 'I was very frightened. He said that if I said anything they would get rid of my family and blow me up. Not him, but they.' In a letter to Mrs Hanmore during her trial, Lamb wrote: 'Jimmy kept saying he was sorry to me. He passed a note to me saying that he hoped I would not hold a grudge against him and that I started as a bit on the side but he grew to love me.' She also told her friend that Andy Masters had been trying to contact her. 'It's a bit late, isn't it? If he hadn't gone off with that barmaid I wouldn't be in this mess.'

In February 1993, Canning was jailed for 30 years at the Old Bailey while Lamb was convicted of possession of rifles and provid-ing her lover with money and other aid knowing it might be used for acts of terrorism. As she was hauled weeping from the dock by prison officers, she sobbed: 'What's it all about?' She served part of a three-year sentence but died shortly after being released from prison. Canning's marriage survived the revelations which emerged during the trial, his wife apparently regarding the story about Lamb as 'all lies'; she continued to take her children to visit their father in the Maze after his transfer there from England in 1995. Republicans argue that Canning's relationship with Lamb was an illustration of the depth of his dedication to the IRA's cause rather than a straightforward example of unfaithfulness. Canning remains an influential IRA man and in 1998 was visited in jail by the Surgeon.

It had not been until the 1980s that South Armagh's impact had first been felt in Britain. On 20 July 1982, Brigadier Peter Morton was at his desk in the Ministry of Defence, where he was advising the Chief of the General Staff on Northern Ireland matters, when he heard a large explosion in Hyde Park. A 25 lb bomb had been detonated by radio control as 16 troopers from the Blues and Royals were riding to Horseguards Parade for the Changing of the Guard. Around the bomb, which had been placed in the boot of a blue Morris Marina, dozens of four-inch and six-inch nails had been packed. Two troopers died at the scene and another two in the days afterwards. Seven horses were killed or put down as a result of their injuries.

Corporal Oliver Pitt was blown over his horse's head and hit in the face and neck by shrapnel. 'I heard screaming around me,' he said in a police statement. 'I saw and felt blood dripping from my head into the road and realised a bomb had exploded. I lay there for a few seconds and started to move my limbs, checking whether I was in one piece. I looked around me and saw what I can only describe as carnage. There were four or five people motionless and about three severely-injured horses.' Although the names of Lieutenant Anthony Daly, Corporal Roy Bright, Lance Corporal Jeffrey Young and Trooper Simon Tipper, the four soldiers killed by the blast, were soon forgotten, the plight of Sefton, the most severely-injured horse, captured the public imagination. Around three million get well cards were sent to the black gelding and the story of his recovery prompted two books: *Sefton – the Story of a Cavalry Horse* and *Sefton – The Horse for Any Year*.

Brigadier Morton was among those who visited the scene of the blast that afternoon. He said:

The bombers had used exactly the same methods they had used in South Armagh. This one was radio-controlled whereas I had encountered command-wire bombs but it was identical in that you had a concealed position where the button point was and a good view of the target area. They had learned from experience that you needed a good guide point such as a telegraph pole or a gate. At Hyde Park I could see immediately there was one line right across the park where you could see a signboard and a fence so that when the standard bearer at the head of the horses was level with that you knew they were absolutely spot on the target area. It was exactly the same principle South Armagh always applied to all their bombs and I don't think they ever changed that.

Two hours after the Hyde Park blast, a bomb fitted with a timer exploded underneath a bandstand at Regent's Park as the band of the Royal Green Jackets gave a lunchtime concert. Six soldiers were killed and a seventh died of his wounds two weeks later.

On the evening of 16 August 1986, Danny McNamee and his fiancée Linda Vize were about to go to bed in their flat overlooking the Square in Crossmaglen when the door was broken down by a platoon of Colonel Spicer's Scots Guards. They had been due to marry six days later but McNamee, 25, was arrested by the RUC and flown to London to be charged with conspiracy to cause explosions. His fingerprints had been found on tape taken from two arms caches. One print had been on the non-adhesive side of a piece of red tape wrapped around a motorcycle repair kit tin which had been adapted into a radio-wave encoder found in Pangbourne Woods in Berkshire in October 1983. Another was on the adhesive side of a piece of grey tape on part of a radio receiver discovered at Salcey Forest in Northamptonshire in January 1984. A third print, also probably McNamee's, had been identified on the gold tip of a 1.5 volt Duracell battery used in a timing and power unit detonated by the bomb squad after being found in Phillimore Gardens in west London in December 1983.

At the Old Bailey in 1987, the prosecution argued that a comparison between the Salcey Forest receiver and a fragment of radio receiver recovered from the debris of the Hyde Park bomb showed 24 similarities and proved they had both been constructed by the same master bomber. McNamee's defence was that there was an innocent explanation for the fingerprints, which must have resulted from his working at a firm called Kimbles Manufacturing in Dundalk. Although he had worked there for seven years, he said in court, he had not realised that James and George McCann, the brothers who ran the business, were IRA men and that the premises were being used to produce parts for bombs. He had simply worked on repairing CB radios and checking circuit boards for gaming machines. 'I work with electrical equipment a lot and repair many things,' he said. 'If my prints are on it [the Salcey Forest receiver], it must have been when I was repairing something.' The jury took five hours to convict McNamee on all counts and he was sentenced to 25 years.

McNamee was regarded by the RUC as the most skilful and prolific IRA bombmaker of his generation. Among the devices he was believed to have constructed was the 500 lb radio-controlled bomb that blew up Major French and two RUC officers at Cornoonagh Hill less than three months before his arrest. The three probably died because French's men were not carrying ECM equipment, which could have jammed the radio signal. Danny McNamee's flat was among the dozen addresses around Crossmaglen searched after the blast. RUC files list the suspected bombmaker as: 'D. McNamee XMG PIRA EO [Explosives Officer] DOB 29 Sep 60'.

Scotland Yard linked McNamee to IRA attacks that killed 19 people in London, including six blown up by the Harrods bomb, between the autumn of 1981 and Christmas 1983 and said his devices had killed dozens in Northern Ireland. His repertoire, they said, included radio-controlled, command-wire, booby-trap, timer and incendiary devices. Although Brendan Burns was believed to have been the main bombmaker who constructed the Narrow Water devices, McNamee's electronics expertise meant it was very possible he too had been involved.

At the age of 14, McNamee had helped pull his father from the rubble of McArdle's pub after a loyalist bomb exploded in the doorway. Thomas McNamee died of abdominal injuries nearly a year later, leaving his eight children to be brought up by an uncle. Scotland Yard officers said that Danny McNamee, who would have

been expected to have left school as soon as possible to help
supplement the meagre family income, was persuaded by the IRA
to continue with his studies because of the aptitude he showed for
maths and science. He had won a place at the Abbey Grammar
School, run by the Christian Brothers, in Newry and went on to pass
11 O Levels and secure three A grades at A Level. He was offered a
place to study Physics at Imperial College, London but left after a
week. His brother Francis later explained: 'Being Irish, he [Danny]
discovered he had little in common with the English and found it hard
to get on with them. He thought them hostile to the Irish people.' In
1979, Danny McNamee went up to Queen's University, Belfast
assisted by a grant from the Southern Education and Library Board
and, according to the RUC, what amounted to sponsorship from the
IRA.

Taking his A level results into account, Queen's University
allowed McNamee straight into the second year of a Physics degree.
He neglected his mainstream studies, although fellow students
remember him as conscientious enough to attend electronics lectures
that had little relevance to his syllabus. According to senior RUC
officers, the explanation for this was that McNamee was working
from a list of the skills he would need for making explosive devices
and during vacations was being coached in bomb-making techniques.
McNamee failed his second year exams and was nearly thrown out of
Queen's. After repeating his final year he scraped a Pass degree and
began to work full-time for the McCann brothers.

McNamee was twice charged under anti-terrorist legislation in the
Irish Republic. In February 1984, he and Aidan Moley, a brother of
Brendan and Séamus Moley, were arrested along with Donal Moyna,
an electronics specialist from Scotstown in County Monaghan. Gardaí
had observed them in the coffee lounge of the Imperial Hotel in
Dundalk as Moyna handed 17 electronic circuit boards to McNamee
and Moley. Charges of possession of explosive substances against the
South Armagh pair were dropped when Moyna argued that he had
designed the circuit boards to stop the fiddling of gaming machines. In
1989, Moyna was arrested at La Guardia airport in New York with
$13,550 in counterfeit notes. The British authorities believed he was in
America to buy electric detonators. Moyna was deported after
pleading guilty and being sentenced to four months in jail.

A high-speed car chase in County Monaghan in July 1985 ended in a second arrest for Danny McNamee. It was later alleged in court that he had been the driver of the vehicle from which two gunmen emerged to hold gardaí hostage. During a bail hearing, Superintendent Michael Lee said he believed McNamee, who had been charged with possession of a firearm, was a member of the Provisional IRA. But in October 1985 McNamee was freed again after defence lawyers argued that he had been held illegally because he had first been arrested under traffic laws and had not been properly released before being re-arrested under the Offences Against the State Act.

At his Hyde Park trial, McNamee took the unusual step of denouncing the IRA in an attempt to be acquitted. 'I was never a member of the IRA and I was never politically involved in support of the IRA,' he said. 'I never had anything to do with explosions or other sorts of violence.' Willie Martin and Paddy McEntee had been cousins of his parents, he said. 'They saw the IRA doing something, picked up the phone and called the police. They were killed.' He asked the court: 'Can you imagine me joining the IRA when they have shot members of my family? Can you imagine the IRA having me as a member when they have shot two of my family as informers?' He added: 'I have always avoided the IRA.' During his 11 years in prison, however, McNamee was accepted as an IRA prisoner. In September 1994, he was one of five IRA men who escaped from Whitemoor jail, shooting and wounding a prison guard as they did so, before being recaptured within two hours. McNamee was transferred to Northern Ireland from Belmarsh jail in May 1997 and elected to serve the remainder of his sentence in the IRA H Blocks in the Maze.

It was not until after he had been freed from the Maze in November 1998 under the terms of the Good Friday Agreement that McNamee, who had consistently protested his innocence, won his legal victory. Six weeks after his release, the Appeal Court in London quashed his conviction on the grounds that it could no longer be proved he made the Hyde Park bomb and fresh evidence meant it was not certain another jury would have found him guilty. Part of the new evidence was that the fingerprints of Dessie Ellis, a senior IRA bombmaker, had been found on items in the Pangbourne cache and that Ellis had said in a statement that the parts of the Hyde

Park circuit boards were similar to those he had constructed. But in a powerful rider to their decision, the three judges stated that 'the Crown makes a strong case that the appellant [McNamee] was guilty of a conspiracy to cause explosions'. They added that despite the quashing of the conviction: 'It does not follow that this appellant is innocent of the charge brought against him or that he has served 11 years' imprisonment for a crime which it has been found he did not commit.' In February 1999, McNamee read the IRA roll of honour at the Burns and Moley commemoration and the following month he sat with the Caraher family during the trial of Volunteer Micheál Caraher and other members of the South Armagh Brigade's sniper team.

T he period when Danny McNamee was involved in supplying bombs for the England campaign marked a step forward from the IRA's 'excursion phase' in the 1970s when small teams of bombers would cross the Irish Sea on specific bombing missions. By 1982, the IRA had built up a logistical structure in Britain comprising arms hides, facilities for building bombs and a support network for 'active service units' which would often spend long periods blending into the community. Assistant Commissioner David Veness, in charge of Scotland Yard's specialist operations branches since 1991, stressed the dangers of underestimating the IRA's capacity for innovation in its campaign to attack Britain. By the time of the Docklands bomb, he said, the IRA had progressed from 'immensely amateur operations likely to result in arrest to very sophisticated attacks on the critical infrastructure like the City of London and Docklands bombs'. This sophistication reached a peak during the IRA campaign of 1996 when South Armagh took centre stage.

On 7 February 1991, as John Major's Gulf War Cabinet sat down in 10 Downing Street to discuss how to deal with Saddam Hussein, an IRA man drove into Whitehall and parked a white Ford Transit van. Peter Gurney, Scotland Yard's chief bomb disposal officer, said afterwards that strips of tape had probably been stuck on the windscreen and lined up with a predetermined spot. In the back of the van were three Mark 10 mortar bombs, the type first used in Newtownhamilton in 1979 and responsible for killing nine RUC officers in Newry in 1985. As the van driver jumped on to the pillion of a motorcycle which had drawn up alongside, the three mortars were launched through a concealed hole in the roof of the van. One of them demolished a cherry tree in the garden of Number 10, causing Major and his colleagues to take cover under the table. Gurney, who defused the other two mortars, said later that the range and angle of firing had been worked out using scale maps and photographs before a reconnaissance run had been carried out. If the van had not been just five degrees out then the Prime Minister might well have been killed.

Although the identity of the volunteer who fired the mortars has never been discovered, the overall intelligence assessment was that he was probably a South Armagh man who had cut his teeth in attacks on Crossmaglen security force base. Seven years later, the event was celebrated in a rebel song entitled *Downing Street*, played to the tune of *On the Street Where You Live* from *My Fair Lady*. It was recorded along with *Sniper's Lament* and *The Fighting Men of Crossmaglen* on tapes being sold at Jonesborough market, where the IRA makes a profit each Sunday by taking a cut from traders selling smuggled alcohol and cigarettes and counterfeit clothes and perfume. 'Now as I walk by, I see mortars fly, I'm glad it's not Downing Street where I live,' intoned the lead singer of a band calling itself the Irish Brigade. 'Now at Number 10, it's like Crossmaglen . . . don't you understand, while you hold Ireland, it's not safe down the street where you live.' It had been the first time the IRA had used mortars in Britain. In March 1994, Mark 6 mortars were fired at Heathrow airport on consecutive days. The Mark 6, modelled on a Chinese two-inch mortar, had been first used in an attack on the Drummuckavall observation post in September 1974.

In April 1993, a second huge fertiliser bomb made in South Armagh exploded at Bishopsgate in the City of London. The 2,200 lb device killed a *News of the World* photographer and caused £500 million worth of damage. The nine warnings for the Bishopsgate bomb were all traced to a telephone box in Forkhill. As with most of the devices planted in England in the 1990s, including the Docklands bomb, the IRA codeword used was Kerrygold. This was thought to have been selected in 1989 after a Kent supermarket owner withdrew Kerrygold butter and other Irish goods from sale in protest at the Deal bombing.

RUC Special Branch established that Bishopsgate had been orga-nised by the Surgeon and Micksey Martin. They had been directed by Tom Murphy to bypass the IRA support network in England because of fears that a breach in security had led to the arrest of Paddy Kelly in November 1992 as he was driving a lorry bomb through Stoke Newington. To do this, they enlisted the help of a South Armagh volunteer who had become rich through smuggling and trading in stolen vehicles throughout the British Isles. Identified here as Volunteer T, he had been an IRA member since the start of the Troubles and had developed extensive criminal contacts in Britain. Micksey Martin had also established contact with members of the London underworld during a spell on remand in Belmarsh prison in 1994.

Although some of the money Volunteer T would make was given to the IRA, much of it he creamed off for himself. He had procured vehicles for the IRA on countless occasions; this time, he was entrusted with delivering a bomb to the City of London. The Ford Iveco tipper truck used at Bishopsgate was stolen from a yard in Newcastle-under-Lyme five weeks before the bombing and re-sprayed from white to dark blue. Volunteer T then arranged to pay two Irish criminals based in England several thousand pounds to drive the bomb to Bishopsgate. The pair parked the lorry on double yellow lines, switched its hazard lights on and then fled on foot towards Aldgate tube station. Volunteer T later fell out with the Surgeon and Martin after arguments about his profiteering from Provisional IRA activities and he subsequently aligned himself with the Real IRA.

South Armagh's central role in the logistic support for the IRA's England Department was illustrated in February 1994 when Feilim O hAdhmaill, a PhD and social policy lecturer at the University of Central Lancashire, was arrested in Accrington. He had just returned from South Mimms service station on the M25 – later used by Séamus McArdle on the eve of the Docklands bomb – after picking up a silver Nissan Stanza which had arrived in England at the port of Fleetwood. Concealed in the seats, under the wheel arches and in the door panels were nearly 3 lbs of Semtex, two booby-trap bombs, a pistol and enough detonators and timers to make 17 more explosive devices. Volunteer T had paid a haulier from Armagh city to deliver it to South Mimms on a low-loader, but the haulier had panicked and left it in a car park in West Thurrock in Essex. Speaking in code in a telephone call to Northern Ireland, O hAdhmaill, a senior IRA quartermaster, reported that the Nissan had not been delivered at the appointed time. The code involved using the names of 31 football teams for days of the month and the names of fictitious relatives for venues. For instance, the message 'Meet at Uncle Cormac's to watch the Derby match' meant a meeting at a motorway service station in Coventry on the fourth of the month. 'Mother-in-law' was the police.

After receiving the message, the South Armagh Brigade arranged for two London-based Irishmen, a father and son, to pick up the car and drive it to South Mimms. In separate operations, MI5 had O hAdhmaill under surveillance while the Nissan were being tracked by MI5. There was some anger within RUC Special Branch when O hAdhmaill, the Armagh city haulier and the London-based Irishmen were all arrested. 'The operation could have been brought off without alerting South Armagh that their supply route had been compromised,' said one anti-terrorist officer. 'It was a classic case of being too keen to grab a headline and get a single conviction rather than waiting and letting things run.' If the watch on O hAdhmaill had continued, he might well have led the authorities to other members of his unit. There was also consternation that the option of recruiting the haulier as an informer was not considered; Volunteer T might well have used him again to transport equipment or explosives to England. O hAdhmaill was sentenced at the Old Bailey to 25 years in November 1994.

The next major IRA bomb destined for England was also built in South Armagh or North Louth and was to act as a prototype for the Docklands bomb. Inside a flatbed Leyland Freighter bought by Volunteer T at auction in Britain, the IRA built two 24-ft-long compartments. Inside were packed bags containing around 4,000 lbs of explosives. After being driven from South Armagh to Warrenpoint on 11 July 1994, the vehicle was left for ferry staff to drive onto the overnight ferry to Heysham in Lancashire. A man in his mid-30s and wearing blue overalls arrived at Heysham port office to pick up the vehicle at 5 a.m. the next day, but left swiftly when told it was in a secure area being examined by sniffer dogs. No one was ever firmly linked to the vehicle but it was believed the bomb would have been detonated later that day, possibly at South Quay.

With no charges being brought against IRA members as a result of the Baltic Exchange, Bishopsgate or Heysham bombs, South Armagh was considered by many anti-terrorist officers to be a safe haven, a 'forensic redoubt' where it was not practical to try to gather evidence. 'It was largely held that it was impossible to go back to the big bomb-makers,' said John Grieve, who had been appointed commander of SO13 just before the Docklands blast. Although Met officers had travelled to Northern Ireland at the start of the Troubles, it had become the practice for the RUC to be the only police force to operate in what was acknowledged as the most hostile environment for the police in the United Kingdom.

Grieve had rushed to New Scotland Yard when the Docklands bomb warnings were received. He said:

> We were standing there talking when there was a boom, the windows rattled and we saw the red glow. So we went down there, saw the devastation and thought: 'Shit, where do you start with this, what on earth do you do?' You couldn't even get in there for the gas and the water and the fire brigade. Well, the words South Armagh appeared at a very early stage and the detective work was done on our hands and knees and with divers in the dock . . . We actually had a vision from day one about going into South Armagh and building up a relationship with the RUC so we could do that. Once we had traced the bomb lorry back to Belfast it was almost as if there was a big finger pointing south from Belfast to South Armagh. By that time we had mapped the history and the component parts of the bomb truck and produced an intelligence map that virtually formed a circle round the McKinley farm.

When the two cars bought at the Carlisle auction on the dummy run were traced to Patrick McKinley, Grieve asked the RUC if he could fly his men over to search for evidence. He said: 'We did a huge project here in London thinking what we might look for, including things like flakes of paint, aluminium extrusion, welding extrusion and paint layering. Tiny things in a huge, complex environment.'

Grieve thought he needed three days in South Armagh to search four premises in Mullaghbawn. But at the briefing to set up Operation Fisherton he was told there was 'zero option' of being allowed to stay there beyond nightfall on the first day. 'The possibility of a soldier or policeman being shot if we let it run any longer was just too strong,' said one RUC officer involved in the planning. More than a thousand soldiers from the Coldstream Guards, Grenadier Guards and Duke of Wellington's Regiment sealed off Mullaghbawn and Forkhill as 90 Met officers were flown in. Several vehicles were removed by Chinook helicopter and taken to England for examination. Grieve felt that the very fact he and his men had travelled to South Armagh was an important breakthrough. 'It stuck a spoke in their wheel,' he said. 'It showed them we were capable of going back to South Armagh and was a way of saying to the IRA: "If you are going to build bomb trucks, you are going to have to take a lot more care, which makes life much more difficult for you in the future."' Three of the men arrested were released without charge and the fourth, McKinley, was acquitted. After his trial, senior anti-terrorist oficers conceded that they had never believed McKinley was an IRA member.

Four months after the Docklands bomb and just eight days after Operation Fisherton, the IRA switched its attentions to Manchester for the biggest bomb attack in England since the Troubles began. Once again, South Armagh Brigade members had mixed the explosives under the supervision of the Surgeon. But rather than building the bomb and driving it to England, it was decided to ship the explosives by freight from Dublin. Between 2.52 p.m. and 5.02 p.m. on 13 June 1996, a mobile phone, registered to a Declan McCann at an address in Castleblaney and codenamed 'Digit 6' by police, was used four times by a man calling himself 'Tom Fox' to contact Arthur Loveridge, a Peterborough motor dealer. Using new technology which can trace the location where a mobile phone call is made by linking it to a 'cell site', police established that two of the four calls were from Manchester and the others from Birmingham and Wisbech in Cambridgeshire. The bombers had been carrying out a final reconnaissance of Manchester city centre before driving south.

Two weeks earlier, 'Fox' had called Loveridge from the Irish Republic and agreed a cash price of £2,000 for a lorry advertised in *Anglian Auto Trader*. The money was sent by registered post but was incorrectly addressed and returned to the Republic; the sender's name and address were false and it ended up in the hands of the Garda. In the meantime, Loveridge had sold the lorry but instead offered 'Fox' another one, a red and white Ford cargo lorry with 'Jack Roberts Transport' painted on the side. A new price of £1,195 was settled and arrangements made for the money to be delivered to Loveridge in Peterborough on 14 June. The cash was handed over by Sabir Khan, a taxi driver who had been approached outside a nearby Tesco store by an Irishman and paid in advance for the journey. At 3 p.m., Loveridge left the lorry at the Nursery Lane parking area in Peterborough, unlocked and with the keys inside, to be picked up by the new owner.

The lorry was then taken to the London area where it was loaded with the bomb. By 7.40 p.m. that evening it was being driven north up the M1 accompanied by a maroon Ford Granada acting as a scout car. Both vehicles were caught on video on the M6 at around 9 p.m. before being parked overnight in either Staffordshire or Cheshire. At 8.31 a.m. on Saturday 15 June, the lorry was seen heading towards Manchester and at 9.22 a.m. being parked on double yellow lines outside Marks and Spencer on Corporation Street in the city centre. Two South Armagh men, whose names are known to the authorities, were filmed by a security camera leaving the lorry and walking a few hundred yards to Cathedral Street where a third man was waiting in the Granada, later abandoned in Preston. The men who left the lorry were wearing cagoules, hooded sweatshirts, baseball caps, and sunglasses. Digit 6 was used to make two calls within four minutes of the lorry being parked. The bomb exploded at 11.15 a.m., causing more than £400 million worth of damage and injuring 206 people.

The two calls made after the lorry was parked were traced to the home of Terence Fitzsimons, 47, in Lisdoney in Castleblaney. Fitzsimons was convicted in June 1997 of helping to produce Ecstasy tablets for a gang with links in Cork, Dublin and England and jailed for 10 years. Dublin's High Court heard that the gang could have expected to make £2 million from an outlay of £50,000. This was not the only link between drugs dealing and the IRA's England campaign. According to Garda sources, Declan Donaghy, a 26-year-old arrested at Dublin port in April 1998 with 101,000 Ecstasy tablets worth £1.5 million, was a lorry driver who occasionally worked for Volunteer T.

Although not an IRA man, Donaghy, from Newtownclogue, had driven explosives to England in the early 1990s. The IRA has always denied any involvement in drugs but security sources on both sides of the border believe that dealers operating in republican areas are forced to hand over a large slice of their profits to the Provisionals. In the underworld inhabited by Volunteer T, the lines between the IRA, 'ordinary' criminals and the drugs trade are often blurred.

The second call to Fitzsimons, who was suspected of making the coded warning calls, was the last made by Digit 6. Twelve days later, a man calling himself Declan McCann reported that the phone had been stolen on 10 June. Seven of the 10 calls made to Digit 6 during its 13-day 'life' were from McCann's home, the last on 13 June, and a number of the 26 calls made from the phone were to McCann's relatives. Even though Digit 6 had supposedly been stolen, Declan McCann, a 29-year-old married man from the Ardross estate in Crossmaglen, paid the £66.40 bill for all calls and rental until August but did not ask for a replacement phone. In May 1999, McCann's solicitor issued a statement denying his client had played any part in the Manchester bombing.

'Manchester didn't have the precision of Docklands,' said Grieve. 'It showed that they are deeply flexible and will try a different thing to see what works. Our successes with CCTV after Docklands had created a very hostile environment so they changed the system. The next one was quick and dirty.' Despite the relative haphazardness of the Manchester bombing, no one was charged as a result of the investigation, which was codenamed Operation Cannon. Docklands, however, was planned almost to perfection but prompted a highly successful police investigation. 'There's almost the sense that they overreached themselves at Docklands,' said Grieve. 'They put such effort into camouflaging what was going on that they set up a tachograph so they could survive a traffic patrol check. But we found it.' The tachograph was only found because McArdle and his colleagues abandoned the tyre and its contents rather than destroying them. Grieve said:

> I think they were going to burn all that stuff and it was the wrong place to do it. You just had some great neighbours and people on that bit of waste ground; it was a bit of waste ground

that trucks used but people didn't like trucks using, if you see what I mean. It looked safe but it was more hostile than they thought. They did make mistakes but only with hindsight and not terribly crass ones. They were living real life in which you turn the wrong way, you bump into the wrong person, you think you're spooked when you're not. You're under enormous pressure.

Curiously, the name on the tachograph was 'J. McCann' and McCann had been the name used for booking the ferry journey on the dummy run. When the two cars had been bought in Carlisle by McArdle and another man, they had used the names Mr Hearty of Kilcurry in County Louth and Mr McCann of Castleblaney in County Monaghan.

South Armagh remained to the fore in the second half of 1996 which saw the IRA lose two bombing teams as its England campaign was brought to an abrupt halt. In July, six IRA men were arrested in south London at the end of Operation Airlines, which involved around 100 police anti-terrorist officers and a similar number of MI5 operatives. Led by Gerry Hanratty, the IRA unit had planned to black out London and the south-east of England by blowing up six electricity substations. It was a modern version of the IRA's 'S Plan' of 1939 designed to paralyse the infrastructure of the capital. Although only Robert Morrow, who had been based in Dundalk, had border connections, the six were effectively controlled from South Armagh. Donal Gannon, a 'fixer' whose fingerprints had been found at the Clapham bomb factory in 1988 and a key figure in the substations plot, was linked to the Manchester bomb. Many of the 134 banknotes recovered by the Garda in the envelope addressed to Arthur Loveridge had serial numbers very close to those found in Gannon's wardrobe. Gannon had also been telephoning Terence Fitzsimons's home.

In September 1996, five members of another IRA unit were arrested and Volunteer Diarmuid O'Neill shot dead during raids in Hammersmith and other parts of London. To psyche them up before the raids, 'Officer Kilo', the police marksman who killed O'Neill, and his colleagues had been shown footage of the Docklands bomb exploding. There were more than 50,000 hours of surveillance tape of the IRA unit being observed by MI5 and SO13 during what was codenamed Operation Tinnitus. Brian McHugh, its leader, had been followed each night as he went to a telephone box to call another public phone in Castleblaney. At one stage, two suspected bomb lorries were tracked from South Armagh via the port of Larne in County Antrim to Cairnryan in Scotland and then south towards London. O'Neill, posing as the owner of a transport firm, had rented a steel storage unit at a warehouse in Hornsey in north London. In it, police found four large wooden crates loaded with 13,800 lbs (6.3 tons) of explosives and booster tubes. The explosives had been packed into clear plastic bags labelled 'spent mushroom compost'.

Bernard McGinn later revealed that these explosives had been mixed on the same day as the Docklands bomb. At the end of the mixing session, the filled compost bags had been placed on five pallets and forklifted onto a blue lorry. Frank McCabe had told him they were then to be driven to Dublin where they would be collected by a freight company and shipped to England. Some 32 lbs of Semtex were also shipped out; this was later made into two briefcase-sized bombs placed under London's Hammersmith Bridge by O'Neill. It had been intended that the bombs, the largest Semtex devices ever used in England, would mark the 80th anniversary of the Easter Rising, but the detonators failed to trigger the main charge.

According to Grieve, the IRA's 'England department' is best understood as a collection of project teams:

> If I was looking at the IRA as a highly effective guerrilla army I would say you don't let things fall into patterns that we can unravel. You have a very broken down devolved system of manufacturing stuff and you give people certain tasks and you know what they are capable of achieving. So you say that at the moment South Armagh like making bombs. They've got the capacity to mix; they can operate across the border; they can frighten farmers into not saying anything; they can ship over here. They've got fertiliser there and booster tubes, Semtex and timers. They can do a bit of welding on the trucks and put it all together. I think South Armagh got the go ahead to put together a big bomb and a project team – that's what Airlines looks like – and were told to keep it as tight as they could.

South Armagh would be a natural area to look to for operations in England not only because of the IRA brigade's expertise, support network and strict security, but also because of the range of skills and materials readily available. Grieve said:

> You normally find guerrilla armies are either urban or rural. South Armagh is rural but can operate very effectively in urban conurbations and that's what they did in England. Although there is farming there, there are also haulage companies, lorry companies and used car businesses. That sort of engineer-farmer thing becomes very interesting. These are people who can do welding and cutting and they've got bits of metal lying about and they've got a mate who runs the metal works. All the ingredients, the scaffolding for the booster tubes, everything is there. Go round farmers over there you'll find all that stuff in their sheds.

Grieve added that a profile of a South Armagh IRA volunteer would be almost impossible to draw up.

> What is the profile of a terrorist? Well, a terrorist is anybody from twelve to seventy, male or female and they range from people with the highest security classification in the United States of America and three PhDs to somebody who claims that he can barely read or write and wouldn't know how to look at a newspaper in his cell. I don't think there is an immediate picture. You look for patterns of behaviour and you see what you can do to create a hostile environment to put them off balance and start leaving evidence for you but you never ever draw any assumptions about who it is because that's when they'll get you.

The South Armagh Brigade's success in planning bomb attacks in England secured its reputation as an élite within the IRA. Volunteer M said: 'Both the expertise and the will for taking the war to England has been here in South Armagh. For one-off spectaculars, the proximity to the ports meant it also made sense from a logistical point of view. If a bomb was made in South Armagh, you could be sure that it would go off. Under Tom Murphy's leadership, since the 1980s it had shed its parochialism and placed itself at the cutting edge of the world's most feared paramilitary organisation. In the meantime, senior IRA men from South Armagh had also become involved in importing weaponry and the technology of war from America to Ireland. By the 1990s, it seemed that whatever the IRA was involved in and wherever it was happening, the influence of Tom Murphy and South Armagh would be there.

Chapter 10

Made in the USA

'As you've probably guessed by now, we're kind of experiencing a slight technical problem at our end . . . we need a new SAM system to counteract low-flying helicopters within an altitude of 300 feet to probably 3,000 feet.'

(Telephone conversation intercepted by FBI, 1988)

'Pop the trunk. This is a Stinger missile.' 'Now we got the son of a bitch. We got it, it works, we've got batteries, we got the case, we got everything you need to go with it.'

(Undercover FBI agents talking to IRA arms dealers, 1989)

Sergeant Peter McCoy was mystified. He had just measured for the third time the dimensions of the animal trailer propped up on a hay bale in the farmyard. Having checked and double checked, his reckoning was that the height on the outside was five feet one inch and on the inside just four feet six inches. The trailer, designed to transport sheep or pigs, had been found in the hayshed next to the farmyard, part of a farm complex on the Cregganduff Road, close to where Lance Corporal Ken Newell had been shot in 1991. It had been sealed off since the SAS operation that had resulted in the arrest of the sniper team the previous day. It was only when McCoy noticed a small nut at the base of the trailer on the tow hitch end that the significance of the seven-inch discrepancy began to dawn on him. Using a spanner to remove the nut and bolt attached to it, he found that this freed a plywood section to slide up within the trailer's steel frame. Calling on a colleague to bring a spade to hold the section in the up position, the RUC man peered into the hidden compartment he had just discovered. Inside, poking out of a nylon coal bag, was the butt of a large bolt action rifle. Moulded into the end of the butt was the word 'Barrett'.

The arrest of the sniper team and recovery of the Barrett Model 90 rifle was the most significant success by the security forces in South Armagh in nearly 30 years of the Troubles. Capable of firing a .50 calibre bullet at nearly three times the speed of sound, the weapon was accurate against a man-sized target at distances of more than a mile. The rifle in the hidden compartment had been made at the Barrett Firearms factory at Murfreesboro, Tennessee as a variant of the Barrett 'Light Fifty', a semi-automatic .50 calibre rifle which had been used by the US Marine Corps to knock out Iraqi vehicles during the Gulf War. Lighter and 16 inches shorter than the Light Fifty, the Barrett 90 had been designed primarily for game hunting or target shooting but a number had been bought by the US Navy to mount on its coastguard vessels.

The serial number 180 on the Barrett found in the animal trailer identified it as one of a pair sold by the company to a firearms dealer on 27 January 1995. A week later, the dealer sold both weapons to Michael Angel Suarez, a 37-year-old Cuban living in Cleveland, Ohio. Suarez, in turn, had passed them to an unknown Irishman. Shortly afterwards, and less than six months into the IRA's 1994 ceasefire, the guns had been shipped to the Irish Republic, along with a quantity of .50 calibre ammunition. By this time, each of the guns had been fitted with a Vari-X III telescopic sight manufactured by Leupold & Stevens in Beaverton, Oregon. The sight, like the rifle, had been designed for the hunter; it could magnify a target 10 times and had both a built-in range estimator and a facility for making windage and elevation adjustments. Two years later, the Barrett that was to be found in the animal trailer fired the brass .50 calibre bullet that killed Lance Bombadier Stephen Restorick at a vehicle checkpoint in Bessbrook.

It was not the first time that a trail had been found linking Bessbrook and the South Armagh Brigade to the USA. At 1.31 a.m. on 3 September 1983, Bessbrook had been shaken by a blast that blew debris over a 150-yard radius, damaging the Presbyterian church and library. Eamon Collins and a group of fellow IRA men had earlier left a stolen Ford Escort outside Dale Terrace; in the boot was a 30 lb radio-controlled device in a metal cylinder. The previous day, Brendan Burns had handed the bomb to Collins outside a house near Donnelly's bar in Silverbridge. Around the explosives had been packed 'dockyard confetti' – jagged metal, nails and bolts – designed to kill and maim members of an Army patrol returning to Bessbrook Mill. The operation had been botched when two 'button men' took over a house that did not have a clear line of sight to the Escort. Collins had telephoned Burns, who reluctantly agreed that the bomb could be detonated at night because it was too dangerous to try to retrieve it.

This decision turned out to be a costly mistake for the IRA because tiny fragments recovered from the debris were to lead the authorities across the Atlantic to Massachusetts and Richard Clark Johnson, a 35-year-old American electronics and defence expert who had worked on the Voyager space probe and Space Shuttle projects. Johnson was also working for the IRA on some of the most technically advanced projects of the Troubles. Forensic scientists investigating the Bessbrook blast identified parts of an FX401 'tone frequency selector switch' which operated on frequencies the Provisionals had never used before. The switch was one of a batch of 430 that bore a data code of 8308 and had been manufactured by Consumer Microcircuits Ltd in Essex. Investigations established that 66 of these had been exported to North Carolina and 50 had then been sold to an electronic parts salesman in California who had placed the order on Johnson's behalf. The device that Burns had entrusted to Collins was Johnson's brainchild. He had come up with the ingenious idea of using the Weather Alert Radio frequency to trigger IRA bombs. The Weather Alert Radio system, activated by satellite to warn mariners or mountaineers of gales or blizzards, was unique to North America. Its frequency of 162.55 MHz was not in use in Europe and was therefore a clear channel for the IRA.

As well as designing the Bessbrook device, Johnson was developing for the South Armagh Brigade a sophisticated method of bringing down helicopters. Ridding the skies of British military aircraft had long been Tom Murphy's dream. In 1981, he had sent

Gerry McGeough, who had been arrested on his farm four years earlier, on a mission to buy Redeye surface-to-air (SAM) missiles in America. After arriving in Florida, McGeough drove through the state with a young American woman and bought dozens of Armalites and Heckler and Koch pistols across the counter in gun shops. The weapons were stored in a camper van before being shipped to Ireland from Newark docks in New Jersey. But a rendezvous in a New Orleans warehouse between McGeough, another IRA man and a group of arms dealers to discuss buying five Redeyes for $50,000 turned out to be an FBI sting. McGeough went on the run and his accomplices were arrested.

The setback did not deter Murphy. In September 1984, he travelled to America with the St Patrick's tug-of-war club from Ballybinaby for a tour culminating in the world tug-of-war championships in Oshkosh, Wisconsin. Tom and Patrick Murphy had been among those who had started the club at a summer fair in Crossmaglen in 1972. Others among the many founder members were Séamus Harvey, the volunteer shot dead by the SAS in 1977, and Patrick Casey, the Murphy farm employee who served a jail term for possession of explosives. The 1984 trip involved more than just sport for Tom Murphy. He used his time in America to slip away from his team-mates to make contact with republicans and arms dealers in Chicago and New York. By the late 1980s, he had initiated two separate operations designed to provide a decisive advantage in the battle for control of the skies. After discussions with the Surgeon and Micksey Martin, .50 calibre rifles suitable for sniping attacks were added to the list of requirements.

According to Army records, since the beginning of the Troubles the IRA has mounted some 23 helicopter attacks in South Armagh, bringing down three, compared with a handful in other areas of Northern Ireland. The first was in September 1974 when four gunmen who had been hiding in a derelict building fired 79 shots at a Scout as it landed an Army patrol at Ballsmill near Silverbridge. As the soldiers returned fire, the gunmen jumped in a car and headed for the border 200 yards away. The Scout was hit eight times but was able to fly back to Forkhill. On 15 April 1976, the same night the SAS shot dead Volunteer Peter Cleary, an RPG-7 glanced off the belly of an RAF Wessex as it hovered over the security force base in

Crossmaglen. At the same time, gunmen opened fire from nearby Conway Crescent before once again escaping across the border by car. The Wessex landed safely.

The threat to aircraft had become more potent by the end of the 1970s when the South Armagh Brigade had acquired light machine-guns such as the American belt-fed M60. In March 1979, Sergeant Petrie, an Army Scout pilot, made a low pass close to Glasdrumman Post Office to investigate a tipper lorry which had been hijacked in Cullaville that day. As he did so, gunmen opened fire from the cover of a hedgerow about 300 yards away, hitting the helicopter nine times and sending shards of Perspex from the cockpit into his face. Major Charles Woodrow, the Grenadier Guards company comman-der in Crossmaglen, was wounded in the leg by two bullets. Petrie managed to regain control and fly back to Crossmaglen. The IRA had used tracer rounds to direct its fire more accurately and an under-cover Army unit which searched the derelict the gunmen had used found 86 empty M60 shell cases as well as others from an SLR and a Garand. The attack had been carefully planned with the tipper lorry being abandoned so a helicopter would swoop low to check whether it was being used for a mortar attack on Glasdrumman watchtower. One of the gunmen had prepared his position by laying a strip of carpet in a dip in the ground.

There were also opportunity shoots at helicopters. Six months after the Scout incident at Glasdrumman, a Gazelle flying low over the Concession Road near Cullaville was engaged by automatic fire from close to O'Neill's garage, where Lance Corporal Newell and Private Lewis were abducted in 1991. One Armalite round hit the helicopter, cutting a number of instrument cables, damaging the radio and starting a small electrical fire. Frank McCabe, who was suspected of being the gunman, was arrested and later released without charge. In May 1981, another Gazelle was flying in the same area when six men next to a red van opened fire, striking the rotor blades of the aircraft.

McCabe, one of the South Armagh Brigade's best marksmen, was sentenced to eight years in May 1982 after being convicted in Dublin's Special Criminal Court of possessing explosives and a firearm. McCabe, along with Francis 'Lucas' Quigley and Pat McNa-mee, a cousin of Danny McNamee and later to become a Sinn Féin councillor, had been arrested near the Slab Murphy farm complex after their hijacked van was rammed by a Garda car. Quigley and McNamee fired shots at the gardaí while McCabe, the driver, tried to grab a Garand rifle as he was arrested. A command wire, several milk churns and beer kegs filled with homemade explosive were found in the van. The three volunteers were believed to have been about to carry out a landmine attack which had been planned by Tom Murphy.

IRA firepower continued to increase and in July 1982, on the same day as the Hyde Park and Regent's Park bombings, an RAF Wessex en route from Forkhill to Bessbrook Mill was hit nine times after being fired at from four different positions at the foot of Croslieve mountain. Some 103 empty shell cases, including 35 ejected from an M60 and two from a .50 calibre weapon, were found. A farmer's description of a distinctive booming noise above the rattle of a machine-gun confirmed that a .50 calibre weapon had been employed; sandbags used to support it had been left behind. Discarded sweet wrappers, cigarette butts and empty Coke cans indicated the gunmen had waited for several hours for a helicopter to fly within range. The .50 cases had been manufactured in 1943 and one possibility considered was that the IRA had recovered a Browning machine-gun from an aircraft shot down over Lough Neagh during the Second World War. An M60 and a .50 Browning were fired at a Wessex from Aughanduff mountain in May 1983. Two years later, two Brownings mounted on the back of a truck and concealed by a wooden frame covered in black binliners were fired from the Dundalk Road in Crossmaglen at another Wessex.

The Libyan shipments further enhanced the IRA's anti-aircraft capability when 18 DShKs were landed between 1985 and 1987. The DShK, or Degtyarova Shapgina Krupnokalibernyi, designed by Degtyarev and Shapgin and manufactured in Russia, had been used against American forces during the Vietnam War. Taking several men to carry, the weapon has an effective range of more than a mile and can fire 575 rounds per minute. A DShK was used for the first time by the IRA in June 1988. This time it was a Lynx flying from Crossmaglen to Bessbrook Mill which was the target. Lieutenant David Richardson, a Royal Navy pilot attached to the Army Air Corps, felt his Lynx go into a spin as it was hit 15 times around the fuselage and rotors, damaging control cables and stopping one engine. Several of the rounds were armour-piercing and the aircraft was forced to make an emergency landing near Cashel Lough Upper. It was later found that the Lynx had been engaged by two DShKs, three M60s and assorted rifles from Aughanduff mountain. An IRA statement said a dozen volunteers had taken part in the attack. They had tried to find the downed aircraft so they could destroy it with an RPG-7 before finishing off the three crew and two passengers with a machine-gun but Army reinforcements arrived before they could do so.

Both DShKs brought out for the helicopter shoot were thought to have been used in an attack in October 1989 in which an RUC armour-plated Sierra was raked by more than 70 bullets fired from DShKs mounted on the back of a lorry. Constables Michael Marshall and Nigel Colmer had been driving from Bessbrook Mill to Belleek, where they had arranged to deliver a court summons. Marshall was killed, his body burned beyond recognition after the petrol tank exploded. Colmer later described seeing what looked like a gravel lorry beside the road just before the attack began:

> We then came under intense gunfire but it didn't sound like any gunfire that I had heard before. I was aware of white and yellow coloured lights striking the car . . . I can remember the dashboard disintegrating in front of me. I was conscious of being hit in both my legs. At this stage, I felt that the police vehicle was being ripped apart and I was still being hit. Michael grabbed the radio and called: '139 to 139A. Attack, attack.' I opened my door and cocked my rifle. Michael shouted at me to close my door. At this stage Michael was trying to get the car started. He was struggling with the ignition and the gearstick. The next thing that I remember was falling out of the car. I must have tried to get out but I can't remember . . . I was convinced that I was going to die. Some time later the shooting stopped and I looked back into the car. Michael was lying slumped in my seat and the car was well on fire.

Although the DShK was an effective and prestigious weapon, it was never going to force the Army out of the skies. But the IRA's hopes that the man behind the Weather Radio Alert devices would help them achieve that aim had been put paid to by Johnson's arrest in July 1989. Charging him with terrorist offences was the culmination of an investigation on both sides of the Atlantic which had begun with the Bessbrook bomb six years earlier.

Johnson, who had a degree in electronic engineering from Washington DC's Catholic University and a Master's from Berkeley, had been working for the Northrop Corporation in California when he had bought the FX401 switches. A year after the Bessbrook bomb, he told the FBI that he had been using the switches for a prototype of a telephone-controlled burglar alarm and that none of them had been sent to Ireland. The following month, another Weather Radio Alert bomb went off in Newry and in 1985 FX401 switches with the code 8308 were found in unexploded devices in Charlestown in County Meath, Cullyhanna and Warrenpoint. In February 1986, the FBI questioned Johnson about the switches once more. He repeated his explanation but this time added that he might have sent some of them to relatives in Ireland.

By this time, Johnson had moved to Massachusetts and joined the Mitre Corporation to work in the fields of radar, ECM and electronic counter-countermeasures (ECCM). His association with the IRA stretched back to at least 1978 when he was observed in the Irish Republic with Stephen Lambert, a Derry Provisional, and had given the false name 'Thomas Clark' when stopped by gardaí. Awkward, unmarried and with no known friends outside work, Johnson was a social misfit whose precise motivation for working for the IRA was never established. Although his IRA links had been noted by the FBI, Johnson's US government security clearance had been upgraded from 'Secret' to 'Top Secret' when he joined Mitre.

The IRA had been using radio-controlled bombs since 1972. The earliest controls were of the type that could be bought in a model shop and used to guide a toy boat or plane; the bomb was triggered when a nail attached to the servomotor made electrical contact. But this method had only a limited range and was liable to interference from static or other signals; they could also be detonated by the Army's electronic sweeps. One of the earliest bands used was 27 MHz – Citizens Band – and IRA engineers soon saw the need to switch frequencies. The result was a chase along the electromagnetic spectrum with the IRA constantly trying to find frequencies which the Army was unable to detect or jam. Eamon Collins said:

> There's a cat and mouse game that goes on between the IRA and the British Army. It's a war of technology. Prior to the Bessbrook bomb, the Army had broken the code of the radio-controlled devices and South Armagh and all the border areas and Belfast were without radio-controlled devices for almost two years. A device had been found on a tractor up near Crossmaglen. I was talking to Slab's number two [the Undertaker] and he said: 'You know, if we'd them radio-controlled devices fucking working we'd be slaughtering troops in South Armagh'. He told me they'd captured the device and had been able to defuse and decode it and that once that happened the whole thing had been fucked.

In 1987, another piece of the jigsaw fell into place when gardaí searching a garage in Clondalkin in Dublin found a bundle of correspondence stuffed into an old stove. The garage was rented by Eamon Maguire, a 49-year-old Aer Lingus electronics engineer who lived in nearby Monastery Rise. The letters, dated between May 1981 and July 1984, were addressed to 'Ed' and signed 'Thomas', 'T' or 'Tom'. They appeared to have been part of a detailed correspondence about the construction of explosive devices, the procurement of parts and radio-control detonation. The sender was soon identified as Johnson and 'Ed' as Maguire. In one letter, Johnson pondered whether to pass equipment to the IRA via a courier in the Mexican border town of Tijuana but warned: 'The area is under watch for drug activities, so one must be careful. The authorities are there. I think another country would be better.'

According to an affidavit sworn by Brendan Cleary, an FBI special agent, Maguire had been involved in the IRA's 'research programme' since the late seventies. He had been arrested by gardaí in 1981 along with six other IRA members suspected of manufacturing radio-controlled bombs and in December that year had been watched by the FBI in New York 'in the company of a PIRA procurement mission'. He had become more prominent within the IRA after Danny McNamee, until then 'chief of PIRA's remote control bomb technology group', was jailed in 1987.

The discrepancy between Johnson's explanations in 1984 and 1986 of what he had done with the 50 FX401 switches led to the FBI bugging the telephone at his apartment in Casco Drive in Nashua, New Hampshire. By November 1988, FBI agents were growing tired of listening to Johnson's phone calls and had noticed nothing unusual about his lifestyle. With the regularity of a metronome, he went to work, came home and spent the weekends with his parents on Cape Cod. The day before the FBI was to stop monitoring his phone, Johnson received a call from a woman in California called 'Chris'. She told him that 'a friend of Ed's' was in San Francisco and would like to meet him. The woman was identified as Christina Reid, 24, an electrical engineering student at San Francisco State University. Johnson's letters to Maguire had referred to her as 'the bird' and described her as a reliable courier.

A conversation between Johnson and the man in San Francisco was arranged for 15 December 1988. Johnson, who was afraid the FBI might be eavesdropping, gave Reid three telephone numbers and told her to dial them in order until she he reached him. The FBI, aware that a telephone box would be used, was sitting across 918 phone lines ready to intercept the call. Two FBI agents watched Johnson as he picked up the receiver at a telephone box in front of the Market Basket supermarket in Nashua. The caller, who introduced himself as 'Michael', was Martin Quigley, a 26-year-old from Dundalk who had entered the country to study computing at Lehigh University in Pennsylvania. He was also listed by the RUC as an IRA member. Quigley explained that he and his colleagues were 'experiencing a slight technical problem' which they needed to solve. 'You've helped us out of these situations before and we're looking to you once again.' Johnson replied: 'Sure, name it.' Quigley said that what was needed was a new surface-to-air missile system capable of bringing down helicopters up to an altitude of 3,000 feet. He then outlined the difficulties the IRA was having in designing a proximity fuse capable of functioning at low altitudes. Johnson suggested that a radar-activated device would be 'the best' and Quigley cautioned that any system would have to be 'quite small' and 'we'll want to be able to manufacture'. After a discussion about triggering mechanisms, Johnson assured his new friend: 'I can start working up something on that immediately.'

Two months later, Maguire and his wife Carol stopped off in New York on their way back from a holiday in the Bahamas and stayed with Johnson in Nashua; by this time, the FBI had bugged Johnson's kitchen. Maguire waited until his wife went shopping before broaching the subject of the IRA's requirements. The American asked about 'the Swimmer', the nickname of Dessie Ellis, an IRA bombmaker arrested with Maguire in 1981 and later linked to Danny McNamee and the Hyde Park bombing. Maguire replied that Ellis was nearing the end of his prison sentence. The two men then discussed means of counteracting Army radio jamming techniques by either overpowering the jamming signal or disguising a transmission signal as background noise. Johnson explained that a radar-activated device could be manufactured from parts of radar detectors in the basement of his parents' home. The detectors were designed to be put on vehicle dashboards to warn drivers of the presence of a police radar gun in time for them to slow down. If attached to a detonator, a radar detector could set off a bomb when activated by a signal from a radar gun. 'This weekend I'm gonna rig up the coffee cans and do the final part of the experiment and see how it goes,' said Johnson. A radar-activated device was used to detonate the proxy bomb that killed Ranger Smith at Cloghogue checkpoint in October 1990. The radar detector had almost certainly been bought across the counter in the United States and was one of many commercially available items adapted by the IRA. During one bugged conversation, Johnson remarked to Quigley that they 'would be nowhere without Radio Shack' — a chain of electronics shops.

In April 1989, Quigley travelled to Nashua to meet Johnson before they went together to his parents' house at Cape Cod to work on equipment Johnson had rigged up in the basement. The Irishman's role was to develop a rocket system to deliver a missile from the ground to within about 25 feet of a helicopter while Johnson had the more complex task of creating a fusing system that would explode because of an aircraft's proximity. Reid was used to buy the rocket motors while a fourth person, Gerald Hoy, a 39-year-old mathematician completing a PhD in computer science at Lehigh, worked on calculating trajectories and fuel burn rates. When they returned to Johnson's apartment at the end of the weekend, the FBI heard Quigley and Johnson arranging their next meeting. 'Just find a picnic table because there's plenty of tables,' said Johnson. 'Sit there like you're having lunch and I'll just come along.'

Three weeks later Quigley spoke to Johnson at a telephone box and recited a brief code: '12, 27 at 32.' The FBI worked out that this meant they should meet at noon on 27 May at the intersection of state highway 32 across which Johnson would have to travel. The next problem for the FBI was how to eavesdrop on the conversation; there were picnic areas on both sides of the intersection, each with 24 tables. It was decided to bug two tables on each side and fill up the others with FBI agents and their families. The tables with bugs underneath them would be the only ones empty and Johnson and Quigley would have no option but to sit at one of them.

But by noon on 27 May, heavy rain had set in. The FBI families, who had all volunteered to give up part of their Memorial Day weekend, picnicked stoically as Quigley and Johnson drew up in their cars. Quigley, wearing brown shorts and a white T-shirt, was dressed for the open air but the two men elected to head for a nearby McDonald's. By a stroke of good fortune for the FBI, the restaurant was too full and Quigley and Johnson decided to talk in Johnson's Subaru station wagon, which had been bugged.

The discussion lasted 85 minutes and ranged from the ways the IRA could develop electronic expertise through to a series of possible schemes for bringing down helicopters in South Armagh. Quigley spoke of the IRA's fears of informers penetrating their ranks:

> We don't really let outsiders in. They're always looking for people to infiltrate. If you were to go out in the morning, say, like go around all the different areas and say 'right, I want a guy with some electronics experience, can you recommend somebody', you might get 10 guys but you can nearly bet your arse two of those guys will be put in there, like, just to infiltrate, to knock you out completely, you know.

Johnson then looked at photos of soldiers in South Armagh carrying electronic jamming equipment. 'This is a standard backpack and this is a little box that they clip onto the frame of the backpack and what it does is that you can programme it to do any kind of different jamming signal,' he said. Such equipment was vital for the

Army to counter the threat of radio-controlled devices. In 1988, patrols in South Armagh carried four ECM devices operating on different frequencies, two of which were codenamed Stripe and Chimp.

Quigley impressed on Johnson the importance to the IRA of the work he was doing:

> You're talking about hitting them [helicopters] within a second or two seconds. Now what can they do in two seconds? They won't have time to blink. Our main aim at the moment is going for the strike straight in as fast as possible. I know that they've changed their tactics a lot now in our area. I think that they're a lot more worried as of late.

He then described his work on two computer programmes for the missile guidance system. 'There's a lot of other applications. It's not just even for an air target.' Getting the right guidance system was 'nearly 50 per cent of the battle . . . like for anything . . . anti-tank, building or whatever it is. So if everything goes okay and this thing comes off it'll be a tremendous boost, there's no doubt about it.' Quigley observed that 'no matter what proximity system you come up with . . . you know yourself like that, what they have built into all those choppers is like some of the best, best stuff available'. Army counter-measures might be able to defeat Johnson's system but he concluded: 'I think you should work ahead with something anyway.'

The two men also discussed bringing down helicopters with machine-guns or hyper-velocity missiles. Quigley described the Kevlar rope theory of hoisting grenades on a line underneath a floating balloon; if the line was entangled in a helicopter's rotor blades, the grenades would be drawn in. He also told Johnson that Maguire wanted him to buy laser equipment. Seven years earlier, Johnson said, he had suggested to Maguire that the IRA should move towards laser rather than radio detonation.

Quigley was right about the concern within the security forces about the IRA's capacity to attack helicopters. By 1986, the attempts of McGeough and others to buy Redeyes had prompted the fitting of infra-red jammers to some Wessex and Pumas. Similar devices had been used by the Americans in Vietnam to counteract SAM-7s and by the late 1980s, when it was clear that the IRA had acquired SAM-7s from Libya, infra-red jammers were fitted to all helicopters operating in South Armagh. Despite the fears of the Army, the only known deployment of a SAM-7 in Northern Ireland was against a Wessex at Kinawley on the County Fermanagh border in July 1991; the missile failed to lock on to the helicopter and exploded on the ground.

Other missile counter-measures included: the use of chaff, tiny metal slivers released in a burst from the aircraft to deceive homing missiles by creating a spurious radar image; and 'bafflers' to disperse exhaust gases into the rotor blades, thereby reducing the helicopter's heat signature. This allowed pilots to fly at high altitudes knowing they were out of range of the DShK and Browning .50 and also had the means to protect themselves from missile attack. Enormous effort also went into creating irregular flight patterns and making a variety of different approaches to the security force bases. The most dangerous moments for the pilots continued to be while landing or taking off, particularly when in the hover.

Two weeks after speaking to Johnson, Quigley confirmed by letter that the IRA had acquired a radar unit which, with modifications by the American, might 'suit our needs' and tentatively arranged a further meeting for 15 July. But on 12 July, the FBI's cover was blown when two agents preparing for the meeting by fitting another bug into Johnson's car were spotted as he walked along a glass corridor from his office to another building. Johnson summoned the Mitre security guards. One of the agents tried to pretend they were fitting a car stereo and had started work on the wrong vehicle but Johnson knew that the equipment on the front seat was not a sound system.

The FBI had no option but to arrest Johnson and move quickly to bring in the remaining conspirators before they could flee or destroy any evidence. Maguire was back in Dublin but warrants authorising searches in Massachusetts, Pennsylvania, California and New Hampshire were obtained. Quigley and Reid were arrested and Hoy turned himself in. In Johnson's parents' basement, the FBI found an almost complete laser detonation system and parts which matched exactly a Weather Radio Alert device found intact in a tartan shopping trolley in Armagh city after being abandoned by North Armagh Brigade volunteers in March 1985. The device contained an FX401 switch, one of around a dozen of the batch of 50 bought by Johnson believed to have been used in bombs in Northern Ireland. At Quigley's apartment in Bethlehem, Pennsylvania, agents discovered the proto-type of a shoulder-held rocket launcher and a video showing two men experimenting with rockets in the Appalachians. On the back of a *Military Helicopters* magazine, Quigley had written a list of those used in Northern Ireland: 'Lynx, Puma, Wessex, Gazelle, Chinook.'

One item the FBI was unable to seize was a Barrett Light Fifty which letters found in Quigley's apartment indicated had been successfully shipped to the Irish Republic. Another Light Fifty had been pieced together in Dublin's Central Sorting Office in August 1986 after its component parts had been sent in parcels from Chicago to addresses in the Irish capital.

In August 1990, Johnson was sentenced to 10 years in prison without remission and Quigley eight years. Maguire, who had fled to Nigeria, was arrested in South Africa in December 1992, extradited from the Irish Republic to the USA the following year and sentenced to six years in April 1994. The fact that the IRA has never killed the occupants of a helicopter in South Armagh is at least partly due to Johnson's incarceration. But while his laser-activation system was never employed, he had already played his part in the IRA's war against the Army and in developing the South Armagh Brigade's deadly efficiency with radio-controlled devices.

The loss of Johnson was a major blow to the IRA but even as he was arrested, leading members of the South Armagh Brigade were planning to add another weapon to their arsenal: the Stinger missile. Five feet long and weighing just 35 lbs, the Stinger was the successor to the Redeye. Resembling a Second World War bazooka, it was designed to be launched from the shoulder and its three-mile range and supersonic speed meant it was capable of homing in on and destroying an airliner. From 1986, the CIA had provided Afghan mujahedin guerrillas with Stingers which were used against Soviet forces with devastating effect; by 1989, an estimated 270 Russian aircraft had been brought down. The latest Stinger model, first produced in 1987, included a 'Passive Optical Seeker Technique' to overcome enemy jamming systems. For Tom

Murphy, the acquisition of the Stinger would have been a way of stepping up the conflict in South Armagh at a time when discussions of ceasefires and political talks were beginning to divert attention from the military struggle. A successful conclusion to Johnson and Quigley's project would have prevented helicopters flying low while Stingers would ensure that high altitudes would no longer be safe. The IRA had been having problems with its detonators so 10,000 of these were also required and Murphy remained determined to acquire .50 calibre sniper rifles.

Micksey Martin was in charge of the operation, which began in July 1989 when Kevin McKinley, a 32-year-old Belfast volunteer who had spent several years on the run in Dundalk, rented a holiday home in North Palm Beach in Florida. He began to look for sources of arms and by the end of the month had made contact with Marvin Jameson, a Vietnam veteran and owner of a gold mine in Santa Cruz County, Arizona. At a meeting at Paradise Marina in Sebastian, Florida, Jameson explained to McKinley that his mine provided a legitimate reason to buy detonators. By September, brochures from the Ireco company, based in Tucson and specialising in electric detonators, were being faxed to South Armagh. On 10 October, McKinley told Jameson he had contacted his superiors about the detonators and they would be sending a man over who would know exactly what type was needed. According to the prosecution in the subsequent court case, three days later two senior South Armagh republicans, Jim Martin, 32, from Mullaghbawn, and Aidan Moley, 27, from Dorsey, had arrived in Toronto. There they met Moley's brother, Séamus, 30, and Denis Leyne, a 50-year-old vice-chairman of a Canadian bank and leading NORAID supporter.

Jim Martin had recently been released from the Maze after serving part of a 15-year sentence for the attempted murder of Gilbert Johnston's brother Samuel in 1973. He had also been given life sentences for the murder of Corporal Steven Harrison and Lance Corporal Terence Brown but these convictions had been quashed on appeal. The Moleys were younger brothers of the late Volunteer Brendan Moley. The youngest Moley brother, Patrick, 24, who was living in Stamford in Connecticut, was later accused of helping to organise funds for the arms deal but charges were dropped. His arrest, he said, was part of the ongoing harassment of his family since his brother's death. Séamus Moley had first come to the attention of the security forces in June 1978 when an informer working for the Army had reported that he was one of two young volunteers who had been put in charge of the body of Constable Turbitt after he had been shot dead in the Sturgan Brae ambush.

The prosecution alleged that Aidan Moley flew on from Toronto to New York where he met a childhood friend from South Armagh who was working in an Irish American pub in Manhattan. In November 1989, Jim Martin visited Florida where McKinley introduced him to Michael Burdof, a 31-year-old gun enthusiast who had been told he could earn a substantial sum by supplying a .50 calibre rifle. The two IRA men told Burdof that they were also interested in Grendel semi-automatic pistols and ammunition capable of penetrating body armour. But Burdof, later revealed to be the FBI's informant number MDO-1077, was being used to set up a sting operation. The meetings in Toronto and New York had already been observed by special agents who had decided to set up a trap. Jim Martin flew home, leaving McKinley to meet 'LJ Connelly' and his colleague 'Greg', whom Burdof had said were arms dealers who might be willing to do business. In fact they were the FBI's Special Agents Larry O'Donnell and Greg Fields, who had been comprehensively briefed about the hardware the IRA was looking for and the black market prices such items could command.

As McKinley was walking towards Big Daddy's Lounge at 4.10 p.m. on 20 November, Fields was turning on his concealed microphone and reporting that he was about to have an undercover meeting with 'a suspected IRA member who is going to attempt to purchase weapons from us'. The music of ZZ Top and Lynyrd Skynyrd blared out in the background as McKinley began to outline what he was looking for. At first, he spoke in code, referring to 'stained glass', shipments of 'Coca Cola' and 'other commodities . . . like cigarette lighters and bottles'. Before long, however, he had spelt out the real aim of his mission.

> McKinley: 'Can you get missiles?'
> Fields: 'That's what we're talking.'
> McKinley: 'Can you get a Stinger?'
> O'Donnell: 'You want a Stinger? You know what a Redeye is?'

McKinley: 'Yeah, I know what it is, yeah. Is it a SAM or something like that?'
O'Donnell: 'Yeah, we can get something like that. '
McKinley: 'That's number one on the list.'

The meeting then moved over the road to Denny's restaurant where McKinley told the agents he also wanted .50 calibre rifles — 'We're probably only talking the two . . . semi and bolt action' — and 100 rounds of ammunition, military mortars and detonators. Returning to the subject of the Stinger, he said he was not looking for small arms or support weapons because the IRA could already 'hit them every day of the week'. What he wanted was 'something more sophisticated' which could be used along the border and was accurate to at least a 'distance of a mile'. O'Donnell and Fields said the .50 calibre rifles could cost anything up to $9,000 dollars and they could offer training for $500 per day plus an extra $200 for ammunition. McKinley said money was not too much of a problem: 'A lot of our support comes from Boston, New York and all that and that's a lot of money . . . millions of dollars.' The IRA would be able to arrange transportation of the weapons, he added. 'We have a ship that can go anywhere.'

Later that week, McKinley, using the alias 'John Reinhartsen', flew from West Palm Beach to Tucson and another meeting with Jameson. Séamus Moley flew in the following day after stopping in New York en route from Canada to pick up money for the detonators. He asked Jameson if he could acquire three or four .50 calibre rifles that could penetrate vehicle and body armour. On 28 November, McKinley and Jameson picked up 2,500 electrical and 400 fuse detonators, bought in Jameson's name, from Ireco's bunker in Rillito. The two men put the detonators into cardboard boxes packed with Styrofoam and took them to the Greyhound bus station in Tucson. A label on the boxes said they contained clothes and they were addressed to a 'Matt Hamner', a terminally ill AIDS patient who had nothing to do with the IRA. The FBI suspected that a man from Cullyhanna picked them up in New York.

On 2 December, McKinley, O'Donnell and Fields met again at Denny's — now the FBI agents' preferred location as Big Daddy's was so noisy that the tapes of their conversations were barely audible. As he tucked into a jumbo hot dog with bacon and cheese, O'Donnell explained he could obtain a Stinger missile from North Carolina within two weeks at a cost of $50,000. Fields said he had 'done a few calls on the two fifties' and these would cost between $3,500 and $4,000 for two. McKinley provisionally agreed to a price of $4,000 including 100 rounds of ammunition per weapon. He would have to telephone Ireland, he said, to be given the final say-so. 'I would say 90 per cent go ahead. I'm expecting 100 per cent in about two to three hours . . . if you can get the weapon we will have the money in cash.' The missile would be used to bring down helicopters in South Armagh. 'This is for a chopper . . . the Brits they can't come in, they can't drive because of landmines . . . the only way they can come in is by air . . . we beat them in the air so they can't come back.' Even though the IRA might have just one Stinger, the British would believe they had more. 'That's why it would be so important in Ireland. We got one, we could just pretend there'd be 20 . . . they're going to have to rethink . . . they keep us thinking all the time, we have to keep them thinking too.' The people at home were 'very excited' about the Stinger, although there were only 'three or four different people knowing about what's happening'.

His tongue loosening as the meeting went on, McKinley was drawn into conversation about IRA operations. When O'Donnell asked him about the type of organisation the weapons were being sold to, McKinley replied:

> Like the Brighton bombing [in 1984] and all that type of thing, that's the people you're dealing with . . . Remember Margaret Thatcher's whole Cabinet going up . . . they checked the whole place monthly, we had done security on that for weeks before Maggie got into it . . . She was in the toilet when it happened . . . That's why she wasn't killed, she went to the toilet.

McKinley also discussed the Hyde Park bombing — 'a friend of mine [Danny McNamee] is doing 25 years for that one' — and the problems with radio-controlled devices which Richard Johnson had been helping to overcome. 'The Brits, they keep going up and down the frequencies and block the remotes,' he said. 'We have to keep switching.' Most important of all, McKinley revealed the source of the detonators he had bought and added that 'what we really need fast is 100 rounds for our fifty', thereby confirming that the IRA had a Barrett rifle. From McKinley's information that 2,500 electrical detonators had been bought from a mine in Arizona, the FBI was able to track down Jameson, who was persuaded to accept an offer of immunity from prosecution in return for testifying against the IRA man. The prosecution later alleged that after the meeting at Denny's restaurant, McKinley telephoned the home of Eugene 'Cannon' Martin in Mullaghbawn and discussed the arrangements for the deal with his brother Micksey. He then rang O'Donnell to tell him that everything could proceed as discussed. 'Okay, that's a green light,' he said. 'They're happy and the only problem will be it will probably be the weekend or so before there can be funds.'

Four days later, the three met again at Denny's with McKinley telling the agents that someone called Séamus from Canada would be arriving soon. 'This'll be the guy that's bringing the money. He'll be examining the stuff, he'll stay here to the end of it . . . he'll be here the whole time until the thing is picked up.' Séamus was 'into the electronics and that type of stuff . . . he's an expert on that type of thing.' It was important not to mention weapons to anyone, McKinley emphasised. 'I import Coca Cola, remember that — Coca Cola.'

Back in Toronto, Séamus Moley was trying to arrange both the shipment of the detonators and the raising of $50,000 in cash for the Stinger. Sorting out the money was proving difficult and Moley was having to resort to unorthodox methods. On a single day in January 1990, he visited the Bank of Ireland and a branch of Chemical Bank in New York, the Spinning Wheel and several other Irish American bars and a number of republican sympathisers. The balance of the $50,000 which he could not raise was wired to American banks from the Irish Republic. On 13 December, Leyne sent a package of detonators to Bundoran in County Donegal. He later referred to the package as 'that Christmas card that you wanted for your first cousin' in a bugged telephone call to Séamus Moley.

In an otherwise carefully planned operation by the FBI, the fact that the 2,900 detonators were all eventually to reach Ireland was a remarkable mistake. McKinley had told O'Donnell and Fields that the detonators were for testing purposes only and the FBI apparently took him at his word and channelled their resources into securing arrests by setting up the Stinger deal. In fact, Ireco detonators, which had been sold legitimately to Chile and South Africa, became one of the mainstays of the Provisional IRA's armoury. They first began to appear in devices in Northern Ireland in 1991 and have since been used in coffee jar bombs, improvised grenades, under-car booby-trap bombs and mortars. The IRA bomb defused at London's Canary Wharf in 1992 contained an Ireco detonator and others were probably used in the Bishopsgate and Baltic Exchange bombs. A number fell into the hands of the Real IRA when Micky McKevitt resigned as the Provisionals' quartermaster general in October 1997. It was believed that one was used to set off the Omagh bomb in August the following year.

The day after Leyne posted the detonators, Séamus Moley drove from Canada into the USA with a shopping list of arms, ammunition, detonators, night-vision glasses and other equipment. In January, the Canadian authorities found a copy of the Winter 1985 issue of the magazine *Gung Ho Special Purpose Weapons*, which featured a cover story on 'Barrett's Fabulous .50 Semi-Auto Sniper Rifle', in Séamus Moley's locker in Toronto.

On 18 December, McKinley introduced Moley to O'Donnell and Field. When Moley asked whether the .50 calibre rifles would be semi-automatic or bolt action, Field replied: 'No, they're not gonna be automatics. They're gonna be single shot, bolt action. That's the cheapest one we could find.' Although Moley did not seem to know, bolt action rifles were much more suited to the IRA's needs than semi-automatics. Smaller and lighter, bolt action rifles such as the Barrett 90 do not eject a cartridge case or the firearms residue that could provide the police with a forensic link between sniper and weapon.

A more senior IRA figure than McKinley, Moley told the agents how hard he had been working on the arrangements for the Stinger deal. 'I talked to Kevin on the phone. Ever since that very day, I've been working on trying to get a good way of getting it out . . . it's a major asset where it's going and it's a lot of money as well.' He rejected an offer from O'Donnell for the missile to be shipped to Ireland before being taken on by the IRA. The shipment would be difficult but he would be able to arrange it. 'There's no direct route. It's very hard to get . . . There's a contact here, there's a contact there, a contact to put it back on there and then back off it . . . we've initiated the plan . . . it's just a matter of someone getting back and saying "okay, everything's laid out".'

Moley outlined his remaining concerns. 'The other thing which puts me a little uneasy is that I've never actually used one of these things. I've never used one . . . and the other things is, you know where the [serial] numbers and things are on it and could you get them off it? . . . that has to be done.' He reassured the Americans that no leaks about the deal would come from the IRA.

> We have a very high security, probably one of the best organised in the world right now. I always want to keep it that way, that's why we spend a lot of time in our shipping methods. Not very much of our equipment gets caught. An awful lot is getting in there and not very much of it is getting caught and if I have to spend an extra week, two weeks making sure that happens, then that'll have to be . . . I don't want it caught. I'd rather see it at the bottom of the ocean.

As the meeting ended, Moley said Mrs Thatcher had been shocked by the Brighton bomb and would be shocked again. 'No doubt she's gonna be more upset before long.' He laughed. 'We like women in anger.' O'Donnell's last comment as he switched off the tape while watching the two Irishmen leaving the restaurant was: 'Piece of cake.'

The prosecution case was that Séamus Moley phoned his brother Aidan from Florida on Christmas Eve to ask him how many .50 calibre rifles were needed. Aidan, it was alleged, said he would find out and added that he wanted more detonators shipped across the Atlantic. A week later, Séamus Moley and Micksey Martin discussed the financing of the missile purchase and whether the middle of January would be 'right' for the purchase of additional detonators. By this time, it had been decided that a third man, Joe McColgan, 39, would join them for the last stage of the deal. A weapons expert and former prisoner living, like McKinley, on the run in Dundalk, he was a brother-in-law of Martin McGuinness and was named in court in October 1990 as having gathered information about members of the

The body of John McAnulty, a smuggler shot dead as an informer and dumped at Cullaville in July 1989. It had been dragged onto the road by the Army in case of booby traps.

The body of Paddy Flood, an IRA man shot dead as an informer and dumped at Newtownhamilton in July 1990. Flood was interrogated for nearly seven weeks but it has since been established that he was not an informer.

The body of John Dignam, an IRA man shot dead as an informer and dumped at Lislea in June 1992. A priest placed a blanket over the body before the security forces arrived.

Above The RUC canteen portacabin at Corry Square station in Newry after it was hit by a Mark 10 mortar bomb, killing nine officers, in February 1985.

The scene of the IRA ambush on the Edenappa Road outside Jonesborough in March 1989, after Chief Superintendent Harry Breen and Superintendent Bob Buchanan had been shot dead. Buchanan's body was still strapped into the passenger seat.

The armour-plated Ford Sierra in which Constable Michael Marshall died in October 1989. Two Russian DShKs brought in from Libya were used to riddle the car with armour-piercing .50 calibre bullets.

security forces who were later shot dead. On 3 January, Séamus Moley and McKinley telephoned Micksey Martin, who indicated that 'John' [McColgan] was getting together the documents he needed for the United States and would bring money with him.

As the final arrangements were being made, Moley and McKinley again met the undercover agents. Moley showed them $15,000 in US currency and gave $2,500 as a down payment. Using the alias Hugh Nolan, he then rented a safe deposit box at the First Union National Bank of Florida and placed $10,500 in it. On 11 January, the four men met to discuss handing over the missile the following day. Moley said:

> I'll explain it to you. I show you, we can all go together, I can show you the money and the safety deposit box that there's one key for. All right? The deal can go down like this. This man goes with LJ to look at it, he phones the hotel room that we're sitting in, whenever you're happy and the man's happy and so okay hand over the money. You know where the money is right at that point. I know where the money is, I take you and hand you the money.

The agents agreed to this arrangement and showed Moley and McKinley the Stinger. The next morning, Moley and O'Donnell opened a joint access safe deposit box at the Barnett Bank and Moley placed $47,500 in it.

McColgan, who had arrived in Florida on 8 January, appeared to have an inkling that all was not right with the deal. On the appointed day, however, he was driven to the warehouse where he was to be shown the missile. He frisked O'Donnell and Fields, who asked whether he always 'went this far on a first date', but found nothing. The handover was being secretly filmed by the FBI, which had borrowed a Stinger from the US Defense Department and removed the rocket fuel and internal warhead. Video footage later shown in an Arizona courtroom captured the few minutes when the IRA believed it had finally secured the means to bring down a helicopter in South Armagh at will. 'Put your cheek up against this and you look through the peephole,' said O'Donnell as McColgan raised the missile to his shoulder. He continued:

Put your hole on your target to acquire your target. Activate. There's an activation switch. This is a loudspeaker . . . when it hits a source that it wants to lock on to it'll give you a tone, you'll hear it and feel it . . . That uncages the gyro, this is gyro stabilised. It'll start to track then. You don't have to keep the tube pointed right at it once you've done that. You've got maybe thirty, forty degrees to play with either way.

McColgan asked about the blowback after the missile was fired and how to fit a battery before satisfying himself with the feel of the weapon.

'Well, do we have a sale?' asked Fields. 'Yeah. Get it,' replied McColgan. He then wrapped the Stinger in a blanket and, when he couldn't get in into the boot of his hire car, jammed it behind the passenger seat. He was arrested as he tried to drive away and the following day was proclaiming his innocence as he was led in handcuffs from the federal court. 'I'm just a poor Irishman here on holiday and I was entrapped by certain people here,' he said. Séamus Moley and McKinley were arrested minutes after McColgan. All three received four-year sentences for attempting to buy the missile with an extra 19 months later being given to Moley and McKinley for buying the 2,900 detonators. Micksey Martin was extradited to America, pleaded guilty and received a 16-month sentence. Eleven others, including Aidan and Patrick Moley and Eugene and Jim Martin were either acquitted or had the charges against them dropped. These four had protested that they had been rounded up simply because their brothers had been implicated and investigators later conceded that not all those charged had been part of the conspiracy. In May 1998, McKinley was arrested after a consignment of £1.7 million worth of smuggled tobacco was tracked by MI6 from South Africa to a warehouse in central Portugal. He had arrived in the Portuguese resort of Cascais with his Texan girlfriend the previous September to set up an import-export business which MI6 believed was linked to the IRA.

Despite his setbacks in America, Tom Murphy had ordered that the search for anti-aircraft weapons be redoubled after the defeats at the hand of the FBI. If the mujahedin could defeat the Russians with Stingers, he reasoned, then South Armagh could do the same against the British. By the time of the July 1997 ceasefire, the IRA had not been able to deploy successfully any type of surface-to-air missile against a helicopter. But while the Libyan connection had been broken, the American one had too many strands to be severed completely. When asked whether it had been a failing on the part of the South Armagh Brigade that more helicopters had not been brought down, Pat Thompson replied: 'It's something that the leadership didn't take unnoticed and I'm sure the leadership are doing their best to overcome such military problems.' These efforts continued to focus on America.

Chapter 11

Sniper's Promise

'I've been waiting for two years or more
Waiting for Major to settle this war
You have done nothing to prove you want peace
That's why your Army will R.I.P.'

(Sniper's Promise signs, Crossmaglen
and Mullaghbawn, March 1997)

'The plan on Thursday was to shoot a soldier anywhere in the South Armagh area . . . I was to ride shotgun with the AK and Micheál was to be the sniper.'

(Volunteer Bernard McGinn to
RUC detectives, April 1997)

Volunteer Micheál Caraher crouched in the back footwell of the car, his stomach resting on the folded rear seat as he adjusted his view through the telescopic sight of the Barrett 90 sniper rifle. He was wearing a pair of ear defenders over his balaclava to prevent him being deafened by the sound of the shot he was about to fire. With him in the maroon Mazda 626 hatchback were two other South Armagh volunteers: Bernard McGinn, who was 'riding shotgun' with an AK-47, and a man nicknamed Tiny, who was driving. The barrel of the Barrett poked out through a foot-square hole cut in an armour-plated shield fitted into the rear.

Tiny had turned the Mazda into a laneway before reversing into position beside a concrete bus shelter. McGinn had jumped out and opened the tailgate. Now, in a dip 120 yards further along the Green Road, Caraher could see the Army checkpoint guarding roads around Bessbrook Mill. The corrugated iron hut protected the sentries but the soldier checking cars was out in the open. Caraher steadied himself and perhaps allowed the memory of his brother Fergal, shot dead by two Royal Marines more than six years earlier, to flit through his mind for a moment. The soldier's back was in the centre of the cross-hairs of the sight as he bent down to a white Vauxhall Cavalier. Caraher breathed out and squeezed the trigger.

Half a minute earlier, at 6.21 p.m. on 12 February 1997, Lorraine McElroy had been driving home to Bessbrook with her husband Tony and their baby David after buying ice cream in Newry when a soldier in helmet and camouflage fatigues waved his red torch to signal she should stop. As she slowed down, she recognised the cheery character who would often crack a joke or pass the time of day. Mrs McElroy handed Lance Bombadier Restorick her driving licence; he smiled, had a quick look at the licence and thanked her as he handed it back. His arm was still lifted at the window when there was a loud crack and a flash as a .50 calibre brass bullet travelling at nearly three times the speed of sound smashed into his SA80 rifle. The bullet broke into three pieces, the largest fragment ripping into Restorick's left buttock, passing through his body and out of his right side. The bullet's impact with the rifle sent part of the gun sight flying into the car, gashing Mrs McElroy's forehead. She heard the soldier groan and slump to the ground. When Bombadier Mark Fountain, the checkpoint commander, rushed over and asked his friend what had happened, Restorick gasped: 'The lady's been hit.' They were the last words he ever spoke.

As the shot rang out, Caraher tugged a length of blue nylon string dislodging a piece of wood propping open the tailgate and slamming it shut. Tiny moved the Mazda into fourth gear as it raced away up the Green Road; in front was a silver-coloured scout car with Séamus McArdle at the wheel. As the cars swung right into Camlough, they passed a telegraph pole on which a Sniper at Work sign had been fixed. Below it was a wooden board with the words of Padraig Pearse, one of the leaders of the Easter Rising in 1916, painted on it: 'Life springs from death and from the graves of patriot men and women spring living nations.' The two cars did not stop until they reached an old quarry close to Cullyhanna where two young volunteers were waiting to take away the vehicles and the guns. McArdle then used his own car to drive Caraher and McGinn to a nearby safe house where they showered to get rid of any firearms residue and put their clothes into a plastic bag for burning.

Restorick was pronounced dead on arrival at Daisy Hill Hospital in Newry. The bullet fragment had perforated his bowel and lacerated blood vessels, a vein and an artery, causing massive internal bleeding. The following day, Mrs McElroy said:

> I sat there in that ambulance and watched a man die. I wanted to go over and take him in my arms because he was all on his own and dying. He was unconscious and he looked all grey. One of my strongest emotions this morning was shame. I felt ashamed that we were going to be tarred with the same brush as the IRA. But they certainly don't stand for any of my family or friends. They say 'we' as if they are talking on my behalf. But they are not 'we'. They are themselves alone.

Mrs McElroy, a 35-year old Catholic, was later threatened by the IRA. Her outspoken attack had angered republicans, particularly because she was a cousin of Donna Maguire, the Newry volunteer who had been active with the IRA on the continent. A year later, the McElroys sold their house in Bessbrook and moved away.

Restorick, the last soldier killed by the IRA before its 1997 ceasefire, was buried on what would have been his 24th birthday. Two months earlier, he had written to his grandparents: 'I am sitting here at the checkpoint for hours on end, doing all the things I shouldn't do, like writing letters, listening to my Walkman. I think what I'll do is settle up some of my loans and go and get a new car . . . I am doing three days off 16 hours on and eight hours off . . . I am knackered. Well, I am going to have to go now to do my stint on the road, checking cars. See you soon. Love, Stephen.'

He was the ninth member of the security forces in South Armagh to be killed by a single high-velocity bullet in five years. The first had been Private Paul Turner, a slightly-built 18-year-old who had decorated his arms with 'England' and 'John Bull' tattoos just before his battalion had flown out for its six-month tour. On 28 August 1992, he had been down on his haunches outside the Northern Bank in the Square in Crossmaglen as other members of his patrol checked a suspect lorry. Beside a white gravestone moulded into the shape of Christ hanging on the cross, Micheál Caraher stood with a .50 calibre rifle resting on a 4-ft-high platform on the edge of St Patrick's churchyard. He had broken branches from a beech tree to give a clear line of sight down to the corner of the Square some 125 yards away. Fixing the crouching figure in the telescopic sight, Caraher fired the rifle, sending a bullet which ripped through the soldier's flak jacket, obliterated his left nipple, passed straight through his heart and pulled part of his liver out of a gaping exit wound in his right side. Death was instantaneous. Turner was still in a squatting position leaning against the wall of the bank when it was discovered his heartbeat and breathing had stopped.

The rifle used in the attack was thought to have been one of those made and sold legitimately in Texas by Ron Freshour, a former Barrett employee, and later bought by the IRA. Stamped with the word 'Tejas' — Spanish for Texas — on the butt, it was fired in west Belfast in June 1993 and seized a month later during an RUC search of a vacant house. The killing of Turner was the third single-shot .50 calibre attack in Crossmaglen; in the first, a bullet had passed between the helmet and head of Lance Corporal Hartsthorne of the Light Infantry as he stood at a checkpoint on the Castleblaney Road in March 1990. A fortnight before Turner was killed, another shot was fired at a foot patrol on the Carran Road in Crossmaglen. By January 1993, there had been further single-shot attacks against foot patrols or cordon positions in Drumintee, Meigh, Jonesborough and Cross-maglen and one against Borucki sangar.

Even though there had been seven misses out of eight single-shot attacks, the Army realised that the sniping tactic posed a major threat and heralded a new phase in the conflict in South Armagh. Having driven the Army off the roads in the 1970s and mortared bases in the 1980s, the IRA had now begun to respond to the success of the watchtowers by using dead ground to mount sniping attacks and attempt to bring down helicopters. The problem for the Army was that preventing mortar attacks meant carrying out mortar baseplate patrols on foot, which in turn provided targets for the sniper. One obvious deterrent was to use helicopters as 'top cover' but this increased the chances of the IRA achieving the coup of bringing down a helicopter. This period marked the zenith of the South Armagh Brigade's power. As the August 1994 ceasefire approached, the contrast between the campaign being waged on all fronts in South Armagh and the IRA's waning efforts elsewhere in Northern Ireland could hardly have been more acute.

The soldier in South Armagh was already at an innate disadvantage because he was operating in an unfamiliar environment for a short period. Colonel Spicer said:

> The army units used to change every four months and inevitably in the four month period you spent the first month finding your feet and you're probably quite cautious and methodical. The second and third months you are probably very productive. And the last one you are trying to stay alert because inevitably, however well you trained, however professional you are, you are on the down, you want to go home. By the fourth month your soldiers are knackered, mentally more than physically. And the commanders therefore have to deal with their own fatigue but also keep kicking the soldiers along to make sure they stay alert, they don't take short cuts, they don't race through gateways. The IRA are there the whole time and they don't have this learning curve. They can observe, they can pick the time, they can pick the place, they can pick the weapons and they know the terrain.

Tours had been extended to six months by the 1990s but a similar cycle still took place.

Even before the single-shot sniping attacks began to take their toll, the capacity of IRA gun teams to engage troops on equal terms had become a major headache for the Army. In May 1990, the Army had mounted Operation Conservation, an elaborate plan to lure the IRA into attacking Light Infantry soldiers dug in around Silverbridge and Cullyhanna. Some 16 COP teams were inserted in a ring around the Light Infantry positions with orders to ambush any IRA team that attempted an attack. But the IRA had pinpointed several of the covert positions and established that a four-man Scots Guards team near Cullyhanna was vulnerable.

The Scots Guards team had been inserted deep into a large area of gorse at 3 a.m. on 3 May. At 2 a.m. on 6 May, an IRA unit some 400 yards away raked the position with gunfire from two GPMGs and a Heckler and Koch G3 rifle. Lance Sergeant Graham Stewart, the team leader, was hit in the head and fatally wounded during a fierce 90-second firefight which saw the IRA expending 188 rounds and the Scots Guards 128. It was later ascertained that two of the IRA men had positioned themselves in a small gully next to a derelict building on the downward slope of a hill. Boulders had been used to build firing ports through which the GPMGs had been pointed; green military face veils had concealed the gun barrels. The G3 had been used to cover the GPMG men as they escaped to the Slatequarry Road where a car was waiting. A radio-controlled bomb had been left between the COP position and the road to catch any soldiers who might have given chase.

'It was another classic South Armagh rural contact: audacious, aggressive and accurate,' reported a senior Army officer who concluded that a well-trained IRA gun team was operating in Cullyhanna, by this time considered to be the most dangerous part of Northern Ireland. 'Once again, the enemy used dead ground to their advantage.' One of the officers who planned Operation Conservation said:

> In military terms, it was one of the IRA's finest attacks in South Armagh. They picked out the COP team in the most exposed position. With hindsight, it was the one weak link in the operation and it says something for the IRA's tactical and field skills that they identified that fact before we did. As soon as Lance Sergeant Stewart was killed, we pulled out all covert and overt troops and abandoned the operation.

As well as the growing threat from what the Army nicknamed the 'Cullyhanna Gun Club', the use of air cover was becoming more dangerous as the IRA stepped up its attacks on helicopters. Since 1989, machine-guns had been mounted on all helicopters flying in South Armagh and pilots were instructed to fly only in pairs. As the threat increased, there was a new requirement to fly with groups of three aircraft, each with two pilots in case one was hit by gunfire.

On the afternoon of 20 February 1990, an RAF Wessex pilot spotted several masked IRA men with light machine guns standing by a van and a car on a track to the east of Newtownhamilton. Realising they had been seen, the IRA men drove off to the south-west with the helicopter in pursuit. There was a chase involving eight different vehicles as the IRA men abandoned cars, hijacked others, threw ammunition boxes onto the road and discarded their weapons. The IRA men split up, some escaped and the helicopter followed a blue Toyota Corolla into Silverbridge. Jim Martin, fresh from his arms buying excursion to Toronto and Florida, was arrested along with two other IRA suspects but a crowd of up to 40 people quickly surrounded the three soldiers and two RUC officers who had been landed by the Wessex. When the crowd began to stone them, the RUC men let go of the suspects, who promptly disappeared into houses nearby. Martin was not recaptured and, eight years later, was still on the run and living at Ballybinaby as a result of the incident.

In searches afterwards, two AKM rifles, two GPMGs and a Heckler and Koch G3 were recovered along with seven CB radios. Intelligence officers researching the sources of IRA weapons noted that one GPMG was Belgian while the other had an Indian body, British working parts made by Enfield, and a Libyan barrel. The G3 was Portuguese and the two AKMs, which had been used to shoot dead Chief Superintendent Breen and Superintendent Buchanan the year before, were Romanian.

An Army report into the helicopter chase concluded that it 'proved that the enemy now operate in large numbers, in quite separate tactical groupings but with sophisticated co-ordination and communications'. It added: 'It is virtually certain that the nucleus of the enemy operation was a helicopter shoot and that the other groups were subordinate to this primary aim.' Up to 20 IRA men had been involved, including gunmen, drivers, scouts and dickers.

In September 1993, the IRA attacked a Puma as it lifted off from Crossmaglen security force base with two Lynxes circling above to protect it. Two DShKs and three GPMGs, mounted on vehicles, opened fire simultaneously from close to St Patrick's Church and the community centre. The Puma and one of the Lynxes were hit but the three aircraft managed to fire 200 rounds during a 10-minute gun battle as the IRA vehicles headed for Cullyhanna. Six soldiers dropped off by a helicopter to intercept a white van saw three masked men jump out of the vehicle and run behind a house. But there were no weapons visible and in these circumstances the Army's rules of engagement prevented them from opening fire. A DShK, two GPMGs and an AKM rifle were recovered afterwards.

Gaz Hunter, then an SAS staff sergeant operating primarily in South Armagh, said:

> It really was the IRA's domain. They'd become so sophisticated they had mobile communications, they had scouts, they had follow wagons. The sniper dominated the area and could take his time. They would take the DShKs up into South Armagh and we would get the intelligence and be trying to react to it. On one occasion where there was a chance that they were going to have a go at a helicopter we had quite a lot of our SAS people down there. We had .50s mounted behind sandbags in the helicopters.

By 1993, the IRA was able to use Mark 15 'barrack buster' mortars to bring down helicopters. Mark 12s had been fired at a helicopter unloading troops at Newtownhamilton in August 1991 and in March 1994 the South Armagh Brigade registered the most successful IRA attack against a helicopter during the Troubles. Early one Saturday evening, a tractor loaded with bales of hay was driven up the Monog Road into Crossmaglen and parked on waste ground 150 yards from the base. At 8.27 p.m., as a Lynx hovered 100 feet above the landing site, all the street lights in the Square suddenly went out and a single Mark 15 mortar scored a direct hit, severing the helicopter's tail boom.

The mortar had been attached to a collapsing circuit and its firing pack plugged into the mains so that it would be launched as soon as the IRA turned off the electricity supply. A Grenadier Guards patrol commander a mile away described seeing an enormous orange flash as the Lynx was hit. The helicopter crashed inside the base and Corporal Wayne Cuckson, who had been marshalling it in, was later awarded the Queen's Gallantry Medal for dragging Constable Peter

Skelly, who was wounded in the chest and stomach, from the wreckage. Beside the landing site where the smouldering remnants were examined at first light was a message which had been painted in large white letters several months before for the benefit of aircrew as they arrived. It read: 'Don't Worry. Be Happy. Welcome to XMG.' Four months later, an RAF pilot managed to crash-land his Puma in Newtownhamilton after its tail was hit by another Mark 15 mortar fired from the back of a tractor. 'My heart was performing the 1812,' he said afterwards.

The growing number of sniper attacks and the South Armagh Brigade's success in downing two helicopters were as much psychological as military blows to the security forces. For the young soldier on foot patrol, there was an almost paralysing fear that at any moment a sniper might strike with a bullet so powerful he would have little chance of survival. Homemade signs designed to mock the Army and sap morale soon began to spring up. In early 1993, a 'Welcome to Crossmaglen Sniper's Alley' notice appeared in the town. Then, alongside the giant letters I-R-A painted green, white and orange and nailed to telegraph poles, there was a new addition to the IRA's version of the Highway Code: a red circle with a stripe across an earthbound helicopter and the legend 'Heli-Buster Control Zone'. The Army could not remove them because of the danger they would be booby-trapped; in 1978, Rifleman Nicky Smith had been blown to pieces as he took down an Irish tricolour from a telegraph pole outside St. Patrick's church.

In September 1993, the first of the infamous Sniper at Work signs was put up in Crossmaglen. Soon, different versions of the sign had been placed on roadsides throughout the South Armagh countryside; after the 1994 ceasefire, boards stating 'On Hold' were nailed in the corners only to be replaced after the Docklands bomb with the message 'I'm Back'. Locals who wanted to remove the signs did so at their own peril. After the first ceasefire, the owner of a guesthouse in Mullaghbawn took down a Sniper at Work sign from a telegraph pole outside St Mary's Church. He returned home the next day to find his windows broken and a new sign back in place. When asked who had thought of the idea of the Sniper at Work signs, Pat Thompson said with a smile: 'I don't know but they fair caught the fucking imagination, didn't they?'

Myths grew up about the sniper attacks. In the bars around the Square in Crossmaglen, the sniper was referred to as 'Goldfinger' or 'the Terminator', terms lapped up by the tabloid press whose readership included the soldiers patrolling in South Armagh. There were tall tales of a former US Marine using a Barrett Light Fifty to kill almost at will from more than a mile away and never wasting a shot. In fact, in 24 recorded attacks between March 1990 and March 1997 there were nine members of the security forces killed, one wounded and 14 misses. There was more than one weapon and probably two snipers – Caraher operating to the west of Slieve Gullion and another volunteer to the east. Among the misses was a two-shot attack on *HMS Signet*, a Royal Navy patrol craft, from a firing point across Carlingford Lough close to where the Narrow Water bombs had been detonated in 1979. Eight of the attacks were with a 7.62 mm weapon, possibly the Belgian FN sniper rifle discovered in an arms hide near Inniskeen in September 1998.

The sniper threat affected different battalions in different ways. Major M, an Army intelligence officer who helped plan counter-sniper operations in South Armagh, said: 'It was very good for soldiers' skills and it made them feel they were doing something that was bloody serious. It made it much, much better for discipline. You still had to get up and leave the barracks and go patrolling whether you liked it or not. You just did it better because of the threat.' Captain Nick Lewis, who served with the Coldstream Guards in Bessbrook and Forkhill in 1996, said:

> The soldiers positively enjoyed patrols as that was the only time they could get out in the fresh air but the down side was that the IRA would try to kill them. Patrolling in South Armagh is a strange experience. You have to pinch yourself to remember where you are sometimes. If you are not careful, the beautiful countryside, rolling hills and small farms can make it seem as if you are rather ludicrously manoeuvring tactically through Gloucestershire. It just seems so bloody normal.

Morale plummeted during 1993 as the South Armagh Brigade perfected its sniping operations and seven members of the security forces were killed in nine single-shot attacks. Towards the end of the year, members of a Scots Guards platoon were disciplined for remaining in their base while on vehicle checkpoint duty because they had opted to falsify car registration details in preference to venturing outside.

Just after midday on St Patrick's Day in 1993, Lance Corporal Lawrence Dickson was leading a patrol along the Bog Road in Forkhill when his patrol commander reported on the radio that a person had been seen running near Church Road. Dickson jumped over the back wall of the disused Protestant churchyard and out through the gates onto Church Road, telling Private Lindsay McWhir to keep his eyes open for anyone acting suspiciously. McWhir heard a shot ring out and saw Dickson lying on the grass verge. 'I asked him if he could feel anything and he said he couldn't feel his legs,' he said in a statement afterwards. 'I found a bullet hole and then he fell unconscious.' The person seen running had lured Dickson to his death.

Three months later, Private John Randall was lying on his bunk in Newtownhamilton security force base composing a letter to his fiancée Michelle Tetley, a nurse he had met in the garrison town of Catterick in Yorkshire. 'When we went out last night I could not concentrate,' he wrote. 'I could only think about you and us. I always think of you . . . and I cannot afford to be like this . . . There are two or three of us that have a bad feeling about tonight's patrol. It has been very quiet for ages so something is due to happen. I hope not.' In the 11 weeks he had been stationed in South Armagh, Randall had sent her more than a hundred letters. At 7.17 p.m. on 26 June, as he patrolled in a field south of Newtownhamilton after crossing the Tullyvallen River, a 7.62 mm bullet fired from behind a hedge hit Randall's light machine gun, sending two lead fragments into his stomach and out of his left side. As he lay in the field while the other patrol members frantically tried to locate his wounds, he said: 'I think I'm dying.' His colleagues tried to reassure him he would pull through but he lost consciousness within seconds. 'When it was on television that a soldier had been killed, I feared the worst,' said Tetley. 'As soon as the phone rang, I just knew what the call was.'

The following month, Lance Corporal Kevin Pullin, also of the Duke of Edinburgh's Royal Regiment, was killed by a single .50 calibre round which hit him in the abdomen as he crouched on the Carran Road in Crossmaglen. The bullet passed straight through his flak jacket and the two identity tags hanging from his neck; its lead core was found embedded in a water bottle inside his rucksack. 'I heard a very loud, sharp bang and I immediately thought it was a .50 calibre going off,' said Private Kenneth Price in a statement. 'I checked down the road from where this bang had come from through the rifle sight and caught a fleeting glimpse of a red car. I then saw that Lance Corporal Pullin had been shot.' Such was the effect on the rest of the battalion that the lieutenant colonel in command at Bessbrook Mill had to address each of his companies to tell them that unless they conquered their fear there would be further casualties in the remaining two months of the tour.

Sixteen of the 24 sniper attacks in South Armagh involved the use of an estate car, van or jeep as a mobile firing platform. To protect the sniper from a patrol returning fire, the rear of the vehicle was fitted with an armour-plated shield with an aperture in the centre for the gun to be fired through. This had been tried successfully in 1978 by the gun team that shot dead the three Grenadiers from Sergeant Garmory's brick.

When driving a sniper vehicle through South Armagh, the IRA protected it with scout cars. Major M said:

> Whenever they're moving anything, they push a vehicle out front to catch any checkpoints. They'd also have a couple of cars out on parallel routes so that they could switch routes. The roads in South Armagh tend to run in parallel from the north-west to the south-east at a 45-degree angle. So if you were running a couple of vehicles up the middle road and a couple of vehicles up the side roads and the vehicle in the lead in the middle road runs into a checkpoint, for example, you can push the vehicle that's following with the snipe team across to one of the side roads and you've already got a car waiting there to take over the job.

The Surgeon was believed to be the driving force behind the sniper attacks and would often be out on the ground with his men for the shoot itself. He was arrested in connection with the murder of Constable Brian Woods, who died after being shot in the neck at a checkpoint in Newry in October 1993, but later released without charge.

A study of the distribution of the attacks showed that they fell into two distinct zones centred around Cullyhanna and Drumintee. 'At first, we believed it was one unit, one weapon and one trigger man,' said Hunter. 'It developed into at least two. It was a process of elimination working out who was involved and eventually we decided there had to be more than one team operating.' The Drumintee sniper team tended to use up to 20 volunteers in a 'dicking screen'. Major M said: 'You'd see dickers coming out on the day of an attack although the volunteers detailed to take part in it might not know whether it's for a bomb, a snipe or even a smuggling operation. Their jobs would range from watching the front gates of barracks to sitting in vehicles at key junctions. They could end up holding down an area of up to five miles.' Caraher, McGinn, McArdle and Martin 'Stove' Mines, who formed the nucleus of the Cullyhanna team, had a *modus operandi* based on predicting when patrols would be using the routes in and out of Crossmaglen. This required fewer dickers. Major M said: 'Crossmaglen was like a shooting gallery with most of the snipes coming straight down one of the six roads leading into the Square.'

Major M was tasked with advising company commanders how to counter the sniper threat. He recalled:

> They would say: 'Tell us something that will save us from the sniper'. My reply was always: 'Just good infantry skills'. They didn't like hearing that because they felt there must be some special recipe but there wasn't. The best way to counter a sniper is to apply the basic battlefield principles that every soldier learns at the depot which are: shape, shine, silhouette, shadow, movement, cam up properly, move tactically, watch your flanks as you're moving, mutual support, move as teams, reserves, defences, all of that. The battalions which had those good infantry skills like the Green Jackets, the Coldstream Guards and the Paras were the ones that avoided sniper casualties.

The Army's main offensive weapon against the sniper was the SAS. Hunter recalled that on one occasion in 1993 there were around 50 SAS soldiers on the ground in South Armagh in an anti-sniper operation. 'You try to dominate the ground so he can't use various sniping positions,' he said. 'The Green Army would patrol less or not go into certain areas and therefore reduce the number of targets the sniper could fire at. Normally he'd have quite a target rich environment.' The defensive measures the Army was forced to take meant that its operations were more constrained than at any time since the 1970s. During a Grenadier Guards tour which ended in March 1994, a third of all RAF and Army helicopter hours world-wide were flown over South Armagh. By 1997, troops were being issued with body armour containing a ceramic plate made from boron carbide, which could protect the trunk from a .50 calibre round; Kevlar flak jackets had proved useless against such a bullet. But a set of boron carbide body armour not only cost £4,000 but weighed 32 lbs, making it too heavy to be worn on patrol; even soldiers at static checkpoints could only wear it for two hours at a time. Major M said:

> Heavier body armour was good for the IRA because it's heavy and hot and that degrades the performance of the individual soldier. We would also insert VCPs by having soldiers slide down ropes from a helicopter straight onto the road rather than have them patrol out from the bases, and then extract them by air. That meant that to some extent the IRA had succeeded in forcing troops off the ground and it made helicopters more vulnerable so we had to guard against using them too much.

Seán MacStiofáin, the Provisional IRA's first Chief of Staff, claimed to have introduced the theory of one-shot sniping to Northern Ireland in 1972. 'One-shot sniping was in fact the theory of the guerrilla rifle,' he wrote in his *Memoirs of a Revolutionary* three years later. 'It turned up, struck once and vanished, presenting no target in return . . . Crossmaglen developed an exceptionally good unit which exploited the terrain and used the sympathy of the local people to the utmost.' Volunteer M was a leading member of this unit; another was Frank McCabe, whose exploits earned him the nickname 'One Shot'. Volunteer M said the sniper attacks of the 1990s represented a natural development from the tactics of the early days of the Troubles and were a response to the Army's success at jamming radio-controlled devices. 'What's special about the Barrett is the huge kinetic energy,' he said. 'The bullet can just walk through a flak jacket. South Armagh was the prime place to use such a weapon because of the availability of Brits. They came to dread it and that was part of its effectiveness.'

McCabe was one of the senior Provisionals behind the Cullyhanna sniper team in the 1990s. McGinn told the RUC that he had been picked up in Castleblaney by McCabe on the morning of one sniper attack; he acted as a lookout for Army patrols from Mullion high ground outside Crossmaglen until McCabe blew his car horn three times to attract his attention and drove him back. On another occasion, McGinn went to an IRA meeting at McCabe's house in Crossmaglen. 'When a shoot takes place at Crossmaglen, all hills to the border are covered to ensure a clear getaway for the team,' said McGinn. 'If the men on the hills see something, they walk to the road. The mobile scouts see them and, by CB radio or mobile phone, report the problem to the team going to do the shoot.' He had also seen the Barrett being tested in 'Cullyhanna country' by Caraher, who needed to zero the weapon so the Leupold sight would be correctly adjusted to suit his eye. 'Caraher lifted me in a two-door car early last year [1996] and left me on high ground to keep dick,' he said.

On 2 December 1993, McGinn was collected by Mines from Castleblaney and driven to Keady. He told detectives: 'My job was to use a mobile phone and to alert the team when the target was in place . . . I did a circle of the town to watch for a patrol going towards Darkley . . . Micheál Caraher was the sniper on the job and Séamus McArdle rode shotgun.' McGinn stood next to a monument overlooking the town and, when he saw an eight-man patrol carrying out mortar baseplate checks, called a mobile phone in the sniper car so that Caraher could be driven into position. At 12.05 p.m., Lance Bombadier Paul Garrett was hit by a .50 calibre bullet which passed through his ammunition pouch, perforated two SA80 magazines and the front of his flak jacket before penetrating his abdomen, exiting through his back and striking the front of 42 Victoria Street behind him.

By this stage, the danger of a sniper attack was much more acute in built-up areas. In the countryside, further modifications to patrolling methods were minimising the chances of casualties. Major M said:

> All the things you see when you have Army teams moving in
> South Armagh are counter-sniper tactics. Having teams satellit-
> ing is the best thing you can do. Then one team's moving along
> the valley but you've got another two teams up on the hill
> moving in parallel. You've got teams bouncing in and out of the
> main patrol route, circling around in front and cutting in behind.
> The IRA can then see one team but they can't see the other two.
> The team they can see might be the decoy with an attack
> coming in from the flank. You're trying to create that uncer-
> tainty in the minds of the enemy.

Caraher had been identified as the principal sniper some four years before he was arrested. Born into one of the staunchest republican families in Ireland, his dedication to the armed struggle had been strengthened when he had been wounded and his brother Fergal shot dead by two Royal Marines on 30 December 1990 outside the Lite 'n' Easy Bar in Cullyhanna. The circumstances of the shooting were hotly disputed with the versions of locals and the Army at complete variance. Lance Corporal Richard Elkington and Marine Andrew Callaghan, who between them fired 20 shots into the white Rover Micheál Caraher was driving, said they had opened fire because the car had collided with another marine, carrying him away on its bonnet. Six local witnesses said the shooting had been entirely without provocation and the willingness of so many Cullyhanna people to come forward drew a wry comment from one senior RUC Special Branch officer. 'No one in South Armagh sees or hears anything if a policeman or soldier is killed but as soon as Caraher was shot there were witnesses coming out of the woodwork every-where,' he said.

Elkington and Callaghan were found not guilty of murder after it was proved through scientific evidence that the locals had lied in the witness box. Fergal Caraher was buried as a Sinn Féin member but RUC Special Branch believed he was an IRA volunteer. 'There was an argument about it within the South Armagh Brigade but it was decided that the propaganda value of the killing would be under-mined if the IRA claimed him as a member,' said one Special Branch man. 'The family's feeling was that they didn't want to give the Brits the satisfaction of knowing they had shot a volunteer.' Micheál

Caraher, whose lung had been damaged after he was hit once in the back, was released from hospital within nine days and soon resumed his IRA activities.

A week after Elkington and Callaghan were acquitted and on the third anniversary of his brother Fergal's death, Micheál Caraher fired the shot which killed Guardsman Daniel Blinco, a 6 ft 6 in-tall Grenadier, as he stood outside Murtagh's Bar in Crossmaglen. The bullet, fired from a car 130 yards away on the Castleblaney Road, went straight through Blinco's trunk from right to left and sent up a cloud of dust when it struck the cement wall of the bar. He cried out 'I've been shot' but only remained conscious for about 20 seconds. Aidan Murtagh, the publican, remembered the other soldiers shouting 'Keep your fucking eyes open, Danny, keep your fucking eyes open' as they tried to revive him.

Afterwards, Lance Sergeant Keith Turner, who had been in charge of Blinco's brick, went into a shop and was shocked that people were continuing with their shopping as if nothing had happened. A guardsman's mother arranged for flowers to be placed outside Murtagh's but 20 minutes later they were found kicked down the street. Jim McAllister said there was little local sympathy when a soldier was killed. 'The general reaction would be sort of a grim one: "Well, if he wasn't there he wouldn't be shot,"' he said. 'You'd get nobody laying flowers, nothing like that. There was two occasions when soldiers were shot in the Square and flowers appeared at the site. In actual fact, other soldiers had taken them from graves in the cemetery.'

Blinco was to be the last sniper casualty before the August 1994 ceasefire, which was bitterly opposed by the South Armagh Brigade. 'The ceasefires have been humiliating,' said Paddy Short a year later. 'Here in Crossmaglen we had the Army and police on the run. All you needed to do was shoot one every six months.' In November 1994, Frank Kerr, a postal worker from Camlough, was shot dead during a £131,000 Post Office robbery in Newry which had been planned by the Surgeon. Kevin Donegan and Declan McComish, leading IRA men from Jonesborough, were captured in Meigh after being pursued by an RUC patrol car which almost certainly would not have been in South Armagh before the ceasefire. Donegan, believed to have been a member of the

Drumintee sniper team, and McComish, later to defect to the Real
IRA, were both jailed.

'The ceasefire meant that for the first time in more than two
decades, we were able to get that vital inroad into the community,'
said one RUC Special Branch officer. 'It was much easier for members
of the various covert agencies to get into the area. Traffic police went
back into South Armagh after 20 years away; but not all of them were
in fact traffic police. Ceasefires are much better for the security forces
than the IRA.' Some volunteers drifted away from the IRA while
even the most experienced became rusty. The Special Branch officer
said:

> Micksey Martin is a case in point. He is an absolute rascal who
> has been stealing and smoking cigarettes since he was eight
> years old. But he has tremendous organisational ability and was
> superb in a war situation. Once the ceasefire came, his crim-
> inality, his 'homers' — raking off money for himself — drinking
> and womanising meant that he lost a lot of respect from people.

After the Docklands bomb brought the ceasefire to an end,
there were remarkably few IRA attacks in South Armagh. In
June 1996, Paddy Murphy, Stephen Murphy and Brendan
Lennon were arrested by the SAS as they prepared to use a stolen
van to carry out a Post Office robbery. During the previous 21
months, there had been seven Post Office robberies in South Armagh
and the security forces believed they had identified the IRA team
responsible. As the volunteers gathered near a barn on Aughanduff
mountain, members of 14 Int were observing them from concealed
positions. A camera had been placed in a barn where, hidden under
hay bales, was an AKM rifle that had been used in the attack on the
three helicopters in Crossmaglen in September 1993.

Paddy Murphy, who had already served a spell in jail as a result of
the incident in 1992 in which Volunteer Mark Flynn had been
blinded, said:

> We were starting the van up when four soldiers came round the
> corner and another two up the lane. We saw them at the last
> minute. They were all masked up and stuff with gas masks and

balaclavas and one of them was coloured. Then helicopters seemed to come in from all directions and there was soldiers screaming 'Army, Army, Army'. It was mad, like. I knew it was the SAS and I thought it was lights out, I was going to be shot. Brendan put the van into reverse but he didn't get too far because they opened fire and burst the tyres. They pulled us down and were shouting and swearing, demanding our names.

Pat and Alice Murphy, Paddy's parents, heard the shooting from their farm and thought the three young volunteers had been killed; a neighbour had seen white forensic capes being produced and assumed they were body bags. 'We thought it was three more on the roll of honour,' said Pat Murphy, who had himself joined the IRA at the start of the Troubles and been jailed in 1974 for setting fire to a customs post. Among his son's earliest memories was the family farm being raided during searches for his uncle, Francie. Paddy Murphy said:

> I remember them coming for Francie. Most of the times they never caught him. He'd hear the helicopters coming and he'd be away out the back door. Even from that age I probably wanted to get back at them. You'd see them taking the house apart and think it was normal because you knew nothing else but at the same time you knew that you didn't want them there.

His mother said: 'I remember them raiding the house and Paddy telling a soldier: "I'll get an explosion and I'll blow you up."' Paddy Murphy had already had his leg broken at the age of two by a Garda officer in Dundalk during a protest in support of IRA hunger strikers. 'These two Garda vans drove up the street,' said Pat Murphy. 'The back doors flew open and they started flailing all round them. I grabbed Paddy up in my arms and the guards come over with the baton and let me have it across the head. He split my head open and then hit Paddy's leg. That was the first encounter Paddy would have had with the forces of law and order.'

Pat and Alice Murphy blamed an informer for the arrest of their son. Pat Murphy said: 'There was talk at the time that the reason they come to know about the van being there was because of this informer. That's how they got on it.' The volunteer in question had been the fourth member of the gang due to carry out the armed robbery but had escaped. He was later badly beaten and ordered out of Ireland; he moved to Manchester to live with an aunt but was allowed to return for his father's funeral and stayed. 'He left the country for a while but he's back again,' said Pat Murphy. The family had discussed the reasons why the informer had not been executed by the IRA. 'I had mixed feelings,' said Alice Murphy. 'South Armagh is a close-knit community and my son's still alive . . . it wouldn't have served any purpose for that informer to be killed as far as I was concerned. It was the political climate at the time that saved Paddy's life and probably saved the informer's life too.'

IRA investigations were held into how the security forces had been able to frustrate a series of operations but no answers were found. Pat Thompson indicated that the period after the Docklands bomb had shaken the South Armagh Brigade out of its feeling of invincibility and complacency that only other brigade areas had a problem with informers. 'Be it in a political struggle, an industrial set-up where one side wants to outdo the other, you'll always have people who will inform,' he said. 'It could be blackmail, money, caught in bed with some other man's wife, millions of reasons. You guard against it by being careful who you recruit, careful who you talk to, careful who you meet, careful where you operate.'

On the evening of 29 March 1997, Gerry and Paula Sheridan were in their sitting room at 13 Carrickasticken Road in Forkhill watching *Stars in Their Eyes* on television. Their children, Christopher, six, and Darren, four, were eating their tea in the kitchen. At about 8.15 p.m., Mrs Sheridan saw the headlights of a car turning into their drive and reversing up beside the house; she assumed a relative had come to see them. The couple heard voices in the kitchen and a moment later Christopher came into the sitting room and said: 'Daddy, there's a man here to see you.' As the little boy spoke, Caraher, McArdle and Mines, who were wearing balaclavas and armed with an AK-47, came into the room. 'Turn off the fucking lights now and get the dog to shut up,' ordered Caraher. 'We are the IRA. Calm your children and wife down. Everything will be all right.' After the house had been darkened and the dog banished to the garage, Caraher and McArdle went into the back yard leaving Mines in the kitchen with the

Sheridans. 'Act normal and turn the TV to whatever station you want,' said Mines. He seemed agitated and checked his watch frequently. The couple noticed that his legs were shaking and at one stage he dropped his radio on the floor.

From the Sheridans' yard, there was a clear view of the entrance to Forkhill security force base. Earlier that day, a senior Drumintee Provisional – later to join the Real IRA – had been seen near the house looking at the base to the west and Romeo Two Three watchtower on Tievecrum mountain to the east; the yard was in dead ground from both. As Mines guarded the Sheridans, Caraher and McArdle pushed a large white dog kennel to the side of the yard and placed a green milk crate on top. They removed a coping stone from the back wall before bringing out the Barrett rifle from the car. Caraher then got on top of the kennel and crouched down with his bottom on the milk crate and the rifle resting in the gap where the coping stone had been.

Inside the base, Major Ben Bathurst, the Welsh Guards company commander, was preparing to accompany Constables Ronnie Galwey and Michael Cochrane and five of his men on the soldiers' first foot patrol of their six-month tour. At 11.40 p.m., the front gate was opened and the soldiers ran out with Galwey and Cochrane walking beside them. Suddenly, there was a loud bang that Cochrane thought was an explosion. Galwey fell to the ground and shouted across at his colleague: 'I'm hit, I'm hit, Michael. The bastards have hit me.' The bullet had struck his right hip, fractured his femur and split his Maglite torch in two before making a large strike mark in the tarmac. By this time, the Sheridans had been under armed guard in their kitchen for three and a half hours. As soon as he heard the shot, Mines jumped off his chair and said: 'Get up and go into the front room and don't call the cops.' Within minutes, the three volunteers and their weapons were safely back across the border. Galwey nearly lost his leg and was off work for a year. He later said that he had tried to cope with the sniper threat by not dwelling on the dangers. 'I worked on the principle it would not be me – and if it was I would know nothing about it.' After having been hit, he refused to feel bitterness towards Caraher. 'I tell myself that he was not shooting at me, he was shooting at a green uniform. His hatred was against the uniform.'

The ceasefire had already enabled the Army and RUC to study the sniper attacks in depth and the fact that the IRA had chosen to carry out such a risky 'static' attack so close to a base – rather than fire at a patrol – indicated that counter-sniper tactics were proving effective. Major M said:

> To prevent attacks, you have to get inside the enemy's decision-making cycle and throw so many changes to the situation at such a rate that he has to break off his operation. He is then being purely reactive. That's something I don't believe we had ever achieved in South Armagh in 25 years. We'd always been reacting to incidents. We could just about contain them but we couldn't work out where and when the next one was going to take place.

All this changed once the IRA halted its operations because the security forces were able to 'go through every single report, every file, every incident, every sighting, every relationship, every address and start to analyse it'. He added: 'Eventually we could take a map and work out everything from where the kit was being picked up, where the mounting areas were, where the dickers were, where the parallel routes were for the scouts, where the operation was likely to take place, under what circumstances, at what sort of range, where the forensic clean-up would be and where the weapon would be returned to.'

The next step for the RUC-led Tasking and Co-ordination Group (South), known by the letters TCG(S), was to use this information to put in members of 14 Int to prepare the ground for an SAS swoop on a sniper team enticed into mounting an attack. Hunter remembered a similar plan being used in 1993:

> We'd work out a place where we could present a target but if he moved in to try to get a shot then we could take him. Then, if we thought we could lure him into somewhere, we'd set a pattern of patrolling activity to try and bring him out into it. Twice we had him on the ground and twice for some reason he called off because he got spooked. But you've got to put people on the ground as decoys to try and worm the sniper out.

This tactic was nicknamed 'the tethered goat option' by one company commander; the danger was that if the sniper was not detected in time he might kill a member of the decoy patrol.

On Monday 7 April 1997, the Cullyhanna sniper team was tracked to a farm complex at Cregganduff Road. Caraher, McArdle, McGinn and Mines arrived at midday and stayed for seven hours waiting for a phone call to tell them there was an Army patrol in the area but no target presented itself. The following day, a detailed arrest plan was drawn up by TCG(S) and, republicans believe, 14 Int members were used to plant listening devices around the farm complex, at the centre of which was a large corrugated iron hayshed divided into three compartments. Welsh Guards platoons were tasked to patrol in an imaginary box drawn up around Silverbridge and on the Wednesday evening, Caraher was observed driving the animal trailer – containing the Barrett 90 and an AKM in its false bottom – back to the Cregganduff Road. The usual network of republican supporters had reported back that there were soldiers on the ground and the IRA had taken the bait. 'We invited them to come out to play,' said one intelligence officer.

If members of an IRA sniper team preparing to kill a soldier had come up against the SAS a decade earlier, they would almost certainly have been shot dead rather than restrained and handed over to the RUC for arrest and questioning. This time the SAS team inserted into South Armagh was directed to carry out the 'arrest option' by swooping on the farm complex before Caraher and his compatriots had brought out their weapons. In 1984, when a very different political climate had prevailed, Lord Justice Sir Maurice Gibson, later to be blown up at Killeen, had remarked that three IRA men shot dead by the security forces had been brought to 'the final court of justice'. But, 13 years on and with MI5 briefing the Government that a second IRA ceasefire was possible, the prevailing philosophy was that the creation of four republican martyrs would be counter-productive.

At 8.30 a.m. on the Thursday, McArdle picked McGinn up in Castleblaney, drove him to Cullyhanna and dropped him at a crossroads so he could look out for patrols. Half an hour later, McArdle, who had been joined by Caraher, returned in the same Mazda used on the night Lance Bombardier Restorick had been killed;

the car had been resprayed blue in the meantime. They then drove to a lean-to shed to collect the armour-plated shield to fit into the rear. Caraher, McArdle and McGinn arrived at the farm complex at around 10.30 a.m., followed shortly afterwards by Mines in his silver Sierra. Frank McCabe was in charge of the scouting teams checking the movements of patrols. 'We were to wait at the sheds until we were contacted on the mobile phone by others who were scouting for a target,' McGinn said afterwards.

Sixteen SAS men under the command of Soldier A, a Glaswegian warrant officer known as Jock, were already waiting in position after having been briefed on the exact layout of the farm complex. Each armed with a Heckler and Koch G3, they had been divided into eight-man teams in two unmarked vans parked in a lay-by close to Cashel Lough Upper. Soldier A, wearing jeans and a dark blue jacket, sat in the passenger seat of a Toyota van waiting for a radio message from Bessbrook Mill. He was also in radio contact with Soldier I, in charge of the second van. It had been decided not to use helicopters for fear of the sniper team aborting the operation. The soldiers sitting in the backs of the vans were wearing standard Army camouflage fatigues. A number had taken part in the arrests of Paddy Murphy and his comrades less than a year earlier and some were veterans of dozens of undercover operations in South Armagh. There were other SAS and COP units dug in around the area in case the sniper team made a move and several helicopters were standing by. When the order from his commanding officer came through, Soldier A told his men: 'Stand by to move forward to carry out the arrest option.'

The two vans drove slowly along the Newry Road towards Crossmaglen, passing a Sniper at Work sign at Ford's Cross before turning onto the Cregganduff Road and into the farm complex on the right. McGinn said afterwards that they had sensed something was wrong a few minutes before the SAS arrived. 'We came to the conclusion it was too quiet. There were no helicopters.' An unfamiliar red car had been spotted driving past the farm and when McGinn went outside to the road and saw two vans coming towards him, he realised the sniper team had been compromised. 'I went back to tell the others to clear out but it was too late,' he said.

'Go, go, go,' Soldier A shouted as his driver, Soldier H, brought the van to a halt. Soldier I's van, driven by Soldier M, arrived about a minute later, crashing into a gatepost as it did so. The plan was for Soldier A's men to enter and search the buildings to the right and Soldier I's men to take the buildings to the left. As the SAS men flooded into the complex, there was panic in the hayshed with McArdle, Mines and McGinn fearing they were about to be shot dead. Mines tried to escape through a small opening at the back but retreated inside when Soldier C, who had run around to the rear with Soldier A, pointed his rifle at him. Mines was punched and wrestled to the ground by Soldier P and Soldier K, who had run in through the front while Soldier L and Soldier E tackled McGinn with their fists and feet. As he lunged at them, McGinn hit his face on the edge of the animal trailer; he hauled himself to his feet and then ran straight into the 6 ft 5 in bulk of Soldier J, who knocked him to the floor.

Soldier H punched McArdle and broke his nose before forcing him down. Within minutes, all three IRA men were on their knees in the 'arrest position' with their legs crossed and wrists tied together with plastic cuffs. Blood was streaming down the faces of McGinn and McArdle while Mines had been hit on the head with a rifle butt. Caraher, who had been outside the hayshed, had sprinted into the fields when the SAS arrived. 'We've got a runner,' shouted Soldier N, who signalled to a Lynx overhead as he pursued him along a hedgerow until he disappeared into a gorse bush. By this time, Soldier I had arrived and the two SAS men pulled Caraher out of the bush, kicking his hands from a branch he was hanging onto. The Mazda was in the far corner of the hayshed and Mines's Sierra, later found to have traces of Semtex in the boot, was parked in front. 'Complex under control,' Soldier A reported. 'Three times suspects detained, gloved and ready to go. Armoured plate in vehicle. No shots fired. No casualties.' His CO asked: 'Got the long [rifle]?' Soldier A replied: 'Negative.' His subordinates reported seperately that Caraher and the owner of the farm complex had also been seized.

The five arrests completed, Soldier A ordered his men to don masks to protect their identities. Each of the soldiers then put on a balaclava and blue baseball cap with 'Army' in luminous letters on the back and front. Minutes later, two dozen officers from an RUC Headquarters Mobile Support Unit (HMSU) arrived by helicopter to take over the suspects. 'Ready to extract on your call,' said Soldier A to his CO. 'Target is secured. We can drive off when required. HMSU are happy.' With that, the 16 SAS men climbed back into their vans and – in studied defiance of the received wisdom that it was suicidal to move by road in South Armagh – drove back through Silverbridge and Camlough to Bessbrook Mill for a debriefing session and, that evening, a major celebration in the SAS bar.

Along with the Barrett and AKM rifles found in the hidden compartment in the animal trailer the next day were a set of ear defenders, 54 live rounds, some of them contained in a Dunnes Stores carrier bag, 30 spent cartridge cases, two balaclavas and a rucksack. The Mazda, which had been stolen in Castleblaney four months earlier, was fitted with JBZ 5212 ringer plates. A green Mazda with that registration was traced to Declan McCann, whose Digit 6 mobile phone had been linked to the Manchester bomb. Mines's Sierra, which he had planned to use as a scout car, and the Mazda each contained a mobile phone and a CB radio switched to channel 26. Complacency on the part of the volunteers had apparently begun to creep in. Caraher had left footprints on top of the dog kennel in the Sheridans' yard and neglected to get rid of his boots as part of the standard post-attack 'forensic clean-up'. The boots he was wearing when he was arrested provided a perfect match. McGinn's confessions and the matching of McArdle's fingerprints with those found by the Met during the Docklands investigation were the icing on the cake for the security forces.

But any lasting sense of triumph on the part of the security forces was tempered by the realisation that it was only after seven soldiers and two RUC men had perished that the sniper attacks had been brought to a halt. There was also a grudging admiration for what the South Armagh Brigade had achieved. Although John Major had said that Private Randall had been 'murdered in a cowardly fashion' and Bill Clinton had described the killing of Lance Bombardier Restorick as 'a cowardly crime', according to Major M the feeling within the Army was rather different:

> The sniper tactic was clever and the attacks were carried out beautifully. It was face-to-face contact with a superior force all of whom are armed. It was not like parking a mortar baseplate and pissing off. It was actually pointing a weapon at a man who's also got one, who's also got fifteen mates around him and pulling the trigger and then getting away. The snipes started at

around 600 yards and came down to less than 200 yards. That's getting really close, close enough for us to be using SA80s and LMGs quite effectively. That's unbelievably ballsy and to work effectively at that sort of range it takes a lot of guts. To control your breathing and your heart in those sort of circumstances is difficult enough but when you know you're taking on those sorts of odds it's even harder. And it's not easy getting away in countryside where there are so many helicopters in the air. I've got a lot of respect for them. It wasn't cowardly in the slightest.

The Cregganduff Road arrests were arguably among the most significant of the Troubles. Three months later, the IRA called another ceasefire; in the intervening period the only operation the South Armagh Brigade mounted was a mortar attack on New-townhamilton security force base in which a single Mark 15 activated by a timer fell 40 yards short of its target. 'The arrests meant they had to curtail their operations and they assisted in bringing the IRA to the negotiating table,' said a senior RUC Special Branch officer. 'It also showed that South Armagh PIRA weren't infallible or untouchable.'

In March 1999, the four members of the sniper team were found guilty of a string of offences. McGinn received life sentences for the murders of Gilbert Johnston, Paul Garrett and Stephen Restorick while Caraher was given 25 years for the attempted murder of Ronnie Galwey; McArdle, already serving 25 years for the Docklands attack, and Mines received 20 years each. As they left the dock, the four volunteers laughed and joked. Mines called 'See you in 18 months' to supporters in the public gallery, a reference to the early release scheme contained in the Good Friday Agreement. Remarkably, McGinn was accepted into the Maze jail by the IRA despite his betrayal of his comrades and the fact he had been prepared to work as an informer. He had been shown mercy because he had pulled back at the last moment and withdrawn the statements he had made. But the IRA would probably never learn the full extent of McGinn's co-operation with the RUC and the South Armagh Brigade would never again admit an outsider into its ranks. For the security forces, the releases, combined with the knowledge that the South Armagh Brigade possessed another Barrett 90 and at least one other .50 calibre rifle, meant that the sniper threat was likely to remain a potent one for some time to come.

Chapter 12

'A Pause in the Solution'

'Tom is a very powerful man . . . if Tom decides I should be killed, I would be killed. That is the power he has at his fingertips.'
(Eamon Collins during the Tom Murphy
libel case, High Court, Dublin, May 1998)

'If it's over, I suppose there could be a sense of relief in some way but there must be an awful sadness because if it's over what was it for?'
(Jim McAllister at Easter Rising
commemoration, Crossmaglen, April 1998)

On the evening of the declaration of the second IRA ceasefire, there was no sign of celebration in Crossmaglen. 'What is there to celebrate?' asked Paddy Short as he washed a pint glass behind his bar. 'There'll be no ceasefire here until the British Army ships out and moves out. It's quite simple: they are the aggressors and we are the defenders. We weren't losing the battle. The soldiers still have to walk backwards and you don't do that if you're winning. Last time they used the ceasefire to reinforce and refurbish their bases. If that happens again, we'll still go about our business and the soldiers will still have to walk backwards.' Arguments about the wisdom of the IRA's move reverberated around the room. 'They should declare a date for withdrawal like they did in Hong Kong,' said one young woman. 'But we have to trust Gerry Adams and the leadership.'

Others were more sceptical. 'The only way that base in the Square will be removed is by a barrack buster,' said Michael, a regular who had lived through the Troubles. 'This ceasefire is not a solution, it's a pause in the solution. It's stalemate not checkmate.' Life in Crossmaglen, he said, was like living under siege. 'They took over our gardens and our Gaelic football pitch. The helicopters fly in all through the night. There's pure hatred towards the British here. Of course, I'll be glad for my children if there is peace. You would always wonder if you might get hurt some time if something went wrong. But the boys from Cross are brave and precise. We've had no civilian casualties here.'

After the arrest of the sniper team, the Metropolitan Police's swoop into Mullaghbawn and the IRA failures in England, there seemed to be a consensus in South Armagh that the ceasefire had been forced by the Belfast leadership at a time when the military wing of the republican movement was on the back foot. 'Ceasefires are dangerous things,' said Peter John Caraher. 'Virtually every man I know from this area who is in jail was arrested either just before or just after a ceasefire. The IRA stopped for almost two years before and there was plenty of talking being done but where was it getting us? Nowhere.'

When the Sinn Féin leadership, which included Gerry Adams, Martin McGuinness, Pat Doherty and Martin Ferris, who were all members of the IRA's Army Council, signed up to the Mitchell Principles of non-violence, the discontent swelled. There were fears within the republican movement that its leadership was preparing to abandon the armed struggle and dissent was most vocal in South Armagh.

Matters came to a head on 10 October 1997 at an IRA General Army Convention held at Falcarragh, near Gweedore in County Donegal, when Micky McKevitt, quartermaster-general and a close ally of Tom Murphy, denounced the leadership and called for an end to the ceasefire. McKevitt was supported by his common-law wife, Bernadette Sands-McKevitt, a sister of Bobby Sands, the IRA hunger striker; both were members of the 12-person IRA executive. Sands-McKevitt had been one of the Belfast refugees who had fled to Dundalk in the 1970s. In an IRA 'comm' smuggled out of the Maze in 1981, Bobby Sands had proposed her as someone who might be good at dealing with the press. 'I've another sister who is 21 and single,' he wrote. 'She's in Dundalk, south of the border – on the run. Firebombs went off in her pocket. She can't come up here, but if groomed would do down there.' While in Dundalk, she had met and fallen in love with McKevitt, then officer commanding the IRA in Dundalk and Newry.

Sands-McKevitt rose to become the most senior woman in the IRA, an organisation dominated by men. In South Armagh, the role of the few women volunteers would normally be limited to gathering intelligence or acting as couriers. According to RUC Special Branch, in 1998 there was only one active female IRA volunteer, a married woman who lived in Drumintee. 'The republican movement has essentially been a male, patriarchal, militaristic one,' said Eamon Collins. 'It doesn't really leave much space for women. That doesn't mean to say that they don't perform a useful role but this idea that there is a vanguard of women is a lot of horse manure.'

In the early 1990s, McKevitt became the IRA's quartermaster-general and assumed control of all the arms dumps in Ireland. By this time, he and Sands-McKevitt had moved to a comfortable bungalow in a smart cul-de-sac in the seaside town of Blackrock and they started a business, Print Junction, which sold t-shirts, souvenirs and photocopying services from the Longwalk shopping centre in Dundalk.

To their fury, the couple were outmanoeuvred by Adams and McGuinness at the Falcarragh convention and left isolated when only one other executive member supported them. Kevin McKenna, a potential ally, was voted off the Army Council and Tom Murphy, while highly sceptical about the leadership's strategy, argued that the IRA should bide its time and see what concessions Sinn Féin could secure. The Surgeon backed the leadership and was voted onto the new executive along with the Undertaker, who had also resisted the temptation to break ranks. The following week, McKevitt and Sands-McKevitt resigned from the IRA executive and formed a dissident paramilitary group that became known as the Real IRA; a number of leading IRA men in Drumintee and Jonesborough sided with McKevitt. The Surgeon was denounced by one dissident as 'the corrupt commander' and accused of failing to represent the views of his volunteers at Falcarragh. Originally calling themselves Óglaigh na hÉireann, the name 'Real IRA' entered common usage when dissidents staged an illegal roadblock in Jonesborough in early 1998 and told motorists: 'We're from the IRA. The Real IRA.'

The following month, Francie Molloy, a Sinn Féin councillor from East Tyrone who commanded a considerable degree of respect among IRA members, was despatched to Cullyhanna to plead with South Armagh volunteers not to follow McKevitt. Speaking to a packed Lite 'n' Easy bar in an address to commemorate the 24th anniversary of the death of Michael McVerry (Appendix C), he mentioned the issue of unity six times and implored the many IRA members present to be 'together united in one fist facing the British government'. He added: 'This phase of negotiations may fall apart, it may not succeed. And whenever that does happen then we simply go back to what we know best. But we don't go back to the same tactics we used maybe 20 years ago. We go back with new tactics, we devise new methods, new strategies and we go back again to face the Brits again in negotiations.' The volunteers and other republicans listened intently and with an air of some scepticism. Molloy departed immediately after the speech, leaving the discussions and drinking to continue late into the night.

A week later, there was enough concern about the situation for the republican leadership in South Armagh to send Dessie Murphy, from Camlough, to deliver a public message at a major Sinn Féin rally at the Europa Hotel in Belfast. As Adams, McGuinness and Molloy looked on from the stage, Murphy told the assembled republicans: 'On behalf of the entire republican movement in South Armagh, and I speak with a little bit of authority, we are 100 per cent, 110 per cent behind the leadership of Sinn Féin.'

In February 1998, at a republican rally in Creggan to commemorate the anniversary of the deaths of Brendan Burns and Brendan Moley, Jim McAllister's address reflected the confusion and uncertainty among volunteers in South Armagh:

> Sadly, folks, it is hard to know what has changed in the 10 years since the two volunteers were killed. There are probably more Brits on the ground than there ever were, we have more prisoners from this area in prison than we have ever had

previously, again very sadly . . . No one can really defeat us, the republican people, except ourselves, and if we remain united, remain strong, we can fulfil the vision of the two Brendans . . . Don't be afraid to speak out, remain part of your movement but have your say.

Most South Armagh volunteers did remain within the movement, although a stream of intelligence reports indicated that Provisionals were helping McKevitt launch car bomb attacks across Northern Ireland. In the weeks before the Burns and Moley commemoration, the Real IRA had devastated the centres of Moira in County Down and Portadown in North Armagh with huge car bombs. Forensic analysis of the 500 lb Real IRA bomb defused in Banbridge in January 1998 confirmed that it contained Semtex-based detonating cord of the type used by the Provisionals and two detonators, one of which was an Ireco type from the batch bought in Tucson in 1989. This provided the security forces with strong circumstantial evidence that McKevitt's former comrades were supplying him with bomb-making equipment. The Banbridge bomb, in common with virtually every other Real IRA device, was constructed in North Louth or South Armagh; the van used was a ringer for an unmarked Army vehicle in use in Bessbrook. Vehicle registration searches showed that Provisional IRA members had scouted at least one Real IRA bomb through Crossmaglen.

On 2 March 1998, a Renault 21 stolen three months earlier from Newtownclogue, near Meigh, was found by gardaí hidden under bales of hay in a barn near Hackballscross, less than half a mile from the Slab Murphy farm complex. 'PIRA-Real IRA co-operation in South Armagh was happening at a frightening rate prior to Omagh and causing great concern within the PIRA hierarchy in Belfast,' one of Northern Ireland's most senior anti-terrorist officers commented several months later. 'Tom Murphy had to be turning a blind eye. I have no evidence to prove it but that's my assessment. He could dominate that place overnight if he wished.' Later in March, a 1,300 lb Real IRA car bomb was seized by gardaí in a shed in Dundalk and the following day there were mortar attacks on Forkhill security force base and Golf Three Zero watchtower at Glasdrumman. Again, Provisionals were believed to have assisted the Real IRA in planning the attacks.

But in Drumintee and Jonesborough a bitter feud was developing between the Surgeon and two brothers who had defected to the Real IRA and become its leaders in South Armagh. The elder of the brothers had been the Surgeon's predecessor as IRA commander in the Drumintee/North Louth area. He was thought to have been one of the gunmen who shot dead Chief Superintendent Breen and Superintendent Buchanan in 1989; as the local quartermaster, he had supplied the weapons beforehand. Although he and the Surgeon had been close at one time, bad blood had developed when he had been moved sideways to make room for the Surgeon and was later overshadowed by him. 'The dispute had nothing to do with ideological differences,' said one senior RUC Special Branch officer. 'It goes back to a power struggle that developed between them in the 1980s. They are like dogs protecting their territory.' Pat Thompson was withering in his criticism of the Real IRA, describing them as 'fish and chip dissidents' who had no vision. 'I feel sad that they don't understand the politics of the IRA,' he said.

After the Good Friday Agreement was signed on 10 April 1998, there was, in the words of Jim McAllister, an 'air of confusion possibly verging on despondency' in South Armagh. Speaking beside St Patrick's Church on Easter Sunday, he said: 'There's an unsureness of where we're going, even a questioning of who we are, which is a new thing. I've read the damn thing and I believe it offers nothing whatsoever for republicans. To say this deal is transitional towards a united Ireland, that is bollocks. People had a genuine belief that this was an attempt to address the core issue of the British presence, which it never was.' When asked about local feelings about the 32-County Sovereignty Committee, the political wing of the Real IRA, he said: 'People around this area have a fair modicum of respect for them and saw them as a ginger group, never saw them as a breakaway or as a splinter group. Now it appears perhaps that the leadership is coming down on them. I know Bernadette Sands, I meet her perhaps once or twice a week out in Dundalk shopping and we have sensible chats and we're inclined to agree on most things.'

The same day, after the reading of the Easter Declaration by Volunteer M, Patsy O'Callaghan, Eugene O'Callaghan's brother, stepped forward to read the names from the Roll of Honour commemorating the fallen dead of the republican movement in

South Armagh. There was then a pause before he looked at the crowd and, pointing at the headstone commemorating 'all the volunteers of the Irish Republican Army Crossmaglen who died in the struggle for freedom', said: 'And the fellows in those graves there give everything and until, as Padraig Pearse said, the English leave this country, there'll be no peace.' Jutting his finger in the air at the Lynx overhead, he added: 'There will be no settlement, there'll be no peace for this country until those people up there leave this country.'

At the Mullaghbawn Easter rally the day before, Conor Murphy, a former IRA prisoner who was soon to become a Sinn Féin assembly-man, had signalled that, despite the republican movement's strong misgivings, Sinn Féin would support the Good Friday Agreement. Rather than attacking the institutions of the state from outside, republicans would destroy them from within. The situation, he said, was similar to that in the Maze after the Hunger Strikes in 1981 when the British thought the IRA was beaten. South Armagh men, along with their comrades, dug allotments and used the facilities in the prison workshops; the authorities believed they had finally accepted the regime enforced on them. In fact, said Murphy, the prisoners were planning the mass breakout of 1983. 'And the IRA later executed the screw in charge of the workshops.' At a Sinn Féin conference in Dublin the following month, all the South Armagh delegates voted to accept the agreement and participate in the new Stormont assembly as a tactic to advance the republican struggle. Among them were Joe Burns and Aidan Moley, brothers of the 'two Brendans' who had blown themselves up a decade earlier.

Real IRA attacks continued after the agreement was endorsed by 71 per cent in the May referendum. In the week before the June assembly elections, a landmine designed to hit an Army foot patrol exploded on the Newry-to-Forkhill road, shattering the windows of the Three Steps. Two days later, Newtownhamilton was devastated by a large car bomb. The Drumintee landmine had been connected to a mobile phone; when it received a call, the electrical signal completed a circuit and set off the detonator. The use of such advanced technology underlined the fact that McKevitt had enlisted some of the best brains of the Provisionals' engineering department to work for him. What he lacked was the experienced volunteers capable of carrying out attacks successfully and without detection.

Both the limitations and the devastating potential of the Real IRA were illustrated by the bomb blast in Omagh on 15 August which killed 29 people. The evening before, the South Armagh Brigade's leadership had gathered at Cullaville to watch the unveiling of a memorial to Malachy Watters, a young volunteer who had committed suicide two years earlier. Tom Murphy, the Undertaker, Micksey Martin, Peter John Caraher and Pat Thompson all watched a nun bless the stone monument and stood to attention as the *Soldier's Song*, the Irish national anthem, was played. The Surgeon moved among his men with an air of authority. Despite the close attentions of a Lynx helicopter, it was a relaxed gathering with Murphy in noticeably good humour.

A few miles away, the final preparations for the Omagh bomb were being made. Two days earlier, a maroon Vauxhall Cavalier had been stolen in Carrickmacross. It had then been loaded with 300 lbs of homemade explosive, a booster tube, detonating cord and a blue plastic lunchbox containing the TPU. The car, fitted with Northern Ireland ringer plates, was seen from watchtowers in Crossmaglen and Cullaville before it was driven north towards Omagh. At about 2.30 p.m., the car was parked by two men in Market Street and there were warnings telephoned from phone boxes in Lurgancullenboy and Aughanduff in South Armagh.

As with previous Real IRA bombs, the codeword used was 'Martha Pope', the name of an American official who liaised with Sinn Féin on behalf of Senator George Mitchell during the negotiations which led to the Good Friday Agreement. The warnings indicated the bomb was outside the courthouse; in fact, it was 300 yards away, outside a school outfitters shop owned by Roy Kells, a prominent Orangeman. Up to this point, the Real IRA operation was similar to scores of commercial bombings by the Provisionals during the Troubles. The warnings had been deliberately imprecise to prevent the security forces defusing the bomb and perhaps also catch RUC men trying to clear the area. For years, the Provisional IRA had played a similar game of cat and mouse with the authorities. This time, it went badly wrong. There appeared to have been a catastrophic breakdown in communication between those who planted the bomb and those who telephoned the warnings. By the time it became apparent that the RUC was moving shoppers towards rather than away from the bomb it was too late.

At 3.10 p.m., the bomb exploded as dozens of people stood around it next to the police cordon. Survivors later wept as they described the scene. 'I've never seen anything like it in my life,' said Dorothy Boyle. 'I saw bodies lying everywhere, dead people being zipped into bags. One boy had half his leg blown off and it was lying there with the wee shoe still on it. He didn't cry or anything. He was just in shock.' Gerard Turbitt, a dentist in the town, said: 'I counted up to nine bodies. I saw bits and pieces of people. I saw a baby not more than two years of age in a shop window just lying there dead. A water main had burst but there were so many injured people that the dead were just left lying face down in the water.'

In the wave of public outrage that followed, the Real IRA was forced to call a ceasefire and the McKevitts were nearly run out of their home. The couple were evicted from Print Junction and Sands-McKevitt, in desperation, rang Father Desmond Campbell, a local priest, to ask for his help. 'She was obviously in some great turmoil mentally,' said the priest. 'She was crying. She was afraid of something happening and her children being hurt. She was stumbling and stuttering about it and then she broke down completely.' More than 400 people attended a candlelit vigil a few hundred yards from the couple's home while the queue to sign the Omagh condolences book in Dundalk Town Hall stretched into the street.

There was anger, too, in South Armagh. For the first time, it became acceptable to condemn a republican group and all it stood for. During one pub conversation after Omagh, a former Official IRA member explained to the author how McKevitt had been involved in the kneecapping of Larry Carragher, a Newry republican, in 1975 during the feud between the Provisionals and Officials; the Officials in Dundalk had retaliated by kneecapping McKevitt. 'We shot the bastard in the knees,' he said. 'We should have aimed a bit higher.' There were nods and murmurs of agreement around the table from people who had been staunch republican supporters throughout the Troubles. But despite this antipathy towards the Real IRA, there were no protest marches in South Armagh and no significant information about the bombers was passed to the RUC. While the people of Dundalk felt allegiance both to their government and their police force, in South Armagh there was still such a degree of alienation from the British state that even Omagh could not break the wall of silence.

The Real IRA's actions damaged Tom Murphy. The Provisional leadership in Belfast reasoned that he had either been supporting the Real IRA and undermining the Provisionals or had lost control of many of his people. His reputation had also been dealt a severe blow by a disastrous libel action in which he had challenged the *Sunday Times* over an article entitled 'Portrait of a Check-in Terrorist' published in June 1985. He had already secured handsome out-of-court settlements from the *Daily Mail* and a book publisher and decided, along with another man, to sue some two years after the article appeared.

Despite legal advice that the paper would never win a libel case against a man who inspired so much fear and had the power to intimidate witnesses, the *Sunday Times* decided to fight. But Brigadier Morton, the Customs officers Seamus Colgan and Denis Byrne, and a number of gardaí were persuaded to give evidence at the High Court in Dublin in March 1990. Afterwards, Ralph Sutton, counsel for the *Sunday Times*, summed up: 'This case began in a pastoral atmosphere of two quiet, peace-loving farmers whose lives had been devastated by the article. We have come a long way since then . . . These men are men of violence, smugglers, big in oil and with very firm links with the IRA.' The jury found that Tom Murphy was a prominent IRA member who sanctioned indiscriminate murder and the bombing of property and awarded him no damages.

For Tom Murphy, however, the 'long war' was a legal as well as a military concept. He lodged an appeal and in 1996 the Irish Supreme Court ordered a retrial. Among those who agreed to act as character witnesses for Tom Murphy was Paddy Short. But things began to go badly wrong for Murphy as soon as he took to the witness stand on the first day of the retrial in May 1998. Affecting the demeanour of a simple country man who owned a 'small wee farm' and knew nothing about the IRA, his evasiveness soon became almost comical. At one point, when he pretended he had never heard of the Maze prison, Mrs Justice Catherine McGuinness exclaimed: 'Oh come on, Mr Murphy, you must have heard of the Maze.' When asked the question again, he replied: 'I do now.'

Murphy appeared muddled about his date of birth and, after admitting attending the funeral of Volunteer Eugene Martin, the young IRA man and nephew of Micksey Martin who was killed in a car crash in April 1996, claimed he had not been aware it was a paramilitary funeral. He had thought, he said, that the IRA guard of honour was something to do with 'football or cycling'. He feigned amnesia when asked about the three times he had been arrested under the Republic's Offences Against the State Act. On the first occasion, on 13 February 1984, Detective Garda Martin Noone had spotted Murphy's car parked in a lay-by in Tallanstown near Ardee in County Louth. In the passenger seat was Kieran Conway, alleged by Sean O'Callaghan in court to have been the IRA's director of finance at that time; Conway's own car was parked 50 yards away. Murphy did not reply when the garda asked what he was doing and Conway gave a false name. The pair were arrested on suspicion of IRA membership and taken to Ardee Garda Station where they remained silent throughout all questioning before being released without charge. In court, Murphy said Conway was a hitchhiker and insisted he had been arrested by Noone because of a motoring offence. 'I was only after giving the man a lift,' he said.

On 1 April 1984, Murphy was arrested again, this time after being seen by two detectives jumping out of a car in Cox's Demesne housing estate in Dundalk. He was searched by Detective Garda Patrick O'Connor and found to be carrying a false driving licence in the name of a Joseph Murphy who lived in Dublin. Murphy told the court that the incident 'never happened as far as I am concerned'. His third arrest took place shortly before midnight on 28 June 1986 when his car was stopped at a Garda checkpoint close to the Three Mile House pub at Togan's Cross in County Monaghan. The checkpoint had been set up following intelligence that Kevin McKenna was holding an IRA meeting nearby. Inspector Noel Cunningham told the court that there had been two other men in the car, Kevin Martin, from Crossmaglen, and Micky McKevitt. All three were arrested on suspicion of IRA membership but freed the next day. In court, Murphy said he vaguely remembered 'being taken into the barracks one night' after giving two strangers a lift to Castleblaney. 'I was taken in because of having alcohol,' he added. Paul Gallagher, senior counsel for the *Sunday Times*, said: 'Did it ever occur to you that you were an extremely unlucky man, constantly being arrested in circumstances where you had passengers in your car whose names you did not know?' Murphy replied: 'You could call it whatever you like.'

A joint RUC-Garda operation on 29 June 1989 to raid the Slab Murphy farm and question Tom Murphy about the murders of Chief Superintendent Breen and Superintendent Buchanan three months earlier was to prove Murphy's undoing in court. 'When I was getting up that morning, I seen men with guns out in front of the house and the back of the house and I thought I was going to be assassinated and I jumped out through the window and left,' Murphy said in cross-examination. The armed men had been wearing 'boiler suits and had blackened faces' and he had leapt through a window into his yard, thereby leaving the Irish Republic and entering Northern Ireland, before escaping through the fields. In his absence, two passports were seized from the farm. The first was in Tom Murphy's name and had expired in March 1989; on page 11, there were stamps indicating he had flown in and out of Athens airport in April and July 1987 after 24-hour stays. The second passport, which was still current, had Tom Murphy's photograph in it but bore the name Jim Faughey. Inside were stamps for day-long visits to Athens in May and November 1986 and a single stamp from Split in Yugoslavia dated May 1989. In court, Murphy claimed he had bought a false passport from a man in Dundalk because he had needed a new identity to escape death threats made to him after the *Sunday Times* article. The real Jim Faughey, who had never applied for a passport or travelled abroad, lived in Kilcurry, a short distance from the Slab Murphy farm complex.

There was worse to come for Murphy. With the help of the Dutch, British and Irish authorities, Jason McCue, the newspaper's solicitor, was able to prove that the Faughey passport had been supplied by the IRA. It had been one of a batch of a hundred from the J series stolen from the Dublin Passport Office in May 1984 shortly before they had been due to be sent to the Irish Embassy in Lusaka. Three from the batch had been recovered in Glasgow in July 1985; they bore false names and the photographs of Peter Sherry, Ella O'Dwyer and Martina Anderson, members of an IRA unit planning a seaside bombing campaign in England. Five more had been seized in Holland the following year when Gerry Kelly and Brendan 'Bik' McFarlane were arrested along with a large quantity of arms and ammunition. Three bore pictures of Gerry Kelly, later to become a senior Sinn Féin figure, who had fled to Holland with McFarlane after they escaped from the Maze. The details on the Faughey passport and the nine seized in Scotland and Holland had all been forged by the same hand.

Also damning was the testimony of Sean O'Callaghan and Eamon Collins, two former IRA men who had met Tom Murphy in very different circumstances. As he entered the court surrounded by plain-clothed gardaí, O'Callaghan blew a kiss at Patrick Murphy, who scowled back. He described how he had met Tom Murphy at a Revolutionary Council meeting in 1983 and two GHQ Staff meetings the following year. When asked to identify him, he pointed his finger at the public gallery and said: 'He is sitting there. The man with the leather jacket and the blue shirt.'

The appearance of Eamon Collins took Tom Murphy's legal team by surprise and the men surrounding him in the public gallery, including Michael Conlon and Michael 'Legs' McLoughlin, glared at the former IRA man as he entered the witness box. As a frightened youth some 19 years earlier, Conlon had bought the motorcycle later used in the Narrow Water attack. McLoughlin had once been arrested by the SAS at the Slab Murphy farm complex before being released without charge. The court listened in silence as Collins told how he had first seen Tom Murphy in 1981 at a social function organised by Len Hardy to 'impress the Generals' and attended by a host of South Armagh IRA men. 'I understood the Generals to be the most significant players in the IRA,' Collins explained. The function had been held in the upstairs room of Mark McLoughlin's bar in Dundalk, a former Official IRA drinking hole which had been bought by Teddy Farmer, a Provisional on the run from South Armagh. Hardy and Brendan Burns had pointed out Tom Murphy to him. 'I saw him drinking orange,' said Collins. 'I was impressed he did not take alcohol.'

According to Collins, the second time he met Murphy was in the house of Malachy Foot, a Sinn Féin activist, in Dundalk in November 1983 following the killing of Sean McShane, who had been shot in a Newry betting shop after being mistaken for an off-duty RUC man. Collins had identified McShane as a Detective Constable Cunningham; in fact, he was a civilian who had been selling spare car parts in police stations. There had been an IRA inquiry into how the error had occurred, during which Collins had been suspended from active service; now Tom Murphy wanted to discuss the matter. According to Collins, he introduced himself by saying: 'I am Tom Murphy and I'm here as a representative of the Army Council.' Collins continued:

> Tom explained he was there as a result of the shooting in Newry in relation to the innocent Catholic civilian and could I go over again what had taken place and how had I targeted. I did that in detail. He asked me how the mistake had been made and the history of it and how did I feel and I explained that I recognised the severity of making such a mistake but as an IRA volunteer I must put it behind me and continue on. He accepted that . . . he told me on behalf of the Army Council I had been completely exonerated. I found what he said quite gratifying and I was extremely impressed by his manner and the way he treated me and his professionalism . . . He shook hands with me and he left in good form. The only interruption was Malachy who put an old rubber boot into the fire to heat up the room. I was quite affected by having met such an important man.

During the trial, Foot issued a statement denying the meeting had ever taken place.

When challenged about his motives for testifying against Murphy, Collins replied: 'My evidence is absolutely true and history will vindicate me.' But he was aware of the possible repercussions and told the court he was in no doubt that if Murphy ordered his execution then he would soon be dead. As he was ushered away to a waiting car after completing his evidence, Collins called out: 'No hard feelings, Slab.' Murphy looked away and his chief bodyguard muttered: 'Judas Iscariot will always appear on these occasions.' Four days later, the jury took just under an hour to find against Murphy, leaving him with a legal bill of more than £1 million. The humiliating defeat had taken place within the Four Courts building, where the Civil War had begun in June 1922 when the Free State forces shelled it after it was occupied by the anti-Treaty IRA.

Despite warnings that his life was in danger, Eamon Collins continued to live with his wife Bernie and their four children in the middle of the republican Barcroft estate in Newry. Shortly after the trial, intelligence was received that the question of what to do about Collins had been discussed at an IRA meeting in South Armagh presided over by Tom Murphy. Four months later, the house in Camlough left to him by his father was burnt to the ground. His children were abused at school and anti-Collins graffiti, including messages such as 'Enjoy the house-warming Eamon! Touts out!' and 'Eamon Collins Brit Agent 1984–99', appeared around the estate. On 27 January 1999, the former IRA man rose at 4.30 a.m. and, taking a pot of black paint, brushes and a ladder, went to cover up the latest daubings; underneath his coat, he was wearing a bullet-proof jacket. An hour or so later, he returned to the house to wash the brushes before setting out for a walk with his two Springer spaniels.

At 6.18 a.m., two men returning from their night shift found Collins's body on the lane that runs up Doran's Hill between the Barcroft estate and the Newry bypass. In an attack reminiscent of those carried out by the loyalist Shankill Butchers in Belfast in the 1970s, he had been stabbed repeatedly in the back and head, the fatal wound penetrating his brain; his face had been obliterated and his injuries were so severe that at first it was thought he had been run over.

The killing had been set up with almost military precision and only the weapon and the almost animal ferocity used distinguished it from any number of meticulously planned paramilitary operations. The killers were believed to have escaped by driving onto the bypass and then through Camlough into South Armagh. RUC and Army intelligence officers had no doubt that the 'execution' had been ordered by Tom Murphy with the full backing of the IRA's Army Council. Given the continuing IRA ceasefire and the possible political repercussions if the Provisionals were held responsible, it had been decided that a gun would not be used. Three months later, the Surgeon, two brothers from Drumintee and another man were arrested and held for questioning about Collins's murder on the basis of intelligence information passed to the RUC from Garda Special Branch. They were freed when their DNA samples failed to match blood thought to have been left at the scene by one of the killers, who had apparently been injured during the struggle with Collins.

*   *   *

Collins's grisly death was another sign that in South Armagh, despite the Good Friday Agreement and tentative steps towards establishing new political structures, the 30-year conflict had not yet run its course. 'Do I believe the politics at the moment is going to achieve a united Ireland? No, I don't,' said Pat Thompson. 'But it's another phase of the struggle. It's a phase that has to reach its final conclusion. Whether there'll be one more phase, two more phases or half a dozen phases after that I don't know. The IRA's prepared for any eventuality. People who fought a campaign for 30 years are not going to just throw the towel in now.' He insisted that the South Armagh Brigade would never countenance surrendering arms. 'There won't be decommissioning,' he said. 'No. Absolutely not. In no form. The IRA volunteers won't allow it. It'd be a very brave man in this area who would drive down with a load of guns and hand them over. It's a non-starter.'

Brian Keenan, Tom Murphy's close ally on the IRA Army Council, received rapturous applause in Cullyhanna in November 1998 when he told hundreds who had gathered to mark the 25th anniversary of the death of Michael McVerry that weapons would not be given up:

> I can say categorically the only time the IRA will decommission, we will decommission in agreement with a government of national democracy, a government that derives from the first Dáil. That's when we will decommission – never, ever before . . . Everybody's saying: 'The prisoners are being released, what's your problem?' Well there's no prisoner was ever in jail to be let out to sell out the struggle and I'm sure none of them would want to be let out if this struggle wasn't going the whole way.

If republican demands were not met, he warned, 'then Tony Blair will carry the consequences' and the British had to realise that the IRA would act:

> So in the future maybe the jails are going to be full again . . . If our enemies don't want peace, there can only be one conclusion: they must want war. We don't want to go back to that. But let there be no mistake: if we don't get equality and if the reasons for conflict are there . . . then the waiting time will soon draw to

a close and republicans will once again have to do anything that is necessary to get a Republic, because that's the goal.

As if to emphasise the continuity of the republican struggle, the man holding the tricolour in the centre of the front rank of the IRA colour party was Tommy McMahon, the man who had blown up Lord Mountbatten's fishing party nearly two decades earlier. At an IRA General Army Convention in County Meath a few weeks later, Murphy offered to step down as chief of staff in favour of Keenan. But the offer, made because of both the amount of dissident activity in South Armagh and the embarrassment caused to the republican movement by the libel case, was refused. Both the Undertaker and the Surgeon were re-elected to the IRA executive; the Army Council remained unchanged.

Looking back on events since 1971, Pat Thompson said he remained as dedicated a republican as the day he joined the IRA:

> Prison made me very strong. I gave most of my life to this struggle. I've no regrets. There's no nice ways to fight a war. It's either you die or they die. You have to fight terror with terror, if they want to use the word terror. I'll not use the word but they'll use it. This stuff about IRA psychopaths and all the rest is just black propaganda. There's no IRA person or republican that glorifies death. Republican resistance sees the enemy as being British in the same way as the British sees an IRA man in uniform or with a weapon as the enemy. The only difference is the SAS stand over Mairéad Farrell after she was dead and blitzed her to pieces. How they can live with their consciences after that beats me. I just fail to understand how a government can train a person to do the likes of that to young women.

He emphasised, however, that the South Armagh Brigade had never underestimated the capabilities of the British Army. 'You're not playing toy soldiers here,' he said. 'The one thing that the IRA in this area would be intelligent enough to have in their heads is that the enemy they're fighting is a very trained enemy and they're no fools. They're good at their job. They just weren't as good as the IRA.'

The Undertaker oversaw the swelling of the IRA's coffers as a result of the increasing profitability of smuggling after the 1997 ceasefire was called. The differential in excise duties between the United Kingdom and the Irish Republic was 29 pence on diesel and 21 pence on unleaded petrol following Gordon Brown's budget of March 1999. Tom Murphy was able to cash in because the Newry and Mourne Regulation Hydrocarbon Traffic Order was only effective when prices were higher in the Republic, as had been the case when it was introduced in 1990. 'Lorries were queuing up along Larkins Road to move fuel from south to north through the Slab farm,' said one anti-terrorist officer. In 1998, Customs and Excise officers in Northern Ireland estimated that at least £100 million a year was lost through smuggling; the South Armagh Brigade was netting a substantial proportion.

But as smuggling revenue was increasing, the tap on another major money-spinner for the IRA was being turned off. The RUC's Operation Saddle (South Armagh Deception over Deceased Livestock Enquiry) began after concerns about the level of compensation paid out by the Ministry of Defence to farmers in South Armagh. Between April 1994 and March 1995, there were 38,643 claims for animals killed or injured as a result of military helicopter activity and over £6.1 million was paid out in compensation. The overall figure for compensation paid out for dead animals, damage to property and requisitioned land between 1991 and 1997 was nearly £9.5 million to claimants in South Armagh compared with less than £1.9 million in the whole of the rest of Northern Ireland. Investigations revealed evidence of massive and systematic fraud, with hundreds of thousands of pounds of the MoD's money ending up in the hands of the IRA. Individuals not connected to the IRA were also involved.

Two men were convicted as a result of Operation Saddle. In February 1998, John Niall Sands, from Camlough, was jailed for ten months for making five bogus compensation claims in 1994. He had claimed low-flying helicopters had caused his cattle to stampede over rocks to their deaths and had driven sheep into a lake or river, where they drowned. He was caught when he claimed for some cattle, which were tagged, a second time and others turned up alive at Camlough market or on other farms. In May 1998, Gerard Cunningham, from Mullaghbawn, was given a suspended sentence of 18 months after pleading guilty to 17 counts of false accounting. One claim had been for £23,500 for a chestnut gelding said to have drowned in a drain after being scared by a helicopter; in fact, the horse had been bought for just £1,000. One of the vets who, it had been claimed, had provided death certificates for the animals was discovered to have been abroad on holiday at the time. After Operation Saddle, during which more than 20 South Armagh farmers were questioned, compensation claims dropped dramatically. Between April 1997 and March 1998, 6,228 animals were claimed for, of which 4,900 were chickens killed in one incident; the amount of money paid out dropped by £6 million to just over £500,000.

Eamon Collins said:

> I was once stopped by a British Army patrol and the officer was talking to me about the claims in South Armagh by all the farmers for damage to their land. He said there were so many claims made and paid out very generously by the British administration for fences that had been cut by soldiers that by now we should be seeing nothing in South Armagh only a gleam of metal from the air; there must be a million yards of it. In South Armagh, practically every second car is a Mercedes or a BMW. You go out and there are three-storey houses being built everywhere. Where's all the money coming from?

The IRA, he said, had taken more than its fair share of that wealth, whereas in Belfast many IRA men lived in relative poverty.

> In South Armagh, practically every IRA activist I know has a fucking good house. You're talking about places worth £100,000 easy. The same house in Dublin would be worth three or four hundred thousand. A lot have several cars, four-wheel drives, the lot. Okay, they worked hard for it, maybe they earned it, I don't know, maybe they did some smuggling. Some of them have good businesses but if we had a situation that justifies war there wouldn't be any of these people living in these decent houses: the British Army would have been out knocking the things down, the same way as they do in Israel. If a Palestinian family has a son who died in a suicide bomb their house is bulldozed. I don't see that happening in South Armagh.

Many of the compensation claims in South Armagh were genuine. Wire fences would be routinely cut by soldiers because of the dangers of gaps and gates being booby-trapped; taking an obvious route in the South Armagh countryside was a short cut to death. There were also difficulties in sending MoD assessors into an area effectively controlled by the IRA. Eamon Collins said he felt the authorities had been happy to pour money into South Armagh and raise the level of prosperity. 'I remember somebody in the States talking about the war in Vietnam and he said the way to deal with the problems in Vietnam was to drown the revolution in baby milk. And I am semi-convinced that South Armagh has been drowned in baby milk over the past 20 years.'

Volunteer M said he had been plunged into the depths of despair by the Omagh bomb and had begun to question the validity of the armed struggle for the first time in 30 years. He said:

> The whole thing created its own momentum and to some extent it ran away from us and led to the conflagration of the past 30 years. I've been shot, I've escaped, I've been on hunger strike, thirst strike, I've been extradited, excluded, I've been through it fucking all and now I do wonder whether it was all worth it. It just gets to the point where the cost of attaining your objectives just isn't worth it. There's no point in killing anybody for what can be achieved now. Saying that goes against my whole republican upbringing. Everything I believed all my life has been just blown away over the past couple of years. It's a very poor tally for what we've been through; we've effectively signed up to a new Stormont, something the republican movement had rejected over the years. The conclusion I've come to is that we can't win this war by shooting and bombing and killing people. We have to deal with this British problem by politics. But if it is not sorted out there is still the potential to go through it all again.

For many, the physical and mental scars of the past three decades in South Armagh will never heal. Twenty-seven years after Sam Malcomson was shot at Drummuckavall as he and Albert McCleary drove back to Crossmaglen, he is paralysed down most of his left side and wears a caliper over his useless left leg. The nerves at the base of his spine are irreparably damaged and bullet fragments are still lodged in his back. His only relief from the pain comes from the doses of morphine he injects into himself several times a day. He was 22 and a keen footballer and marathon runner when he was shot. Hardest of all are the memories of his mother, who collapsed and died at his bedside. He said:

> My father and I have never been able to bring ourselves to talk about it. She was only 48 but she died of a heart attack brought on by seeing me lying there with all the tubes and things coming out of me. One of my last memories of my mother is her giving me a wee leather travelling case to take with me to Crossmaglen. My dad's still a very active man, out two or three nights a week bowling and whatever. Him and I would go to motorbike races and do quite a bit together but I could never sit down and ask him a direct question like: 'When you were rushing down to the hospital what conversation did you have?'; 'Those last few miles, what was my mum like, was she panicky or was she calm?' I have never been able to do it and I suppose I never will. There's not a day that passes that I don't think about what my father's journey back home was like. And then there were my two sisters at home. He obviously had to break the news to them. Maybe they waved mum and dad off to see me and then he came home without her. How did they feel? They can't talk about it either.

Although Malcomson was given a medical discharge from the RUC, McCleary was able to remain in the force. 'One day Albert walked into the ward and he seemed to have made a reasonable recovery,' said Malcomson. 'Yet he had a scar which ran about two feet down his back where this Armalite bullet went in, tore up a lung and did a lot of damage. He came in and used to get me out of bed, put me into a wheelchair and take me over to the cafe. We sat and chatted, and him and my father got to know each other quite well. Him and I went over to Buckingham Palace to receive British Empire Medals for services in South Armagh.' But McCleary never came to terms with his injuries and nearly 25 years later he died suddenly. 'To this day I believe that he never fully left the past behind him,' said Malcomson. 'I don't want to go as far as saying that he hid behind drink but he was in his house and he banged his head and as a result he died. I remember being at the funeral and thinking: "My goodness, you made the recovery at a certain stage and I was a bit envious that you were able to continue on and yet I'm at your funeral."'

Malcomson also often thinks about the two IRA men — one of them believed to have been Tommy McMahon — who shot him:

> I'm still determined to ask those guys how they felt when the news broke that my mother had died. I need to know if they showed any signs of remorse. I wonder if that turned either of them away from terrorism, the fact that an innocent person, my mother, had died. I want a straight answer. They can say: 'We struck a double blow, we went after you, we got you and we got your mother too.' Or they can say: 'If we could have apologised to you about your mother's death we would.' Those are the thoughts that niggle away in your mind day and daily. Most people, if they had to put down a cat or a dog, they would come away with some feeling. That makes me wonder what a person must feel like if they've gone out and murdered somebody. How can they live with it? Would it maybe help if people like us got together and talked? There's maybe a common denominator, something there that would put it out of our minds and would lay the whole thing to rest.

As the 20th anniversary of the Narrow Water massacre approached, Tom Caughey, too, was still finding it difficult to come to terms with what had happened to him. His legs were so badly burned that the wounds had never healed. After leaving the Army in 1982, he turned to drink and was married and divorced before eventually settling down and taking a clerical job within the civil service in his native Northern Ireland. He said:

> At the time of the bomb, life was one adventure. We knew in the back of our heads what could happen but we never dwelt on it. Everybody thinks they know what bombs can do. But to see it actually on top of you, what a body ends up like, takes the

romantic side of being a soldier out of it. I resent the Army, although not the Parachute Regiment, in a sense because of the alcohol side of things. In hospital our beds were covered with alcohol, whatever we wanted. I had money, which was wrong as well. At age 20 I had thousands of pounds in the bank plus getting paid. It was just drink after drink. It affected my temper and made me violent. It was just all the anger in me coming out. Even today, if I have too much alcohol and a remark is made then all the sense can go out the window. It's like lighting a touch paper.

Some of Caughey's contemporaries subsequently rose through the ranks while he was doomed to lead the rest of his life wondering what might have been. At a regimental dinner, Caughey shook the hand of a friend who had just been promoted to Regimental Sergeant Major and congratulated him. 'I said: "At least one of us done it." And he replied: "You know, I think you would have done it two years before me." Well, I'll never know if that's true and that is the chip on my shoulder. I often wonder whether I would have still been in the regiment, what rank I would have been or whether I'd have been a complete arsehole. It's something I'll never know.'

Like many victims, Caughey had found the prisoner release scheme contained in the Good Friday Agreement difficult to stomach. Among those freed early was Joe Brennan, one of the Narrow Water bombers, who had been jailed after being caught following a mortar attack in 1994 and sentenced to 16 years. Caughey said:

I can't understand all this talk about there being a war here. Conflict, certainly, but if it was a war they would have a uniform on and come out and fight you. But they won't hit you unless they've done a dry run 20 times. It's nice doing it from a distance but they don't like doing it close up. The difference between me and them is I wore a uniform. But enough is enough. And if it takes the people that done this to me and my friends being released from prison and walking the streets then so be it. It's hard but I'll accept it. As long as it never happens again.

Shortly before his death, Eamon Collins was hoping that South Armagh's notoriety would be consigned to the past. 'The other day, I was driving back from Carrickmacross through South Armagh to Newry, through that rugged landscape, and I realised that it was now alien to me. I thought about the people who have been killed and I thought: "Won't it be great if there's peace and this place sinks into the obscurity that it deserves." They ran that place with a reign of terror.' Weeks later, a group of Provisionals were to drive part of the same route on their way to kill him.

For Peter John Caraher and Pat Thompson, the IRA's work would only be complete when a British withdrawal was finally secured. 'It'll keep going on because Irish history shows it,' said Caraher. 'Every decade from 1916 there was a rising. There'll come other young lads and I don't know who they'll be. They could be IRA, they could be Continuity IRA. They could be INLA. They could be anything. But you mark my words: if this is not over, in ten years it'll be on as hard as ever again.' Pat Thompson too gave little indication he or his comrades were prepared to let South Armagh lapse into obscurity, deserved or not. 'There'll be no settlement until the Brits are out of this country,' he said. 'They've no right to be here in the first place and while there's a British presence there'll always be armed republican resistance. It's a long road yet.'

Over the course of nearly three decades, the British Army and RUC have arguably learned how to contain the South Armagh Brigade. 'We've had a lot of success in South Armagh,' said one senior anti-terrorist officer. 'By the last ceasefire, we were preventing four out of five operations. Prevention alone means success.' But this 'success', achieved at a massive human and financial cost, was largely reactive and only scratched at the surface. Despite the ring of watchtowers, still being refurbished and upgraded as the millennium drew to a close, and an enormous concentration of intelligence resources, the forces of law and order are still on the outside looking in. A real understanding of South Armagh – and perhaps of Irish republicanism – remains elusive.

From 1997, after years of treating the IRA and Sinn Féin as beyond the Pale, the British government began to view the republican movement as a potential coalition member of a new liberal democratic structure. Officials had been seduced by the language used by republicans into believing that they had somehow accepted British rule. Yet, as the historian Robert Darnton suggested when considering 18th century French peasant society, a common language can mask fundamentally different thought structures. 'They do not think the way we do,' he wrote. 'And if we want to understand their way of thinking, we should set out with the idea of capturing otherness.' This meant finding out 'how they construed the world, invested it with meaning, and infused it with emotion'.

In Northern Ireland, the 'otherness' was more pronounced in South Armagh than anywhere else and the fact that by the end of 1999 most IRA men there had remained within the mainstream Provisional movement showed that republicans were not about to become constitutional nationalists. There was no one from South Armagh in Sinn Féin's negotiating team during the talks which led to the Good Friday Agreement and during the political stalemate which followed, Conor Murphy, providing a blood link back to Frank Aiken, was the only South Armagh representative close to the Belfast leadership. But Tom Murphy, who kept himself well briefed on political matters, continued to support Adams and McGuinness and the South Armagh Brigade was content to bide its time. Men whose primary pastime for many years had been to dream up more and more ingenious schemes for killing soldiers and policemen were waiting for the moment when their skills would be called upon again. In the meantime, the border was still providing the means to make plenty of money and their power and hold on the community in South Armagh remained largely unchallenged.

Looking ahead to the new millennium, a senior Army officer who had spent much of his career with the SAS operating in South Armagh expressed the hope that during his retirement he might be able to enjoy a pint in the Three Steps with the Surgeon or drive through Ballybinaby and pay Tom Murphy a visit. 'I'd like to go down there and do a bit of walking, climb Slieve Gullion and visit the passage tomb,' he said. 'If it were a clear day, perhaps I'd be able to look down and see that there were no more watchtowers and that there wasn't a helicopter in the sky. In the pub, maybe I would talk to the locals about the Troubles, which by that time would be consigned to history.' He added that the term 'Bandit Country' had been entirely counter-productive for it had fuelled the South Armagh

Brigade's sense of invincibility and planted fear in every soldier's mind.

But while myth and propaganda have played their part in cementing the notoriety of South Armagh, so too has a terrible reality. Even to Irish nationalists, the area remains 'neither fish nor flesh', a borderland where strangers fear to tread. South Armagh's quarrel is with authority *per se* rather than just British rule, and even a genuine political accommodation in Northern Ireland is unlikely to bring to an end a rebellion that has already lasted centuries.

Appendix A

A list of the military, RUC, IRA and civilian killings in South Armagh or carried out by the IRA's South Armagh Brigade since the modern Troubles began in 1969.

1970

12 August
Constable Sam Donaldson, 23, Royal Ulster Constabulary
Constable Roy Millar, 26, Royal Ulster Constabulary
Died the day after being blown up by IRA booby-trap gelignite bomb in abandoned car on Lisseraw Road outside Crossmaglen.

1971

29 August
Corporal Ian Armstrong, 33, 14th/20th Hussars
Shot dead by IRA at Shelagh near Crossmaglen after Ferret scout cars had crossed border at Courtbane in County Louth.

27 November
Ian Hankin, 27, Customs official
James O'Neill, 39, Customs official
Shot dead by IRA gunmen firing at an Army patrol which had arrived at Killeen Customs Post following a bomb attack.

29 November
Private Robert Benner, 25, Queen's Regiment
Abducted by IRA while visiting his girlfriend in Dundalk and found
shot dead at Teer near Crossmaglen. Off duty.

1972

21 January
Private Philip Stentiford, 18, Devon and Dorset Regiment
Blown up by IRA landmine detonated by command wire from across
the border while on foot patrol at Derrynoose near Keady.

6 February
David Seaman, 31, civilian
Found shot dead on the Concession Road near Cullaville. Former
soldier who claimed he had been working as a double agent. Official
IRA believed responsible.

9 February
Patrick Casey, 26, civilian
Eamon Gamble, 27, civilian
Died three days after receiving severe burns in explosion at
temporary council offices in Keady. No group claimed reponsi-
bility.

10 February
Sergeant Ian Harris, 26, Devon and Dorset Regiment
Private David Champ, 23, Devon and Dorset Regiment
Died after their Land Rover was blown up by IRA landmine at
Freeduff near Cullyhanna.

2 March
Sergeant Roy Morrow, 28, Royal Ulster Constabulary
Died of head wounds two days after being shot by IRA gunmen as he
investigated a report of intruders at the Bairnswear factory in
Camlough.

17 April
Corporal James Elliott, 33, Ulster Defence Regiment
Abducted by IRA near Killeen while driving his firm's lorry and shot dead. Booby-trapped body found two days later at Altnamackin near Newtownhamilton. Off duty.

17 May
Sapper Ronald Hurst, 25, Royal Electrical and Mechanical Engineers
Shot dead by IRA sniper while working on perimeter fence at Crossmaglen security force base.

15 July
Captain John Young, 27, Royal Army Ordnance Corps
Blown up while attempting to defuse IRA bomb at Silverbridge.

16 July
Lance Corporal Terence Graham, 24, Duke of Wellington's Regiment
Private James Lee, 25, Duke of Wellington's Regiment
Blown up by IRA landmine detonated by command wire while on patrol in Ferret scout car on the Carran Road in Crossmaglen.

24 August
Trooper Ian Caie, 19, Scots Dragoon Guards
Blown up by IRA landmine packed into a beer barrel and detonated by command wire while on patrol in Ferret scout car at Richardson's crossroads in Moybane near Crossmaglen.

18 September
Edmund Woolsey, 32, civilian
Blown up by IRA booby-trap bomb attached to his car, which had been stolen and abandoned at Glasdrumman.

22 September
Second Lieutenant Stewart Gardiner, 23, Argyll and Sutherland Highlanders
Shot dead by IRA gunmen while investigating report of landmine at Moybane.

20 November
Captain Bill Watson, 28, Argyll and Sutherland Highlanders
Colour Sergeant James Strothers, 31, Argyll and Sutherland Highlanders
Blown up by IRA booby-trap bomb hidden in chimney of derelict house in Cullyhanna and attached to butt of rifle placed on hay bales.

1973

8 March
Corporal Joseph Leahy, 31, Duke of Edinburgh's Regiment
Died of wounds two days after being injured by IRA booby-trap bomb in derelict house at Mullaghbawn.

13 March
Private John King, 22, Royal Hampshire Regiment
Blown up while on foot patrol by IRA booby-trap bomb left in a parcel on Coolderry Bridge near Crossmaglen.

26 March
Samuel Martin, 33, civilian
Accidentally shot outside his home in Newtownhamilton by Army. A soldier was acquitted of his manslaughter.

7 April
Corporal Steven Harrison, 26, Parachute Regiment
Lance Corporal Terence Brown, 26, Parachute Regiment
Blown up by IRA command-wire culvert bomb as their Land Rover drove along the Carrickrovaddy Road in Tullygallaghan near Newtownhamilton. Volunteer Jim Martin found guilty of two murders but convictions quashed on appeal.

5 May
Company Sergeant Major William Vines, 37, Parachute Regiment
Blown up by IRA command-wire landmine while on foot patrol at Moybane near Crossmaglen.

5 May
Corporal Terence Williams, 25, 17th/21st Lancers
Trooper John Gibbons, 22, 17th/21st Lancers
Blown up by IRA booby-trap bomb attached to command wire used
to detonate device which had killed CSM Vines three and a half hours
earlier.

24 May
Warrant Officer (Second Class) Ian Donald, 35, Royal Engineers
Sergeant John Wallace, 32, Parachute Regiment.
Blown up by IRA radio-controlled bomb while searching house in St
Bridget's Park in Cullaville

10 July
Isaac Scott, 41, former member of Ulster Defence Regiment
Shot dead by IRA gunmen outside Tully's Bar in Belleek.

20 July
Private Sidney Watt, 36, Ulster Defence Regiment
Shot dead by IRA gunmen as he got out of his car outside his home at
Ballintemple near Newtownhamilton. Off duty.

23 August
Margaret Meeke, 52, civilian
Shot dead by IRA sniper at McGuffin's Cross, near Newtown-
hamilton. Her car was mistaken for that of an Ulster Defence
Regiment member.

25 October
Séamus Larkin, 34, civilian
Disappeared from his home in Derrybeg, Newry and found shot dead
in laneway at Flagstaff near Killeen. One-time Official IRA member
thought to have been killed by his former comrades.

28 October
Private Stephen Hall, 27, Light Infantry
Shot dead by IRA sniper while on foot patrol in the Square,
Crossmaglen.

6 November
Corporal John Aikman, 25, Royal Signals
Shot dead by IRA gunmen firing from upstairs room of bar while he was on foot patrol outside the courthouse in Newtownhamilton.

15 November
Volunteer Michael McVerry, 23, Provisional Irish Republican Army
Shot dead by RUC during IRA gun attack on Keady security force base.

24 November
Guardsman David Roberts, 25, Welsh Guards
Blown up by IRA radio-controlled bomb while on foot patrol on the Monog Road outside Crossmaglen.

1974

18 February
Staff Sergeant Alan Brammagh, Royal Army Ordnance Corps
Blown up by IRA bomb after lifting sod of earth at end of command wire close to scene of another explosion at Moybane near Crossmaglen.

10 March
Michael McCreesh, 15, civilian
Michael Gallagher, 18, civilian
Blown up by IRA booby-trap bomb in abandoned car at Drumintee intended for Army foot patrol. McCreesh was killed instantly while Gallagher died four days later.

16 March
Private Roy Bedford, 22, Royal Horse Artillery
Lance Corporal Phillip James, 22, Royal Horse Artillery
Shot dead in IRA ambush on the Dundalk Road outside Crossmaglen shortly after carrying out vehicle checkpoint.

16 April
Constable Thomas McCall, 34, Royal Ulster Constabulary
Shot dead outside Newtownhamilton RUC station by IRA sniper.

22 April
Muhammad Khalid, 18, civilian
Shot dead by IRA gunmen at Ford's Cross while driving home after finishing work in the canteen at Crossmaglen security force base.

2 July
Sapper John Walton, 27, Royal Engineers
Blown up while trying to defuse IRA booby-trap bomb in derelict house at Whitecross.

13 August
Corporal Dennis Leach, 24, Royal Marines
Marine Michael Southern, 19, Royal Marines
Blown up by radio-controlled IRA bomb buried under covert observation post position at Drummuckavall.

5 October
Eugene McQuaid, 35, civilian
Blown up at Killeen by rockets he was transporting across the border on a motorbike for the IRA.

6 November
Corporal Stephen Windsor, 26, Duke of Edinburgh's Royal Regiment
Private Brian Allen, 20, Duke of Edinburgh's Royal Regiment
Shot by IRA sniper while on foot patrol in the Square in Crossmaglen. Windsor died of wounds inside Crossmaglen security force base and Windsor at Musgrave Park hospital in Belfast.

14 December
Constable Jim McNeice, 19, Royal Ulster Constabulary
Rifleman Michael Gibson, 20, Royal Green Jackets
Shot dead by IRA gunmen on the Drumintee Road in Meigh during ambush after investigating a bogus burglary.

1975

19 January
Patrick Toner, 7, civilian
Blown up by IRA command-wire bomb in field next to Main Street in Forkhill as security forces were defusing proxy bomb contained in a car. A cow was also killed.

24 March
William Elliot, 51, Post Office worker
Shot dead by IRA when he arrived at the scene of a robbery at Silverbridge Post Office. Mistaken for RUC detective.

3 June
Sergeant Alfred Doyle, 24, Ulster Defence Regiment
John Presha, 30, civilian
David Thompson, 34, civilian
Bodies found in car at Killeen after being shot dead by IRA. Doyle was off duty.

4 June
Volunteer Francis Jordan, 21, Provisional Irish Republican Army
Shot dead by Army while planting bomb outside the Pit Bar near Bessbrook.

17 July
Major Peter Willis, 36, Green Howards
Warrant Officer (Second Class) Gus Garside, 34, Royal Army Ordnance Corps
Sergeant Sammy McCarter, 33, Royal Engineers
Corporal Calvert Brown, 25, Royal Army Ordnance Corps
Blown up by IRA command-wire bomb at Cortreasla Bridge in Tullydonnell. Volunteer Pat Thompson convicted of four murders.

15 August
William Meaklin, 28, former member of Royal Ulster Constabulary Reserve

Abducted by IRA in Dorsey or Cullyhanna area as he delivered groceries in his van, shot dead and found the following day lying in a ditch next to McKenna's crossroads in Tullyvallen near Newtownhamilton.

24 August
Colm McCartney, 22, civilian
Sean Farmer, 30, civilian
Abducted by loyalists while driving through Altnamackin near Newtownhamilton and found shot dead. Both were Catholics.

30 August
Corporal Robert Frazer, Ulster Defence Regiment
Shot dead by IRA gunmen after being pulled from car while off duty as he drove away from friend's farm near Whitecross. Off duty. Suspected Ulster Volunteer Force member.

31 August
Lance Corporal Joseph Reid, Ulster Defence Regiment
Shot dead by IRA at his farm at Fernaloy near Keady. Off duty.

1 September
James McKee, 70, civilian, former member of B-Specials
Ronald McKee, 40, civilian, former member of B-Specials
John Johnson, 80, civilian
Nevin McConnell, 40, civilian
William Herron, 63, civilian
Shot dead by IRA gunmen in attack on Tullyvallen Orange Hall near Newtownhamilton. All were members of the Orange Order. Herron died two days later. Attack claimed by Republican Action Force, a cover name for the IRA.

9 October
Corporal Edward Gleeson, 28, Royal Regiment of Fusiliers
Blown up by IRA culvert bomb while in Saracen armoured personnel carrier at Lurgancullenboy near Crossmaglen.

6 November
Lance Corporal John Bell, 59, Ulster Defence Regiment
Shot dead by IRA gunmen while travelling home from work at
Ballymoyer near Whitecross. Off duty.

10 November
Colour Sergeant Joseph Nesbitt, 54, Ulster Defence Regiment
Shot dead by IRA at Carramoyle near Keady on his way to Gough
security force base in Armagh city.

15 November
Thomas McNamee, 55, civilian
Died of injuries nearly a year after loyalist bomb attack on McArdle's
pub in Crossmaglen.

21 November
Sergeant Simon Francis, 29, Royal Regiment of Fusiliers
Blown up by rifle booby-trapped by IRA and left near abandoned car
at Shean, near Forkhill.

22 November
Fusilier James Duncan, 19, Royal Regiment of Fusiliers
Fusilier Peter McDonald, 19, Royal Regiment of Fusiliers
Fusilier Michael Sampson, 20, Royal Regiment of Fusiliers
Shot dead during IRA gun attack on covert observation post at
Drummuckavall.

6 December
Volunteer James Lochrie, 20, Provisional Irish Republican Army
Volunteer Sean Campbell, 19, Provisional Irish Republican Army
Blown up when IRA landmine they were preparing at Kelly's Road in
Killeen exploded prematurely.

19 December
Trevor Bracknell, 35, civilian
Patrick Donnelly, 24, civilian
Michael Donnelly, 14, civilian

Catholics shot dead during loyalist bomb and gun attack on Donnelly's bar in Silverbridge.

1976

4 January
John Reavey, 24, civilian
Brian Reavey, 22, civilian
Anthony Reavey, 17, civilian
Catholic brothers shot dead by loyalists at their home in Whitecross.
Anthony Reavey died just over three weeks later.

5 January
James McWhirter, 58, civilian
Robert Freeburn, 50, civilian
John Bryans, 46, civilian
Joseph Lemon, 46, civilian
Robert Walker, 46, civilian
Reginald Chapman, 25, civilian
Kenneth Wharton, 24, civilian
Walter Chapman, 23, civilian
John McConville, 20, civilian
Robert Chambers, 19, civilian
Protestant workers taken from their bus at Kingsmills and shot dead
by IRA gunmen. Attack claimed by Republican Action Force.

22 February
Marjorie Lockington, 55, civilian
Shot dead by IRA during attempted hijacking of her car at Killeen.

26 February
Private Joseph McCullough, 57, Ulster Defence Regiment
Stabbed in throat and stomach by IRA as he arrived at his farm at
Tullygeasy near Newtownhamilton to feed his dog. Off duty.
Anthony McCooey convicted of murder.

31 March
Private Roderick Bannon, 25, Royal Scots

Private John Pearson, 23, Royal Scots
Private David Ferguson, 20, Royal Scots
Blown up by IRA culvert bomb contained in milk churns and detonated by command wire while patrolling in Land Rover at Carrickgallogly near Belleek.

5 April
Corporal Robert McConnell, 32, Ulster Defence Regiment
Shot dead by IRA outside his home at Tullyvallen near Newtown-hamilton while off duty. Suspected Ulster Volunteer Force member. Anthony McCooey convicted of murder.

15 April
Volunteer Peter Cleary, 25, Provisional Irish Republican Army
Shot dead by SAS as he allegedly tried to escape after being captured and arrested at Tievecrum near Forkhill.

12 June
Liam Prince, 26, civilian
Accidentally shot dead by Army in aftermath of explosion of IRA command-wire bomb on the Newry Road between Drumintee and Meigh.

28 June
Private William Snowdon, 18, Parachute Regiment
Died from wounds five days after being injured by IRA radio-controlled bomb while on foot patrol at Drumlougher near Cullyhanna.

29 July
Reserve Constable George Johnston, Royal Ulster Constabulary
Shot dead by Army when he produced his gun during argument at checkpoint in Bessbrook. Off duty.

8 August
Private James Borucki, 19, Parachute Regiment
Blown up by IRA radio-controlled bomb contained in basket of bicycle in the Square, Crossmaglen as he returned from foot patrol. Golf Five Zero Army watchtower named after him.

14 August
Majella O'Hare, 12, civilian
Shot dead when Army opened fire on suspected IRA gunman near
Whitecross. A soldier was acquitted of her manslaughter.

16 August
Elizabeth McDonald, 38, civilian
Gerard McGleenan, 22, civilian
Catholics blown up by loyalist car bomb outside Step Inn in Keady.

1977

2 January
Lance Corporal David Hind, 23, Royal Highland Fusiliers
Shot dead by IRA sniper while on foot patrol on the Dundalk Road in
Crossmaglen.

16 January
Volunteer Séamus Harvey, 20, Provisional Irish Republican Army
Shot dead by SAS during ambush of IRA unit at Coolderry near
Crossmaglen.

2 April
Hugh Clarke, 30, civilian
Protestant shot dead by IRA members after being pulled off tractor at
Tullymacrieve near Mullaghbawn. Body found dumped in car at
nearby Redmond's Cross.

14 May
Captain Robert Nairac, 29, Grenadier Guards
Abducted and beaten outside Three Steps pub in Drumintee and shot
dead by IRA near Ravensdale Forest, Co Louth. Body never found.

22 August
William Martin, 60, civilian
Abducted from his home in Crossmaglen by the IRA, shot dead and
found dumped on the Castleblaney Road. Alleged informer.

1978

4 March
Rifleman Nicky Smith, 20, Royal Green Jackets
Blown up by IRA booby-trap bomb while trying to remove Irish tricolour from telegraph pole on the Newry Road in Crossmaglen.

3 June
Volunteer Daniel McErlaine, Official Irish Republican Army
Abducted by IRA and found shot dead on the Edenappa Road outside Jonesborough the following day. Alleged to have been a criminal who had misused IRA guns.

17 June
Constable William Turbitt, 42, Royal Ulster Constabulary
Constable Hugh McConnell, 32, Royal Ulster Constabulary
Shot dead in IRA ambush of their car at Sturgan Brae near Camlough. Turbitt's body found dumped two weeks later at Drumlougher.

25 June
Patrick McEntee, civilian
Abducted from his car at Drummuckavall by the IRA and found shot dead at Ballsmill near Crossmaglen the following day. Alleged informer.

12 July
Private Jack Fisher, 19, Parachute Regiment
Blown up by IRA radio-controlled bomb hidden in manhole while patrolling in Ferret scout car on the Dundalk Road in Crossmaglen.

17 August
Corporal Robert Miller, 22, Royal Marines
Blown up by IRA radio-controlled car bomb car while on foot patrol on Main Street in Forkhill.

19 August
Gilbert Johnston, former Ulster Defence Regiment member
Shot dead by IRA in parked car outside shop in Victoria Street in Keady. Volunteer Bernard McGinn convicted of murder.

12 November
Marine Gareth Wheedon, 19, Royal Marines
Died from head injuries four days after being injured by IRA radio-controlled bomb while on foot patrol in Castleblaney Street, Crossmaglen.

21 December
Guardsman Graham Duggan, 22, Grenadier Guards
Guardsman Kevin Johnson, 20, Grenadier Guards
Guardsman Glen Ling, 18, Grenadier Guards
Shot dead by IRA gunmen who opened fire on Army foot patrol from back of van parked on the Newry Road in Crossmaglen.

1979

24 January
Martin McGuigan, 16, civilian
James Keenan, 16, civilian
Blown up by IRA radio-controlled bomb hidden in trailer near Darkley. Mistaken for Army personnel.

19 March
Private Peter Woolmore, 21, Queen's Regiment
Blown up by IRA mortar bomb which landed on ablutions block in Newtownhamilton security force base.

17 April
Constable Noel Webb, 30, Royal Ulster Constabulary
Constable Alan Baird, 28, Royal Ulster Constabulary
Constable Paul Gray, 25, Royal Ulster Constabulary
Reserve Constable Bobby Lockhart, 44, Royal Ulster Constabulary
Blown up by IRA radio-controlled bomb while driving along the Millvale Road outside Bessbrook in Land Rover. Volunteer Pat Trainor convicted of four murders.

3 June
Superintendent Stanley Hanna, 47, Royal Ulster Constabulary
Constable Kevin Thompson, 22, Royal Ulster Constabulary

Blown up by radio-controlled IRA milk churn bomb during clearance operation around Shelagh Youth Club, near Crossmaglen. Volunteer Eugene Byrne found not guilty of two murders.

9 June
Volunteer Peadar McElvenna, 24, Provisional Irish Republican Army
Shot dead by Army during gun battle near Keady.

8 July
Private Alan MacMillan, 18, Queen's Own Highlanders
Died from wounds a day after being injured by IRA radio-controlled bomb while on foot patrol in the Square, Crossmaglen.

27 August
Lieutenant Colonel David Blair, 40, Queen's Own Highlanders
Major Peter Fursman, 35, Parachute Regiment
Warrant Officer (Second Class) Walter Beard, 33, Parachute Regiment
Sergeant Ian Rogers, 31, Parachute Regiment
Corporal Leonard Jones, 26, Parachute Regiment
Corporal Nicholas Andrews, 24, Parachute Regiment
Corporal John Giles, 22, Parachute Regiment
Lance Corporal Christopher Ireland, 25, Parachute Regiment
Lance Corporal Victor MacLeod, 24, Queen's Own Highlanders
Lance Corporal Donald Blair, 23, Parachute Regiment
Private Thomas Vance, 23, Parachute Regiment
Private Robert England, 23, Parachute Regiment
Private Raymond Dunn, 20, Parachute Regiment
Private Anthony Wood, 19, Parachute Regiment
Private Gary Barnes, 18, Parachute Regiment
Private Dylan Jones, 18, Parachute Regiment
Private Jeffrey Jones, 18, Parachute Regiment
Private Michael Woods, 18, Parachute Regiment
Michael Hudson, 29, civilian
Blown up by two IRA radio-controlled bombs at Narrow Water Castle near Warrenpoint detonated from Omeath. Hudson shot dead on Omeath shore by Army as he looked across Carlingford Lough at the scene.

5 October
Martin Rowland, 26, civilian
Catholic shot dead on Quarter Road in Camlough by loyalists.

13 November
Guardsman Paul Fryer, 18, Welsh Guards
Blown up by IRA booby-trap bomb attached to telegraph pole at Ford's Cross near Crossmaglen.

16 December
Private Peter Grundy, 21, Parachute Regiment
Blown up by IRA command-wire bomb in milk churn at covert observation post in derelict house at Tullydonnell near Forkhill.

1980

1 January
Lieutenant Simon Bates, 23, Parachute Regiment
Private Gerald Hardy, 18, Parachute Regiment
Shot dead near Forkhill by fellow members of the Parachute Regiment when they walked into ambush set for IRA.

2 January
Clifford Lundy, 62, former member of Ulster Defence Regiment
Shot dead by IRA at workplace in Kingsmills.

15 March
Private John Bateman, 18, King's Own Border Regiment
Shot dead by IRA sniper while on foot patrol on the Newry Road in Crossmaglen.

21 March
Private Sean Walker, 18, King's Own Border Regiment
Died two weeks after being injured by IRA radio-controlled car bomb while on foot patrol in North Street in Crossmaglen.

25 March
Gerard Evans, 23, civilian

Disappeared after last being seen hitching a lift from Castleblaney back to his home in Crossmaglen and body never found. IRA believed responsible.

13 May
Anthony Shields, 57, civilian
Abducted from his car at Drummuckavall by the IRA, shot dead and booby-trapped body found dumped close to border at Mounthill two days later. Alleged informer.

9 August
Sergeant Brian Brown, 29, Parachute Regiment
Blown up by IRA radio-controlled bomb at vehicle checkpoint on the Shean Road in Forkhill.

20 August
Frank McGrory, 52, civilian
Blown up by INLA booby-trap nail bomb hidden in undergrowth beside Castleblaney Road at Carnagh near Keady.

31 August
Reserve Constable Wallace Allen, 49, Royal Ulster Constabulary
Abducted by IRA while off duty and driving milk lorry along Whitecross Road near Newtownhamilton. Body found on Trainor's Bridge, 20 yards from border, 13 days later.

12 November
Oliver Walsh, 39, civilian
Blown up by IRA bomb at Lislea. Car mistaken for RUC vehicle.

1981

19 January
Volunteer Maurice Gilvarry, 24, Provisional Irish Republican Army (Belfast Brigade)
Abducted by IRA and found shot dead at Jonesborough. Alleged informer.

19 March
Gerry Rowland, 40, civilian
Shot dead by IRA sniper while driving in car with UDR member at Mounthill near Crossmaglen. Mistaken for UDR member.

2 April
Constable Kenneth Acheson, 23, Royal Ulster Constabulary
Blown up by IRA booby-trap bomb placed under his car outside his home in Derrywilligan Road in Bessbrook. Off duty.

19 April
Lance Corporal Grenville Winstone, Royal Green Jackets
Rifleman Michael Bagshaw, 25, Royal Green Jackets
Rifleman John King, 20, Royal Green Jackets
Rifleman Andrew Gavin, 19, Royal Green Jackets
Driver Paul Bulman, 19, Royal Corps of Transport
Blown up by IRA radio-controlled bomb while travelling in Saracen along Chancellor's Road outside Bessbrook.

28 May
Mervyn Robinson, 47, Royal Ulster Constabulary
Shot dead by IRA as he left Wayside Inn in Whitecross. Off duty.

16 July
Lance Corporal Gavin Dean, 21, Royal Green Jackets
Shot dead during IRA gun attack on Army close observation platoon position in scrapyard at Mounthill near Crossmaglen.

16 August
Charles Armstrong, 56, civilian
Disappeared from Crossmaglen. Car found in Dundalk the following day but body never discovered. IRA believed responsible.

1982

5 March
Volunteer Séamus Morgan, Provisional Irish Republican Army (East Tyrone Brigade)

Abducted by IRA and found shot dead on Carrickasticken Road, Forkhill. Alleged informer.

29 October
Sergeant Thomas Cochrane, 55, Ulster Defence Regiment
Found shot dead five days after being knocked off motorcycle at Lislea near Camlough by IRA members while driving to work. Off duty.

1983

13 April
Trevor Elliott, 38, Territorial Army
Shot dead by IRA gunmen at his shop in Keady while off duty.

7 May
Eric Dale, 43, Irish National Liberation Army
Abducted by INLA in Inniskeen in County Monaghan and found shot dead at Killeen. Alleged informer.

13 July
Eamon McMahon, 35, Irish National Liberation Army
Patrick Mackin, 37, Irish National Liberation Army
Shot dead in Dundalk by INLA members after being suspected of siphoning off money from robberies. Bodies found in McMahon's car on Lurgan Road outside Crossmaglen.

7 November
Lance Corporal Stephen Taverner, 24, Devon and Dorset Regiment
Died of wounds two weeks after being injured by IRA radio-controlled bomb while on foot patrol in the Square in Crossmaglen.

20 November
David Wilson, 44, civilian
Harold Brown, 59, civilian
Victor Cunningham, 39, civilian
Shot dead by group calling itself the Catholic Reaction Force, a cover name for the INLA, in the entrance hall to Mountain Lodge Pentecostal Church in Darkley near Keady.

1984

31 January
Sergeant William Savage, 27, Royal Ulster Constabulary
Constable Thomas Bingham, 29, Royal Ulster Constabulary
Blown up by IRA command-wire bomb packed into four beer kegs
as they drove along the Newry Road between Drumintee and
Meigh.

13 February
Volunteer James Young, Provisional Irish Republican Army (Belfast
Brigade)
Abducted by IRA and found shot dead on Corliss Road near
Crossmaglen. Alleged informer.

18 May
Reserve Constable Trevor Elliott, 29, Royal Ulster Constabulary
Constable Neville Gray, 25, Royal Ulster Constabulary
Blown up by IRA command-wire culvert bomb while driving
armoured car along Hall Road at Lislea near Camlough.

29 May
Lance Corporal Stephen Anderson, 23, Staffordshire Regiment
Blown up by IRA booby-trap bomb while on foot patrol at Mounthill
near Crossmaglen.

26 July
Volunteer Brian McNally, 25, former member of Provisional Irish
Republican Army (South Down Brigade)
Shot dead by IRA following interrogation in Dundalk and body
dumped in ditch beside the Carn Road near Meigh. Alleged informer
who had been dismissed from IRA two months earlier.

1985

28 February
Chief Inspector Alex Donaldson, 41, Royal Ulster Constabulary
Sergeant John Dowd, 31, Royal Ulster Constabulary

Constable Rosemary McGookin, 27, Royal Ulster Constabulary
Constable Ivy Kelly, 29, Royal Ulster Constabulary
Constable David Topping, 22, Royal Ulster Constabulary
Reserve Constable Paul McFerran, 33, Royal Ulster Constabulary
Reserve Constable Geoffrey Campbell, 24, Royal Ulster Constabulary
Reserve Constable Denis Price, 22, Royal Ulster Constabulary
Reserve Constable Sean McHenry, 19, Royal Ulster Constabulary
Killed when IRA mortar bomb hit temporary canteen in Corry Square
RUC station in Newry.

20 May
Inspector William Wilson, 28, Royal Ulster Constabulary
Constable David Baird, 22, Royal Ulster Constabulary
Constable Tracy Doak, 21, Royal Ulster Constabulary
Reserve Constable Steven Rodgers, 19, Royal Ulster Constabulary
Blown up in patrol car at Killeen by IRA radio-controlled bomb
detonated from across the border.

9 September
James Burnett, 28, Irish National Liberation Army
Abducted by INLA and found shot dead at Killeen. Alleged informer.

15 November
Constable David Hanson, 24, Royal Ulster Constabulary
Blown up by IRA radio-controlled bomb while on foot patrol on the
Castleblaney Road outside Crossmaglen.

1986

20 May
Colm McKevitt, civilian
Abducted by IRA from sister's home in Killeen and shot dead on
nearby Jack's Road. Alleged informer and petty criminal with close
links to IRA.

22 May
Major Andrew French, 35, Royal Anglian Regiment
Constable David McBride, 27, Royal Ulster Constabulary
Constable William Smyth, 25, Royal Ulster Constabulary

Blown up by IRA radio-controlled bomb hidden in stone wall while conducting a search at Cornoonagh Hill near Crossmaglen.

16 June
Terence McKeever, 30, civilian
Abducted by IRA and found shot dead at Mullaghduff Bridge near Cullyhanna. Contractor to security forces.

9 July
Private Carl Davies, 24, Royal Anglian Regiment
Private Mitchell Bertram, 20, Royal Anglian Regiment
Blown up by IRA radio-controlled van bomb at Army position next to site where Glasdrumman watchtower was being built.

9 September
Volunteer David McVeigh, Provisional Irish Republican Army (North Armagh Brigade)
Abducted by IRA and found shot dead on Flagstaff Road near Killeen. Alleged informer.

1987

7 March
Thomas Maguire, 19, Irish People's Liberation Organisation
Abducted by INLA in Newry and found shot dead at Killeavey. Victim of feud between INLA and IPLO.

14 March
Fergus Conlon, 31, Irish National Liberation Army
Abducted by INLA in Newry and found shot dead on the Ferryhill Road near Forkhill. Alleged informer.

12 April
Volunteer Francis McIlmurray, 30, Provisional Irish Republican Army (Belfast Brigade)
Abducted by IRA and found shot dead in van abandoned behind McKevitt's filling station on the Dublin Road in Killeen. Alleged informer.

25 April
Lord Justice Sir Maurice Gibson, 74, civilian
Lady Cecily Gibson, 67, civilian
Blown up as they drove past IRA radio-controlled bomb packed into a parked car at Killeen.

1 September
Eamon Maguire, former member of Provisional Irish Republican Army
Abducted by IRA in Dublin and found shot dead on the Concession Road at Clonalig near Cullaville a week later. Alleged informer.

4 October
James McDaid, 30, civilian
Abducted by INLA and found shot dead in car on the Castleblaney Road outside Crossmaglen. Alleged criminal.

1988

29 February
Volunteer Brendan Burns, 30, Provisional Irish Republican Army
Volunteer Brendan Moley, 30, Provisional Irish Republican Army
Blown up when IRA radio-controlled bomb they were loading into a van near Donaldson's Road in Creggan exploded prematurely.

21 May
Corporal Derek Hayes, 28, Royal Pioneer Corps
Blown up with his sniffer dog, Ben, by IRA radio-controlled bomb placed in biscuit tin in dry stone wall while searching field at Tullyard Hill near the Castleblaney Road outside Crossmaglen.

23 July
Robin Hanna, 44, civilian
Maureen Hanna, 44, civilian
David Hanna, 6, civilian
Blown up by IRA radio-controlled bomb hidden behind wall at Killeen as they returned from holiday in family car. Bomb was intended for Judge Higgins.

28 July
Sergeant Michael Matthews, 27, Parachute Regiment
Died of wounds a day after being injured by IRA radio-controlled
bomb while on foot patrol on Skerriff Road near Cullyhanna.

1989

20 March
Chief Superintendent Harry Breen, 51, Royal Ulster Constabulary
Superintendent Robert Buchanan, 55, Royal Ulster Constabulary
Shot dead when car ambushed by an IRA unit on the Edenappa Road
outside Jonesborough as they returned from meeting with gardaí in
Dundalk.

4 May
Corporal Russell McGonigle, 30, Worcestershire and Sherwood
Foresters
Blown up by IRA radio-controlled bomb attached to telegraph pole
while on foot patrol at Cashel near Silverbridge.

18 July
John McAnulty, 48, civilian
Abducted by IRA outside Rosewood Country Club in Ravensdale
and found shot dead on Loughross Road in Cullaville. Alleged
informer.

20 October
Constable Michael Marshall, 25, Royal Ulster Constabulary
Shot dead during IRA gun attack on armoured patrol car as he drove
along the Newry Road outside Belleek.

1990

15 April
Volunteer Eoin Morley, Irish People's Liberation Army
Shot dead at girlfriend's house in Iveagh Crescent in Newry as he
tried to escape IRA punishment gang.

7 May
Lance Sergeant Graham Stewart, 25, Scots Guards
Died of wounds two days after being shot by IRA gunman during
attack on close observation platoon position next to Slatequarry
Road near Cullyhanna.

26 July
Volunteer Patrick Flood, Provisional Irish Republican Army (Derry
Brigade)
Abducted by IRA in Derry and found shot dead on the Coach
Road in Newtownhamilton seven and a half weeks later. Alleged
informer.

16 September
Detective Constable Louis Robinson, 42, Royal Ulster Constabulary
Abducted at Killeen by IRA unit while returning from fishing trip in
Dingle, Co Kerry. Body found in laneway off Foxfield Road in
Crossmaglen.

24 October
Ranger Cyril Smith, 21, Royal Irish Rangers
Blown up by IRA proxy bomb contained in van detonated by
radar gun at Romeo One Five permanent vehicle checkpoint at
Cloghogue.

30 December
Fergal Caraher, Sinn Féin member
Shot dead by Royal Marines as the car he was in was driven away
from Lite 'n' Easy Bar on Tullynavall Road in Cullyhanna by his
brother Micheál.

1991

21 July
Tom Oliver, 43, civilian
Abducted by IRA near Omeath and later found shot dead on
Newtownhamilton Road in Belleek. Alleged informer.

17 August
Lance Corporal Simon Ware, 22, Coldstream Guards
Blown up by IRA booby-trap bomb buried in grass bank while on foot patrol in Carrickrovaddy Wood near Belleek.

27 November
Lance Corporal Ken Newell, 31, Ulster Defence Regiment
Abducted while off duty and delivering soft drinks to a garage on the Concession Road at Cullaville. Shot dead and body dumped on Cregganduff Road near Crossmaglen.

1992

10 April
Thomas Casey, 49, civilian
Paul Butt, 29, civilian
Danielle Carter, 15, civilian
Blown up by IRA van bomb set on timer and left outside Baltic Exchange in City of London. Bomb mixed by South Armagh Brigade.

1 May
Fusilier Andrew Grundy, 22, Royal Fusiliers
Blown up by IRA van bomb pushed along railway line into Romeo One Five permanent vehicle checkpoint at Cloghogue and detonated by command wire.

1 July
Volunteer Gregory Burns, 34, Provisional Irish Republican Army (North Armagh Brigade)
Volunteer John Dignam, 32, Provisional Irish Republican Army (North Armagh Brigade)
Volunteer Aidan Starrs, 29, Provisional Irish Republican Army (North Armagh Brigade)
Abducted by IRA. Burns found shot dead near Cullaville Road, Crossmaglen, Dignam on Mountain Road, Belleek and Starrs near Dundalk Road, Newtownhamilton. Alleged informers.

28 August
Private Paul Turner, 18, Light Infantry
Shot dead outside Northern Bank in the Square in Crossmaglen by
IRA sniper firing .50 calibre rifle from St Patrick's churchyard.

1993

25 February
Constable Jonathan Reid, 30, Royal Ulster Constabulary
Shot dead at vehicle checkpoint on the Castleblaney Road outside
Crossmaglen by IRA sniper firing 7.62 mm calibre rifle from car.

8 March
Nigel McCollum, 25, civilian
Blown up during IRA mortar bomb attack on Keady security force
base. Construction worker.

17 March
Lance Corporal Lawrence Dickson, 26, Royal Scots
Shot dead while on foot patrol in Church Road in Forkhill by IRA
sniper firing 7.62 mm calibre sniper rifle from vehicle.

24 April
Ed Henty, 34, civilian photographer
Blown up by IRA lorry bomb left at Bishopsgate in City of London
and activated by timer. Bomb mixed by South Armagh Brigade.

26 June
Private John Randall, 19, Duke of Edinburgh's Royal Regiment
Shot dead while on foot patrol in field next to Carrickacullion Road
outside Newtownhamilton by IRA sniper firing a 7.62 mm calibre
rifle from fence next to the Dundalk Road.

17 July
Lance Corporal Kevin Pullin, 28, Duke of Edinburgh's Royal Regiment
Shot dead while on foot patrol on Carran Road in Crossmaglen by
IRA sniper firing .50 calibre rifle from vehicle.

2 November
Reserve Constable Brian Woods, 30, Royal Ulster Constabulary
Shot at vehicle checkpoint in Upper Edward Street in Newry by IRA
sniper in vehicle using .50 calibre rifle. Died in Craigavon hospital
two days later.

2 December
Lance Bombadier Paul Garrett, 23, Royal Artillery
Shot dead while on foot patrol in Victoria Street, Keady by IRA
sniper firing .50 calibre rifle from car. Volunteer Micheál Caraher
named in court as the sniper and Volunteer Bernard McGinn
convicted of murder.

30 December
Guardsman Daniel Blinco, 23, Grenadier Guards
Shot dead outside Murtagh's Bar on corner of Newry Street and
North Street next to the Square in Crossmaglen by IRA sniper firing
.50 calibre rifle from vehicle.

1994

30 April
Volunteer Michael Brown, Provisional Irish Republican Army (South
Down Brigade)
Abducted in Kilkeel in County Down and found shot dead on the
Omeath Road near Newry.

14 May
Lance Corporal David Wilson, 27, Royal Logistics Corps
Blown up by IRA bomb detonated outside observation post in
Keady.

10 November
Frank Kerr, civilian Post Office worker
Shot dead during IRA robbery at main Post Office sorting office,
Clanrye, Newry. Volunteer Kevin Donegan and Volunteer Declan
McComish convicted of participating in robbery and disposing of
Kerr's clothing.

1996

9 February
Inam Bashir, 29, civilian
John Jefferies, 31, civilian
Blown up by IRA lorry bomb parked outside Bashir's newsagents shop at South Quay in London's Docklands and set on a timer. Bomb mixed and transported by South Armagh Brigade.

1997

12 February
Lance Bombadier Stephen Restorick, 23, Royal Horse Artillery
Shot by IRA sniper in car using Barrett 90 .50 calibre rifle while talking to motorist at vehicle checkpoint at Green Road in Bessbrook. Volunteer Micheál Caraher named in court as sniper and Volunteer Bernard McGinn convicted of murder.

1998

22 June
Corporal Gary Fenton, 29, Royal Gloucestershire, Berkshire and Wiltshire Regiment
Run over on the Castleblaney Road outside Crossmaglen by oil smuggler driving away from Army checkpoint. Patrick Belton charged with causing death by dangerous driving.

1999

27 January
Eamon Collins, 44, former member of Provisional Irish Republican Army (South Down Brigade)
Abducted, beaten and stabbed to death on Doran's Hill near his home in Barcroft estate in Newry. No claim of responsibility but Provisional IRA believed responsible.

28 May
Volunteer Eamon Molloy, Provisional Irish Republican Army

Alleged informer who was abducted in Belfast and shot dead in 1975. Remains left in coffin in Faughart graveyard after being disinterred by IRA members. First of 'the Disappeared' to be recovered.

13 June
Paul Downey, 36, civilian
Abducted from outside Canal Court Hotel in Newry, shot dead and body dumped the next day beside the Carrowmannon Road near Belleek. Alleged drugs dealer. Provisional IRA believed responsible.

29 June
Brian McKinney, 23, civilian
John McClory, 18, civilian
Abducted by IRA in Belfast and shot dead in 1978. Remains dug up by gardaí at Colgagh near Culloville in County Monaghan. Second and third of 'the Disappeared' to be recovered.

Appendix B

Talking To People In South Armagh
by Captain Robert Nairac

1. Just as it is important to regard everyone with serious suspicion, it is also important to regard any local as a possible source of information. Most people (possibly 80 per cent) are sick of the violence and would like to see the Troubles end. Some would go as far as to do something about it, if approached in the right way. Among fringe PIRA (or even active terrorists) there are those who might be 'turned' by the right approach. Generally speaking, four factors prevent this:
   a. Fear of PIRA
   b. Fear and mistrust of the Army
   c. Genuine sympathy for the 'republican' cause
   d. Tradition
2. Most of the points in this paper are applicable to the RC communities throughout NI.

Aim

3. The aim of this paper is to suggest how best to overcome these four difficulties.

Fear of PIRA

4. Fear is the most important factor in keeping people's mouths shut. They look at everyone — fathers, mothers, sons, neighbours

— as possible dangers. To have been seen talking to soldiers may often mean a 'visit' and some sharp questioning. All too often a friendly nod from a local has resulted in uniformed soldiers openly halting or greeting them. If this goes on, a beating or a knee or head job is the end result. Therefore, if you wish to talk to someone, follow these points carefully:

a. Do not single them out for attention. If you visit their home, visit at least four or five others, before and after. Try to make your visit to your subject as normal as possible.

b. Make sure that your subject realises that he/she is not being singled out — even if they are.

c. Give them an excuse for your visit. They will certainly be asked why the 'Brits' visited. Find a plausible excuse and tell them straight away e.g. 'We are calling on all the houses around here because . . .' Obviously, use the same story for all the visits on the operation.

d. If, after the interview, they appear at all friendly, give them the opportunity to ask you back e.g. 'We often check the houses around here so we will see you again if that's okay?' This gives them the chance to say how they would like you to come e.g. 'Fine, but come after dark', or 'when the kids are out'. If you get this then you have a contact.

5. If you can convince your subject that you are totally discreet and will not put them on the spot, many people will help.

Mistrust of the Army

6. Many innocent people fear and mistrust the Army. Some, no doubt, have excellent reason to do so. The Army is, inevitably, a 'Brit' instrument, and harmless people suffer inconvenience, or worse, after an incident. Furthermore, we are seen as outsiders and interlopers. When faced with sincere complaints, blind denial is worse than useless. One is merely calling your plaintiff a liar! They may well be, but a far better line is to switch to the attack e.g. 'I agree it is bad, but when you have seen your friends blown to bits . . .'. Also try the 'young eighteen soldier' line. Any soldier who has been killed must be either eighteen years old, fresh from home, or married with a new baby. It is possible to

gain sympathy and genuine emotion from these very emotional people. Nonetheless, the best way is to avoid giving useless offence. Admittedly, if a totally committed PROVO gets a beating, it may not do any harm. However, it creates a bad impression. In any case, it is very difficult to tell who are Provos, and many totally innocent people have traces. It is always worth mentioning that some who are openly anti SF [security forces] in public, are probably putting on an act to impress the real terrorists.

Genuine Republicanism

7. At heart, all Catholic men and women in South Armagh have some sympathy for the Provo cause. It is a complete waste of time, and totally unproductive, to heap abuse and pour scorn on PIRA. Remember that you are an outsider and are probably talking about their son, neighbour etc. 'Misguided and misled' is a much better line of attraction than 'foul bastards'. Then once again attack their sympathy. Try the 'young soldier' line. Be wary of using accidents — South Armagh PIRA have a good record of not causing civilian casualties. If that does not succeed, move onto 'Kingsmills' or the 'Tullyvallen Orange Hall Massacre'. You could suggest to them that these two incidents were unlikely to win over the Protestants. It is useful to use three lines of attack for different age groups:

a. The Young (14–25 years). These days this age group is very up on history so know your facts. The best line of approach is to try and share their convictions. Attack PIRA propaganda and use all the Provo nastiness you can think of. Some of them have consciences, if so they will have some doubts. One good line from you could shake them out of their attitudes. Try and get them to argue politics with you. The hard facts of Protestant determination and military power always shakes them e.g. 'If we pull out, do you think anyone can control the Prot paramilitaries' or 'If 20,000 British soldiers are pushed to defeat the Provos, who the hell is going to control 20,000 UVF men?' Ask them for their solutions — but know your facts; they will know theirs.

b. The 26–38 year olds. All the above arguments can work well for this age group. If they are newly-married or have young kids try 'Is this a fit place to bring up kids?' Also, this age group is also very financially aware. The advantage of British social security etc can be used: be careful not to patronise. Try talking very much 'man to man', or indeed 'man to woman'. You will often get a favourable reaction by talking about 'wild tearaway kids'. c. The parents (40s . . .) In this age group you probably have the greatest chance of success. Undoubtedly the emotional 'eighteen-year-old soldier — just like your Danny' line can work well. Also try the 'Evil men leading young lads astray' line. Above all with this generation play on their parental worries, use the picture of sinister, hard men pushing young republicans getting irretrievably enmeshed in an organisation which lost its decency. Ask if they worry about their kids. A great deal of success will come to you with experience. If you are very sure of your ground, hint darkly that you saw young Pat in dubious company. Finally and most powerfully, ask them if they would like the evil and hard men of the PIRA to rule their lives if we pulled out.

Tradition

8. South Armagh is traditionally a lawless and independent-minded area. It is resentful of authority of any kind. Furthermore, certain things are taboo. It is said that if you raped your next door neighbour it will soon be forgotten: if your grandfather had been an 'INFORMER' you would be an outcast. It follows that there are certain deep-rooted things that will shut up people like a clam. Never ever use the words INFORM, INFORMATION, WITNESS or INTIMIDATE. Never write anything down; it smacks of police work. Never offer money for 'INFORMATION'. (It may come to that after months of cultivation, but to offer it is fatal.) There are ways around these taboos. 'May I call for a chat?' 'Can you help?' Avoid the direct question, hint, suggest and work round the subject. If you wish to say 'It is high time the bad men were locked up' try to get them to say it for you. Ask their advice, opinion, in very general terms.

Security

9. Finally, be very wary of giving away any more than you get. Always consult 'Int' to see whose name you may mention. Do not ever use information from MISRs or 'P' Cards directly. You could be talking to the local PIRA IO!

Useful Euphemisms

10. No

No	Yes
'Can you give me any information?'	'Perhaps you might be able to help'
'The Provos are stupid murderers'	'Some of the boys have gone too far'
'Your son is a terrorist'	'Your son is taking up with a bad crowd'
'Did you see that shooting/bombing?'	'Terrible business that bomb, it must have given you a fright'
'Will our visit lead to intimidation?'	'We don't want to embarrass you.'
'We have come to see you.'	'We are calling on all the houses round here because . . .'
'We want to ask you some questions'	'We've just come for a chat.'
'How can we see you without fingering you?'	'We'll call again but we don't want to embarrass you.'

Useful Lines to Take

11. a. That a young soldier that was killed — only eighteen and a half — just arrived — left a mother and baby etc.
b. There are some evil men working on the lads and leading them on etc.
c. THE WOMEN FOR PEACE — Would you like your lives to be run by the PROVOS? 25,000 marchers attended the peace march in Belfast. — 400 people were at the Provo rally in Camlough.
d. Every bomb that goes off and every shot that is fired puts peace another ten years further off.
e. The Provos are the worst republicans we have ever seen.
f. The Easter proclamation: 'Let no rapine cowardice or inhumanity dishonour our cause.'
g. Cite various Provo murders of policemen off duty in front of their wives/kids etc.

h. When genuine complaints are made: 'Well I agree, but when you have seen a young boy (like that soldier etc.) blown apart . . . What if it was your Danny/Pat etc, etc.'

Some Answers

12. Question:
'Who are the Army protecting in XMG?'
Answer:
'Well I agree; but face it if the boys stopped shooting and bombing we could go.' OR: 'I agree but shooting and bombing for six years has meant more soldiers/SAS/searchers/VCPs.' OR: 'Yes but do you want those Provo boys running your lives.' OR: 'Yes, but how long would an unarmed policeman last in XMG — you must have some law.'

Conclusion

13. Throughout South Armagh there are many people who have vital bits of information. With skill and professionalism it is possible to extract life-saving titbits. If approached the right way, the fence-sitters (probably 60 per cent of the community) will come down on our side. When that happens we have won.

R L NAIRAC
Captain
SAS LO

Appendix C

Speech by Francie Molloy, a senior Sinn Féin negotiator from East Tyrone, at the Lite 'N' Easy Bar, Cullyhanna on 16 November 1997 to mark the 24th anniversary of the death of Volunteer Michael McVerry. Recorded by the author.

Michael McVerry's name is known throughout South Armagh and the republican movement and without question is one of the notable names of the volunteers who paid a very high price for the sacrifice that he made for the battle that he was carrying on for you and I, the ordinary people.

Looking at this young audience tonight and some not so young, it's certainly heartening to see so many young people here, many who wouldn't have known Michael McVerry and wouldn't have been around or if they were would have been very young at the time and that is the continuity of this struggle in the fact that this struggle has gone on for more than 24 years, this struggle has continued and has grown and strengthened throughout those 24 years.

If we look back at previous phases of struggle, we look at 1916 to 1921, five years and even going on to the other couple of years of civil war, a very short time, a very short stretch. This struggle has gone on for 30 years and the people who were involved at the very start of that struggle, the people who went out and fought for basic civil rights are still part of that struggle.

And that is our strength, the unity of purpose, the dedication to the cause, that is what has kept that struggle together and that's what we need to continue to keep together. There are divisions in every grouping. There are people who for various different reasons disagree, dispute and debate. And criticism is healthy provided it is criticism with a purpose, provided people are playing a part. (sporadic applause)

The history of Michael McVerry. I didn't know Michael McVerry but I know in dealing with the same issues in Tyrone this part of the country was very lucky because despite very severe losses at different times there were still very few who actually lost their lives. If you look at the Roll of Honour for Tyrone, so many casualties, so many big numbers of people who actually died at the one time, all tragedies, the kind of community you had here, the very competent and courageous organisation, the commitment and dedication and no loss of life is very important.

That's why Michael McVerry's name stands out, so important was he at a time when this struggle was at its height is the name of a volunteer who lost his life. Sometimes we get into a way of talking of volunteers losing their lives, laying down their lives. But Michael McVerry didn't want to die. Like any other volunteer he wanted to live in this struggle. He fought a hard struggle, brought the struggle to the Brits. He didn't sit back and wait for the Brits coming but led from the front, contained the struggle within the area but also brought it out of this area and took on the Brits.

There were many obstacles to volunteers 24 to 30 years ago, a great many obstacles. But the volunteers didn't allow those obstacles to stop them carrying on their struggle and the very fact that Michael McVerry was caught in crossfire and gunfire taking on the British in a fortified barracks, overwhelmed with numbers, the fear of gunfire, big fortifications, with all of that locality around them, that didn't stop the volunteers from going to try to attack the Brits.

They weren't deterred by high walls and barbed wire fences, by the strong defences and we have to do the same in every aspect of this struggle. We can't be deterred by the obstacles that are placed in front of us. If the volunteers of Óglaigh na hÉireann every time they saw a high wall around a barracks simply turned away and said well there's no purpose. They went back with a good strategy, they came up with new methods and if they couldn't get over physically then they sent something else over physically and they blew it up. (loud applause)

And that's what we, the ordinary people in this struggle, have to do. We have to take on all the obstacles placed in front of us. And one of those obstacles in some senses is trying to negotiate a peace out of this conflict because no matter how long any conflict goes on, we have to negotiate and we should try to negotiate it at a time of our strength not of weakness. We have to try and face the enemy and try to outwit it in every way possible, by every means possible. And negotiations is simply another phase in that struggle.

Negotiations is taking on the Brits, again against all the fortifications, all the technicalities, with all the superior forces they may have, the negotiating skills they may have, whatever. But we take them on because we're as good as they are and we're better and this is our country and we want it free (applause) And again, unity is our strength. We see the obstacles and try to counteract them.

If we put up one finger it's a very weak and delicate piece of our bodies. But with our clenched fists it's very strong, hard to break open and we will be strong when we're all together united in one fist facing the British government whether it be Óglaigh na hÉireann, Sinn Féin, the prisoners, all of the different aspects of this struggle, all contained in one body facing the Brits and taking them on, the might that they have.

So, this whole struggle contains a high risk strategy and that has been said by Gerry Adams and Martin McGuinness in negotiations.

Yes, this is a high risk strategy. But the volunteers of Óglaigh na hÉireann have been taking high risks for the last 30 years on our behalf. They have been facing and taking the risk of death, destruction every time they take up arms, every time they try to grasp a situation, every time they send someone across to take action in England or wherever it's a very high risk strategy and the one thing that's facing all the volunteers is either prison or death.

There is no one going to the negotiating table who is facing that particular thing but what it can do it can weaken our position if we allow the Brits to manipulate or to use the media, allow them to use divisions within ourselves so that they penetrate our defences and catch us in a weakness.

We have to be strong, we have to be united to withstand all of that. The one thing that is certain is that nobody is going to negotiate on behalf of this movement who has any less aspirations than anyone here or anyone outside or anyone in the rest of the six counties or beyond. Every one of those people has took part in the struggle, they've played in different roles within it, they're committed and confident and the confidence of the nationalist community is what'll take this through to a final end.

This phase of negotiations may fall apart, it may not succeed. And whenever that does happen then we simply go back to what we know best. But we don't go back to the same tactics we used maybe 20 years ago. We go back with new tactics, we devise new methods, new strategies and we go back again to face the Brits again in negotiations.

We have to continue to strive to bring this conflict to an end because for the people who suffered imprisonment, families who have suffered death, lost loved ones for a number of years, for those people to have any meaning out of this struggle they have to see success and the only success that any of those people want to see is the Brits out of our country.

It's really no use if it's the next generation that get that. Okay, it might finish up that way but we want to live in the freedom and Michael McVerry when he was taking on the British Army, the RUC, he wanted to live for that freedom, he wanted to walk the hills of South Armagh, to walk the roads without being stopped and harassed and harangued by British occupation forces for that's what they are. They're not security. We don't need security. We need the freedom to walk our own roads, our own fields, to live in our house without harassment.

That's what people are fighting to achieve: freedom and justice and peace and there's no one who needs peace more than republicans because for generations we have been trying to remove the British occupation forces from this country. We could do it. The confidence within the nationalist community is higher now than it's been for some time so let's take that high risk, let's get involved in aspects of it.

There's no one asking everyone to take on the role of the volunteer. Those who want, still there's certainly a role for them to play as a volunteer of Óglaigh na hÉireann. But there's many other different aspects. We need people mobilising and putting the pressure on. We need people campaigning for the release of all political prisoners. It may not be achieved right away but we need that campaigning to start to ensure the prisoners know that people support them and the people know that those prisoners are there because of the political circumstances of this country not because they're criminals, they're there because of us, they're the people who had a conscience, who took on the might of the British Empire, who fought the British Empire and who are now in jail.

For those are people who have played an active role in this struggle. We need to get behind that, the Saioirse campaign is there for people who want to play that role. The political campaign of Sinn Féin is equally as important. All strands coming together build that fist which will take on the British Empire.

And whatever role people want to play to then there are places there for them to do so but it is very important at this particular time that we don't fragment, that we see the problem, that we keep in front of us the task that is the British.

The enemy in this struggle is the British. Not ourselves, not individualists, not the Unionists even to that extent but the British people, the British government who are governing and occupying our country. If we keep that task ahead of us then we can win this struggle but we need leadership to do that.

Michael McVerry was a man who led from the front. He didn't ask anyone else to do what he wouldn't do himself. He didn't stay behind and wait for others, he brought the struggle to the Brits and he led the offensive. Everyone here can play a role in bringing this struggle to a successful conclusion by leading from the front in whatever way you can do. Let's get together, let's put the Brits out of our country.

Interviews

The following people gave interviews to the author during his period of research; for reasons of personal security or protection from prosecution, some requested that their names not be used. Unless otherwise stated, all the quotations in the book from those listed here were recorded during those interviews. Many other republicans, serving and former members of the security forces and civilians spoke only on the condition that they remain anonymous.

Republicans

Pat Thompson, former IRA prisoner
Peter John Caraher, senior South Armagh republican
Jim McAllister, former Sinn Féin councillor for Crossmaglen
Volunteer M, IRA member and former prisoner
Volunteer G, IRA member
Owen Caraher, former IRA prisoner during Border Campaign
Joe Farrell, former member of IRA's 4th Northern Division
Pat Murphy, former IRA prisoner
Paddy Murphy, former IRA prisoner
Alice Murphy, wife of Pat and mother of Paddy Murphy
Eamon Larkin, Republican Sinn Féin organiser in South Armagh
Paddy Short, Crossmaglen publican
Maurice Healy, former IRA member later abducted and beaten
Eamon Collins, former IRA member (died January 1999)

Sean O'Callaghan, former head of IRA's Southern Command
Vincent McKenna, former IRA member
Henry McElroy, farmer, member of South Armagh Farmers' and
    Residents' Association
Séamus Murphy, leading Official republican

Members of the Security Forces

Sir John Hermon, former RUC Chief Constable
David Veness, Assistant Commissioner, Metropolitan Police
John Grieve, former Head of SO13, Metropolitan Police
Eric Anderson, RUC detective chief superintendent
Paul Murfitt, RUC chief inspector
Monty Alexander, former RUC sergeant
Sam Malcomson, former RUC constable
Constable E, member of RUC
Ronnie Galwey, RUC constable
Officer D, former member of MI5
Detective Inspector L, former member of Garda Special Branch
Roger Brunt, brigadier and commander of 3 Brigade
Peter Morton, former Parachute Regiment brigadier
Tim Spicer, former Scots Guards lieutenant colonel
Major C, former SAS major
Major M, Army intelligence officer
Nick Lewis, former Coldstream Guards captain
Gaz Hunter, former SAS warrant officer
Staff Sergeant P, former SAS member
Frank Gillan, former Scots Guards corporal
Tom Caughey, former Parachute Regiment private

Others

Lord Merlyn Rees, former Secretary of State for Northern
    Ireland
Professor Jack Crane, State Pathologist for Northern Ireland
Mervyn Kingston, Rector of Church of Ireland parish of
    Creggan
Lorraine McElroy, Bessbrook resident injured in sniper attack

Gabrielle Nairac, sister of Captain Robert Nairac
Billy McCaughey, former Ulster Volunteer Force prisoner
William Frazer, South Armagh loyalist
Billy Wright, Loyalist Volunteer Force leader (died December
1997)

Glossary

ARF – Airborne Reaction Force

Army Convention – The IRA's supreme authority made up of delegates from throughout Ireland

Army Council – The IRA's seven-man ruling body

Army Executive – The IRA's 12-man body elected by the Army Convention to appoint the Army Council and oversee its activities

Baseplate – Place where mortar frame is set up in advance of mortar attack

BBK – Bessbrook

BCP – Border Crossing Point

Black and Tans – Former members of the British Army recruited to the Royal Irish Constabulary from 1920 who gained a reputation for brutality

Booster tube – Piece of scaffolding pole drilled with holes and filled with PETN and RDX to boost explosive power of fertiliser-based bomb

Brick – Four-man Army patrol

B-Specials – Part-time members of the Ulster Special Constabulary, formed in 1920 to supplement the Royal Irish Constabulary

BSU – Bessbrook Support Unit

Cam up – To cover one's face and hands with dark camouflage cream

CO – Commanding Officer

COP – Close Observation Platoon

Cumann na mBan – Female section of the IRA

Dáil – Irish parliament

DDK – Dundalk

Dead ground – An area which cannot be seen from a given point such as a watchtower

Det – Detachment, the colloquial name for 14 Int

Dickers – Republican supporters used to report on the movements of the security forces

E4A – The RUC's undercover surveillance unit

FBI – Federal Bureau of Investigation

Fianna na hÉireann – Junior wing of the IRA

FKL – Forkhill

GAA – Gaelic Athletic Association

Garda Síochana – Irish police force

Garda – Irish police officer

Gardaí – Plural of Garda

GHQ Staff – IRA's General Headquarters Staff appointed by the Chief of Staff to control day-to-day IRA activities

GPMG – General Purpose Machine-Gun

HBX – Hackballscross

HMSU – Headquarters Mobile Support Unit

Int – Intelligence

IVCP – Illegal Vehicle Checkpoint

LMG – Light Machine-Gun

LO – Liaison Officer

Long – Army slang for a rifle

LS – Landing Site

MISR – Military Intelligence Source Report

NCO – Non-Commissioned Officer

NORAID – Northern Aid, the American organisation which raised funds for the Irish republican movement

Northern Command – IRA grouping in control of Northern Ireland and border counties

NTH – Newtownhamilton

OC – Officer Commanding

Official IRA – Marxist rump of IRA from which Provisionals split in 1970

Óglaigh na hÉireann – Irish for the IRA (literally 'Soldiers of Ireland')

OP – Observation Post

OTR – On the Run

P Card – Personality Card used by Army to record details of terrorist suspects

PETN – Pentaerythritol Tetranitrate, a constituent element of Semtex

RDX – Research Development Explosive, codename for cyclonite, a constituent element of Semtex

Real IRA – Dissident republican group founded in October 1997

Recce patrol – Reconnaissance patrol (forerunner of COPs)

RIC – Royal Irish Constabulary

Ringer vehicle – Vehicle with false numberplates matching registration of another similar vehicle

RSF – Republican Sinn Féin. Formed in 1986 when the republican movement split over the issue of taking seats in the Dáil

RTÉ – Radio Teilifeís Éireann, state broadcasting corporation in the Irish Republic

RUC – Royal Ulster Constabulary

SAS – Special Air Service

Scout car – A car used to accompany and protect a vehicle containing a bomb or gunman

Scouts – IRA members used to clear routes for vehicles containing bombs or gunmen. Also used to monitor movements of security forces. An integral part of most IRA attacks

Screw – Slang for prison officer

SDLP – Social Democratic and Labour Party

Short – Army slang for a handgun

SLR – Self Loading Rifle

SMG – Sub Machine-Gun

Southern Command – IRA grouping which controls non-border counties in Irish Republic and the supply of weapons

SPG – Special Patrol Group, the RUC's mobile anti-terrorist unit

Supergrass – Paramilitary who agrees to supply evidence on former comrades in return for a degree of immunity from prosecution.

SO13 – Anti-terrorist branch of Metropolitan Police

TCG – Tasking and Co-ordination Group

Tout – Derogatory slang for informer

TPU – Timing and Power Unit for explosive device

UDA – Ulster Defence Association

UDR – Ulster Defence Regiment
UVF – Ulster Volunteer Force
VCP – Vehicle Checkpoint
XMG – Crossmaglen
14 Int – 14th Intelligence and Security Company

List of Illustrations

Section I

Notices offering rewards for the capture of the Ribbonmen who murdered
  George McFarland in 1837 and Thomas Bateson in 1851
B-Specials at Lisdrumliska in June 1922
Frank Aiken in 1957
Members of the Northern Border Commission in 1922
The remnants of a booby-trapped Ford Cortina blown up in 1970
Tom and Patrick Murphy in Roche Emmets Gaelic football team
Tom Murphy in action for Roche Emmets
Slab Murphy farm at Ballybinaby
The van in which Harry Thornton was killed in 1971
Saracen armoured car blown up at Lurgancullenboy in 1975
The Caraher family in 1986 (*Mike Abrahams*)
Captain Robert Nairac in cermonial Grenadier Guards uniform
Nairac at Bessbrook Mill before he was killed in May 1977 (*Kelvin Boyes*)
Liam Townson
Danny O'Rourke
The Three Steps pub in Drumintee
An RUC montage of IRA suspects in South Armagh from the 1970s
Tom Murphy at the Four Courts in Dublin in May 1998
'The Undertaker'
Micksey Martin
'The Surgeon'
'The Undertaker'
RUC and Army casualties after Forkhill explosion in January 1978 (*Alan Lewis*)
The scene at Narrow Water (*Kelvin Boyes*)

'Bandit Country'

The truck blown up at Narrow Water (*Kelvin Boyes*)
Tom Murphy's passport; Greek stamps from trips to arrange Libyan arms
    deals; a false passport in the name of Jim Faughey
South Armagh Brigade volunteers with machine gun and rifles
IRA volunteer steps forward to read Easter statement in Crossmaglen in
    1995 (*Crispin Rodwell*)
IRA volunteer reading Easter statement in 1997 (*Frankie Quinn*)

Section II

The body of John McAnulty in 1989 (*Kelvin Boyes*)
The body of Paddy Flood in 1990 (*Kelvin Boyes*)
The body of John Dignam in 1992 (*Kelvin Boyes*)
RUC canteen bombing in Newry in 1985 (*Kelvin Boyes*)
Scene of IRA ambush outside Jonesborough in 1989 (*Kelvin Boyes*)
Ford Sierra in which Constable Michael Marshall died in 1989 (*Kelvin Boyes*)
IRA volunteers preparing a mortar attack in 1982
The body of Private Ken Newell in 1991 (*Kelvin Boyes*)
Killeen in 1987 after Lord Chief Justice Sir Maurice Gibson and his wife
    were blown up (*Kelvin Boyes*)
Army Air Corps Lynx takes off from Crossmaglen (*Frankie Quinn*)
IRA signs and Borucki sangar in Crossmaglen (*Rebecca Peters*)
Eamon Maguire and Richard Johnson
Martin Quigley
Members of a Parachute Regiment in Crossmaglen in 1987 (*Laurie Sparham*)
Golf Three Zero watchtower at Glasdrumman (*Kelvin Boyes*)
Sign at Mullaghbawn (*Rebecca Peters*)
Soldiers on Jonesborough Mountain (*Pacemaker*)
Commander John Grieve surveys damage caused by the Docklands bomb
    in 1986 (*Eddie Mulholland*)
Sniper at Work sign near Crossmaglen warning soldiers of sniper attacks
Secret compartment in bottom of animal trailer containing rifle used to kill
    Lance Bombadier Stephen Restorick in 1997 (*Kelvin Boyes*)
Identity tag belonging to Lance Corporal Kevin Pullin (*Kelvin Boyes*)
Reconstruction of how Mícheál Caraher fired the rifle through an aperture
    of the Mazda 626 (*Kelvin Boyes*)
IRA sniper team photographs taken in Gough barracks (*Kelvin Boyes*)
View from inside the barn in Cregganduff Road farm complex in 1997
    (*Kelvin Boyes*)

(*All photographs from a private collection unless otherwise stated*)

• 388

Bibliography

Books

Andrews, C.S., *Dublin Made Me: An Autobiography*; Mercier Press, Dublin, 1979

Arthur, Max, *Northern Ireland Soldiers Talking*; Sidgwick & Jackson, London, 1987

Asher, Michael, *Shoot to Kill: A Soldier's Journey through Violence*; Penguin Books, London, 1991

Bardon, Jonathan, *A History of Ulster*; Blackstaff Press, Belfast, 1992

Bartlett, Thomas and Jeffery, Keith (eds), *A Military History of Ireland*; Cambridge University Press, 1996

Barzilay, David, *The British Army in Ulster, Volumes 1-4*; Century Books, Belfast, 1973, 1975, 1978, 1981

Bassett, George Henry, *The Book of County Armagh*; Sealey, Bryers and Walker, London, 1888

Bassett, George Henry, *Louth County Guide and Directory*; Sealey, Bryers and Walker, London, 1886

Beevor, Antony, *Inside the British Army*; Chatto & Windus, London, 1990

Bowyer Bell, J., *In Dubious Battle: the Dublin and Monaghan Bombings 1972–1974*; Poolbeg, Dublin, 1996

Bowyer Bell, J., *IRA Tactics and Targets*; Poolbeg, Dublin, 1990

Bradley, Anthony, *Requiem for a Spy: the Killing of Robert Nairac*; Mercier Press, Dublin, 1992

Carragher, Peter, *The Rusted Roof*; Banbridge Chronicle Press Ltd, Banbridge, 1999

Chadwick, Nora, *The Celts*; Penguin, London, 1971

Clark, Samuel and Donnelly, James S. Jnr (eds), *Irish Peasants: Violence and Political Unrest 1780–1914*; Gill and Macmillan, Dublin, 1983

Clarke, A.F.N., *Contact*; Secker and Warburg, London, 1983

Clarke, Gerry and O'Sullivan, Harold, *Dundalk and North Louth: Paintings and Stories from Cúchulainn's Country*; Cottage Publications, Donaghadee, 1997

Collins, Eamon, *Killing Rage*; Granta Press, London, 1997

Coogan, Tim Pat, *The Troubles*; Hutchinson, London, 1995

Coogan, Tim Pat, *Michael Collins*; Hutchinson, London, 1990

Corrigan, Peter, *Soldier U SAS: Bandit Country*; 22 Books, Rochester, Kent, 1995

Crawford, Steve, *The SAS at Close Quarters*; Sidgwick & Jackson, London, 1993

Crawford, Steve, *The SAS Encyclopedia*; Sidgwick & Jackson, London, 1996

Darby, John, *Dressed to Kill: Cartoonists and the Northern Ireland Conflict*; Appletree Press, Belfast, 1983

Darnton, Robert, *The Great Cat Massacre and Other Episodes in French Cultural History*; Allen Lane, London, 1984

de Rís, Seán (ed.), *Peadar Ó Doirnín*; Clóchuallacht Chathail Teoranta, Dublin, 1969

Devereux, Steve, *Terminal Velocity*; Smith Gryphon, London, 1997

Devlin, Crónán (ed.), *1798: A Union of Wills? Proceedings of Scoil Shliabh gCuillinn 1997*; Tí Chulainn, Mullaghbawn, 1998

Dewar, Colonel Mike, *The British Army in Northern Ireland*; Arms and Armour, London, 1985

Dillon, Martin, *The Dirty War*; Hutchinson, London, 1990

Donaldson, John, *A Historical and Statistical Account of the Barony of Upper Fews in the County of Armagh 1838*; Creggan Local History Society, Crossmaglen, 1993 (reprint)

Estyn Evans, E. (ed.), *Harvest Home: The Last Sheaf – A selection from the writings of T.G.F.Paterson*; Dundalgan Press, Dundalk, 1975

Falconer, Duncans *First Into Action: A Dramatic Personal Account of Life in the SBS*; Little, Brown and Company, London, 1998

Foot, M.L.R., *Fighting for Ireland*; Routledge, London, 1995

Gantz, Jeffrey (transl), *Early Irish Myths and Sagas*; Penguin Books, London, 1981

Geraghty, Tony, *The Irish War: The Military History of a Domestic Conflict*; HarperCollins, London, 1998

Gibson, Brian, *The Birmingham Bombs*; Barry Rose (Publishers) Ltd, Chichester and London, 1976

Gillespie, Raymond and O'Sullivan, Harold, *The Borderlands: Essays on the History of the Ulster-Leinster Border*; Institute of Irish Studies, Queen's University, Belfast, 1989

Gurney, Peter, *Braver Men Walk Away: Memoirs of the World's Top Bomb-Disposal Expert*; HarperCollins, London, 1993

Halstock, Max, *Rats: The Story of a Dog Soldier*; Victor Gollancz, London, 1981

Hamill, Desmond, *Pig in the Middle: The Army in Northern Ireland 1969–1984*; Methuen, London, 1985

Hart, Peter, *The IRA and its Enemies: Violence and Community in Cork 1916–1923*; Clarendon Press, Oxford, 1998

Hayes-McCoy, G.A., *Irish Battles: A Military History of Ireland*; Appletree Press, Belfast, 1969

Hayward, Richard, *Border Foray*; Arthur Barker, London, 1957

Her Majesty's Stationery Office, *Ring of Gullion: Area of Outstanding Natural Beauty*; HMSO, London, 1991

Hermon, Sir John, *Holding the Line*; Gill and Macmillan, Dublin, 1997

Heslinga, Dr M.W., *The Irish Border as a Cultural Divide*; Van Gorcum Assen, the Netherlands, 1979

Hezlet, Sir Arthur, *The 'B' Specials: A History of the Ulster Special Constabulary*; Pan Books, London, 1973

Hockey, John, *Squaddies: Portrait of a Subculture*; University of Exeter, 1986

Hoffman, Bruce, *Inside Terrorism*; Victor Gollancz, London, 1998

Holland, Jack, *Too Long a Sacrifice: Life and Death in Northern Ireland Since 1969*; Dodd, Mead and Company, New York, 1981

Holland, Jack, *The American Connection*; Viking Penguin, New York, 1987

Holland, Jack and McDonald, Henry, *INLA: Deadly Divisions*; Poolbeg, Dublin, 1994

Holland, Jack and Phoenix, Susan, *Phoenix: Policing the Shadows*; Hodder & Stoughton, London, 1996

Hunter, Gaz, *The Shooting Gallery*; Victor Gollancz, London, 1998

Insight Team, The Sunday Times, *Ulster*; Andre Deutsch, London, 1972

Kinsella, Thomas (transl), *The Táin: from the Irish epic Táin Bó Cúailnge*; Oxford University Press, 1969

Kitson, General Frank, *Low Intensity Operations*; Faber, London, 1971

Knox, Oliver, *Rebels and Informers: Stirrings of Irish Independence*; John Murray, London, 1997

Lindsay, Oliver, *Once a Grenadier: The Grenadier Guards 1945–1995*; Leo Cooper, London, 1996

McArdle, Brendan, Treacy, Willie and Craven, Niall, *Football Feats of Faughart 1884–1997: Roche Emmets G.F.C. Fifty Golden Years*; Anglo Printers Ltd, Drogheda, 1997

McArdle, Patsy, *The Secret War*; Mercier Press, Dublin, 1984

McCreary, Alf, *Survivors*; Century Books, Belfast, 1976

McDonald, Peter, *The SAS in Action*; Sidgwick & Jackson, London, 1990

MacEoin, Uinseann, *Harry: the Story of Harry White*; Argenta Publications, Dublin, 1985

MacEoin, Uinseann, *The IRA in the Twilight Years 1923–48*; Argenta Publications, Dublin, 1997

McGeough, Gerry, *The Ambush and Other Stories: A Selection of Prison Writings*; Jay Street Publishers, New York, 1996

McGuire, Maria, *To Take Arms: A Year in the Provisional IRA*; Macmillan, London, 1973

McNab, Andy, *Immediate Action*; Bantam Press, London, 1995

McShane, Michael (ed.), *Naomh Malachi and the Shelagh Story*; Bellew Print, Dundalk, 1994

MacStiofáin, Seán, *Memoirs of a Revolutionary*; Gordon Cremonesi, Edinburgh, 1975

Mallory, J.P. (ed.), *Aspects of the Táin*; December Publications, Belfast, 1992

Miller, David W., *Peep O'Day Boys and Defenders: Selected Documents on the County Armagh Disturbances 1784–96*; Public Record Office of Northern Ireland, Belfast, 1990

Morton, Brigadier Peter, *Emergency Tour: 3 Para in South Armagh*; William Kimber, Wellingborough, 1989

Murphy, Dervla, *A Place Apart*; John Murray, London, 1978

Murphy, Michael J., *At Slieve Gullion's Foot*; Dundalgan Press, Dundalk, 1941

Murphy, Michael J., *Ulster Folk of Field and Fireside*; Dundalgan Press, Dundalk, 1983

Murphy, Michael J., *Sayings and Stories from Slieve Gullion*; Dundalgan Press, Dundalk, 1990

Murphy, Michael J., *The Rising of Yalla Ned and Other Stories*; Dundalgan Press, Dundalk, 1992

Murray, Raymond, *The SAS in Ireland*; Mercier Press, Dublin, 1990

Northern Ireland Human Rights Commission (NIHRC), *The Erosion of Human Rights in Crossmaglen*; NIHRC, Washington DC, 1994

O'Callaghan, Sean, *The Informer*; Bantam Press, London, 1998

O Connor, Fionnuala, *In Search of a State: Catholics in Northern Ireland*; Blackstaff Press, Belfast, 1993

O'Doherty, Malachi, *The Trouble with Guns*; Blackstaff Press, Belfast, 1998

O'Farrell, Padraic, *Who's Who in the Irish War of Independence and Civil War 1916–1923*; The Lilliput Press, Dublin, 1997

O'Kelly, Michael J., *Early Ireland: An Introduction to Irish Prehistory*; Cambridge University Press, 1989

Ormsby, Frank (ed.), *A Rage for Order: Poetry of the Northern Ireland Troubles*; Blackstaff Press, Belfast, 1992

Parker, John, *Death of a Hero: Captain Robert Nairac GC and the Undercover War in Northern Ireland*; Metro, London, 1999

Parker, John, *Who Dares Wins: The Special Air Service, 1950 to the Gulf War*; Little, Brown and Company, London, 1992

Patrick, Lieutenant Colonel Derrick, *Fetch Felix: The Fight Against the Ulster Bombers 1976–77*; Hamish Hamilton, London, 1981

Pogatchnik, Shawn, *Bordering on Reality: Competition and Consensus Among Catholic Nationalists in Bandit Country*; Unpublished MA thesis, Queen's University, Belfast, 1991

Provisional IRA, *Freedom Struggle*; Irish Republican Publicity Bureau, Dublin, 1973

Rees, Merlyn, *Northern Ireland: A Personal Perspective*; Methuen, London, 1985

Rennie, James, *The Operators: Inside 14 Intelligence Company*; Century, London, 1996

Robinson, Anthony (ed.), *Weapons of the Vietnam War*; Bison Books, Greenwich, Connecticut, 1983

Room, Adrian, *A Dictionary of Irish Place-Names*; Appletree Press, Belfast, 1986

Ryder, Chris, *The Ulster Defence Regiment: An Instrument of Peace?*; Methuen, London, 1991

Short, Con, Murray, Peter and Smyth, Jimmy, *Ard Mhacha 1884–1984: A Century of GAA Progress*; Coiste Chonndae Ard Mhacha CLG, Armagh, 1985

Sjoestedt, Marie-Louise, *Gods and Heroes of the Celts*; Methuen, London, 1949

Skinner, Liam C., *Politicians by Accident*; Metropolitan Publishing Co. Ltd, Dublin, 1946

Smith, Michael, *New Cloak, Old Dagger: How Britain's Spies Came in from the Cold*; Victor Gollancz, London, 1996

Stevenson, Jonathan, *'We Wrecked the Place': Contemplating an End to the Northern Irish Troubles*; The Free Press, New York, 1996

Stewart, A.T.Q., *The Narrow Ground: Aspects of Ulster 1609–1969*; Faber and Faber, London, 1977

Sutton, Malcolm, *An Index of Deaths from the Conflict in Ireland 1969–1993*; Beyond the Pale Publications, Belfast, 1994

Taylor, Peter, *Beating the Terrorists? Interrogation in Omagh, Gough and Castlereagh*; Penguin, London, 1980

Taylor, Peter, *Families at War*; BBC Books, London, 1989

Taylor, Peter, *Provos: The IRA and Sinn Fein*; Bloomsbury, London, 1997

Taylor, Peter, *States of Terror*; BBC Books, London, 1993

Thatcher, Margaret, *The Downing Street Years*; HarperCollins, London, 1993

Tóibín, Colm, *Walking Along the Border*; Queen Anne Press, London, 1987

Toolis, Kevin, *Rebel Hearts: Journeys within the IRA's Soul*; Picador, London, 1995

Trench, W. Steuart, *Realities of Irish Life*; McGibbon and Kee, London, 1966. First published in 1868

Turner, Colin and Smyth, Austin, *Newry: An Illustrated History and Companion*; Cottage Publications, Donaghadee, 1996

Urban, Mark, *Big Boys Rules: The SAS and the Secret Struggle against the IRA*; Faber and Faber, London, 1992

Urban, Mark, *UK Eyes Alpha: The Inside Story of British Intelligence*; Faber and Faber, London, 1996

Wallace, Colin (ed.), *Facts about Northern Ireland*; Army Headquarters Northern Ireland, Lisburn, 1970
Weale, Adrian, *The Real SAS*; Sidgwick & Jackson, London, 1998
Weale, Adrian, *Secret Warfare: Special Operations Forces from the Great Game to the SAS*; Hodder & Stoughton, London, 1997
Wilson, Andrew J., *Irish America and the Ulster Conflict 1968–1995*; Blackstaff Press, Belfast, 1995
Wragg, David, *Helicopters at War*; Robert Hale, London, 1983
Wright, Frank, *Two Lands on One Soil: Ulster Politics before Home Rule*; Gill and Macmillan, Dublin, 1996

Articles

Bilton, Michael, *The Killing of Stephen Restorick*; Sunday Times Magazine, 6 July 1997
Bowcott, Owen, *Second Front: 'We will strike at will'*; Guardian, 11 February 1993
Burns, Jimmy, *Perspectives: Robert Nairac and Other Unsolved Mysteries*; Financial Times, 11 April 1998
Burton, Nigel, *Separated Forever by a Sniper's Bullet* and *Sad Soldier's Premonition*; The Northern Echo, 29 June 1993
Cathcart, Brian, *It all began with a line on the map*; Independent on Sunday, 22 May 1994
Clarke, Liam and Millar, Peter, *Focus Special: They've Not Gone Away*; Sunday Times, 11 February 1996
McAleer, Phelim, *Massacre of the Innocent in a Quiet Country Town*; Sunday Times, 16 August 1998
McCann, Eamonn, *The Eye of the Storm*; Sunday Times Magazine, 1975
McMahon, Kevin, *Agrarian Disturbances around Crossmaglen 1835–55*; Creggan Journal, 1987
McMahon, Kevin, *Cal Mór*; Creggan Journal, 1990
McMahon, Kevin, *The 'Crossmaglen Conspiracy' Case Parts I, II and III*; Seanchas Ard Mhacha, 1972, 1973, 1974
McMahon, Kevin, *The United Irishmen in Creggan Parish*; Creggan Journal, 1997/98
Panter, Steve, *We Name Manchester Bomb Suspect, How Police Hunt Tracked Bombers and Lorry* and *Mobile Phone Call that Plotted a Trail to Terror*; Manchester Evening News, 22 April 1999

Television Programmes

Bandit Country; BBC1 *Panorama*, 12 January 1976

The British Connection: Crossmaglen; BBC1, 9 April 1978

Spotlight: The American Connection; presented by Mark Devenport, BBC Northern Ireland, 18 October 1990

Spotlight: On Trial in Tucson; presented by Mark Devenport, BBC Northern Ireland, 21 April 1994

Index

399 •